Microsoft®
ACCESS® 2013
INTRODUCTORY

Philip J. Pratt

Mary Z. Last

CENGAGE
Learning®

SHELLY
CASHMAN
SERIES®

Australia • Brazil • Japan • Korea • Mexico • Singapore • Spain • United Kingdom • United States

Microsoft® Access® 2013: Introductory
Philip J. Pratt and Mary Z. Last

Executive Editor: Kathleen McMahon

Product Manager: Jon Farnham

Associate Product Manager: Crystal Parenteau

Editorial Assistant: Sarah Ryan

Print Buyer: Julio Esperas

Director of Production: Patty Stephan

Content Project Manager: Matthew Hutchinson

Development Editor: Amanda Brodkin

Senior Brand Manager: Elinor Gregory

Market Development Manager: Kristie Clark

Market Development Manager:
    Gretchen Swann

Marketing Coordinator: Amy McGregor

QA Manuscript Reviewers: Jeffrey Schwartz,
    John Freitas, Serge Palladino, Susan Pedicini,
    Danielle Shaw, Susan Whalen

Art Director: GEX Publishing Services, Inc.

Text Design: Joel Sadagursky

Cover Design: Lisa Kuhn, Curio Press, LLC

Cover Photo: Tom Kates Photography

Compositor: PreMediaGlobal

Copyeditor: Michael Beckett

Proofreader: Kim Kosmatka

Indexer: Rich Carlson

Microsoft and the Office logo are either registered trademarks or trademarks of Microsoft Corporation in the United States and/or other countries. Cengage Learning is an independent entity from the Microsoft Corporation, and not affiliated with Microsoft in any manner.

For product information and technology assistance, contact us at
Cengage Learning Customer & Sales Support, 1-800-354-9706

For permission to use material from this text or product,
submit all requests online at **cengage.com/permissions**
Further permissions questions can be emailed to
permissionrequest@cengage.com

Library of Congress Control Number: 2013937123

ISBN-13: 978-1-285-16903-3
ISBN-10: 1-285-16903-4

Cengage Learning
20 Channel Center Street
Boston, MA 02210
USA

Cengage Learning is a leading provider of customized learning solutions with office locations around the globe, including Singapore, the United Kingdom, Australia, Mexico, Brazil, and Japan. Locate your local office at:
international.cengage.com/region

Cengage Learning products are represented in Canada by Nelson Education, Ltd.

To learn more about Cengage Learning, visit **www.cengage.com**

Purchase any of our products at your local college bookstore or at our preferred online store at **www.cengagebrain.com**

Printed in the United States of America
2 3 4 5 6 7 18 17 16 15 14

Microsoft® ACCESS® 2013
INTRODUCTORY

Contents

Preface

The Shelly Cashman Series® offers the finest textbooks in computer education. We are proud that since Mircosoft Office 4.3, our series of Microsoft Office textbooks have been the most widely used books in education. With each new edition of our Office books, we make significant improvements based on the software and comments made by instructors and students. For this Microsoft Access 2013 text, the Shelly Cashman Series development team carefully reviewed our pedagogy and analyzed its effectiveness in teaching today's Office student. Students today read less, but need to retain more. They need not only to be able to perform skills, but to retain those skills and know how to apply them to different settings. Today's students need to be continually engaged and challenged to retain what they're learning.

With this Microsoft Access 2013 text, we continue our commitment to focusing on the users and how they learn best.

Objectives of This Textbook

Microsoft Access 2013: Introductory is intended for a first course on Access 2013. No experience with a computer is assumed, and no mathematics beyond the high school freshman level is required. The objectives of this book are:

- To offer an introduction to Microsoft Access 2013

- To expose students to practical examples of the computer as a useful tool

- To acquaint students with the proper procedures to create databases suitable for coursework, professional purposes, and personal use

- To help students discover the underlying functionality of Access 2013 so they can become more productive

- To develop an exercise-oriented approach that allows learning by doing

The Shelly Cashman Approach

A Proven Pedagogy with an Emphasis on Project Planning

Each chapter presents a practical problem to be solved within a project planning framework. The project orientation is strengthened by the use of the Roadmap, which provides a visual framework for the project. Step-by-step instructions with supporting screens guide students through the steps. Instructional steps are supported by the Q&A, Experimental Step, and BTW features.

A Visually Engaging Book that Maintains Student Interest

The step-by-step tasks, with supporting figures, provide a rich visual experience for the student. Call-outs on the screens that present both explanatory and navigational information provide students with information they need when they need to know it.

Supporting Reference Materials (Quick Reference)

With the Quick Reference, students can quickly look up information about a single task, such as keyboard shortcuts, and find page references to where in the book the task is illustrated.

Integration of the World Wide Web

The World Wide Web is integrated into the Access 2013 learning experience with (1) BTW annotations; (2) BTW, Q&A, and Quick Reference Summary Web pages; and (3) the Learn Online resources for each chapter.

End-of-Chapter Student Activities

Extensive end-of-chapter activities provide a variety of reinforcement opportunities for students to apply and expand their skills through individual and group work. To complete some of these assignments, you will be required to use the Data Files for Students. Visit www.cengage.com/ct/studentdownload for detailed access instructions or contact your instructor for information about accessing the required files.

New to this Edition

Enhanced Coverage of Critical Thinking Skills

A New Consider This element poses thought-provoking questions throughout each chapter, providing an increased emphasis on critical thinking and problem-solving skills. Also, every task in the project now includes a reason *why* the students are performing the task and *why* the task is necessary.

Enhanced Retention and Transference

A new Roadmap element provides a visual framework for each project, showing students where they are in the process of creating each project, and reinforcing the context of smaller tasks by showing how they fit into the larger project.

Integration of Office with Cloud and Web Technologies

A new Lab focuses entirely on integrating cloud and web technologies with Access 2013, using technologies like SkyDrive and Web Apps.

More Personalization

Each chapter project includes an optional instruction for the student to personalize his or her solution, if required by an instructor, making each student's solution unique.

More Collaboration

A new Research and Collaboration project has been added to the Consider This: Your Turn assignment at the end of each chapter.

Instructor Resources

The Instructor Resources include both teaching and testing aids and can be accessed via CD-ROM or at www.cengage.com/login.

Instructor's Manual Includes lecture notes summarizing the chapter sections, figures and boxed elements found in every chapter, teacher tips, classroom activities, lab activities, and quick quizzes in Microsoft Word files.

Syllabus Easily customizable sample syllabi that cover policies, assignments, exams, and other course information.

Figure Files Illustrations for every figure in the textbook in electronic form.

Powerpoint Presentations A multimedia lecture presentation system that provides slides for each chapter. Presentations are based on chapter objectives.

Solutions to Exercises Includes solutions for all end-of-chapter and chapter reinforcement exercises.

Test Bank & Test Engine Test banks include 112 questions for every chapter, featuring objective-based and critical thinking question types, and including page number references and figure references, when appropriate. Also included is the test engine, ExamView, the ultimate tool for your objective-based testing needs.

Data Files for Students Includes all the files that are required by students to complete the exercises.

Additional Activities for Students Consists of Chapter Reinforcement Exercises, which are true/false, multiple-choice, and short answer questions that help students gain confidence in the material learned.

Learn Online

CengageBrain.com is the premier destination for purchasing or renting Cengage Learning textbooks, eBooks, eChapters, and study tools at a significant discount (eBooks up to 50% off Print). In addition, CengageBrain.com provides direct access to all digital products, including eBooks, eChapters, and digital solutions, such as CourseMate and SAM, regardless of where purchased. The following are some examples of what is available for this product on www.cengagebrain.com.

Student Companion Site The Student Companion Site reinforces chapter terms and concepts using true/false questions, multiple choice questions, short answer questions, flash cards, practice tests, and learning games, all available for no additional cost at www.cengagebrain.com.

SAM: Skills Assessment Manager Get your students workplace-ready with SAM, the market-leading proficiency-based assessment and training solution for Microsoft Office! SAM's active, hands-on environment helps students master Microsoft Office skills and computer concepts that are essential to academic and career success, delivering the most comprehensive online learning solution for your course!

Through skill-based assessments, interactive trainings, business-centric projects, and comprehensive remediation, SAM engages students in mastering the latest Microsoft Office programs on their own, giving instructors more time to focus on teaching. Computer concepts labs supplement instruction of important technology-related topics and issues through engaging simulations and interactive, auto-graded assessments. With enhancements including streamlined course setup, more robust grading and reporting features, and the integration of fully interactive MindTap Readers containing Cengage Learning's premier textbook content, SAM provides the best teaching and learning solution for your course.

MindLinks MindLinks is a new Cengage Learning Service designed to provide the best possible user experience and facilitate the highest levels of learning retention and outcomes, enabled through a deep integration of Cengage Learning's digital suite into an instructor's Learning Management System (LMS). MindLinks works on any LMS that supports the IMS Basic LTI open standard. Advanced features, including gradebook exchange, are the result of active, enhanced LTI collaborations with industry-leading LMS partners to drive the evolving technology standards forward.

course|notes™
quick reference guide

CourseNotes

Cengage Learning's CourseNotes are six-panel quick reference cards that reinforce the most important and widely used features of a software application in a visual and user-friendly format. CourseNotes serve as a great reference tool during and after the course. CourseNotes are available for software applications, such as Microsoft Office 2013. There are also topic-based CourseNotes available, such as Best Practices in Social Networking, Hot Topics in Technology, and Web 2.0. Visit www.cengagebrain.com to learn more!

About Our Covers

The Shelly Cashman Series is continually updating our approach and content to reflect the way today's students learn and experience new technology. This focus on student success is reflected on our covers, which feature real students from The University of Rhode Island using the Shelly Cashman Series in their courses, and reflect the varied ages and backgrounds of the students learning with our books. When you use the Shelly Cashman Series, you can be assured that you are learning computer skills using the most effective courseware available.

Textbook Walk-Through

The Shelly Cashman Series Pedagogy: Project-Based — Step-by-Step — Variety of Assessments

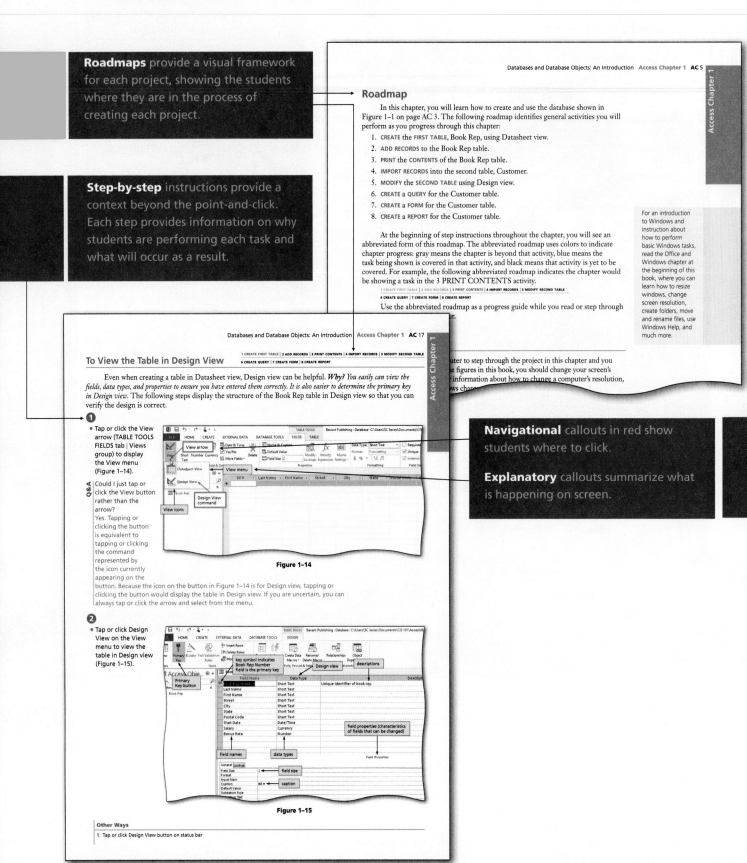

Roadmaps provide a visual framework for each project, showing the students where they are in the process of creating each project.

Step-by-step instructions provide a context beyond the point-and-click. Each step provides information on why students are performing each task and what will occur as a result.

Navigational callouts in red show students where to click.

Explanatory callouts summarize what is happening on screen.

Roadmap

In this chapter, you will learn how to create and use the database shown in Figure 1–1 on page AC 3. The following roadmap identifies general activities you will perform as you progress through this chapter:

1. CREATE the FIRST TABLE, Book Rep, using Datasheet view.
2. ADD RECORDS to the Book Rep table.
3. PRINT the CONTENTS of the Book Rep table.
4. IMPORT RECORDS into the second table, Customer.
5. MODIFY the SECOND TABLE using Design view.
6. CREATE a QUERY for the Customer table.
7. CREATE a FORM for the Customer table.
8. CREATE a REPORT for the Customer table.

At the beginning of step instructions throughout the chapter, you will see an abbreviated form of this roadmap. The abbreviated roadmap uses colors to indicate chapter progress: gray means the chapter is beyond that activity, blue means the task being shown is covered in that activity, and black means that activity is yet to be covered. For example, the following abbreviated roadmap indicates the chapter would be showing a task in the 3 PRINT CONTENTS activity.

| 1 CREATE FIRST TABLE | 2 ADD RECORDS | 3 PRINT CONTENTS | 4 IMPORT RECORDS | 5 MODIFY SECOND TABLE |
| 6 CREATE QUERY | 7 CREATE FORM | 8 CREATE REPORT |

Use the abbreviated roadmap as a progress guide while you read or step through...

For an introduction to Windows and instruction about how to perform basic Windows tasks, read the Office and Windows chapter at the beginning of this book, where you can learn how to resize windows, change screen resolution, create folders, move and rename files, use Windows Help, and much more.

...uter to step through the project in this chapter and you ...e figures in this book, you should change your screen's ... information about how to change a computer's resolution,

To View the Table in Design View

| 1 CREATE FIRST TABLE | 2 ADD RECORDS | 3 PRINT CONTENTS | 4 IMPORT RECORDS | 5 MODIFY SECOND TABLE |
| 6 CREATE QUERY | 7 CREATE FORM | 8 CREATE REPORT |

Even when creating a table in Datasheet view, Design view can be helpful. *Why? You easily can view the fields, data types, and properties to ensure you have entered them correctly. It is also easier to determine the primary key in Design view.* The following steps display the structure of the Book Rep table in Design view so that you can verify the design is correct.

1
- Tap or click the View arrow (TABLE TOOLS FIELDS tab | Views group) to display the View menu (Figure 1–14).

Q&A
Could I just tap or click the View button rather than the arrow?
Yes. Tapping or clicking the button is equivalent to tapping or clicking the command represented by the icon currently appearing on the button. Because the icon on the button in Figure 1–14 is for Design view, tapping or clicking the button would display the table in Design view. If you are uncertain, you can always tap or click the arrow and select from the menu.

Figure 1–14

2
- Tap or click Design View on the View menu to view the table in Design view (Figure 1–15).

Figure 1–15

Other Ways
1. Tap or click Design View button on status bar

Textbook Walk-Through

The Shelly Cashman Series Pedagogy: Project-Based — Step-by-Step — Variety of Assessments

Q&A boxes anticipate questions students may have when working through the steps and provide additional information about what they are doing right where they need it.

Experiment Steps within the step-by-step instructions encourage students to explore, experiment, and take advantage of the features of the Office 2013 user interface. These steps are not necessary to complete the projects, but are designed to increase confidence with the software and build problem-solving skills.

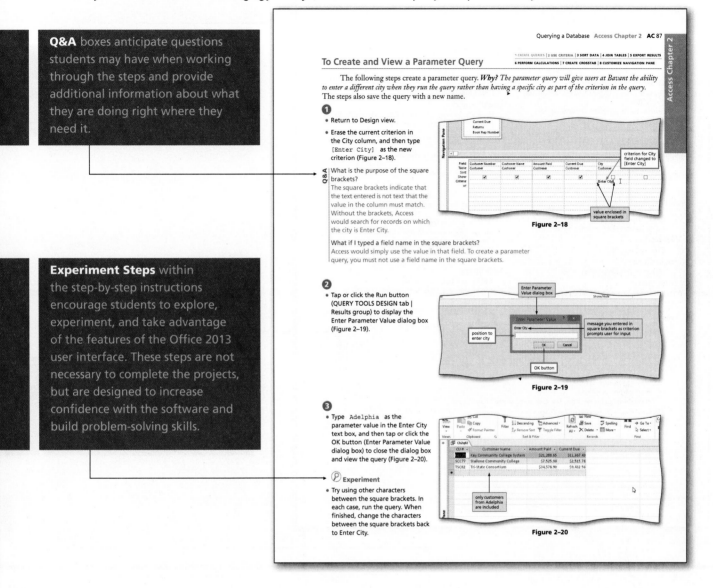

Querying a Database **Access Chapter 2** **AC 87**

Access Chapter 2

1 CREATE QUERIES | 2 USE CRITERIA | 3 SORT DATA | 4 JOIN TABLES | 5 EXPORT RESULTS
6 PERFORM CALCULATIONS | 7 CREATE CROSSTAB | 8 CUSTOMIZE NAVIGATION PANE

To Create and View a Parameter Query

The following steps create a parameter query. **Why?** *The parameter query will give users at Bavant the ability to enter a different city when they run the query rather than having a specific city as part of the criterion in the query. The steps also save the query with a new name.*

1
- Return to Design view.
- Erase the current criterion in the City column, and then type [Enter City] as the new criterion (Figure 2–18).

Q&A What is the purpose of the square brackets?
The square brackets indicate that the text entered is not text that the value in the column must match. Without the brackets, Access would search for records on which the city is Enter City.

What if I typed a field name in the square brackets?
Access would simply use the value in that field. To create a parameter query, you must not use a field name in the square brackets.

Figure 2–18

2
- Tap or click the Run button (QUERY TOOLS DESIGN tab | Results group) to display the Enter Parameter Value dialog box (Figure 2–19).

Figure 2–19

3
- Type Adelphia as the parameter value in the Enter City text box, and then tap or click the OK button (Enter Parameter Value dialog box) to close the dialog box and view the query (Figure 2–20).

Experiment
- Try using other characters between the square brackets. In each case, run the query. When finished, change the characters between the square brackets back to Enter City.

Figure 2–20

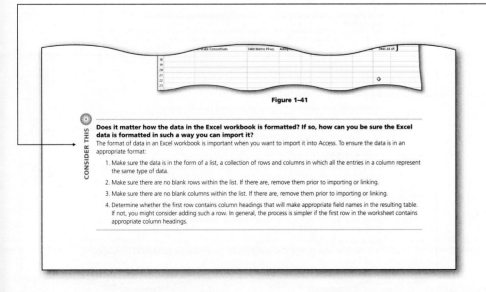

Figure 1–41

Does it matter how the data in the Excel workbook is formatted? If so, how can you be sure the Excel data is formatted in such a way you can import it?

The format of data in an Excel workbook is important when you want to import it into Access. To ensure the data is in an appropriate format:

1. Make sure the data is in the form of a list, a collection of rows and columns in which all the entries in a column represent the same type of data.

2. Make sure there are no blank rows within the list. If there are, remove them prior to importing or linking.

3. Make sure there are no blank columns within the list. If there are, remove them prior to importing or linking.

4. Determine whether the first row contains column headings that will make appropriate field names in the resulting table. If not, you might consider adding such a row. In general, the process is simpler if the first row in the worksheet contains appropriate column headings.

Consider This boxes pose thought-provoking questions with answers throughout each chapter, promoting critical thought along with immediate feedback.

Chapter Summary

In this chapter you have learned to create an Access database, create tables and add records to a database, print the contents of tables, import data, create queries, create forms, create reports, and change database properties. You also have learned how to design a database. The items listed below include all the new Access skills you have learned in this chapter, with tasks grouped by activity.

Database Object Management
Delete a Table or Other Object in the Database (AC 58)
Rename an Object in the Database (AC 58)

Database Properties
Change Database Properties (AC 55)

File Management
Run Access (AC 5)
Create a Database (AC 6)
Create a Database Using a Template (AC 7)
Exit Access (AC 24)
Open a Database from Access (AC 25)
Back Up a Database (AC 56)
Compact and Repair a Database (AC 57)
Close a Database without Exiting Access (AC 57)
Save a Database with Another Name (AC 57)

Form Creation
Create a Form (AC 45)

Import Data
Import an Excel Worksheet (AC 33)

Print Objects
Preview and Print the Contents of a Table (AC 30)

Query Creation
Print the Results of a Query (AC 45)
Print a Report (AC 54)

Query Creation
Use the Simple Query Wizard to Create a Query (AC 40)
Use a Criterion in a Query (AC 43)

Report Creation
Create a Report (AC 48)
Modify Report Column Headings and Resize Columns (AC 50)
Add Totals to a Report (AC 53)

Table Creation
Modify the Primary Key (AC 11)
Define the Remaining Fields in a Table (AC 14)
Save a Table (AC 16)
View the Table in Design View (AC 17)
Change a Field Size in Design View (AC 18)
Close the Table (AC 20)
Resize Columns in a Datasheet (AC 28)
Modify a Table in Design View (AC 37)

Table Update
Add Records to a Table (AC 20)
Add Records to a Table that Contains Data (AC 26)

What decisions will you need to make when creating your next database?
Use these guidelines as you complete the assignments in this chapter and create your own databases outside of this class.

1. Identify the tables that will be included in the database.

2. Determine the primary keys for each of the tables.

3. Determine the additional fields that should be included in each of the tables.

4. Determine relationships between the tables.

   a) Identify the "one" table.
   b) Identify the "many" table.
   c) Include the primary key of the "one" table as a field in the "many" table.

5. Determine data types for the fields in the tables.

6. Determine additional properties for fields.

   a) Determine if a special caption is warranted.
   b) Determine if a special description is warranted.
   c) Determine field sizes.
   d) Determine formats.

7. Identify and remove any unwanted redundancy.

8. Determine a storage location for the database.

9. Determine the best method for distributing the database objects.

CONSIDER THIS

How should you submit solutions to questions in the assignments identified with a ⊛ symbol?
Every assignment in this book contains one or more questions identified with a ⊛ symbol. These questions require you to think beyond the assigned database. Present your solutions to the questions in the format required by your instructor. Possible formats may include one or more of these options: write the answer; create a document that contains the answer; present your answer to the class; discuss your answer in a group; record the answer as audio or video using a webcam, smartphone, or portable media player; or post answers on a blog, wiki, or website.

CONSIDER THIS

Apply Your Knowledge

Reinforce the skills and apply the concepts you learned in this chapter.

Adding a Caption, Changing a Data Type, Creating a Query, a Form, and a Report
Note: To complete this assignment, you will be required to use the Data Files for Students. Visit www.cengage.com/ct/studentdownload for detailed instructions or contact your instructor for information about accessing the required files.

Instructions: Cosmetics Naturally Inc. manufactures and sells beauty and skin care products made with only natural ingredients. The company's products do not contain any synthetic chemicals, artificial fragrances, or chemical preservatives. Cosmetics Naturally has a database that keeps track of its sales representatives and customers. Each customer is assigned to a single sales rep, but each sales rep may be assigned to many customers. The database has two tables. The Customer table contains data on the customers who purchase Cosmetics Naturally products. The Sales Rep table contains data on the sales reps. You will add a caption, change a data type, create two queries, a form, and a report, as shown in Figure 1–83 on the next page.

Perform the following tasks:
1. Start Access, open the Apply Cosmetics Naturally database from the Data Files for Students, and enable the content.

2. Open the Sales Rep table in Datasheet view, add SR # as the caption for the Sales Rep Number field, and resize all columns to .... to the layout of the table and

STUDENT ASSIGNMENTS Access Chapter 1

Textbook Walk-Through

Extend Your Knowledge projects at the end of each chapter allow students to extend and expand on the skills learned within the chapter. Students use critical thinking to experiment with new skills to complete each project.

Apply Your Knowledge continued

Figure 1–83

Extend Your Knowledge

Extend the skills you learned in this chapter and experiment with new skills. You may need to use Help to complete the assignment.

Using a Database Template to Create a Contacts Database

Note: To complete this assignment, you will be required to use the Data Files for Students. Visit www.cengage.com/ct/studentdownload for detailed instructions or contact your instructor for information about accessing the required files.

Instructions: Access includes both desktop database templates and web-based templates. You can use a template to create a beginning database that can be modified to meet your specific needs. You will use a template to create a Contacts database. The database template includes sample tables, queries, forms, and reports. You will modify the database and create the Contacts Query shown in Figure 1–84.

Perform the following tasks:

1. Start Access.
2. Select the Desktop contacts template in the template gallery and create a new database with the file name Extend Contacts.
3. Enable the content. If requested to do so by your instructor, watch the videos in the Getting Started with Contacts dialog box. Close the Getting Started with Contacts dialog box.
4. Close the Contact List form.
5. Open the Contacts table in Datasheet view and delete the Fax Number field and the Attachments field in the table. The Attachments field has a paperclip as the column heading.
6. Change the data type for the ID field to Short Text, change the field name to Contact ID, and change the field size to 4. Change the column width so that the complete field name is

[...] acts table and close the table.

[...] d to create the Contacts Query shown in Figure 1–84. Close the

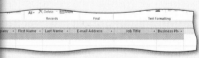

Figure 1–84

9. Open the Phone Book report in Layout view. Delete the control containing the date. Change the title of the report to Contact Phone List.
10. Save the changes to the report.
11. If requested to do so by your instructor, add your first and last names to the end of the title and save the changes to the report.
12. Submit the revised database in the format specified by your instructor.
13. a. Why would you use a template instead of creating a database from scratch with just the fields you need?
    b. The Attachment data type allows you to attach files to a database record. If you were using this database for a job search, what specific documents might you attach to a Contacts record?

Analyze, Correct, Improve

Analyze a database, correct all errors, and improve the design.

Correcting Errors in the Table Structure

Note: To complete this assignment, you will be required to use the Data Files for Students. Visit www.cengage.com/ct/studentdownload for detailed instructions or contact your instructor for information about accessing the required files.

Instructions: Analyze SciFi Movies is a database containing information on classic science fiction movies that your film professor would like to use for teaching. The Movie table shown in Figure 1–85 contains errors to the table structure. Your professor has asked you to correct the errors and make some improvements to the database. Start Access and open the Analyze SciFi Movies database from the Data Files for Students.

Figure 1–85

1. Correct Movie Number should be the primary key for the Movie table. The ID field should not be a field in the table. The Rating field represents a numerical rating system of one to four to indicate the quality of the movie. Your instructor wants to be able to find the average rating for films directed by a particular director. Only integers should be stored in both the Rating and the Length (Minutes) fields.

2. Improve The default field size for Short Text fields is 255. Changing the field size to more [...]tely represent the maximum [...]ored in a field is one way [...]

Analyze, Correct, Improve projects call on the students to analyze a file, discover errors in it, fix the errors, and then improve upon the file using the skills they learned in the chapter.

In the Lab Three in-depth assignments in each chapter that require students to apply the chapter concepts and techniques to solve problems. One Lab is devoted entirely to Cloud and Web 2.0 integration.

In the Labs

Design, create, modify, and/or use a database following the guidelines, concepts, and skills presented in this chapter. Labs are listed in order of increasing difficulty. Labs 1 and 2, which increase in difficulty, require you to create solutions based on what you learned in the chapter; Lab 3 requires you to create a solution, which uses cloud and web technologies, by learning and investigating on your own from general guidance.

Lab 1: Creating Objects for the Dartt Offsite Services Database

Problem: Dartt Offsite Services is a local company that provides offsite data services and solutions. The company provides remote data backup, disaster recovery planning and services, website backup, and offsite storage of paper documents for small businesses and nonprofit organizations. Service representatives are responsible for communicating data solutions to the client, scheduling backups and other tasks, and resolving any conflicts. The company recently decided to store its client and service rep data in a database. Each client is assigned to a single service rep, but each service rep may be assigned many clients. The database and the Service Rep table have been created, but the Monthly Salary field needs to be added to the table. The records shown in Table 1–6 must be added to the Service Rep table. The company plans to import the Client table from the Excel worksheet shown in Figure 1–86. Dartt would like to finish storing this data in a database and has asked you to help.

Figure 1–86

Note: To complete this assignment, you will be required to use the Data Files for Students. Visit www.cengage.com/ct/studentdownload for detailed instructions or contact your instructor for information about accessing the required files.

Instructions: Perform the following tasks:
1. Start Access and open the Lab 1 Dartt Offsite Services database from the Data Files for Students.
2. Open the Service Rep table in Datasheet view and add the Monthly Salary field to the end of the table. The field has the Currency data type. Assign the caption SR # to the Service Rep Number field.
3. Add the records shown in Table 1–6.
4. Resize the columns to best fit the data. Save the changes to the layout of the table.

Table 1–6 Data for Service Rep Table

Service Rep Number	Last Name	First Name	Street	City	State	Postal Code	Start Date	Monthly Salary
21	Kelly	Jenna	25 Paint St.	Kyle	SC	28797	5/14/2012	$3,862.45
45	Scott	Josh	1925 Pine Rd.	Byron	SC	28795	4/28/2014	$3,062.08
24	Liu	Mia	265 Marble Dr.	Kyle	SC	28797	1/7/2013	$3,666.67
37	Martinez	Mike	31 Steel St.	Georgetown	SC	28794	5/13/2013	$3,285.00

© 2014 Cengage Learning

✺ Consider This: Your Turn

Apply your creative thinking and problem solving skills to design and implement a solution.

Consider This: Your Turn exercises call on students to apply creative thinking and problem solving skills to design and implement a solution.

1: Maintaining the Craft Database
Personal/Academic

Instructions: Open the Craft database you used in Chapter 2 on page AC 133. If you did not create this database, contact your instructor for information about accessing the required files.

Part 1: Use the concepts and techniques presented in this chapter to modify the database as follows:
   a. The minimum price of any item is $4.00.
   b. The Description field should always contain data.
   c. Ten oven pulls have been sold. Use an update query to change the on hand value from 25 to 15. Save the update query.
   d. Tom Last (student code 4752) has created the items shown in Table 3–4. Use a split form to add these items to the Item table.

Table 3–4 Additional Records for Item table

Item Number	Description	Price	On Hand	Student Code
W128	Child's Stool	$115.00	3	4752
W315	Harmony Stool	$81.00	4	4752
W551	Skittle Pins	$4.00	15	4752

© 2014 Cengage Learning

   e. A Total Value (On Hand * Price) calculated field should be added to the Item table before the Student Code field. Set the Result Type to Currency and the Decimal Places to 2. (*Hint:* Result Type is a field property for calculated fields.)
   f. Specify referential integrity. Cascade the delete but not the update.
   g. Add the Total Value field to the Wood Crafts for Sale report created in Chapter 1.
   h. All the magazine ___ ___ not want to make any m___

Office 2013 and Windows 8: Essential Concepts and Skills

Microsoft product screen shots used with permission from Microsoft Corporation.

Objectives

You will have mastered the material in this chapter when you can:

- Use a touch screen
- Perform basic mouse operations
- Start Windows and sign in to an account
- Identify the objects in the Windows 8 desktop
- Identify the apps in and versions of Microsoft Office 2013
- Run an app
- Identify the components of the Microsoft Office ribbon

- Create folders
- Save files
- Change screen resolution
- Perform basic tasks in Microsoft Office apps
- Manage files
- Use Microsoft Office Help and Windows Help

Office 2013 and Windows 8: Essential Concepts and Skills

This introductory chapter uses Access 2013 to cover features and functions common to Office 2013 apps, as well as the basics of Windows 8.

Roadmap

In this chapter, you will learn how to perform basic tasks in Windows and Access. The following roadmap identifies general activities you will perform as you progress through this chapter:

1. SIGN IN to an account
2. USE WINDOWS
3. USE Features in Access that are Common across Office APPS
4. FILE and Folder MANAGEMENT
5. SWITCH between APPS
6. SAVE and Manage FILES
7. CHANGE SCREEN RESOLUTION
8. EXIT APPS
9. USE ADDITIONAL Office APP FEATURES
10. USE Office and Windows HELP

At the beginning of the step instructions throughout the chapter, you will see an abbreviated form of this roadmap. The abbreviated roadmap uses colors to indicate chapter progress: gray means the chapter is beyond that activity, blue means the task being shown is covered in that activity, and black means that activity is yet to be covered. For example, the following abbreviated roadmap indicates the chapter would be showing a task in the 3 USE APPS activity.

1 SIGN IN | 2 USE WINDOWS | 3 USE APPS | 4 FILE MANAGEMENT | 5 SWITCH APPS | 6 SAVE FILES
7 CHANGE SCREEN RESOLUTION | 8 EXIT APPS | 9 USE ADDITIONAL APP FEATURES | 10 USE HELP

Use the abbreviated roadmap as a progress guide while you read or step through the instructions in this chapter.

Introduction to the Windows 8 Operating System

Windows 8 is the newest version of Microsoft Windows, which is a popular and widely used operating system. An **operating system** is a computer program (set of computer instructions) that coordinates all the activities of computer hardware, such as memory, storage devices, and printers, and provides the capability for you to communicate with the computer.

The Windows operating system simplifies the process of working with documents and apps by organizing the manner in which you interact with the computer. Windows is used to run apps. An **app** (short for application) consists of programs designed to make users more productive and/or assist them with personal tasks, such as database management or browsing the web.

The Windows 8 interface begins with the **Start screen**, which shows tiles (Figure 1). A **tile** is a shortcut to an app or other content. The tiles on the Start screen include installed apps that you use regularly. From the Start screen, you can choose which apps to run using a touch screen, mouse, or other input device.

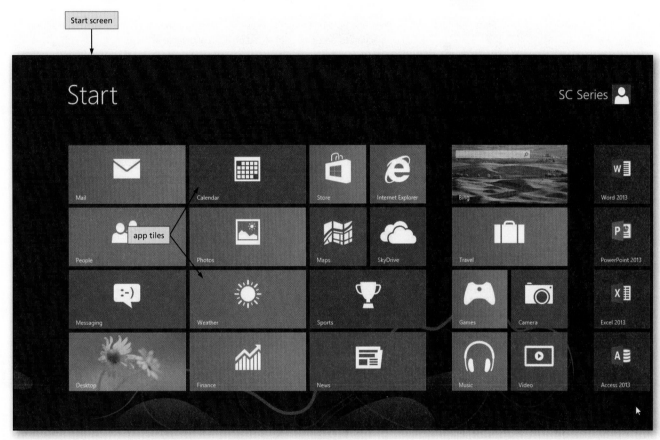

Figure 1

Using a Touch Screen and a Mouse

Windows users who have computers or devices with touch screen capability can interact with the screen using gestures. A **gesture** is a motion you make on a touch screen with the tip of one or more fingers or your hand. Touch screens are convenient because they do not require a separate device for input. Table 1 on the next page presents common ways to interact with a touch screen.

If you are using your finger on a touch screen and are having difficulty completing the steps in this chapter, consider using a stylus. Many people find it easier to be precise with a stylus than with a finger. In addition, with a stylus you see the pointer. If you still are having trouble completing the steps with a stylus, try using a mouse.

Table 1 Touch Screen Gestures		
Motion	**Description**	**Common Uses**
Tap	Quickly touch and release one finger one time.	Activate a link (built-in connection) Press a button Run a program or an app
Double-tap	Quickly touch and release one finger two times.	Run a program or an app Zoom in (show a smaller area on the screen, so that contents appear larger) at the location of the double-tap
Press and hold	Press and hold one finger to cause an action to occur, or until an action occurs.	Display a shortcut menu (immediate access to allowable actions) Activate a mode enabling you to move an item with one finger to a new location
Drag, or slide	Press and hold one finger on an object and then move the finger to the new location.	Move an item around the screen Scroll
Swipe	Press and hold one finger and then move the finger horizontally or vertically on the screen.	Select an object Swipe from edge to display a bar such as the Charms bar, Apps bar, and Navigation bar (all discussed later)
Stretch	Move two fingers apart.	Zoom in (show a smaller area on the screen, so that contents appear larger)
Pinch	Move two fingers together.	Zoom out (show a larger area on the screen, so that contents appear smaller)

© 2014 Cengage Learning

CONSIDER THIS

Will your screen look different if you are using a touch screen?
The Windows and Microsoft Office interface varies slightly if you are using a touch screen. For this reason, you might notice that your Windows or Access screens look slightly different from the screens in this book.

Windows users who do not have touch screen capabilities typically work with a mouse that has at least two buttons. For a right-handed user, the left button usually is the primary mouse button, and the right mouse button is the secondary mouse button. Left-handed people, however, can reverse the function of these buttons.

Table 2 explains how to perform a variety of mouse operations. Some apps also use keys in combination with the mouse to perform certain actions. For example, when you hold down the CTRL key while rolling the mouse wheel, text on the screen may become larger or smaller based on the direction you roll the wheel. The function of the mouse buttons and the wheel varies depending on the app.

Table 2 Mouse Operations

Operation	Mouse Action	Example*
Point	Move the mouse until the pointer on the desktop is positioned on the item of choice.	Position the pointer on the screen.
Click	Press and release the primary mouse button, which usually is the left mouse button.	Select or deselect items on the screen or run an app or app feature.
Right-click	Press and release the secondary mouse button, which usually is the right mouse button.	Display a shortcut menu.
Double-click	Quickly press and release the primary mouse button twice without moving the mouse.	Run an app or app feature.
Triple-click	Quickly press and release the primary mouse button three times without moving the mouse.	Select a paragraph.
Drag	Point to an item, hold down the primary mouse button, move the item to the desired location on the screen, and then release the mouse button.	Move an object from one location to another or draw pictures.
Right-drag	Point to an item, hold down the right mouse button, move the item to the desired location on the screen, and then release the right mouse button.	Display a shortcut menu after moving an object from one location to another.
Rotate wheel	Roll the wheel forward or backward.	Scroll vertically (up and down).
Free-spin wheel	Whirl the wheel forward or backward so that it spins freely on its own.	Scroll through many pages in seconds.
Press wheel	Press the wheel button while moving the mouse.	Scroll continuously.
Tilt wheel	Press the wheel toward the right or left.	Scroll horizontally (left and right).
Press thumb button	Press the button on the side of the mouse with your thumb.	Move forward or backward through webpages and/or control media, games, etc.

*Note: The examples presented in this column are discussed as they are demonstrated in this chapter.

© 2014 Cengage Learning

Scrolling

A **scroll bar** is a horizontal or vertical bar that appears when the contents of an area may not be visible completely on the screen (Figure 2). A scroll bar contains **scroll arrows** and a **scroll box** that enable you to view areas that currently cannot be seen on the screen. Tapping or clicking the up and down scroll arrows moves the screen content up or down one line. You also can tap or click above or below the scroll box to move up or down a section, or drag the scroll box up or down to move to a specific location.

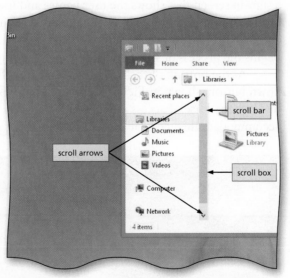

Figure 2

What should you do if you are running Windows 7 instead of Windows 8?

Although Windows 8 includes several user interface and feature enhancements, many of the steps in this book work in both Windows 7 and Windows 8. If you have any questions about differences between the two operating systems or how to perform tasks in an earlier version of Windows, contact your instructor.

CONSIDER THIS

BTW

BTWs

For a complete list of the BTWs found in the margins of this book, visit the BTW resource on the Student Companion Site located on www.cengagebrain.com. For detailed instructions about accessing available resources, visit www.cengage.com/ct/studentdownload or contact your instructor for information about accessing the required files.

Keyboard Shortcuts

In many cases, you can use the keyboard instead of the mouse to accomplish a task. To perform tasks using the keyboard, you press one or more keyboard keys, sometimes identified as a **keyboard shortcut**. Some keyboard shortcuts consist of a single key, such as the F1 key. For example, to obtain help in many apps, you can press the F1 key. Other keyboard shortcuts consist of multiple keys, in which case a plus sign separates the key names, such as CTRL+ESC. This notation means to press and hold down the first key listed, press one or more additional keys, and then release all keys. For example, to display the Start screen, press CTRL+ESC, that is, hold down the CTRL key, press the ESC key, and then release both keys.

Starting Windows

It is not unusual for multiple people to use the same computer in a work, educational, recreational, or home setting. Windows enables each user to establish a **user account**, which identifies to Windows the resources, such as apps and storage locations, a user can access when working with the computer.

Each user account has a user name and may have a password and an icon, as well. A **user name** is a unique combination of letters or numbers that identifies a specific user to Windows. A **password** is a private combination of letters, numbers, and special characters associated with the user name that allows access to a user's account resources. An icon is a small image that represents an object, thus a **user icon** is a picture associated with a user name.

When you turn on a computer, Windows starts and displays a **lock screen** consisting of the time and date (Figure 3a). To unlock the screen, swipe up or click the lock screen. Depending on your computer's settings, Windows may or may not display a sign-in screen that shows the user names and user icons for users who have accounts on the computer (Figure 3b). This **sign-in screen** enables you to sign in to your user account and makes the computer available for use. Tapping or clicking the user icon begins the process of signing in, also called logging on, to your user account.

At the bottom of the sign-in screen is the 'Ease of access' button and a Shut down button, shown in Figure 4. Tapping or clicking the 'Ease of access' button displays the Ease of access menu, which provides tools to optimize a computer to accommodate the needs of the mobility, hearing, and vision impaired users. Tapping

Figure 3a

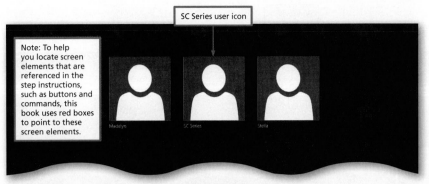

SC Series user icon

Note: To help you locate screen elements that are referenced in the step instructions, such as buttons and commands, this book uses red boxes to point to these screen elements.

Figure 3b

BTW

Q&As

For a complete list of the Q&As found in many of the step-by-step sequences in this book, visit the Q&A resource on the Student Companion Site located on www.cengagebrain.com. For detailed instructions about accessing available resources, visit www.cengage.com/ct/studentdownload or contact your instructor for information about accessing the required files.

or clicking the Shut down button displays a menu containing commands related to restarting the computer, putting it in a low-power state, and shutting it down. The commands available on your computer may differ.

- The Sleep command saves your work, turns off the computer fans and hard disk, and places the computer in a lower-power state. To wake the computer from sleep mode, press the power button or lift a laptop's cover, and sign in to your account.
- The Shut down command exits running apps, shuts down Windows, and then turns off the computer.
- The Restart command exits running apps, shuts down Windows, and then restarts Windows.

To Sign In to an Account

1 SIGN IN | 2 USE WINDOWS | 3 USE APPS | 4 FILE MANAGEMENT | 5 SWITCH APPS | 6 SAVE FILES
7 CHANGE SCREEN RESOLUTION | 8 EXIT APPS | 9 USE ADDITIONAL APP FEATURES | 10 USE HELP

The following steps, which use SC Series as the user name, sign in to an account based on a typical Windows installation. *Why? After starting Windows, you might be required to sign in to an account to access the computer's resources.* You may need to ask your instructor how to sign in to your account. If you are using Windows 7, skip these steps and instead perform the steps in the yellow box that immediately follows these Windows 8 steps.

- Swipe up or click the lock screen (shown in Figure 3a) to display a sign-in screen (shown in Figure 3b).
- Tap or click the user icon (for SC Series, in this case) on the sign-in screen, which depending on settings, either will display a second sign-in screen that contains a Password text box (Figure 4) or will display the Windows Start screen (shown in Figure 5 on the next page).

Q&A

Why do I not see a user icon?
Your computer may require you to type a user name instead of tapping or clicking an icon.

What is a text box?
A text box is a rectangular box in which you type text.

Why does my screen not show a Password text box?
Your account does not require a password.

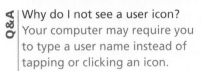

Password text box

SC Series

Password

Submit button

'Ease of access' button

Shut down button

Figure 4

- If Windows displays a sign-in screen with a Password text box, type your password in the text box.

2

- Tap or click the Submit button (shown in Figure 4 on the previous page) to sign in to your account and display the Windows Start screen (Figure 5).

Q&A

Why does my Start screen look different from the one in Figure 5?
The Windows Start screen is customizable, and your school or employer may have modified the screen to meet its needs. Also, your screen resolution, which affects the size of the elements on the screen, may differ from the screen resolution used in this book. Later in this chapter, you learn how to change screen resolution.

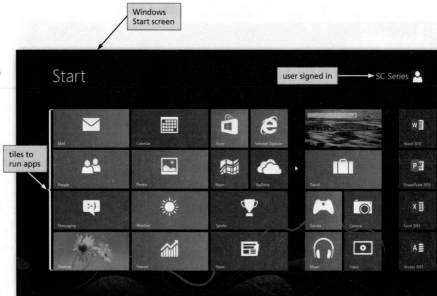

Figure 5

How do I type if my tablet has no keyboard?
You can use your fingers to press keys on a keyboard that appears on the screen, called an on-screen keyboard, or you can purchase a separate physical keyboard that attaches to or wirelessly communicates with the tablet.

TO SIGN IN TO AN ACCOUNT USING WINDOWS 7

If you are using Windows 7, perform these steps to sign in to an account instead of the previous steps that use Windows 8.

1. Click the user icon on the Welcome screen; depending on settings, this either will display a password text box or will sign in to the account and display the Windows 7 desktop.

2. If Windows 7 displays a password text box, type your password in the text box and then click the arrow button to sign in to the account and display the Windows 7 desktop.

The Windows Start Screen

BTW
Modern UI
The new Windows 8 user interface also is referred to as the Modern UI (user interface).

The Windows Start screen provides a scrollable space for you to access apps that have been pinned to the Start screen (shown in Figure 5). Pinned apps appear as tiles on the Start screen. In addition to running apps, you can perform tasks such as pinning apps (placing tiles) on the Start screen, moving the tiles around the Start screen, and unpinning apps (removing tiles) from the Start screen.

If you swipe up from the bottom of or right-click an open space on the Start screen, the App bar will appear. The **App bar** includes a button that enables you to display all of your apps. When working with tiles, the App bar also provides options for manipulating the tiles, such as resizing them.

CONSIDER THIS

How do you pin apps, move tiles, and unpin apps?

- To pin an app, swipe up from the bottom of the Start screen or right-click an open space on the Start screen to display the App bar, tap or click the All apps button on the App bar to display the Apps list, swipe down on or right-click the app you want to pin, and then tap or click the 'Pin to Start' button on the App bar. One way to return to the Start screen is to swipe up from the bottom or right-click an open space in the Apps list and then tap or click the All apps button again.

- To move a tile, drag the tile to the desired location.

- To unpin an app, swipe down on or right-click the app to display the App bar and then tap or click the 'Unpin from Start' button on the App bar.

Introduction to Microsoft Office 2013

Microsoft Office 2013 is the newest version of Microsoft Office, offering features that provide users with better functionality and easier ways to work with the various files they create. These features include enhanced design tools, such as improved picture formatting tools and new themes, shared notebooks for working in groups, mobile versions of Office apps, broadcast presentations for the web, and a digital notebook for managing and sharing multimedia information.

Microsoft Office 2013 Apps

Microsoft Office 2013 includes a wide variety of apps such as Word, PowerPoint, Excel, Access, Outlook, Publisher, OneNote, InfoPath, SharePoint Workspace, and Lync:

- **Microsoft Word 2013**, or Word, is a full-featured word processing app that allows you to create professional-looking documents and revise them easily.
- **Microsoft PowerPoint 2013**, or PowerPoint, is a complete presentation app that enables you to produce professional-looking presentations and then deliver them to an audience.
- **Microsoft Excel 2013**, or Excel, is a powerful spreadsheet app that allows you to organize data, complete calculations, make decisions, graph data, develop professional-looking reports, publish organized data to the web, and access real-time data from websites.
- **Microsoft Access 2013**, or Access, is a database management system that enables you to create a database; add, change, and delete data in the database; ask questions concerning the data in the database; and create forms and reports using the data in the database.
- **Microsoft Outlook 2013**, or Outlook, is a communications and scheduling app that allows you to manage email accounts, calendars, contacts, and access to other Internet content.
- **Microsoft Publisher 2013**, or Publisher, is a desktop publishing app that helps you create professional-quality publications and marketing materials that can be shared easily.
- **Microsoft OneNote 2013**, or OneNote, is a note taking app that allows you to store and share information in notebooks with other people.
- **Microsoft InfoPath Designer 2013**, or InfoPath, is a form development app that helps you create forms for use on the web and gather data from these forms.
- **Microsoft SharePoint Workspace 2013**, or SharePoint, is a collaboration app that allows you to access and revise files stored on your computer from other locations.
- **Microsoft Lync 2013** is a communications app that allows you to use various modes of communications such as instant messaging, videoconferencing, and sharing files and apps.

Microsoft Office 2013 Suites

A **suite** is a collection of individual apps available together as a unit. Microsoft offers a variety of Office suites, including a stand-alone desktop app (boxed software), Microsoft Office 365, and Microsoft Office Web Apps. **Microsoft Office 365**, or Office 365, provides plans that allow organizations to use Office in a mobile setting while also being able to communicate and share files, depending upon the type of plan selected by the organization. **Microsoft Office Web Apps**, or Web Apps, are apps that allow you to edit and share files on the web using the familiar Office interface. Table 3 on the next page outlines the differences among these Office suites.

Table 3 Office Suites					
Apps/ Licenses	Office 365 Home Premium	Office 365 Small Business Premium	Office Home & Student	Office Home & Business	Office Professional
Word	✔	✔	✔	✔	✔
PowerPoint	✔	✔	✔	✔	✔
Excel	✔	✔	✔	✔	✔
Access	✔	✔			✔
Outlook	✔	✔		✔	✔
Publisher	✔	✔			✔
Lync		✔			
OneNote			✔	✔	✔
InfoPath		✔			
Licenses	5	5	1	1	1

© 2014 Cengage Learning

During the Office 365 installation, you select a plan, and depending on your plan, you receive different apps and services. Office Web Apps do not require a local installation and are accessed through SkyDrive and your browser. **SkyDrive** is a cloud storage service that provides storage and other services, such as Office Web Apps, to computer users.

How do you sign up for a SkyDrive account?

• Use your browser to navigate to skydrive.live.com.

• Create a Microsoft account by tapping or clicking the 'Sign up now' link (or a similar link) and then entering your information to create the account.

• Sign in to SkyDrive using your new account.

Apps in a suite, such as Microsoft Office, typically use a similar interface and share features. Once you are comfortable working with the elements and the interface and performing tasks in one app, the similarity can help you apply the knowledge and skills you have learned to another app(s) in the suite. For example, the process for saving a file in Word is the same in PowerPoint, Excel, and the other Office apps. While briefly showing how to use Access, this chapter illustrates some of the common functions across the Office apps and identifies the characteristics unique to Access.

Running and Using an App

To use an app, such as Access, you must instruct the operating system to run the app. Windows provides many different ways to run an app, one of which is presented in this section (other ways to run an app are presented throughout this chapter). After an app is running, you can use it to perform a variety of tasks. The following pages use Access to discuss some elements of the Office interface and to perform tasks that are common to other Office apps.

Access

The term **database** describes a collection of data organized in a manner that allows access, retrieval, and use of that data. **Access** is a database management system. A **database management system** is software that allows you to use a computer to create a database; add, change, and delete data in the database; create queries that allow you to ask questions concerning the data in the database; and create forms and reports using the data in the database.

To Run Access from the Start Screen

1 SIGN IN | 2 USE WINDOWS | 3 USE APPS | 4 FILE MANAGEMENT | 5 SWITCH APPS | 6 SAVE FILES
7 CHANGE SCREEN RESOLUTION | 8 EXIT APPS | 9 USE ADDITIONAL APP FEATURES | 10 USE HELP

The Start screen contains tiles that allow you to run apps, some of which might be stored on your computer. *Why? When you install an app, for example, tiles are added to the Start screen for the various Office apps included in the suite.*

The following steps, which assume Windows is running, use the Start screen to run Access based on a typical installation. You may need to ask your instructor how to run an Office app on your computer. Although the steps illustrate running the Access app, the steps to run any Office app are similar. If you are using Windows 7, skip these steps and instead perform the steps in the yellow box that immediately follows these Windows 8 steps.

1

• If necessary, scroll to display the Access tile on the Start screen (Figure 6).

Q&A

Why does my Start screen look different?
It might look different because of your computer's configuration. The Start screen may be customized for several reasons, such as usage requirements or security restrictions.

What if the app I want to run is not on the Start screen?
You can display all installed apps by swiping up from the bottom of the Start screen or right-clicking an open space on the Start screen and then tapping or clicking the All apps button on the App bar.

How do I scroll on a touch screen?
Use the slide gesture; that is, press and hold your finger on the screen and then move your finger in the direction you wish to scroll.

Figure 6

2

• Tap or click the Access 2013 tile to run the Access app (Figure 7).

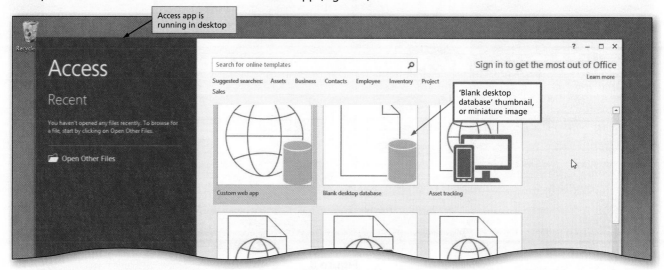

Figure 7

TO RUN AN APP USING THE START MENU USING WINDOWS 7

If you are using Windows 7, perform these steps to run an app using the Start menu instead of the previous steps that use Windows 8.

1. Click the Start button on the Windows 7 taskbar to display the Start menu.
2. Click All Programs at the bottom of the left pane on the Start menu to display the All Programs list.
3. If the app you wish to start is located in a folder, click, or scroll to and then click, the folder in the All Programs list to display a list of the folder's contents.
4. Click, or scroll to and then click, the app name in the list to run the selected app.

Windows Desktop

When you run an app in Windows, it may appear in an on-screen work area app, called the **desktop** (shown in Figure 8). You can perform tasks such as placing objects in the desktop, moving the objects around the desktop, and removing items from the desktop.

Some icons also may be displayed in the desktop. For instance, the icon for the **Recycle Bin**, the location of files that have been deleted, appears in the desktop by default. A **file** is a named unit of storage. Files can contain text, images, audio, and video. You can customize your desktop so that icons representing apps and files you use often appear in the desktop.

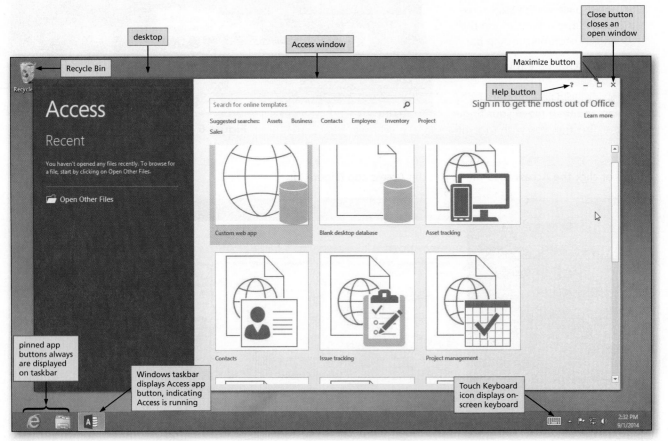

Figure 8

To Switch between an App and the Start Screen

While working with an app such as the Desktop app, you easily can return to the Start screen. The following steps switch from the Desktop app to the Start screen. *Why? Returning to the Start screen allows you to run any of your other apps.* If you are using Windows 7, read these steps without performing them because Windows 7 does not have a Start screen.

1

- Swipe in from the left edge of the screen, and then back to the left, or point to the lower-left corner of the desktop to display a thumbnail of the Start screen (Figure 9).

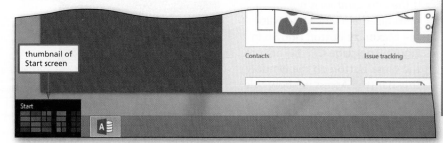

Figure 9

2

- Tap or click the thumbnail of the Start screen to display the Start screen (Figure 10).

3

- Tap or click the Desktop tile to redisplay the Desktop app (shown in Figure 8).

Figure 10

Other Ways

1. Press WINDOWS to display Start screen

To Maximize a Window

Sometimes content is not visible completely in a window. One method of displaying the entire contents of a window is to **maximize** it, or enlarge the window so that it fills the entire screen. The following step maximizes the Access window; however, any Office app's window can be maximized using this step. *Why?* *A maximized window provides the most space available for using the app.*

- If the app window is not maximized already, tap or click the Maximize button (shown in Figure 8 on page OFF 12) next to the Close button on the window's title bar (the Access window title bar, in this case) to maximize the window (Figure 11).

Q&A

What happened to the Maximize button?
It changed to a Restore Down button, which you can use to return a window to its size and location before you maximized it.

How do I know whether a window is maximized?
A window is maximized if it fills the entire display area and the Restore Down button is displayed on the title bar.

Figure 11

Other Ways

1. Double-tap or double-click title bar   2. Drag title bar to top of screen

Access Unique Elements

BTW
Navigation Pane Style
The onscreen area known as the navigation pane is capitalized when referring to the Access Navigation Pane. When referring to the File Management navigation pane, the term is not capitalized.

You work on objects such as tables, forms, and reports in the **Access work area**. Figure 12 shows a work area with multiple objects open. **Object tabs** for the open objects appear at the top of the work area. You select an open object by tapping or clicking its tab. In the figure, the Client Form is the selected object. To the left of the work area is the Navigation Pane, which contains a list of all the objects in the database. You use this pane to open an object. You also can customize the way objects are displayed in the Navigation Pane.

Because the Navigation Pane can take up space in the window, you may not have as much open space for working as you would with Word or Excel. You can use the Shutter Bar Open/Close button to minimize the Navigation Pane when you are not using it, which allows more space to work with tables, forms, reports, and other database elements.

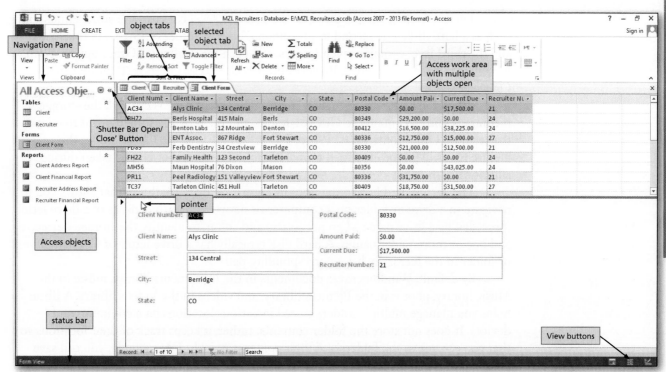

Figure 12

Saving and Organizing Files

Before starting to work in Access, you must either create a new database or open an existing database. When you create a database, the computer places it on a storage medium such as a hard disk, solid state drive (SSD), USB flash drive, or optical disc. The storage medium can be permanent in your computer, may be portable where you remove it from your computer, or may be on a web server you access through a network or the Internet.

A database or other saved document is referred to as a file. A **file name** is the name assigned to a file when it is saved. When saving files, you should organize them so that you easily can find them later. Windows provides tools to help you organize files.

Organizing Files and Folders

You should organize and store databases and other files in folders to help you find the databases or other files quickly.

If you are taking an introductory computer class (CIS 101, for example), you may want to design a series of folders for the different subjects covered in the class. To accomplish this, you can arrange the folders in a hierarchy for the class, as shown in Figure 13.

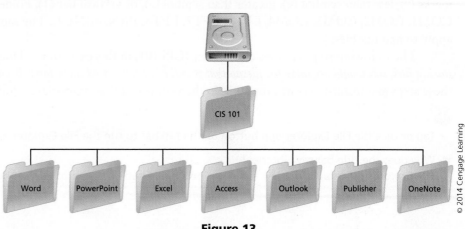

Figure 13

The hierarchy contains three levels. The first level contains the storage medium, such as a hard disk. The second level contains the class folder (CIS 101, in this case), and the third level contains seven folders, one each for a different Office app that will be covered in the class (Word, PowerPoint, Excel, Access, Outlook, Publisher, and OneNote).

When the hierarchy in Figure 13 on the previous page is created, the storage medium is said to contain the CIS 101 folder, and the CIS 101 folder is said to contain the separate Office folders (i.e., Word, PowerPoint, Excel, etc.). In addition, this hierarchy easily can be expanded to include folders from other classes taken during additional semesters.

The vertical and horizontal lines in Figure 13 form a pathway that allows you to navigate to a drive or folder on a computer or network. A **path** consists of a drive letter (preceded by a drive name when necessary) and colon, to identify the storage device, and one or more folder names. A hard disk typically has a drive letter of C. Each drive or folder in the hierarchy has a corresponding path.

By default, Windows saves documents in the Documents library, music in the Music library, photos in the Pictures library, and videos in the Videos library. A **library** helps you manage multiple folders stored in various locations on a computer and devices. It does not store the folder contents; rather, it keeps track of their locations so that you can access the folders and their contents quickly. For example, you can save pictures from a digital camera in any folder on any storage location on a computer. Normally, this would make organizing the different folders difficult. If you add the folders to a library, however, you can access all the pictures from one location regardless of where they are stored.

The following pages illustrate the steps to organize the folders for this class and create a database in one of those folders:

1. Create the folder identifying your class.
2. Create the Access folder in the folder identifying your class.
3. Create the remaining folders in the folder identifying your class.
4. Save a file in the Access folder.
5. Verify the location of the saved file.

To Create a Folder

1 SIGN IN | 2 USE WINDOWS | 3 USE APPS | 4 FILE MANAGEMENT | 5 SWITCH APPS | 6 SAVE FILES
7 CHANGE SCREEN RESOLUTION | 8 EXIT APPS | 9 USE ADDITIONAL APP | 10 USE HELP

When you create a folder, such as the CIS 101 folder shown in Figure 13, you must name the folder. A folder name should describe the folder and its contents. A folder name can contain spaces and any uppercase or lowercase characters, except a backslash (\), slash (/), colon (:), asterisk (*), question mark (?), quotation marks ("), less than symbol (<), greater than symbol (>), or vertical bar (|). Folder names cannot be CON, AUX, COM1, COM2, COM3, COM4, LPT1, LPT2, LPT3, PRN, or NUL. The same rules for naming folders also apply to naming files.

The following steps create a class folder (CIS 101, in this case) in the Documents library. *Why? When storing files, you should organize the files so that it will be easier to find them later.* If you are using Windows 7, skip these steps and instead perform the steps in the yellow box that immediately follows these Windows 8 steps.

- Tap or click the File Explorer app button on the taskbar to run the File Explorer app (Figure 14).

Q&A | Why does the title bar say Libraries?
File Explorer, by default, displays the name of the selected library or folder on the title bar.

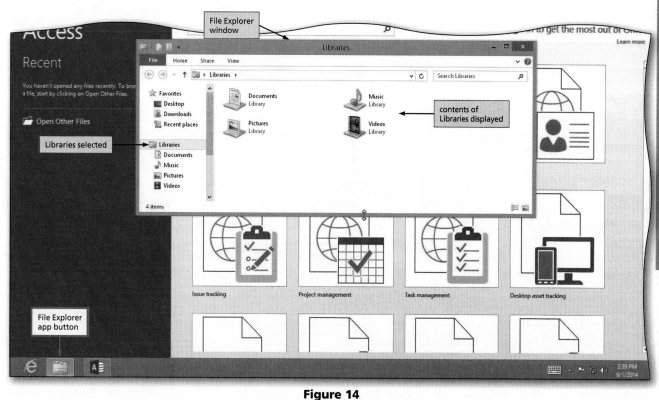

Figure 14

②

• Tap or click the Documents library in the navigation pane to display the contents of the Documents library in the file list (Figure 15).

Q&A What if my screen does not show the Documents, Music, Pictures, and Videos libraries? Double-tap or double-click Libraries in the navigation pane to expand the list.

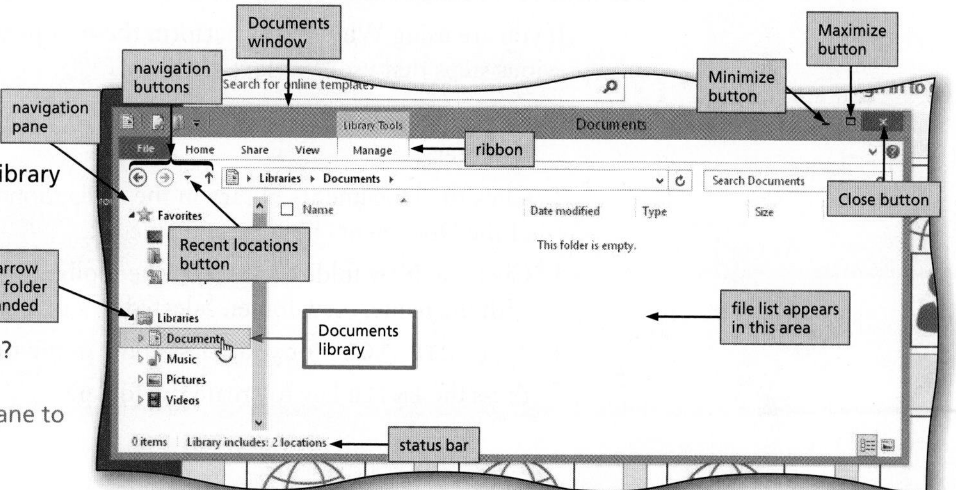

Figure 15

③

• Tap or click the New folder button on the Quick Access Toolbar to create a new folder with the name, New folder, selected in a text box (Figure 16).

Q&A Why is the folder icon displayed differently on my computer? Windows might be configured to display contents differently on your computer.

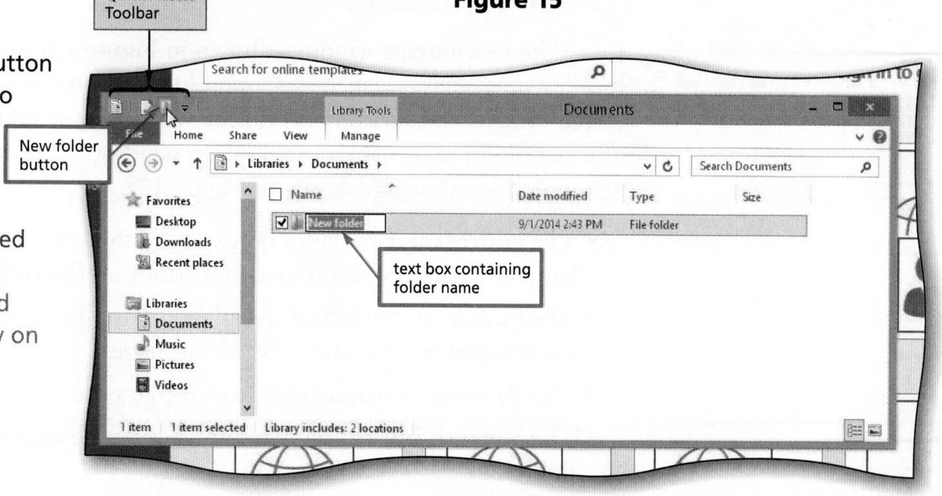

Figure 16

4

- Type **CIS 101** (or your class code) in the text box as the new folder name.
- If requested by your instructor, add your last name to the end.
- Press the ENTER key to change the folder name from New folder to a folder name identifying your class (Figure 17).

Q&A What happens when I press the ENTER key?
The class folder (CIS 101, in this case) is displayed in the file list, which contains the folder name, date modified, type, and size.

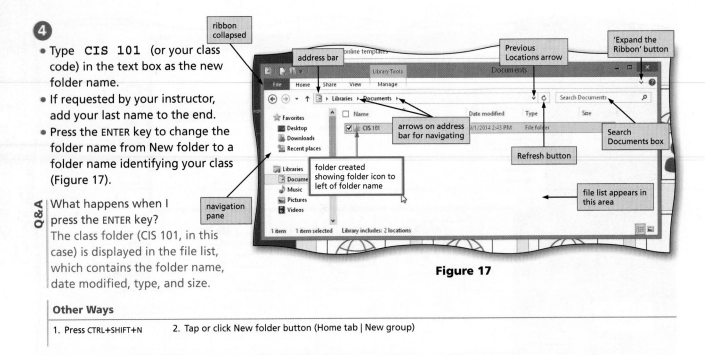

Figure 17

Other Ways

1. Press CTRL+SHIFT+N   2. Tap or click New folder button (Home tab | New group)

TO CREATE A FOLDER USING WINDOWS 7

If you are using Windows 7, perform these steps to create a folder instead of the previous steps that use Windows 8.

1. Click the Windows Explorer button on the taskbar to run Windows Explorer.
2. Click the Documents library in the navigation pane to display the contents of the Documents library in the file list.
3. Click the New folder button on the toolbar to display a new folder icon with the name, New folder, selected in a text box.
4. Type **CIS 101** (or your class code) in the text box to name the folder.
5. Press the ENTER key to create the folder.

Folder Windows

The Documents window (shown in Figure 17) is called a folder window. Recall that a folder is a specific named location on a storage medium that contains related files. Most users rely on **folder windows** for finding, viewing, and managing information on their computers. Folder windows have common design elements, including the following (shown in Figure 17).

- The **address bar** provides quick navigation options. The arrows on the address bar allow you to visit different locations on the computer.
- The buttons to the left of the address bar allow you to navigate the contents of the navigation pane and view recent pages.
- The **Previous Locations arrow** displays the locations you have visited.
- The **Refresh button** on the right side of the address bar refreshes the contents of the folder list.

- The **search box** contains the dimmed words, Search Documents. You can type a term in the search box for a list of files, folders, shortcuts, and elements containing that term within the location you are searching. A **shortcut** is an icon on the desktop that provides a user with immediate access to an app or file.

- The **ribbon** contains five tabs used to accomplish various tasks on the computer related to organizing and managing the contents of the open window. This ribbon works similarly to the ribbon in the Office apps.

- The **navigation pane** on the left contains the Favorites area, Libraries area, Homegroup area, Computer area, and Network area.

- The **Favorites area** shows your favorite locations. By default, this list contains only links to your Desktop, Downloads, and Recent places.

- The **Libraries area** shows folders included in a library.

To Create a Folder within a Folder

1 SIGN IN | 2 USE WINDOWS | 3 USE APPS | 4 FILE MANAGEMENT | 5 SWITCH APPS | 6 SAVE FILES
7 CHANGE SCREEN RESOLUTION | 8 EXIT APPS | 9 USE ADDITIONAL APP | 10 USE HELP

With the class folder created, you can create folders that will store the files you create using each Office app. The following steps create an Access folder in the CIS 101 folder (or the folder identifying your class). *Why? To be able to organize your files, you should create a folder structure.* If you are using Windows 7, skip these steps and instead perform the steps in the yellow box that immediately follows these Windows 8 steps.

- Double-tap or double-click the icon or folder name for the CIS 101 folder (or the folder identifying your class) in the file list to open the folder (Figure 18).

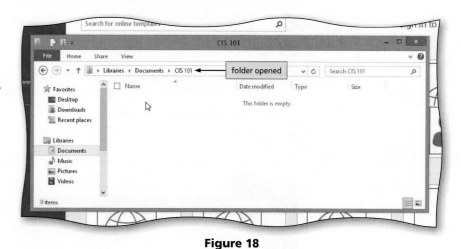

Figure 18

❷

- Tap or click the New folder button on the Quick Access Toolbar to create a new folder with the name, New folder, selected in a text box folder.
- Type **Access** in the text box as the new folder name.
- Press the ENTER key to rename the folder (Figure 19).

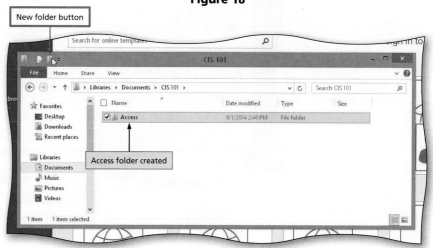

Figure 19

Other Ways

1. Press CTRL+SHIFT+N   2. Tap or click New folder button (Home tab | New group)

TO CREATE A FOLDER WITHIN A FOLDER USING WINDOWS 7

If you are using Windows 7, perform these steps to create a folder within a folder instead of the previous steps that use Windows 8.

1. Double-click the icon or folder name for the CIS 101 folder (or the folder identifying your class) in the file list to open the folder.
2. Click the New folder button on the toolbar to display a new folder icon and text box for the folder.
3. Type **Access** in the text box to name the folder.
4. Press the ENTER key to create the folder.

To Create the Remaining Folders

Even though you will only use the Access folder in this chapter, for practice you will create some of the remaining folders in the folder identifying your class (in this case, CIS 101). If you are using Windows 7, skip these steps and instead perform the steps in the yellow box that immediately follows these Windows 8 steps.

1 Tap or click the New folder button on the Quick Access Toolbar to create a new folder with the name, New folder, selected in a text box.

2 Type **Excel** in the text box as the new folder name.

3 Press the ENTER key to rename the folder.

4 Repeat Steps 1 through 3 to create each of the remaining folders, using OneNote, Outlook, PowerPoint, and Publisher as the folder names (Figure 20).

Q&A | Do I need to create all of the folders?
    | No, the only one you need to create is the Access folder.

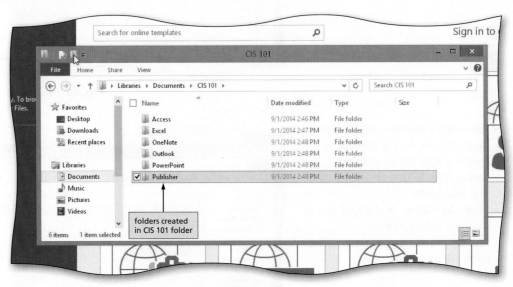

Figure 20

TO CREATE THE REMAINING FOLDERS USING WINDOWS 7

If you are using Windows 7, perform these steps to create the remaining folders instead of the previous steps that use Windows 8.

1. Click the New folder button on the toolbar to create a new folder with the name, New folder, selected in a text box.
2. Type **Access** in the text box as the new folder name.
3. Press the ENTER key to rename the folder.
4. Repeat Steps 1 through 3 to create each of the remaining folders, using Excel, OneNote, Outlook, PowerPoint, and Publisher as the folder names.

To Expand a Folder, Scroll through Folder Contents, and Collapse a Folder

1 SIGN IN | 2 USE WINDOWS | 3 USE APPS | 4 FILE MANAGEMENT | 5 SWITCH APPS | 6 SAVE FILES
7 CHANGE SCREEN RESOLUTION | 8 EXIT APPS | 9 USE ADDITIONAL APP | 10 USE HELP

Folder windows display the hierarchy of items and the contents of drives and folders in the file list. You might want to expand a library or folder in the navigation pane to view its contents, slide or scroll through its contents, and collapse it when you are finished viewing its contents. *Why? When a folder is expanded, you can see all the folders it contains. By contrast, a collapsed folder hides the folders it contains.* The following steps expand, slide or scroll through, and then collapse the folder identifying your class (CIS 101, in this case).

1

- Double-tap or double-click the Documents library in the navigation pane, which expands the library to display its contents and displays a black arrow to the left of the Documents library icon (Figure 21).

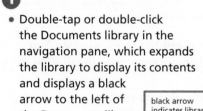

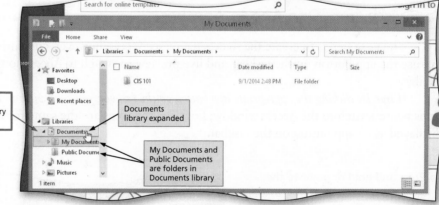

Figure 21

2

- Double-tap or double-click the My Documents folder, which expands the folder to display its contents and displays a black arrow to the left of the My Documents folder icon.

Q&A What is the My Documents folder?
When you save files on your hard disk, the My Documents folder is the default save location.

- Double-tap or double-click the CIS 101 folder, which expands the folder to display its contents and displays a black arrow to the left of the folder icon (Figure 22).

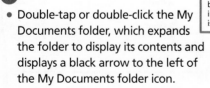

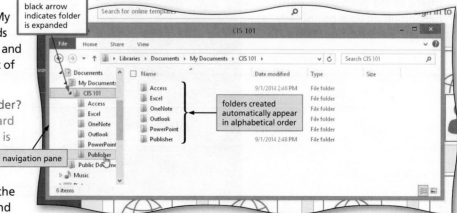

Figure 22

 **Experiment**

- Slide the scroll bar down or click the down scroll arrow on the vertical scroll bar to display additional folders at the bottom of the navigation pane. Slide the scroll bar up or click the scroll bar above the scroll box to move the scroll box to the top of the navigation pane. Drag the scroll box down the scroll bar until the scroll box is halfway down the scroll bar.

- Double-tap or double-click the folder identifying your class (CIS 101, in this case) to collapse the folder (Figure 23).

Q&A Why are some folders indented below others? A folder contains the indented folders below it.

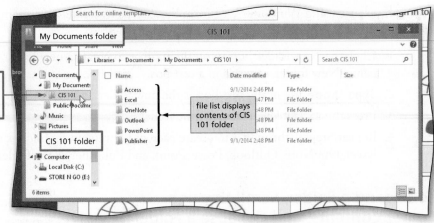

Figure 23

Other Ways

1. Point to display arrows in navigation pane, tap or click white arrow to expand or tap or click black arrow to collapse

2. Select folder to expand or collapse using arrow keys, press RIGHT ARROW to expand; press LEFT ARROW to collapse

To Switch from One App to Another

The next step is to create the Access database. Access, however, currently is not the active window. You can use the app button on the taskbar and live preview to switch to Access so that you can create the desired database.

Why? *By clicking the appropriate app button on the taskbar, you can switch to the open app you want to use.* The steps below switch to the Access window; however, the steps are the same for any active Office app currently displayed as an app button on the taskbar.

- Press and hold or point to the Access app button on the taskbar to see a live preview of the open database(s) or the window title(s) of the open database(s), depending on your computer's configuration (Figure 24).

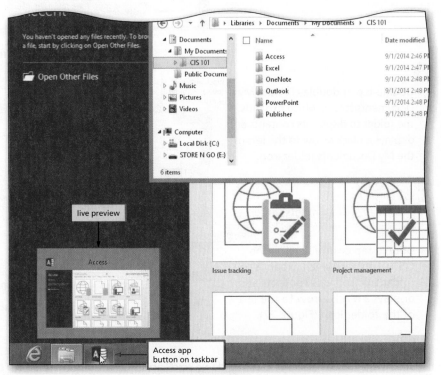

Figure 24

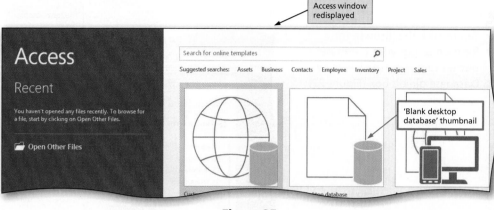

Figure 25

Break Point: If you wish to take a break, this is a good place to do so. To resume at a later time, continue to follow the steps from this location forward.

Creating an Access Database

Unlike the other Office apps, Access saves a database when you first create it. When working in Access, you will add data to an Access database. As you add data to a database, Access automatically saves your changes rather than waiting until you manually save the database or exit Access. In other apps, you first enter data and then save it.

Because Access automatically saves the database as you add and change data, you do not always have to click the Save button on the Quick Access Toolbar. Instead, the Save button in Access is used for saving the objects (including tables, queries, forms, reports, and other database objects) a database contains. You can use either the 'Blank desktop database' option or a template to create a new database. If you already know the organization of your database, you would use the 'Blank desktop database' option. If not, you can use a template. Templates can guide you by suggesting some commonly used database organizations.

To Create a Database in a Folder

1 SIGN IN | 2 USE WINDOWS | 3 USE APPS | 4 FILE MANAGEMENT | **5 SWITCH APPS** | **6 SAVE FILES**
7 CHANGE SCREEN RESOLUTION | **8 EXIT APPS** | **9 USE ADDITIONAL APP** | **10 USE HELP**

The following steps use the 'Blank desktop database' option to create a database named PJP Marketing in the Access folder in the class folder (CIS 101, in this case) in the Documents library. **Why?** *If you want to maintain data for a company, a database is perfect for the job.*

With the folders for storing your files created, you can create the database. The following steps create a database in the Access folder contained in your class folder (CIS 101, in this case) using the file name, PJP Marketing.

- Tap or click the 'Blank desktop database' thumbnail (shown in Figure 25) to select the database type.
- Type **PJP Marketing** in the File Name text box to enter the new file name. Do not press the ENTER key after typing the file name because you do not want to create the database yet (Figure 26).

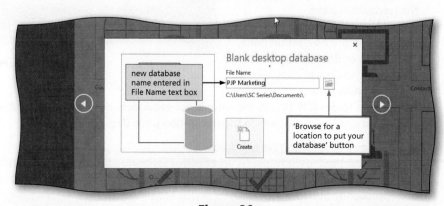

Figure 26

2

- Tap or click the 'Browse for a location to put your database' button to display the File New Database dialog box (Figure 27).

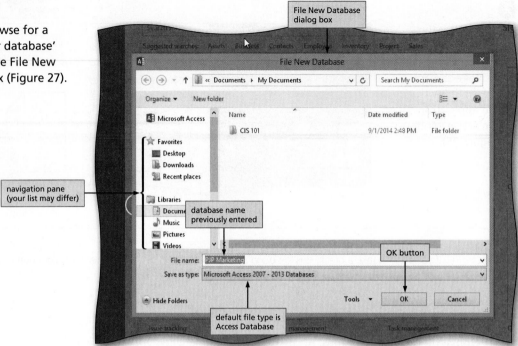

Figure 27

3

- Navigate to the desired save location (in this case, the Access folder in the CIS 101 folder [or your class folder] in the My Documents folder in the Documents library) by performing the tasks in Steps 3a and 3b.

3a

- If the Documents library is not displayed in the navigation pane, slide to scroll or drag the scroll bar in the navigation pane until Documents appears.
- If the Documents library is not expanded in the navigation pane, double-tap or double-click Documents to display its folders in the navigation pane.
- If the My Documents folder is not expanded in the navigation pane, double-tap or double-click My Documents to display its folders in the navigation pane.

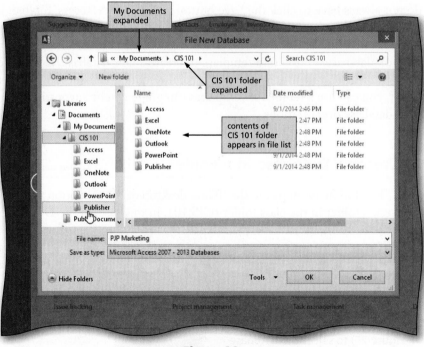

Figure 28

- If your class folder (CIS 101, in this case) is not expanded, double-tap or double-click the CIS 101 folder to select the folder and display its contents in the navigation pane (Figure 28).

Q&A What if I do not want to save in a folder?

Although storing files in folders is an effective technique for organizing files, some users prefer not to store files in folders. If you prefer not to save this file in a folder, select the storage device on which you wish to save the file and then proceed to Step 5.

- Tap or click the Access folder in the navigation pane to select it as the new save location and display its contents in the file list (Figure 29).

Q&A Why does the 'Save as type' box say Microsoft Access 2007–2013 Databases?
Microsoft Access database formats change with some new versions of Microsoft Access. The most recent format is the Microsoft Access 2007–2013 Databases format.

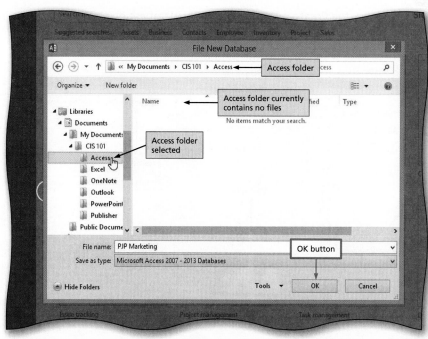

Figure 29

4
- Tap or click the OK button (File New Database dialog box) to select the Access folder as the location for the database and close the dialog box (Figure 30).

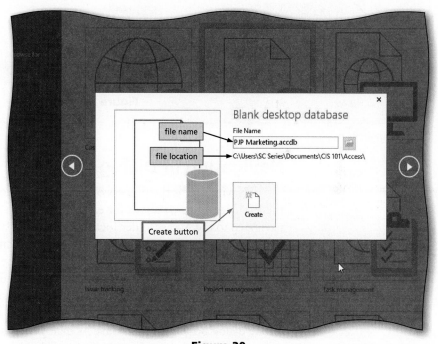

Figure 30

5

- Tap or click the Create button to create the database on the selected drive in the selected folder with the file name, PJP Marketing (Figure 31).

Q&A How do I know that the PJP Marketing database is created?

The file name of the database appears on the title bar.

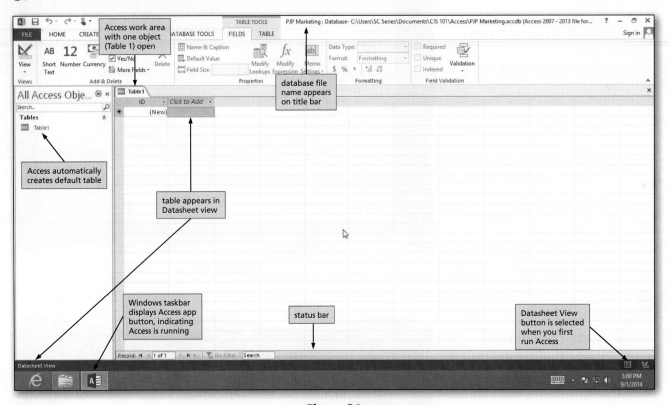

Figure 31

Navigating in Dialog Boxes

Navigating is the process of finding a location on a storage device. While creating the PJP Marketing database, for example, Steps 3a and 3b in the previous set of steps navigated to the Access folder located in the CIS 101 folder in the My Documents folder in the Documents library. When performing certain functions in Windows apps, such as saving a file, opening a file, or inserting a picture in a database object, you most likely will have to navigate to the location where you want to save the file or to the folder containing the file you want to open or insert. Most dialog boxes in Windows apps requiring navigation follow a similar procedure; that is, the way you navigate to a folder in one dialog box, such as the Save As dialog box, is similar to how you might navigate in another dialog box, such as the Open dialog box. If you chose to navigate to a specific location in a dialog box, you would follow the instructions in Steps 3a and 3b.

The Access Window

The Access window consists of a variety of components to make your work more efficient. These include the Navigation Pane, Access work area, ribbon, shortcut menus, and Quick Access Toolbar. Some of these components are common to other Office apps; others are unique to Access.

Navigation Pane and Access Work Area

You work on objects such as tables, forms, and reports in the **Access work area**. In the work area in Figure 31, a single table, Table1, is open in the work area. **Object tabs** for the open objects appear at the top of the work area. If you have multiple objects open at the same time, you can select one of the open objects by tapping or clicking its tab. To the left of the work area is the Navigation Pane. The **Navigation Pane** contains a list of all the objects in the database. You use this pane to open an object. You also can customize the way objects are displayed in the Navigation Pane.

Status Bar   The **status bar**, located at the bottom of the Access window, presents information about the database object, the progress of current tasks, and the status of certain commands and keys; it also provides controls for viewing the object. As you enter data or perform certain commands, various indicators may appear on the status bar. The left edge of the status bar in Figure 31 shows that the table object is open in **Datasheet view**. In Datasheet view, the table is represented as a collection of rows and columns called a **datasheet**. Toward the right edge are View buttons, which you can use to change the view that currently appears.

Scroll Bars   You use a scroll bar to display different portions of an object. If an object is too long to fit vertically, a vertical scroll bar will appear at the right edge of the work area. If an object is too wide to fit, a horizontal scroll bar also appears at the bottom of the work area. On a scroll bar, the position of the scroll box reflects the location of the portion of the object that is displayed in the work area.

Ribbon   The ribbon, located near the top of the window below the title bar, is the control center in Access and other Office apps (Figure 32). The ribbon provides easy, central access to the tasks you perform while creating a database. The ribbon consists of tabs, groups, and commands. Each **tab** contains a collection of groups, and each **group** contains related functions. When you run an Office app, such as Access, it initially displays several main tabs, also called default or top-level tabs. All Office apps have a HOME tab, which contains the more frequently used commands.

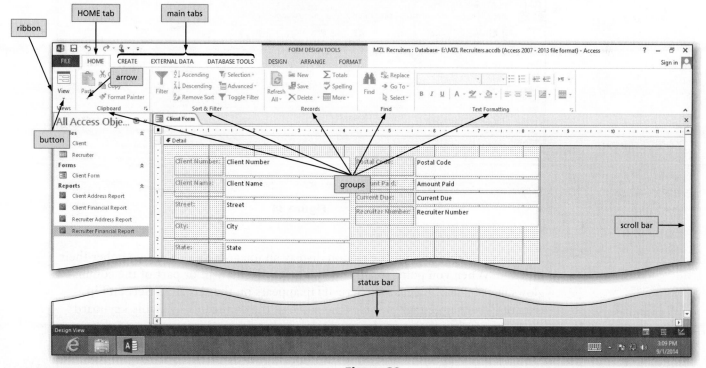

Figure 32

In addition to the main tabs, the Office apps display **tool tabs**, also called contextual tabs (Figure 33), when you perform certain tasks or work with objects such as pictures or tables. If you modify the design of a form, for example, the FORM DESIGN TOOLS tab and its related subordinate DESIGN tab appear, collectively referred to as the FORM DESIGN TOOLS DESIGN tab. When you are finished working with the form, the FORM DESIGN TOOLS DESIGN tab disappears from the ribbon. Access and other Office apps determine when tool tabs should appear and disappear based on tasks you perform.

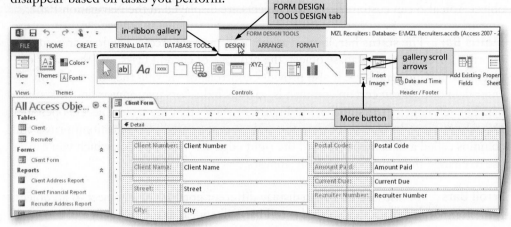

Figure 33

Items on the ribbon include buttons, boxes, and galleries (shown in Figure 32 on the previous page). A **gallery** is a set of choices, often graphical, arranged in a grid or in a list. You can scroll through choices in an in-ribbon gallery by tapping or clicking the gallery's scroll arrows. Or, you can tap or click a gallery's More button to view more gallery options on the screen at a time.

Some buttons and boxes have arrows that, when tapped or clicked, also display a gallery; others always cause a gallery to be displayed when tapped or clicked (Figure 34).

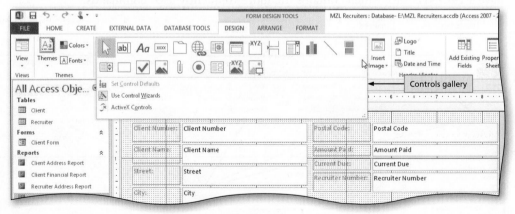

Figure 34

Some commands on the ribbon display an image to help you remember their function. When you point to a command on the ribbon, all or part of the command glows in a shade of blue, and a ScreenTip appears on the screen. A **ScreenTip** is an on-screen note that provides the name of the command, available keyboard shortcut(s), a description of the command, and sometimes instructions for how to obtain help about the command (Figure 35).

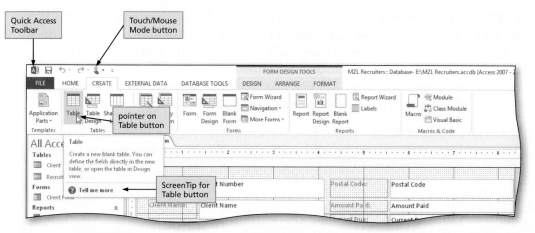

Figure 35

Some groups on the ribbon have a small arrow in the lower-right corner, called a **Dialog Box Launcher**, that when tapped or clicked, displays a dialog box or a task pane with additional options for the group (Figure 36). When presented with a dialog box, you make selections and must close the dialog box before returning to the document. A **task pane**, in contrast to a dialog box, is a window that can remain open and visible while you work in the document.

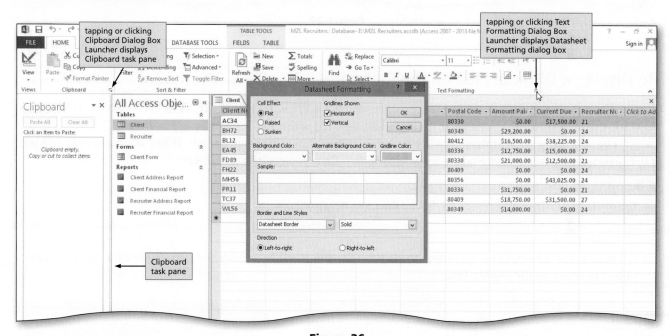

Figure 36

Quick Access Toolbar   The **Quick Access Toolbar**, located initially (by default) above the ribbon at the left edge of the title bar, provides convenient, one-tap or one-click access to frequently used commands (shown in Figure 35). The commands on the Quick Access Toolbar always are available, regardless of the task you are performing. The Touch/Mouse Mode button on the Quick Access Toolbar allows you to switch between Touch mode and Mouse mode. If you primarily are using touch gestures, Touch mode will add more space between commands on menus and on the ribbon so that they are easier to tap. While touch gestures are convenient ways to interact with Office apps, not all features are supported when you are using Touch mode. If you are using a mouse, Mouse mode will not add the extra space between buttons and commands. The Quick Access Toolbar is discussed in more depth later in the chapter.

BTW

Touch Mode
The Office and Windows interfaces may vary if you are using Touch mode. For this reason, you might notice that the function or appearance of your touch screen in Access differs slightly from this book's presentation.

KeyTips   If you prefer using the keyboard instead of the mouse, you can press the ALT key on the keyboard to display **KeyTips**, or keyboard code icons, for certain commands (Figure 37). To select a command using the keyboard, press the letter or number displayed in the KeyTip, which may cause additional KeyTips related to the selected command to appear. To remove KeyTips from the screen, press the ALT key or the ESC key until all KeyTips disappear, or tap or click anywhere in the app window.

Microsoft Account Area   In this area, you can use the Sign in link to sign in to your Microsoft account. Once signed in, you will see your account information as well as a picture if you have included one in your Microsoft account.

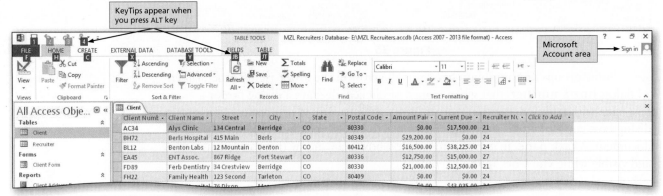

Figure 37

To Display a Different Tab on the Ribbon

1 SIGN IN | 2 USE WINDOWS | 3 USE APPS | 4 FILE MANAGEMENT | 5 SWITCH APPS | 6 SAVE FILES
7 CHANGE SCREEN RESOLUTION | 8 EXIT APPS | 9 USE ADDITIONAL APP FEATURES | 10 USE HELP

When you run Access, the ribbon displays five main tabs: FILE, HOME, CREATE, EXTERNAL DATA, and DATABASE TOOLS. The tab currently displayed is called the **active tab**.

The following step displays the CREATE tab, that is, makes it the active tab. ***Why?*** *When working with an Office app, you may need to switch tabs to access other options for working with a document.*

1

- Tap or click CREATE on the ribbon to display the CREATE tab (Figure 38).

🔍 **Experiment**

- Tap or click the other tabs on the ribbon to view their contents. When you are finished, tap or click CREATE on the ribbon to redisplay the CREATE tab.

Q&A | If I am working in a different Office app, such as PowerPoint or Word, how do I display a different tab on the ribbon?
Follow this same procedure; that is, tap or click the desired tab on the ribbon.

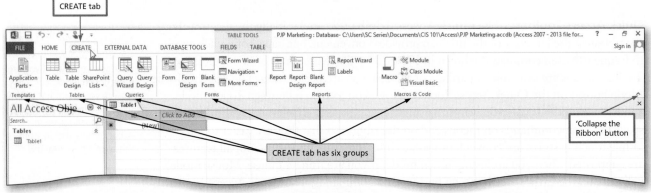

Figure 38

To Collapse and Expand the Ribbon

To display more of a document or other item in the window of an Office app, some users prefer to collapse the ribbon, which hides the groups on the ribbon and displays only the main tabs. Each time you run an Office app, such as Access, the ribbon appears the same way it did the last time you used that Office app. The chapters in this book, however, begin with the ribbon appearing as it did at the initial installation of Office or Access.

The following steps collapse, expand, and restore the ribbon in Access. *Why? If you need more space on the screen to work with your database, you can collapse the ribbon to gain additional workspace.*

1

- Tap or click the 'Collapse the Ribbon' button on the ribbon (shown in Figure 38) to collapse the ribbon (Figure 39).

Q&A What happened to the groups on the ribbon?
When you collapse the ribbon, the groups disappear so that the ribbon does not take up as much space on the screen.

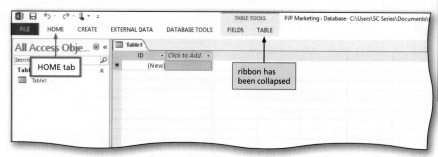

Figure 39

What happened to the 'Collapse the Ribbon' button?
The 'Pin the ribbon' button replaces the 'Collapse the Ribbon' button when the ribbon is collapsed. You will see the 'Pin the ribbon' button only when you expand a ribbon by tapping or clicking a tab.

2

- Tap or click HOME on the ribbon to expand the HOME tab (Figure 40).

Q&A Why would I click the HOME tab?
If you want to use a command on a collapsed ribbon, tap or click the main tab to display the groups for that tab. After you select a command on the ribbon, the groups will be collapsed once again. If you decide not to use a command on the ribbon, you can collapse the groups by tapping or clicking the same main tab or tapping or clicking in the app window.

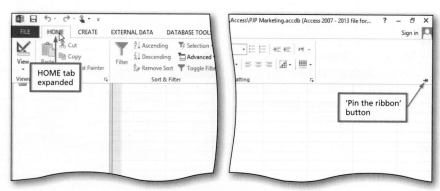

Figure 40

 Experiment

- Tap or click HOME on the ribbon to collapse the groups again. Tap or click HOME on the ribbon to expand the HOME tab.

3

- Tap or click the 'Pin the ribbon' button on the expanded HOME tab to restore the ribbon.

Other Ways

1. Double-tap or double-click a main tab on the ribbon   2. Press CTRL+F1

To Use a Shortcut Menu to Relocate the Quick Access Toolbar

When you press and hold or right-click certain areas of the Access and other Office app windows, a shortcut menu will appear. A **shortcut menu** is a list of frequently used commands that relate to an object. *Why? You can use shortcut menus to access common commands quickly.* When you press and hold or right-click the status bar, for example, a shortcut menu appears with commands related to the status bar. When you press and hold or right-click the Quick Access Toolbar, a shortcut menu appears with commands related to the Quick Access Toolbar. The following steps use a shortcut menu to move the Quick Access Toolbar, which by default is located on the title bar.

1

- Press and hold or right-click the Quick Access Toolbar to display a shortcut menu that presents a list of commands related to the Quick Access Toolbar (Figure 41).

Q&A What if I cannot make the shortcut menu appear using the touch instruction?

When you use the press and hold technique, be sure to release your finger when the circle appears on the screen to display the shortcut menu. If the technique still does not work, you might need to add more space around objects on the screen, making it easier for you to press or tap them. Click the 'Customize Quick Access Toolbar' button and then click 'Touch/Mouse Mode' on the menu. Another option is to use the stylus.

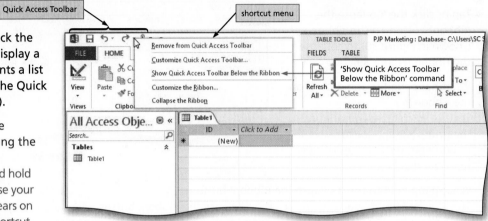

Figure 41

2

- Tap or click 'Show Quick Access Toolbar Below the Ribbon' on the shortcut menu to display the Quick Access Toolbar below the ribbon (Figure 42).

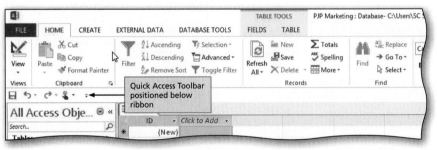

Figure 42

3

- Press and hold or right-click the Quick Access Toolbar to display a shortcut menu (Figure 43).

4

- Tap or click 'Show Quick Access Toolbar Above the Ribbon' on the shortcut menu to return the Quick Access Toolbar to its original position (shown in Figure 41).

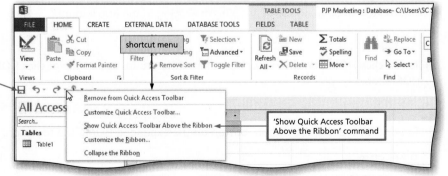

Figure 43

Other Ways

1. Tap or click 'Customize Quick Access Toolbar' button on Quick Access Toolbar, tap or click 'Show Below the Ribbon' or 'Show Above the Ribbon'

To Customize the Quick Access Toolbar

1 SIGN IN | 2 USE WINDOWS | 3 USE APPS | 4 FILE MANAGEMENT | 5 SWITCH APPS | 6 SAVE FILES
7 CHANGE SCREEN RESOLUTION | 8 EXIT APPS | 9 USE ADDITIONAL APP FEATURES | 10 USE HELP

The Quick Access Toolbar provides easy access to some of the more frequently used commands in the Office apps. By default, the Quick Access Toolbar contains buttons for the Save, Undo, and Redo commands. You can customize the Quick Access Toolbar by changing its location in the window, as shown in the previous steps, and by adding more buttons to reflect commands you would like to access easily. The following steps add the Quick Print button to the Quick Access Toolbar in the Access window. *Why?* *Adding the Quick Print button to the Quick Access Toolbar speeds up the process of printing.*

1

- Tap or click the 'Customize Quick Access Toolbar' button to display the Customize Quick Access Toolbar menu (Figure 44).

Q&A Which commands are listed on the Customize Quick Access Toolbar menu?

It lists commands that commonly are added to the Quick Access Toolbar.

What do the check marks next to some commands signify?

Check marks appear next to commands that already are on the Quick Access Toolbar. When you add a button to the Quick Access Toolbar, a check mark will be displayed next to its command name.

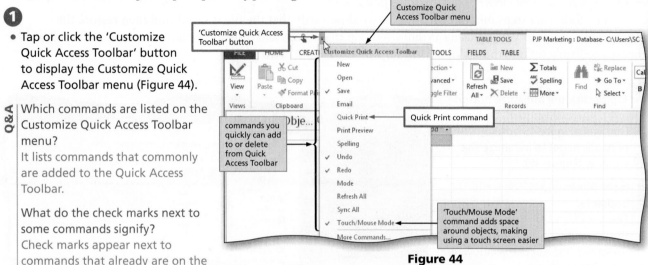

Figure 44

2

- Tap or click Quick Print on the Customize Quick Access Toolbar menu to add the Quick Print button to the Quick Access Toolbar (Figure 45).

Q&A How would I remove a button from the Quick Access Toolbar?

You would press and hold or right-click the button you wish to remove and then tap or click 'Remove from Quick Access Toolbar' on the shortcut menu or tap or click the 'Customize Quick Access Toolbar' button on the Quick Access Toolbar and then click the button name in the Customize Quick Access Toolbar menu to remove the check mark.

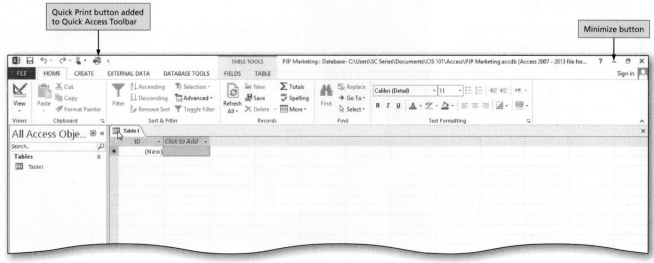

Figure 45

To Minimize and Restore a Window

Before continuing, you can verify that the Access file was saved properly. To do this, you will minimize the Access window and then open the CIS 101 window so that you can verify the file is stored in the CIS 101 folder on the hard disk. A **minimized window** is an open window that is hidden from view but can be displayed quickly by clicking the window's app button on the taskbar.

In the following example, Access is used to illustrate minimizing and restoring windows; however, you would follow the same steps regardless of the Office app you are using. *Why? Before closing an app, you should make sure your file saved correctly so that you can find it later.*

The following steps minimize the Access window, verify that the file is saved, and then restore the minimized window. If you are using Windows 7, skip these steps and instead perform the steps in the yellow box that immediately follows these Windows 8 steps.

- Tap or click the Minimize button on the Access window title bar (shown in Figure 45 on the previous page) to minimize the window (Figure 46).

Q&A Is the minimized window still available?
The minimized window, Access in this case, remains available but no longer is the active window. It is minimized as an app button on the taskbar.

- If the File Explorer window is not open on the screen, tap or click the File Explorer app button on the taskbar to make the File folder window the active window.

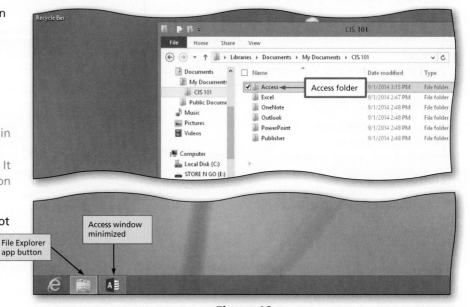

Figure 46

- Double-tap or double-click the Access folder in the file list to select the folder and display its contents (Figure 47).

Q&A Why does the File Explorer app button on the taskbar change?
A selected app button indicates that the app is active on the screen. When the button is not selected, the app is running but not active.

- After viewing the contents of the selected folder, tap or click the Access app button on the taskbar to restore the minimized window (as shown in Figure 47).

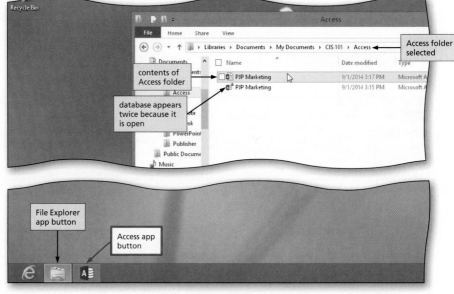

Figure 47

Other Ways

1. Press and hold or right-click title bar, tap or click Minimize on shortcut menu, tap or click taskbar button in taskbar button area

2. Press WINDOWS+M, press WINDOWS+SHIFT+M

TO MINIMIZE AND RESTORE A WINDOW USING WINDOWS 7

If you are using Windows 7, perform these steps to minimize and restore a window instead of the previous steps that use Windows 8.

1. Click the Minimize button on the app's title bar to minimize the window.

2. If the Windows Explorer window is not open on the screen, click the Windows Explorer button on the taskbar to make the Windows Explorer window the active window.

3. Double-click the Access folder in the file list to select the folder and display its contents.

4. After viewing the contents of the selected folder, click the Access button on the taskbar to restore the minimized window.

To Sign Out of a Microsoft Account

If you are using a public computer or otherwise wish to sign out of your Microsoft account, you should sign out of the account from the Account gallery in the Backstage view. Signing out of the account is the safest way to make sure that nobody else can access online files or settings stored in your Microsoft account. *Why? For security reasons, you should sign out of your Microsoft account when you are finished using a public or shared computer. Staying signed in to your Microsoft account might enable others to access your files.*

The following steps sign out of a Microsoft account from Access. You would use the same steps in any Office app. If you do not wish to sign out of your Microsoft account, read these steps without performing them.

1 Tap or click FILE on the ribbon to open the Backstage view.

2 Tap or click the Account tab to display the Account gallery (Figure 48 on the next page).

3 Tap or click the Sign out link, which displays the Remove Account dialog box. If a Can't remove Windows accounts dialog box appears instead of the Remove Account dialog box, tap or click the OK button and skip the remaining steps.

Q&A Why does a Can't remove Windows accounts dialog box appear?
If you signed in to Windows using your Microsoft account, then you also must sign out from Windows, rather than signing out from within Access. When you are finished using Windows, be sure to sign out at that time.

4 Tap or click the Yes button (Remove Account dialog box) to sign out of your Microsoft account on this computer.

Q&A Should I sign out of Windows after removing my Microsoft account?
When you are finished using the computer, you should sign out of Windows for maximum security.

5 Tap or click the Back button in the upper-left corner of the Backstage view to return to the document.

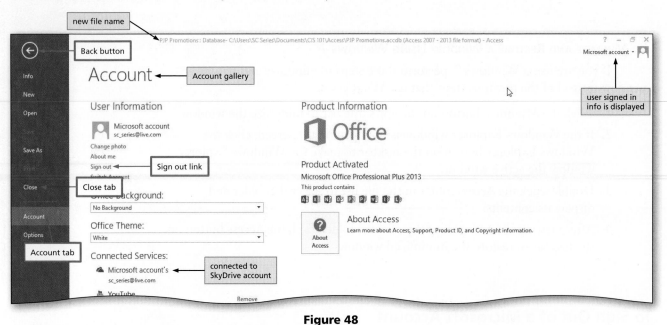

Figure 48

Screen Resolution

Screen resolution indicates the number of pixels (dots) that the computer uses to display the letters, numbers, graphics, and background you see on the screen. When you increase the screen resolution, Windows displays more information on the screen, but the information decreases in size. The reverse also is true: as you decrease the screen resolution, Windows displays less information on the screen, but the information increases in size.

Screen resolution usually is stated as the product of two numbers, such as 1366 × 768 (pronounced "thirteen sixty-six by seven sixty-eight"). A 1366 × 768 screen resolution results in a display of 1366 distinct pixels on each of 768 lines, or about 1,050,624 pixels. Changing the screen resolution affects how the ribbon appears in Office apps and some Windows dialog boxes. Figure 49, for example, shows the Access ribbon at screen resolutions of 1366 × 768 and 1024 × 768. All of the same commands are available regardless of screen resolution. The app (Access, in this case), however, makes changes to the groups and the buttons within the groups to accommodate the various screen resolutions. The result is that certain commands may need to be accessed differently depending on the resolution chosen. A command that is visible on the ribbon and available by tapping or clicking a button at one resolution may not be visible and may need to be accessed using its Dialog Box Launcher at a different resolution.

Comparing the two ribbons in Figure 49, notice the changes in content and layout of the groups and galleries. In some cases, the content of a group is the same in each resolution, but the layout of the group differs. For example, the same gallery and buttons appear in the Text Formatting groups in the two resolutions, but the layouts differ. In other cases, the content and layout are the same across the resolution, but the level of detail differs with the resolution.

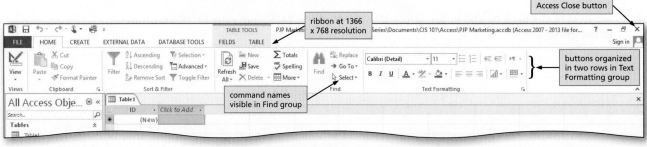

Figure 49 (a) Ribbon at 1366 × 768 Resolution

ribbon at 1024 x 768 resolution

buttons organized in three rows in Text Formatting group

not all command names visible in Find group

Figure 49 (b) Ribbon at 1024 × 768 Resolution

To Change the Screen Resolution

1 SIGN IN | 2 USE WINDOWS | 3 USE APPS | 4 FILE MANAGEMENT | 5 SWITCH APPS | 6 SAVE FILES
7 CHANGE SCREEN RESOLUTION | 8 EXIT APPS | 9 USE ADDITIONAL APP FEATURES | 10 USE HELP

If you are using a computer to step through the chapters in this book and you want your screen to match the figures, you may need to change your screen's resolution. *Why? The figures in this book use a screen resolution of 1366 × 768.* The following steps change the screen resolution to 1366 × 768. Your computer already may be set to 1366 × 768. Keep in mind that many computer labs prevent users from changing the screen resolution; in that case, read the following steps for illustration purposes.

- Tap or click the Show desktop button, which is located at the far-right edge of the taskbar, to display the Windows desktop.

Q&A I cannot see the Show desktop button. Why not?
When you point to the far-right edge of the taskbar, a small outline appears to mark the Show desktop button.

- Press and hold or right-click an empty area on the Windows desktop to display a shortcut menu that contains a list of commands related to the desktop (Figure 50).

Q&A Why does my shortcut menu display different commands?
Depending on your computer's hardware and configuration, different commands might appear on the shortcut menu.

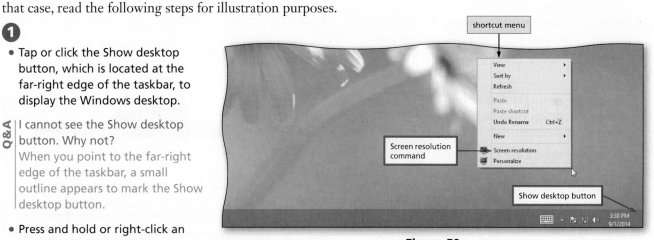

shortcut menu

Screen resolution command

Show desktop button

Figure 50

- Tap or click Screen resolution on the shortcut menu to open the Screen Resolution window (Figure 51).

- Tap or click the Resolution button in the Screen Resolution window to display the resolution slider.

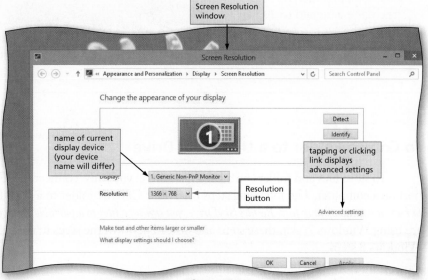

Screen Resolution window

name of current display device (your device name will differ)

tapping or clicking link displays advanced settings

Resolution button

Figure 51

4

- If necessary, drag the resolution slider until the desired screen resolution (in this case, 1366 × 768) is selected (Figure 52).

Q&A

What if my computer does not support the 1366 × 768 resolution?

Some computers do not support the 1366 × 768 resolution. In this case, select a resolution that is close to the 1366 × 768 resolution.

What is a slider?

A **slider** is an object that allows users to choose from multiple predetermined options. In most cases, these options represent some type of numeric value. In most cases, one end of the slider (usually the left or bottom) represents the lowest of available values, and the opposite end (usually the right or top) represents the highest available value.

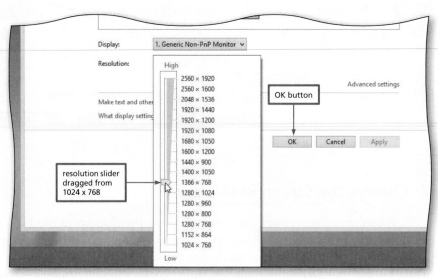

Figure 52

5

- Tap or click an empty area of the Screen Resolution window to close the resolution slider.

- Tap or click the OK button to change the screen resolution and display the Display Settings dialog box (Figure 53).

- Tap or click the Keep changes button (Display Settings dialog box) to accept the new screen resolution.

Q&A

Why does a message display stating that the image quality can be improved?

Some computer monitors or screens are designed to display contents better at a certain screen resolution, sometimes referred to as an optimal resolution.

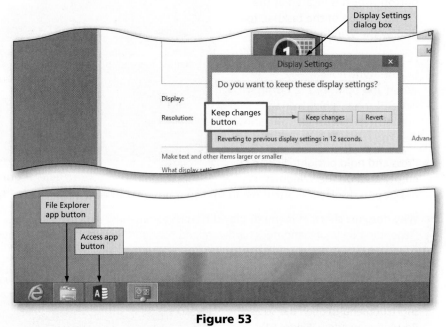

Figure 53

To Copy a Folder to a USB Flash Drive

1 SIGN IN | 2 USE WINDOWS | 3 USE APPS | **4 FILE MANAGEMENT** | 5 SWITCH APPS | 6 SAVE FILES
7 CHANGE SCREEN RESOLUTION | 8 EXIT APPS | **9 USE ADDITIONAL APP FEATURES** | 10 USE HELP

To store files and folders on a USB flash drive, you must connect the USB flash drive to an available USB port on a computer. The following steps copy your CIS 101 folder to a USB flash drive. *Why? It often is good practice to have a backup of your files. Besides SkyDrive, you can save files to a portable storage device, such as a USB flash drive.* If you are using Windows 7, skip these steps and instead perform the steps in the yellow box that immediately follows these Windows 8 steps.

- Insert a USB flash drive in an available USB port on the computer to connect the USB flash drive.

Q&A How can I ensure the USB flash drive is connected?
In File Explorer, you can use the navigation bar to find the USB flash drive. If it is not showing, then it is not connected properly.

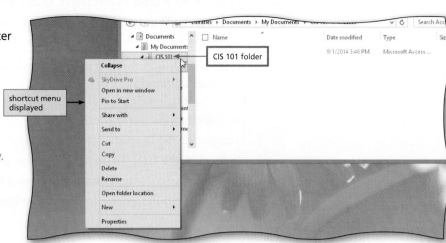

Figure 54

- Tap or click the File Explorer app button on the taskbar (shown in Figure 53) to make the folder window the active window.

- If necessary, navigate to the CIS 101 folder in the File Explorer window (see Step 3a on page OFF 24 for instructions about navigating to a folder location).

- Press and hold or right-click the CIS 101 folder to display a shortcut menu (Figure 54).

- Tap or point to Send to, which displays the Send to submenu (Figure 55).

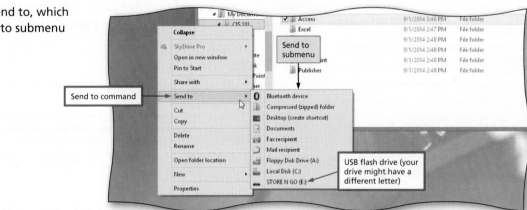

Figure 55

- Tap or click the USB flash drive to copy the folder to the USB flash drive (Figure 56).

Q&A Why does the drive letter of my USB flash drive differ?
Windows assigns the next available drive letter to your USB flash drive when you connect it. The next available drive letter may vary by computer, depending on the number of storage devices that currently are connected.

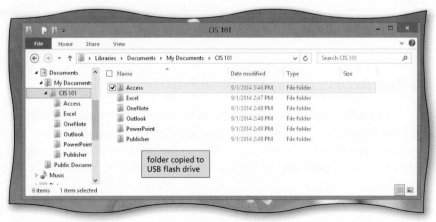

Figure 56

To Copy a Folder to a USB Flash Drive Using Windows 7

If you are using Windows 7, perform these steps to copy a folder to a USB flash drive instead of the previous steps that use Windows 8.

1. Insert a USB flash drive in an available USB port on the computer to open the AutoPlay window.
2. Click the 'Open folder to view files' link in the AutoPlay window to open the Windows Explorer window.
3. Navigate to the Documents library.
4. Right-click the CIS 101 folder to display a shortcut menu.
5. Point to Send to, which causes a submenu to appear.
6. Click the USB flash drive to copy the folder to the USB flash drive.

To Use the Backstage View to Close a Database

1 SIGN IN | 2 USE WINDOWS | 3 USE APPS | 4 FILE MANAGEMENT | 5 SWITCH APPS | 6 SAVE FILES
7 CHANGE SCREEN RESOLUTION | 8 EXIT APPS | 9 USE ADDITIONAL APPS | 10 USE HELP

Assume you need to close the Access database and return to it later. *Why? You no longer need to work with the PJP Marketing database, so you may close it.* The following step closes an Access database.

- Tap or click FILE on the ribbon to open the Backstage view and then click Close in the Backstage view (shown in Figure 48 on page OFF 36) to close the open file (PJP Marketing, in this case) without exiting Access.

Q&A | Why is Access still on the screen?
When you close a database, the app remains running.

To Exit an Office App

1 SIGN IN | 2 USE WINDOWS | 3 USE APPS | 4 FILE MANAGEMENT | 5 SWITCH APPS | 6 SAVE FILES
7 CHANGE SCREEN RESOLUTION | 8 EXIT APPS | 9 USE ADDITIONAL APPS | 10 USE HELP

You are finished using Access. The following step exits Access. *Why? It is good practice to exit an app when you are finished using it.*

- Tap or click the Close button on the right side of the title bar (shown in Figure 49a on page OFF 36) to close the file and exit the Office app.

Break Point: If you wish to take a break, this is a good place to do so. To resume at a later time, continue to follow the steps from this location forward.

To Run Access Using the Search Box

The following steps, which assume Windows is running, use the search box to run the Access app based on a typical installation. *Why? Sometimes an app does not appear on the Start screen, so you can find it quickly by searching.* You may need to ask your instructor how to run apps for your computer. If you are using Windows 7, skip these steps and instead perform the steps in the yellow box that immediately follows these Windows 8 steps.

1

- Swipe in from the right edge of the screen or point to the upper-right corner of the screen to display the Charms bar (Figure 57).

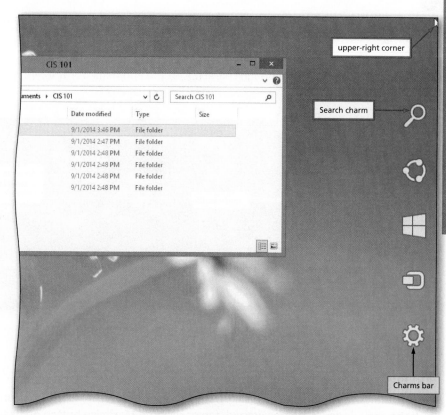

Figure 57

2

- Tap or click the Search charm on the Charms bar to display the Search menu (Figure 58).

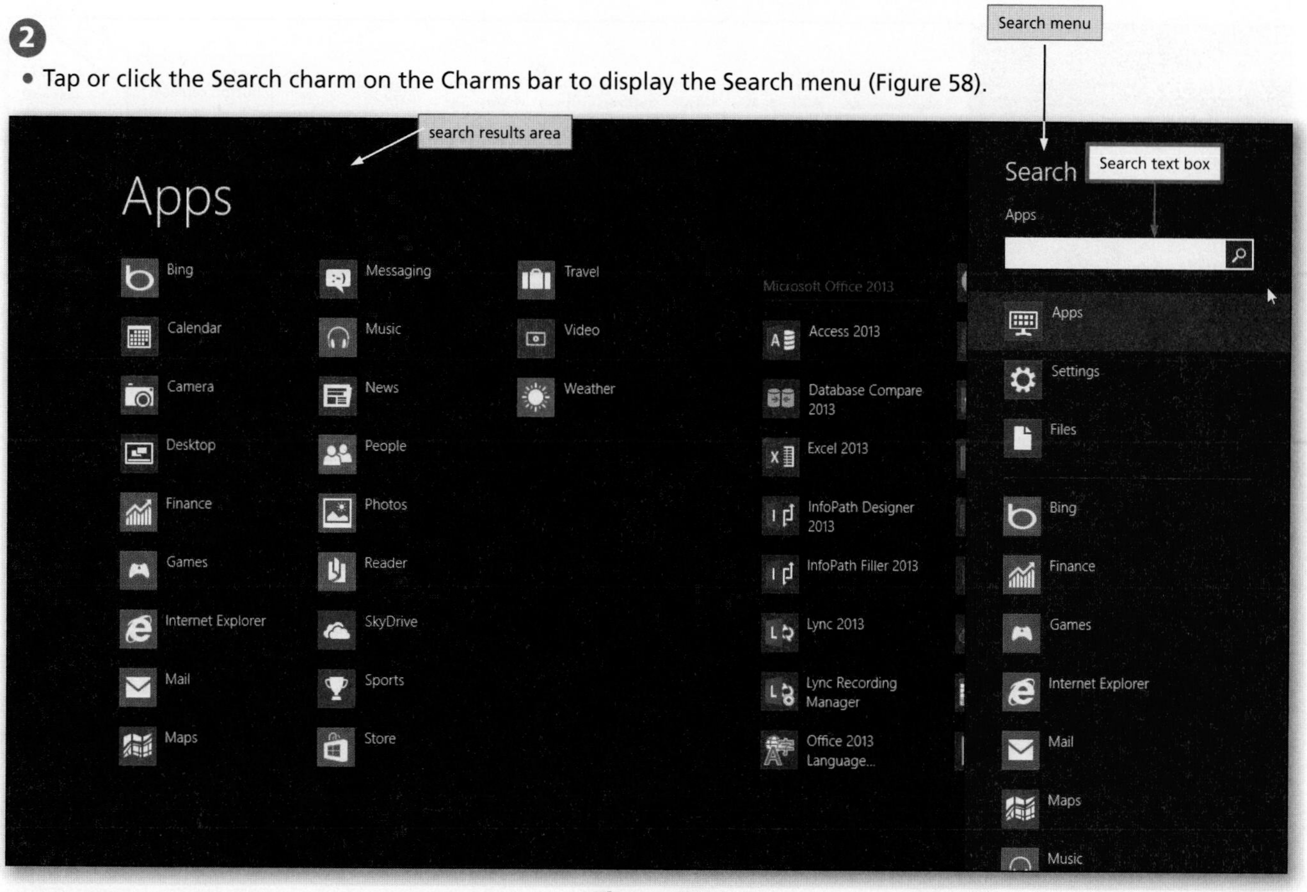

Figure 58

3

- Type **Access 2013** as the search text in the Search text box and watch the search results appear in the Apps list (Figure 59).

Q&A Do I need to type the complete app name or use correct capitalization?

No, you need to type just enough characters of the app name for it to appear in the Apps list. For example, you may be able to type Access or access, instead of Access 2013.

Figure 59

4

- Tap or click the app name, Access 2013 in this case, in the search results to run Access.
- If the app window is not maximized, tap or click the Maximize button on its title bar to maximize the window (Figure 60).

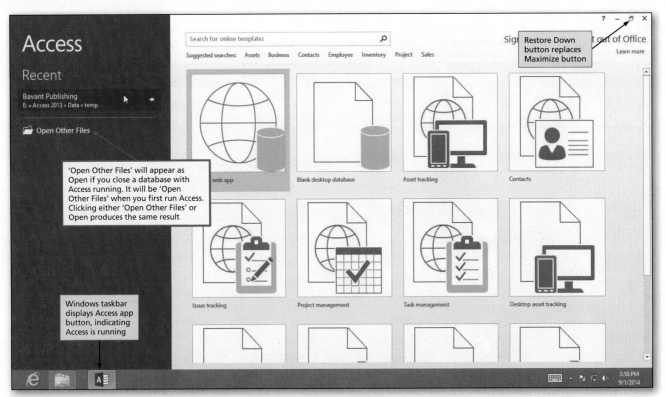

Figure 60

TO RUN AN APP USING THE SEARCH BOX USING WINDOWS 7

If you are using Windows 7, perform these steps to run an app using the search box instead of the previous steps that use Windows 8.

1. Click the Start button on the Windows 7 taskbar to display the Start menu.
2. Type `Access 2013` as the search text in the 'Search programs and files' text box and watch the search results appear on the Start menu.
3. Click the app name, Access 2013 in this case, in the search results on the Start menu to run Access.
4. If the app window is not maximized, click the Maximize button on its title bar to maximize the window.

To Open an Existing Database

To work on an existing database, that is, a database you previously created, you must open the database. To do so, you will use the Backstage view. The following step opens an existing database, specifically the PJP Marketing database. ***Why?*** *Because the database has been created already, you just need to open it.*

- If you have just run Access, tap or click Open Other Files to display the Open gallery in the Backstage view. If not, tap or click FILE on the ribbon to open the Backstage view and then tap or click Open in the Backstage view to display the Open gallery (Figure 61).

Q&A

I see the name of the database I want to open in the Recent list in Backstage view. Can I just tap or click the name to open the file?
Yes. That is an alternative way to open a database, provided the name of the database is included in the Recent list.

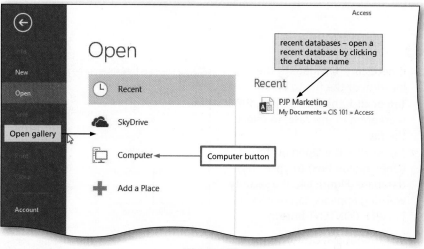

Figure 61

- Tap or click Computer to display recent folders accessed on your computer as well as the Browse button (Figure 62).

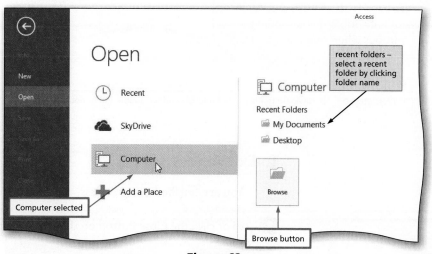

Figure 62

- Tap or click the Browse button to display the Open dialog box (Figure 63).

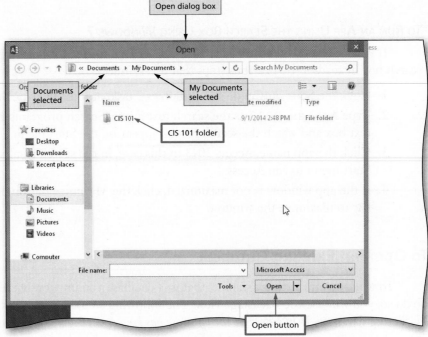

Figure 63

- If necessary, navigate to the location of the file to open.
- Tap or click the file to open, PJP Marketing in this case, to select the file.
- Tap or click the Open button (Open dialog box) to open the database (Figure 64). If a security warning appears, tap or click the ENABLE CONTENT button.

Q&A Why might a Security Warning appear?
A Security Warning appears when you open a database that might contain harmful content. The files you create in this chapter are not harmful, but you should be cautious when opening files from other people.

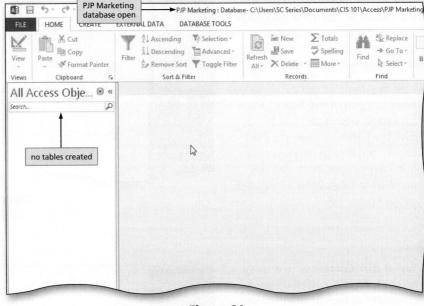

Figure 64

Other Ways

1. Press CTRL+O   2. Navigate to file in File Explorer window, double-tap or double-click file

To Exit Access

You are finished using Access. The following step exits Access.

1 Tap or click the Close button on the right side of the title bar to close the file and exit Access.

To Create a New Access Database from File Explorer

File Explorer provides a means to create an Access database without running an Office app. The following steps use File Explorer to create an Access database. *Why? Sometimes you might need to create a database and then return to it later for editing.* If you are using Windows 7, skip these steps and instead perform the steps in the yellow box that immediately follows these Windows 8 steps.

1

- Double-tap or double-click the File Explorer app button on the taskbar to make the folder window the active window.

- If necessary, double-tap or double-click the Documents library in the navigation pane to expand the Documents library.

- If necessary, double-tap or double-click the My Documents folder in the navigation pane to expand the My Documents folder.

- If necessary, double-tap or double-click your class folder (CIS 101, in this case) in the navigation pane to expand the folder.

- Tap or click the Access folder in the navigation pane to display its contents in the file list.

- With the Access folder selected, press and hold or right-click an open area in the file list to display a shortcut menu.

- Tap or point to New on the shortcut menu to display the New submenu (Figure 65).

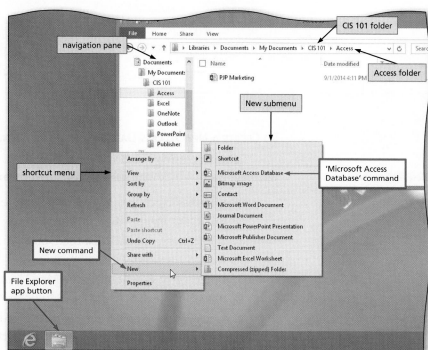

Figure 65

2

- Tap or click 'Microsoft Access Database' on the New submenu to display an icon and text box for a new file in the current folder window with the file name, New Microsoft Access Database, selected (Figure 66).

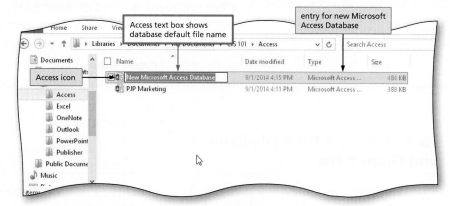

Figure 66

• Type `PJP Promotions` in the text box and then press the ENTER key to assign a new name to the new file in the current folder (Figure 67).

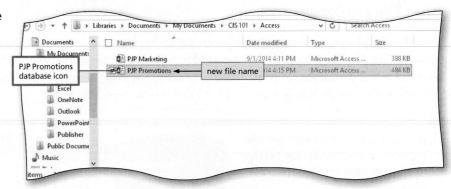

Figure 67

To Create a New Access Database from Windows Explorer Using Windows 7

If you are using Windows 7, perform these steps to create a new Access database from Windows Explorer instead of the previous steps that use Windows 8.

1. If necessary, click the Windows Explorer button on the taskbar to make the folder window the active window.

2. If necessary, double-click the Documents library in the navigation pane to expand the Documents library.

3. If necessary, double-click the My Documents folder in the navigation pane to expand the My Documents folder.

4. If necessary, double-click your class folder (CIS 101, in this case) in the navigation pane to expand the folder.

5. Click the Access folder in the navigation pane to display its contents in the file list.

6. With the Access folder selected, right-click an open area in the file list to display a shortcut menu.

7. Point to New on the shortcut menu to display the New submenu.

8. Click 'Microsoft Access Database' on the New submenu to display an icon and text box for a new file in the current folder window with the name, New Microsoft Access Database, selected.

9. Type `PJP Promotions` in the text box and then press the ENTER key to assign a new name to the new file in the current folder.

To Run an App from File Explorer and Open a File

1 SIGN IN | 2 USE WINDOWS | 3 USE APPS | 4 FILE MANAGEMENT | 5 SWITCH APPS | 6 SAVE FILES
7 CHANGE SCREEN RESOLUTION | 8 EXIT APPS | 9 USE ADDITIONAL APP FEATURES | 10 USE HELP

Previously, you learned how to run Access using the Start screen and the Search charm. The following steps, which assume Windows is running, use File Explorer to run Access based on a typical installation. *Why? Another way to run an Office app is to open an existing file from File Explorer, which causes the app in which the file was created to run and then open the selected file.* You may need to ask your instructor how to run Access for your computer. If you are using Windows 7, follow the steps in the yellow box that immediately follows these Windows 8 steps.

- If necessary, display the file to open in the folder window in File Explorer (shown in Figure 67).

- Press and hold or right-click the file icon or file name (PJP Promotions, in this case) to display a shortcut menu (Figure 68).

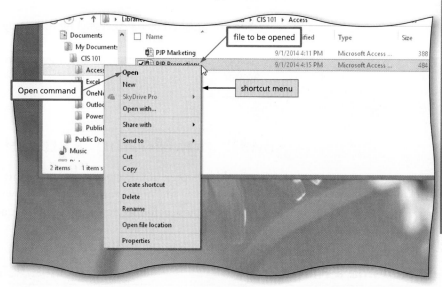

Figure 68

2

- Tap or click Open on the shortcut menu to open the selected file in the app used to create the file, Access in this case (Figure 69). If a security warning appears, tap or click the ENABLE CONTENT button.

- If the Access window is not maximized, tap or click the Maximize button on the title bar to maximize the window.

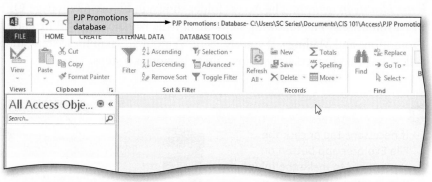

Figure 69

TO RUN AN APP FROM WINDOWS EXPLORER AND OPEN A FILE USING WINDOWS 7

If you are using Windows 7, perform these steps to run an app from Windows Explorer and open a file instead of the previous steps that use Windows 8.

1. Display the file to open in the folder window in Windows Explorer.

2. Right-click the file icon or file name (PJP Promotions, in this case) to display a shortcut menu.

3. Click Open on the shortcut menu to open the selected file in the app used to create the file, Access in this case.

4. If the Access window is not maximized, click the Maximize button on the title bar to maximize the window.

To Exit Access

You are finished using Access. The following step exits Access.

 Tap or click the Close button on the right side of the title bar to close the file and exit Access.

Renaming, Moving, and Deleting Files

Earlier in this chapter, you learned how to organize files in folders, which is part of a process known as **file management**. The following sections cover additional file management topics including renaming, moving, and deleting files.

To Rename a File

1 SIGN IN │ 2 USE WINDOWS │ 3 USE APPS │ **4 FILE MANAGEMENT** │ 5 SWITCH APPS │ 6 SAVE FILES
7 CHANGE SCREEN RESOLUTION │ 8 EXIT APPS │9 USE ADDITIONAL APP FEATURES │ **10 USE HELP**

In some circumstances, you may want to change the name of, or rename, a file or a folder. *Why? You may want to distinguish a file in one folder or drive from a copy of a similar file, or you may decide to rename a file to better identify its contents.* The Access folder shown in Figure 67 on page OFF 46 contains the Access database, PJP Promotions. The following steps change the name of the PJP Promotions file in the Access folder to PJP Promotions and Mailings. If you are using Windows 7, skip these steps and instead perform the steps in the yellow box that immediately follows these Windows 8 steps.

1

- If necessary, tap or click the File Explorer app button on the taskbar to make the folder window the active window.

- If necessary, navigate to the location of the file to be renamed (in this case, the Access folder in the CIS 101 [or your class folder] folder in the My Documents folder in the Documents library) to display the file(s) it contains in the file list.

- Press and hold or right-click the PJP Promotions icon or file name in the file list to select the PJP Promotions file and display a shortcut menu that presents a list of commands related to files (Figure 70).

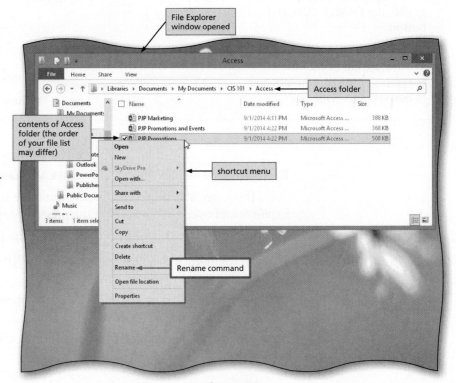

Figure 70

2

- Tap or click Rename on the shortcut menu to place the current file name in a text box.

- Type **PJP Promotions and Mailings** in the text box and then press the ENTER key (Figure 71).

Q&A Are there any risks involved in renaming files that are located on a hard disk?

If you inadvertently rename a file that is associated with certain apps, the apps may not be able to find the file and, therefore, may not run properly. Always use caution when renaming files.

Can I rename a file when it is open?

No, a file must be closed to change the file name.

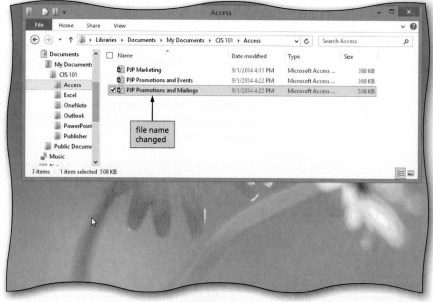

Figure 71

Other Ways

1. Select file, press F2, type new file name, press ENTER   2. Select file, tap or click Rename (Home tab | Organize group), type new file name, press ENTER

To Rename a File Using Windows 7

If you are using Windows 7, perform these steps to rename a file instead of the previous steps that use Windows 8.

1. If necessary, click the Windows Explorer app button on the taskbar to make the folder window the active window.

2. Navigate to the location of the file to be renamed (in this case, the Access folder in the CIS 101 [or your class folder] folder in the My Documents folder in the Documents library) to display the file(s) it contains in the file list.

3. Right-click the PJP Promotions icon or file name in the file list to select the PJP Promotions file and display a shortcut menu that presents a list of commands related to files.

4. Click Rename on the shortcut menu to place the current file name in a text box.

5. Type **PJP Promotions and Mailings** in the text box and then press the ENTER key.

To Save a File with a New File Name

You might want to save a file with a different name or to a different location. For example, you might start a homework assignment with a data file and then save it with a final file name for submission to your instructor, saving it to a location designated by your instructor. The following steps save a file with a different file name.

1 Tap or click the FILE tab to open the Backstage view.

2 Tap or click the Save As tab to display the Save As gallery.

BTW

New File Names and Renaming

Saving a file with a new name makes a copy of the file with a different name while retaining the original version of the file with its original name. Renaming a file changes its name but does not create a new version of the file.

3 With Save Database As and Access Database selected, tap or click the Save As button.

4 Type **PJP Promotions and Events** in the File name box (Save As dialog box) to change the file name. Do not press the ENTER key after typing the file name because you do not want to close the dialog box at this time.

5 If necessary, navigate to the desired save location (in this case, the Access folder in the CIS 101 folder [or your class folder] in the My Documents folder in the Documents library). For specific instructions, perform the tasks in Steps 3a and 3b on pages OFF 24 and 25.

6 Tap or click the Save button (Save As dialog box) to save the document in the selected folder on the selected drive with the entered file name.

To Move a File

Why? At some time, you may want to move a file from one folder, called the *source folder*, to another, called the *destination folder*. When you move a file, it no longer appears in the original folder. If the destination and the source folders are on the same media, you can move a file by dragging it. If the folders are on different media, then you will need to press and hold and then drag, or right-drag the file, and then click Move here on the shortcut menu. The following step moves the PJP Promotions and Mailings file from the Access folder to the CIS 101 folder. If you are using Windows 7, skip this step and instead perform the steps in the yellow box that immediately follows this Windows 8 step.

1

- In File Explorer, if necessary, navigate to the location of the file to be moved (in this case, the Access folder in the CIS 101 folder [or your class folder] in the Documents library).

- If necessary, tap or click the Access folder in the navigation pane to display the files it contains in the right pane.

- Drag the PJP Promotions and Mailings file in the right pane to the CIS 101 folder in the navigation pane and notice the ScreenTip as you drag the mouse (Figure 72).

Experiment

- Click the CIS 101 folder in the navigation pane to verify that the file was moved.

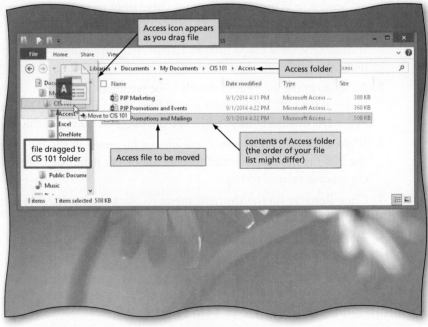

Figure 72

Other Ways

1. Press and hold or right-click file to move, tap or click Cut on shortcut menu, press and hold or right-click destination folder, tap or click Paste on shortcut menu

2. Select file to move, press CTRL+X, select destination folder, press CTRL+V

TO MOVE A FILE USING WINDOWS 7

If you are using Windows 7, perform these steps to move a file instead of the previous steps that use Windows 8.

1. In Windows Explorer, navigate to the location of the file to be moved (in this case, the Access folder in the CIS 101 folder [or your class folder] in the Documents library).

2. Click the Access folder in the navigation pane to display the files it contains in the right pane.

3. Drag the PJP Promotions and Mailings file in the right pane to the CIS 101 folder in the navigation pane.

To Delete a File

1 SIGN IN | 2 USE WINDOWS | 3 USE APPS | **4 FILE MANAGEMENT** | 5 SWITCH APPS | 6 SAVE FILES
7 CHANGE SCREEN RESOLUTION | 8 EXIT APPS | 9 USE ADDITIONAL APP FEATURES | **10 USE HELP**

A final task you may want to perform is to delete a file. Exercise extreme caution when deleting a file or files. When you delete a file from a hard disk, the deleted file is stored in the Recycle Bin where you can recover it until you empty the Recycle Bin. If you delete a file from removable media, such as a USB flash drive, the file is deleted permanently. The next steps delete the PJP Promotions and Mailings file from the CIS 101 folder. *Why?* *When a file no longer is needed, you can delete it to conserve space in your storage location.* If you are using Windows 7, skip these steps and instead perform the steps in the yellow box that immediately follows these Windows 8 steps.

- In File Explorer, navigate to the location of the file to be deleted (in this case, the CIS 101 folder [or your class folder] in the Documents library).

- Press and hold or right-click the PJP Promotions and Mailings icon or file name in the right pane to select the file and display a shortcut menu (Figure 73).

- Tap or click Delete on the shortcut menu to delete the file.

- If a dialog box appears, tap or click the Yes button to delete the file.

Q&A Can I use this same technique to delete a folder?
Yes. Right-click the folder and then click Delete on the shortcut menu. When you delete a folder, all of the files and folders contained in the folder you are deleting, together with any files and folders on lower hierarchical levels, are deleted as well.

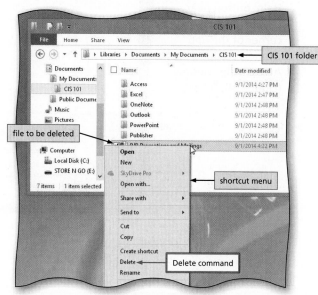

Figure 73

Other Ways

1. Select icon, press DELETE

TO DELETE A FILE USING WINDOWS 7

If you are using Windows 7, perform these steps to delete a file instead of the previous steps that use Windows 8.

1. In Windows Explorer, navigate to the location of the file to be deleted (in this case, the CIS 101 folder [or your class folder] in the Documents library).

2. Right-click the PJP Promotions and Mailings icon or file name in the right pane to select the file and display a shortcut menu.

3. Click Delete on the shortcut menu to delete the file.

4. If a dialog box appears, click the Yes button to delete the file.

Microsoft Office and Windows Help

At any time while you are using one of the Office apps, such as Access, you can use Office Help to display information about all topics associated with the app. This section illustrates the use of Access Help. Help in other Office apps operates in a similar fashion.

In Office, Help is presented in a window that has browser-style navigation buttons. Each Office app has its own Help home page, which is the starting Help page that is displayed in the Help window. If your computer is connected to the Internet, the contents of the Help page reflect both the local help files installed on the computer and material from Microsoft's website.

To Open the Help Window in an Office App

1 SIGN IN | 2 USE WINDOWS | 3 USE APPS | 4 FILE MANAGEMENT | 5 SWITCH APPS | 6 SAVE FILES
7 CHANGE SCREEN RESOLUTION | 8 EXIT APPS | 9 USE ADDITIONAL APP FEATURES | 10 USE HELP

The following step opens the Access Help window. *Why? You might not understand how certain commands or operations work in Access, so you can obtain the necessary information using help.* The step to open a Help window in other Office programs is similar.

- Run Access.

- Tap or click the 'Microsoft Access Help' button near the upper-right corner of the app window to open the Access Help window (Figure 74).

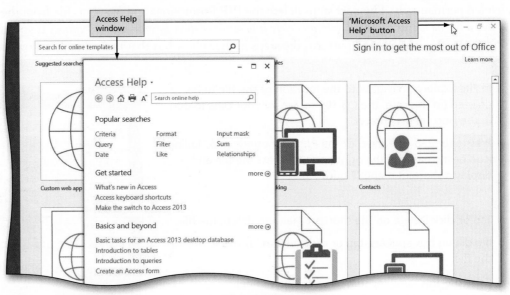

Figure 74

Other Ways

1. Press F1

Moving and Resizing Windows

At times, it is useful, or even necessary, to have more than one window open and visible on the screen at the same time. You can resize and move these open windows so that you can view different areas of and elements in the window. In the case of the Help window, for example, it could be covering database objects in the Access window that you need to see.

To Move a Window by Dragging

1 SIGN IN | 2 USE WINDOWS | 3 USE APPS | 4 FILE MANAGEMENT | 5 SWITCH APPS | 6 SAVE FILES
7 CHANGE SCREEN RESOLUTION | 8 EXIT APPS | 9 USE ADDITIONAL APP FEATURES | 10 USE HELP

You can move any open window that is not maximized to another location on the desktop by dragging the title bar of the window. *Why? You might want to have a better view of what is behind the window or just want to move the window so that you can see it better.* The following step drags the Access Help window to the upper-left corner of the desktop.

- Drag the window title bar (the Access Help window title bar, in this case) so that the window moves to the upper-left corner of the desktop, as shown in Figure 75.

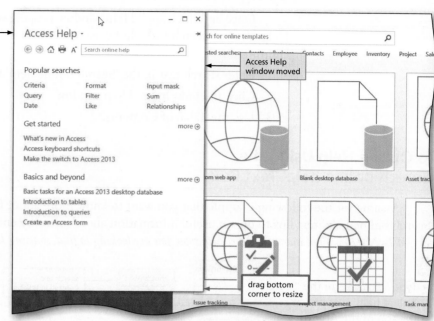

Figure 75

To Resize a Window by Dragging

1 SIGN IN | 2 USE WINDOWS | 3 USE APPS | 4 FILE MANAGEMENT | 5 SWITCH APPS | 6 SAVE FILES
7 CHANGE SCREEN RESOLUTION | 8 EXIT APPS | 9 USE ADDITIONAL APP FEATURES | 10 USE HELP

A method used to change the size of the window is to drag the window borders. The following step changes the size of the Access Help window by dragging its borders. *Why? Sometimes, information is not visible completely in a window, and you want to increase the size of the window.*

- If you are using a mouse, point to the lower-right corner of the window (the Access Help window, in this case) until the pointer changes to a two-headed arrow.

- Drag the bottom border downward to display more of the active window (Figure 76).

Q&A

Can I drag other borders on the window to enlarge or shrink the window?
Yes, you can drag the left, right, and top borders and any window corner to resize a window.

Will Windows remember the new size of the window after I close it?
Yes. When you reopen the window, Windows will display it at the same size it was when you closed it.

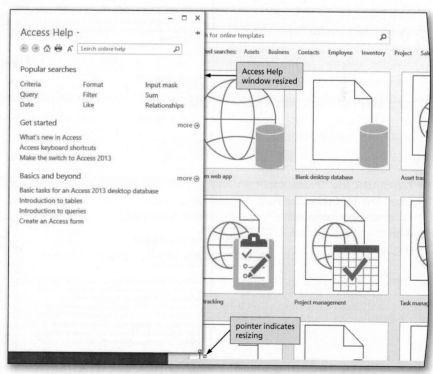

Figure 76

Using Office Help

Once an Office app's Help window is open, several methods exist for navigating Help. You can search for help by using any of the three following methods from the Help window:

1. Enter search text in the 'Search online help' text box.
2. Click the links in the Help window.
3. Use the Table of Contents.

To Obtain Help Using the 'Search online help' Text Box

1 SIGN IN | 2 USE WINDOWS | 3 USE APPS | 4 FILE MANAGEMENT | 5 SWITCH APPS | 6 SAVE FILES
7 CHANGE SCREEN RESOLUTION | 8 EXIT APPS | 9 USE ADDITIONAL APP FEATURES | **10 USE HELP**

Assume for the following example that you want to know more about forms. The following steps use the 'Search online help' text box to obtain useful information about forms by entering the word, forms, as search text. ***Why?*** *You may not know the exact help topic you are looking to find, so using keywords can help narrow your search.*

❶

- Type **forms** in the 'Search online help' text box at the top of the Access Help window to enter the search text.

- Tap or click the 'Search online help' button to display the search results (Figure 77).

Q&A
Why do my search results differ?
If you do not have an Internet connection, your results will reflect only the content of the Help files on your computer. When searching for help online, results also can change as material is added, deleted, and updated on the online Help webpages maintained by Microsoft.

Why were my search results not very helpful?
When initiating a search, be sure to check the spelling of the search text; also, keep your search specific to return the most accurate results.

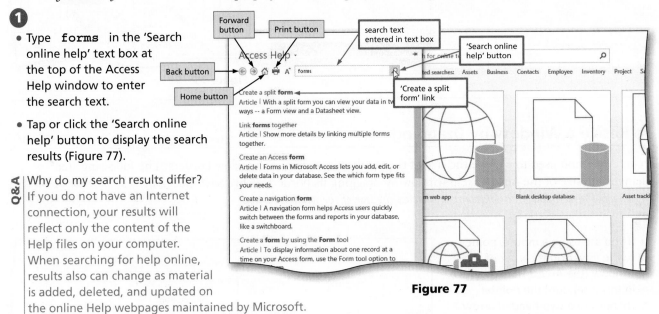

Figure 77

❷

- Tap or click the 'Create a split form' link to display the Help information associated with the selected topic (Figure 78).

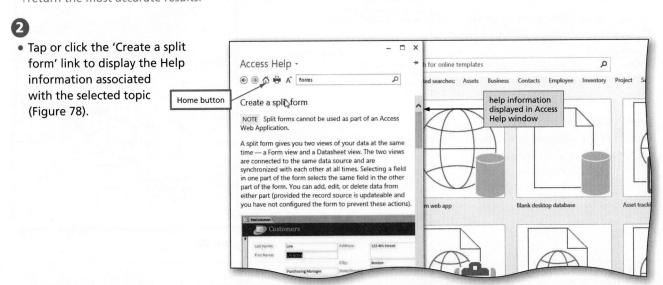

Figure 78

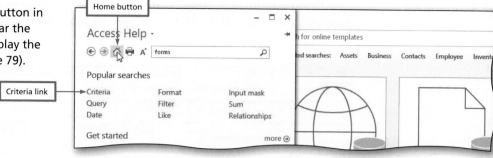

3

- Tap or click the Home button in the Help window to clear the search results and redisplay the Help home page (Figure 79).

Figure 79

To Obtain Help Using Help Links

If your topic of interest is listed in the Help window, you can click the link to begin browsing the Help categories instead of entering search text. *Why? You browse Help just as you would browse a website. If you know which category contains your Help information, you can use these links.* The following step finds the Criteria information using the Criteria link from the Access Help home page.

- Tap or click the Criteria link on the Help home page (shown in Figure 79) to display the Criteria help links (Figure 80).

- After reviewing the page, tap or click the Close button to close the Help window.

- Tap or click Access's Close button to exit Access.

Q&A Why does my Help window display different links?

The content of your Help window might differ because Microsoft continually updates its Help information.

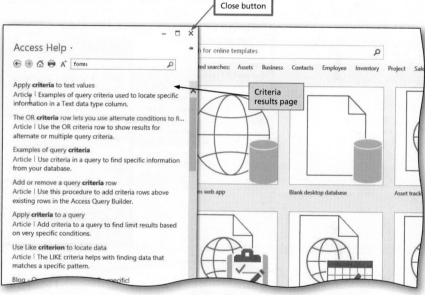

Figure 80

Obtaining Help while Working in an Office App

Help in the Office apps, such as Access, provides you with the ability to obtain help directly, without opening the Help window and initiating a search. For example, you might be unsure about how a particular command works, or you may be presented with a dialog box that you do not know how to use.

Figure 81 shows one option for obtaining help while working in an Office app. If you want to learn more about a command, point to its button and wait for the ScreenTip to appear. If the Help icon appears in the ScreenTip, press the F1 key while pointing to the button to open the Help window associated with that command.

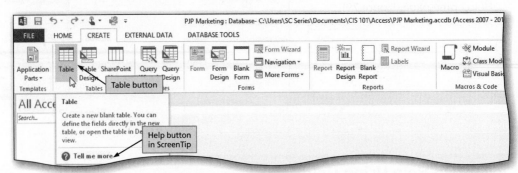

Figure 81

Figure 82 shows a dialog box that contains a Help button. Pressing the F1 key while the dialog box is displayed opens a Help window. The Help window contains help about that dialog box, if available. If no help file is available for that particular dialog box, then the main Help window opens.

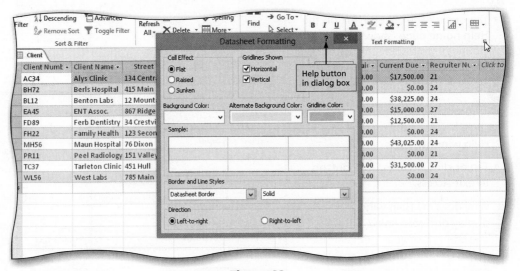

Figure 82

Using Windows Help and Support

One of the more powerful Windows features is Windows Help and Support. **Windows Help and Support** is available when using Windows or when using any Microsoft app running in Windows. The same methods used for searching Microsoft Office Help can be used in Windows Help and Support. The difference is that Windows Help and Support displays help for Windows, instead of for Microsoft Office.

To Use Windows Help and Support

1 SIGN IN | 2 USE WINDOWS | 3 USE APPS | 4 FILE MANAGEMENT | 5 SWITCH APPS | 6 SAVE FILES
7 CHANGE SCREEN RESOLUTION | 8 EXIT APPS | 9 USE ADDITIONAL APP FEATURES | 10 USE HELP

The following steps use Windows Help and Support and open the Windows Help and Support window, which contains links to more information about Windows. *Why? This feature is designed to assist you in using Windows or the various apps.* If you are using Windows 7, skip these steps and instead perform the steps in the yellow box that immediately follows these Windows 8 steps.

- Swipe in from the right edge of the screen or point to the upper-right corner of the screen to display the Charms bar (Figure 83).

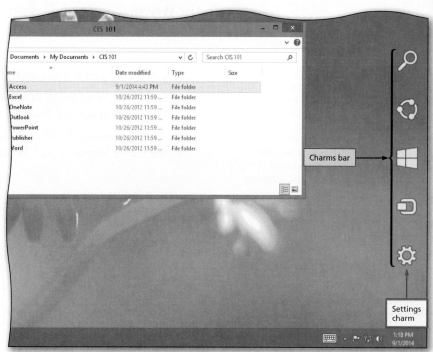

Figure 83

- Tap or click the Settings charm on the Charms bar to display the Settings menu (Figure 84).

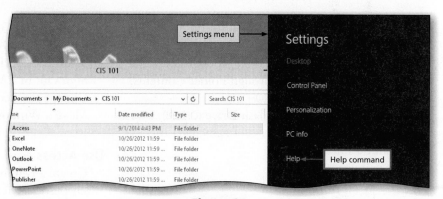

Figure 84

- Tap or click Help to open the Windows Help and Support window (Figure 85).

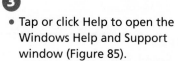

- After reviewing the Windows Help and Support window, tap or click the Close button to close the Windows Help and Support window.

Figure 85

Other Ways

1. Press WINDOWS + F1

BTW
Certification
The Microsoft Office Specialist (MOS) program provides an opportunity for you to obtain a valuable industry credential — proof that you have the Microsoft Office 2013 skills required by employers. For more information, visit the Certification resource on the Student Companion Site located on www.cengagebrain.com. For detailed instructions about accessing available resources, visit www.cengage .com/ct/studentdownload or contact your instructor for information about accessing the required files.

BTW
Quick Reference
For a table that lists how to complete the tasks covered in this book using touch gestures, the mouse, ribbon, shortcut menu, and keyboard, see the Quick Reference Summary at the back of this book, or visit the Quick Reference resource on the Student Companion Site located on www. cengagebrain.com. For detailed instructions about accessing available resources, visit www.cengage.com/ct/studentdownload or contact your instructor for information about accessing the required files.

TO USE WINDOWS HELP AND SUPPORT WITH WINDOWS 7

If you are using Windows 7, perform these steps to start Windows Help and Support instead of the previous steps that use Windows 8.

1. Click the Start button on the taskbar to display the Start menu.
2. Click Help and Support on the Start menu to open the Windows Help and Support window.
3. After reviewing the Windows Help and Support window, click the Close button to exit Windows Help and Support.

Chapter Summary

In this chapter, you learned how to use the Windows interface, several touch screen and mouse operations, and file and folder management. You also learned some basic features of Access and discovered the common elements that exist among Microsoft Office apps. The items listed below include all of the new Windows and Access skills you have learned in this chapter, with the tasks grouped by activity.

File Management
Create a Folder (OFF 16)
Create a Folder within a Folder (OFF 19)
Expand a Folder, Scroll through Folder Contents, and Collapse a Folder (OFF 21)
Copy a Folder to a USB Flash Drive (OFF 38)
Use the Backstage View to Close a Database (OFF 40)
Rename a File (OFF 48)
Move a File (OFF 50)
Delete a File (OFF 51)

Use Help
Open the Help Window in an Office App (OFF 52)
Obtain Help Using the 'Search online help' Text Box (OFF 54)
Obtain Help Using Help Links (OFF 55)
Use Windows Help and Support (OFF 56)

Use Windows
Sign In to an Account (OFF 7)
Run Access from the Start Screen (OFF 11)
Switch between an App and the Start Screen (OFF 13)

Maximize a Window (OFF 14)
Switch from One App to Another (OFF 22)
Minimize and Restore a Window (OFF 34)
Sign Out of a Microsoft Account (OFF 35)
Change the Screen Resolution (OFF 37)
Move a Window by Dragging (OFF 52)
Resize a Window by Dragging (OFF 53)

Use Access
Create a Database in a Folder (OFF 23)
Display a Different Tab on the Ribbon (OFF 30)
Collapse and Expand the Ribbon (OFF 31)
Use a Shortcut Menu to Relocate the Quick Access Toolbar (OFF 32)
Customize the Quick Access Toolbar (OFF 33)
Exit an Office App (OFF 40)
Run Access Using the Search Box (OFF 40)
Open an Existing Database (OFF 43)
Create a New Access Database from File Explorer (OFF 45)
Run an App from File Explorer and Open a File (OFF 46)

What guidelines should you follow to plan your projects?

The process of communicating specific information is a learned, rational skill. Computers and software, especially Microsoft Office 2013, can help you develop ideas and present detailed information to a particular audience and minimize much of the laborious work of drafting and revising projects. No matter what method you use to plan a project, it is beneficial to follow some specific guidelines from the onset to arrive at a final product that is informative, relevant, and effective. Use some aspects of these guidelines every time you undertake a project, and others as needed in specific instances.

1. Determine the project's purpose.
    a) Clearly define why you are undertaking this assignment.
    b) Begin to draft ideas of how best to communicate information by handwriting ideas on paper; composing directly on a laptop, tablet, or mobile device; or developing a strategy that fits your particular thinking and writing style.

2. Analyze your audience.
    a) Learn about the people who will read, analyze, or view your work.
    b) Determine their interests and needs so that you can present the information they need to know and omit the information they already possess.
    c) Form a mental picture of these people or find photos of people who fit this profile so that you can develop a project with the audience in mind.

3. Gather possible content.
    a) Locate existing information that may reside in spreadsheets, databases, or other files.
    b) Conduct a web search to find relevant websites.
    c) Read pamphlets, magazine and newspaper articles, and books to gain insights of how others have approached your topic.
    d) Conduct personal interviews to obtain perspectives not available by any other means.
    e) Consider video and audio clips as potential sources for material that might complement or support the factual data you uncover.

4. Determine what content to present to your audience.
    a) Write three or four major ideas you want an audience member to remember after reading or viewing your project.
    b) Envision your project's endpoint, the key fact you wish to emphasize, so that all project elements lead to this final element.
    c) Determine relevant time factors, such as the length of time to develop the project, how long readers will spend reviewing your project, or the amount of time allocated for your speaking engagement.
    d) Decide whether a graph, photo, or artistic element can express or enhance a particular concept.
    e) Be mindful of the order in which you plan to present the content, and place the most important material at the top or bottom of the page, because readers and audience members generally remember the first and last pieces of information they see and hear.

How should you submit solutions to questions in the assignments identified with a symbol?

Every assignment in this book contains one or more questions identified with a symbol. These questions require you to think beyond the assigned file. Present your solutions to the questions in the format required by your instructor. Possible formats may include one or more of these options: write the answer; create a document that contains the answer; present your answer to the class; discuss your answer in a group; record the answer as audio or video using a webcam, smartphone, or portable media player; or post answers on a blog, wiki, or website.

Apply Your Knowledge

Reinforce the skills and apply the concepts you learned in this chapter.

Creating a Folder and a Database

Instructions: You will create an Access folder and then create an Access database and save it in the folder.

Perform the following tasks:

1. Open the File Explorer window and then double-tap or double-click to open the Documents library.

2. Tap or click the New folder button on the Quick Access Toolbar to display a new folder icon and text box for the folder name.

Continued >

Apply Your Knowledge *continued*

3. Type **Access** in the text box to name the folder. Press the ENTER key to create the folder in the Documents library.

4. Run Access.

5. Use the 'Blank desktop database' option to create a database with the name Apply 1. Do not press the ENTER key after typing the file name.

6. If requested by your instructor, name the database Apply 1 Lastname where Lastname is your last name.

7. Tap or click the 'Browse for a location to put your database' button and navigate to the Access folder in the Documents library. Tap or click the OK button to select the Access folder as the location for the database and close the dialog box. Tap or click the Create button to create the database.

8. If your Quick Access Toolbar does not show the Quick Print button, add the Quick Print button to the Quick Access Toolbar (Figure 86).

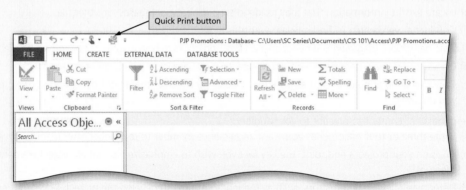

Figure 86

9. Exit Access.

10. Open the File Explorer window, open the Documents library, and then open the Access folder you created in Step 3.

11. Double-tap or double-click the Apply 1 database to start Access and open the Apply 1 database.

12. Remove the Quick Print button from the Quick Access Toolbar. Exit Access.

13. Submit the database in the format specified by your instructor.

14. ⚙ What other commands might you find useful to include on the Quick Access Toolbar?

Extend Your Knowledge

Extend the skills you learned in this chapter and experiment with new skills. You will use Help to complete the assignment.

Using Help
Instructions: Use Access Help to perform the following tasks.

Perform the following tasks:
1. Run Access.

2. Tap or click the Microsoft Access Help button to open the Access Help window (Figure 87).

3. Search Access Help to answer the following questions.

   a. What shortcut keys are available for finding and replacing text or data?

   b. What type of training courses are available through Help?

   c. What are the steps to add a new group to the ribbon?

Figure 87

d. What are Quick Parts?

e. What are three features that have been discontinued in Access 2013?

f. What is a template?

g. What is a primary key?

h. How do you back up a database?

i. What is the purpose of compacting and repairing a database?

j. What is the purpose of the Navigation Pane?

4. Type the answers from your searches in a new blank Word document. Save the document with a new file name and then submit it in the format specified by your instructor.

5. If requested by your instructor, enter your name in the Word document.

6. Exit Access and Word.

7. ✷ What search text did you use to perform the searches above? Did it take multiple attempts to search and locate the exact information for which you were searching?

Analyze, Correct, Improve

Analyze a file structure, correct all errors, and improve the design.

Organizing Vacation Photos

Note: To complete this assignment, you will be required to use the Data Files for Students. Visit www.cengage.com/ct/studentdownload for detailed instructions or contact your instructor for information about accessing the required files.

Instructions: Traditionally, you have stored photos from past vacations together in one folder. The photos are becoming difficult to manage, and you now want to store them in appropriate folders. You will create the folder structure shown in Figure 88. You then will move the photos to the folders so that they will be organized properly.

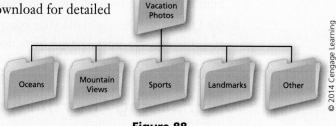

Figure 88

© 2014 Cengage Learning

1. Correct Create the folder structure in Figure 88 so that you are able to store the photos in an organized manner. If requested by your instructor, add another folder using your last name as the folder name.

2. Improve View each photo and drag it to the appropriate folder to improve the organization. Submit the assignment in the format specified by your instructor.

3. ✷ In which folder did you place each photo? Think about the files you have stored on your computer. What folder hierarchy would be best to manage your files?

In the Labs

Use the guidelines, concepts, and skills presented in this chapter to increase your knowledge of Windows 8 and Access 2013. Labs 1 and 2, which increase in difficulty, require you to create solutions based on what you learned in the chapter; Lab 3 requires you to create a solution, which uses cloud and web technologies, by learning and investigating on your own from general guidance.

Lab 1: Creating Folders for a Video Store

Problem: Your friend works for Ebaird Video. He would like to organize his files in relation to the types of videos available in the store. He has six main categories: drama, action, romance, foreign, biographical, and comedy. You are to create a folder structure similar to Figure 89.

Instructions: Perform the following tasks:

1. Insert a USB flash drive in an available USB port and then open the USB flash drive window.

2. Create the main folder for Ebaird Video.

3. Navigate to the Ebaird Video folder.

4. Within the Ebaird Video folder, create a folder for each of the following: Drama, Action, Romance, Foreign, Biographical, and Comedy.

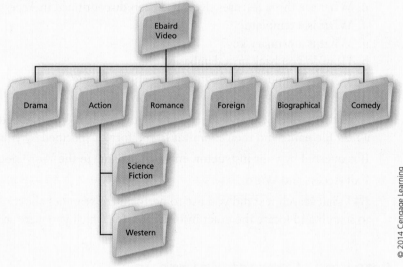

© 2014 Cengage Learning

Figure 89

5. Within the Action folder, create two additional folders, one for Science Fiction and the second for Western.

6. If requested by your instructor, add another folder using your last name as the folder name.

7. Submit the assignment in the format specified by your instructor.

8. ✻ Think about how you use your computer for various tasks (consider personal, professional, and academic reasons). What folders do you think will be required on your computer to store the files you save?

Lab 2: Saving Files in Folders

Creating Access Databases and Saving Them in Appropriate Folders

Problem: You are taking a class that requires you to complete three Access chapters. You will save the work completed in each chapter in a different folder (Figure 90).

Instructions: Create the folders shown in Figure 90. Then, using Access, create three databases to save in each folder.

1. Create the folder structure shown in Figure 90.

2. Navigate to the Chapter 1 folder.

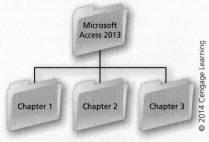

© 2014 Cengage Learning

Figure 90

3. Create an Access database named My Chapter 1 Access Database and then save it in the Chapter 1 folder.

4. Navigate to the Chapter 2 folder.

5. Create another Access database named My Chapter 2 Access Database, and then save in the Chapter 2 folder.

6. Navigate to the Chapter 3 folder.

7. Create another Access database named My Chapter 3 Access Database, and then save it in the Chapter 3 folder.

8. If requested by your instructor, add your name to each of the three Access databases using the Rename command.

9. Submit the assignment in the format specified by your instructor.

10. ✹ Based on your current knowledge of Windows and Access, how will you organize folders for assignments in this class? Why?

Lab 3: Expand Your World: Cloud and Web Technologies
Creating Folders on SkyDrive and Using the Word Web App

Problem: You are taking a class that requires you to create folders on SkyDrive (Figure 91).

Instructions: Perform the following tasks:

1. Sign in to SkyDrive in your browser.

2. Use the Create button to create the folder structure shown in Figure 91.

3. If requested by your instructor, rename the Notes folder as your name Notes.

4. Submit the assignment in the format specified by your instructor.

5. ✹ Based on your current knowledge of SkyDrive, do you think you will use it? Explain why you answered the way you did.

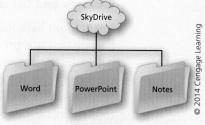

Figure 91

© 2014 Cengage Learning

✹ Consider This: Your Turn

Apply your creative thinking and problem solving skills to design and implement a solution.

1: Creating Beginning Files for Classes
Personal/Academic

Part 1: You are taking the following classes: Introduction to Sociology, Chemistry, Calculus, and Marketing. Create folders for each of the classes. Create a folder structure that will store the databases for each of these classes. In the Introduction of Sociology folder, use Access to create a database named Media and Gender. In the Chemistry folder, use Access to create a database named Periodic Table. In the Calculus folder, use Access to create a database with the name of the class. In the Marketing folder, create an Access database named Data Mining Information. If requested by your instructor, add your name to each of the databases. Use the concepts and techniques presented

Continued >

Consider This: Your Turn *continued*

in this chapter to create the folders and files, and store the files in their respective locations. Submit your assignment in the format specified by your instructor.

Part 2: ⚙ You made several decisions while determining the folder structure in this assignment. What was the rationale behind these decisions? Are there any other decisions that also might have worked?

2: Creating Folders
Professional

Part 1: Your manager at the media store where you work part-time has asked for help with organizing her files. After looking through the files, you decided upon a file structure for her to use, including the following folders: CDs, DVDs, and general merchandise. Within the CDs folder, create folders for music, books, and games. Within the DVDs folder, create folders for movies and television. Within the general merchandise folder, create folders for clothing, portable media players, and cases. If requested by your instructor, add your name to each of the CDs, DVDs, and general merchandise folders. Use the concepts and techniques presented in this chapter to create the folders. Submit your assignment in the format specified by your instructor.

Part 2: ⚙ You made several decisions while determining the folder structure in this assignment. What was the rationale behind these decisions? Justify why you feel this folder structure will help your manager organize her files.

3: Using Help
Research and Collaboration

Part 1: You have just installed a new computer with the Windows operating system and want to be sure that it is protected from the threat of viruses. You ask two of your friends to help research computer viruses, virus prevention, and virus removal. In a team of three people, each person should choose a topic (computer viruses, virus prevention, and virus removal) to research. Use the concepts and techniques presented in this chapter to use Help to find information regarding these topics. Create a document that contains steps to properly safeguard a computer from viruses, ways to prevent viruses, as well as the different ways to remove a virus should your computer become infected. Submit your assignment in the format specified by your instructor.

Part 2: ⚙ You made several decisions while searching Windows Help and Support for this assignment. What decisions did you make? What was the rationale behind these decisions? How did you locate the required information about viruses in help?

Learn Online

Reinforce what you learned in this chapter with games, exercises, training, and many other online activities and resources.

Student Companion Site   Reinforcement activities and resources are available at no additional cost on www.cengagebrain.com. Visit www.cengage.com/ct/studentdownload for detailed instructions about accessing the resources available at the Student Companion Site.

SAM   Put your skills into practice with SAM Projects! If you have a SAM account, go to www.cengage.com/sam2013 to access SAM assignments for this chapter.

Office 365 Essentials

Microsoft product screen shots used with permission from Microsoft Corporation.

Objectives

You will have mastered the material in this chapter when you can:

- Describe the components of Office 365

- Compare Office 2013 to Office 365 subscription plans

- Understand the productivity tools of Office 365

- Sync multiple devices using Office 365

- Describe how business teams collaborate using SharePoint

- Describe how to use a SharePoint template to design a public website

- Describe how to conduct an online meeting with Lync

Explore Office 365

Introduction to Office 365

Microsoft Office 365 uses the cloud to deliver a subscription-based service offering the newest Office suite and much more. The Microsoft cloud provides Office software and information stored on remote servers all over the world. Your documents are located online or on the cloud, which provides you access to your information anywhere using a PC, Mac, tablet, mobile phone, or other device with an Internet connection. For businesses and students alike, Office 365 offers significant cost savings compared to the traditional cost of purchasing Microsoft Office 2013. In addition to the core desktop Office suite, Office 365 provides access to email, calendars, conferencing, file sharing, and website design, which sync across multiple devices.

Cloud Computing

Cloud computing refers to a collection of computer servers that house resources users access through the Internet (Figure 1). These resources include email messages, schedules, music, photos, videos, games, websites, programs, apps, servers, storage, and more. Instead of accessing these resources on your computer or mobile device, you access them on the cloud.

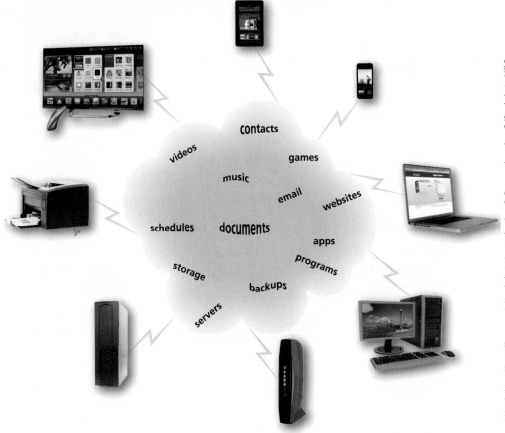

contacts
videos
games
music
email
websites
schedules documents
apps
storage
programs
backups
servers

Figure 1

Cloud computing can help businesses be more efficient and save them money by shifting usage and the consumption of resources, such as servers and programs, from a local environment to the Internet. For example, an employee working during the day in California could use computing resources located in an office in London that is closed for the evening. When the company in California uses the computing resources, it pays a fee that is based on the amount of computing time and other resources it consumes, much in the same way that consumers pay utility companies for the amount of electricity they use.

Cloud computing is changing how users access and pay for software applications. Fading fast are the days when software packages were sold in boxes at a physical store location with a one-time purchase software license fee. Instead, the new pricing structure is a subscription-based model, where users pay a monthly or annual fee for the software that you can use on multiple devices. The cloud-based Office 365 offers the Office suite with added features that allow you to communicate and collaborate with others in real time.

When you create a free Microsoft account, do you get free cloud storage space?
Yes, when you create a free Microsoft account at Outlook.com, you have access to 7 GB of cloud storage for any type of files.

CONSIDER THIS

What Is Office 365?

Office 365 (Office365.com) is a collection of programs and services, which includes the Microsoft Office 2013 suite, file storage, online collaboration, and file synchronization, as shown in Figure 2 on the next page. You can access these services using your computer, browser, or supported mobile device. For example, a business has two options for providing Office to their employees. A business could purchase Office 2013 and install the software on company computers and servers; however, this traditional Office 2013 package with perpetual licensing does not include the communication and collaboration tools. Employees could not access the Office software if they were not using their work computers. In contrast, if the business purchases a monthly subscription to Office 365, each employee has access to the Office suite on up to five different computers, whether at home or work; company-wide email; web conferencing; website creation capabilities; cloud storage; and shared files. For a lower price, Office 365 provides many more features. In addition, a business may prefer a subscription plan with predictable monthly costs and no up-front infrastructure costs.

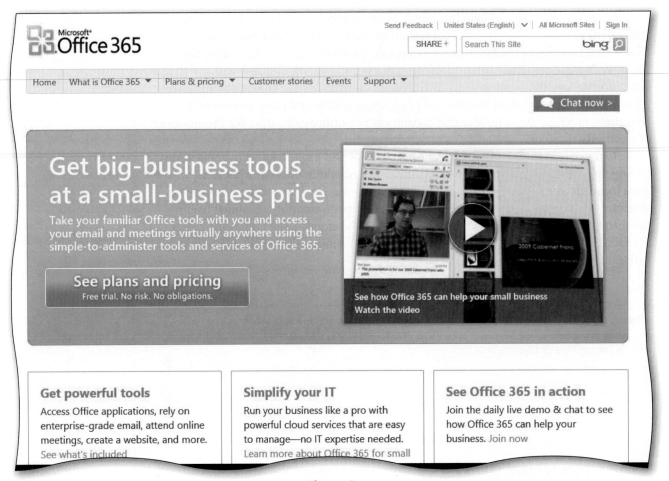

Figure 2

Office 2013 and Office 365 Features Comparison

Office 2013 is the name of the perpetual software package that includes individual applications that can be installed on a single computer. An Office 365 subscription comes with a license to install the software on multiple PCs or Macs at the same time, giving you more flexibility to use your Office products in your home, school, or workplace, whether on a computer or a mobile device. Office 365 provides the Office 2013 programs as part of a subscription service that includes online storage, sharing, and syncing via Microsoft cloud services as shown in Table 1.

Office 365 is available in business, consumer, education, and government editions. Office 365 combines the full version of the Microsoft Office desktop suite with cloud-based versions of Microsoft's communications and collaboration services. The subscription package includes:

- Microsoft Exchange online for shared email and calendars
- Microsoft SharePoint Online for shared file access and public website creation
- Microsoft Office Web apps for browser viewing
- Microsoft Lync Online for communication services

Table 1 Office 2013 and Office 365 Feature Comparison	
Office 2013 Professional (Installed on a single device)	**Office 365 Subscription** (Installed on 2 to 5 devices)
Microsoft Word	Microsoft Word
Microsoft Excel	Microsoft Excel
Microsoft PowerPoint	Microsoft PowerPoint
Microsoft Access	Microsoft Access
Microsoft Outlook	Microsoft Outlook
Microsoft Publisher	Microsoft Publisher
Microsoft OneNote	Microsoft OneNote
	email and calendars (Exchange Online)
	file sharing (SharePoint Online)
	public website design and publishing (SharePoint Online)
	browser-based Office Web Apps
	instant messaging (Lync Online)
	audio and video web conferencing (Lync Online)
	screen sharing with shared control (Lync Online)
	technical support

© 2014 Cengage Learning

Subscription-Based Office 365 Plans

Microsoft provides various subscription plans for Office 365 with different benefits for each individual or organization. Subscription plans include Office 365 Home Premium for home users, Office 365 University for students, Office 365 Small Business, Office 365 Small Business Premium, Office 365 Midsize Business, and Office 365 Enterprise and Government. During the Office 365 sign-up process, you create a Microsoft email address and password to use on your multiple devices. A single subscription to an Office 365 Home Premium account can cover an entire household. The Office 365 Home Premium subscription allows up to five concurrent installations by using the same email address and password combination. This means that your mother could be on the main family computer while you use your tablet and smartphone at the same time. You each can sign in with your individual Microsoft accounts using your settings and accessing your own documents using a single Office 365 subscription.

The Office 365 University subscription plan is designed for higher-education full-time and part-time students, faculty, and staff. By submitting the proper credentials, such as a school email address, students and faculty can purchase Office 365 University, including Word, PowerPoint, Excel, Access, Outlook, Publisher, and OneNote. A one-time payment covers a four-year subscription. In addition, Office 365 University provides users with 27 GB of SkyDrive cloud storage rather than the free 7 GB provided by a Microsoft account, and 60 Skype world minutes per month for videoconferencing. Students have the option of renewing for another four years, for a total of eight years. The Office 365 University edition is limited to two computers (PC or Mac).

The Microsoft Office 365 Business Plans can provide full support for employees to work from any location, whether they are in their traditional business office, commuting to and from work across the country, or working from a home office. Office 365 small business plans (Small Business and Small Business Premium) are best for companies with up to 10 employees, but can accommodate up to 25 users. Office 365 Midsize Business accommodates from 11 to 300 users. Office 365 Enterprise Plan fits organizations ranging in size from a single employee to 50,000-plus users. Each employee can install Microsoft Office 365 on five different computers.

First Look at Office 365

Microsoft Office 365 subscription plans offer all the same applications that are available in the Microsoft Office Professional 2013 suite in addition to multiple communication and collaboration tools. With Office 365 you can retrieve, edit, and save Office documents on the Office 365 cloud, coauthor documents in real time with others, and quickly initiate computer-based calls, instant messages, and web conferences with others.

Productivity Tools

Whether you are inserting audio and video into a Word document to create a high-impact business plan proposal or utilizing the visualization tools in Excel to chart the return on investment of a new mobile marketing program, Office 365 premium plans deliver the full Office product with the same features as the latest version of Microsoft Office. Office 365 uses a quick-start installation technology, called **Click-to-Run**, that downloads and installs the basics within minutes, so that users are able to start working almost immediately. It also includes **Office on Demand**, which streams Office to Windows 7- and Windows 8-based PCs for work performed on public computers. The single-use copy that is installed temporarily on the Windows computer does not count toward the device limit. No installation is necessary when using Office on Demand, and the applications disappear from the computer once you are finished using them. If you have a document on a USB drive or on SkyDrive that you need to edit on another PC, you can use Office on Demand to get the full version of Word in just a few minutes.

In effect, the Office 365 subscription provides access to the full Office applications wherever you are working. When you access your Office 365 account management panel, three choices are listed: 32- and 64-bit versions of Office 2013, and Office for Mac. Selecting the third option will initiate a download of an installer that must be run in the standard OS X fashion. When you install Office 365 on a Mac, the most current Mac version of Office is installed.

CONSIDER THIS

Unlike Google, which offers online documents, spreadsheets, and presentations called Google Docs, Microsoft Office 365 installs locally on your computer in addition to being available online. Google Docs is entirely browser based, which means if you are not connected to the Internet, you cannot access your Google Docs files.

Email and Calendars

In business, sharing information is essential to meeting the needs of your customers and staff. Office 365 offers shared access to business email, calendars, and contacts using **Exchange Online** from a computer, tablet, phone, and browser. The cloud-based Exchange Online enables business people to access Outlook information from anywhere at any time, while eliminating the cost of purchasing and maintaining servers to store data. If you need to meet with a colleague about a new project, you can compare calendars to view availability, confirm conference room availability, share project contacts, search email messages related to the project, and send email invitations to the project meeting. Exchange Online also allows you to search and access your company's address list.

Online Meetings

When you are working with a team on a project that requires interaction, email and text communications can slow the communications process. Microsoft Lync connects you with others by facilitating real-time, interactive presentations and meetings over the Internet using both video and audio calling. As shown in Figure 3, you can conduct an online meeting with a team member or customer that includes an instant messaging conversation, audio, high-definition video, virtual whiteboards, and screen sharing. If the customer does not have an Office 365 subscription, they still can join the meeting through the invitation link, which runs the Lync Web App.

Skype is another tool in the Office 365 subscription, which enables users to place video calls to computers and smartphones and voice calls to landlines. Skype also supports instant message and file sharing to computers and mobile devices. While Skype may be adequate for simple communication, Lync provides for more robust, comprehensive communications. These robust features include high-definition (HD) videoconferencing capabilities, a whiteboard, and a larger audience. Using Lync, meeting attendees simultaneously can view up to five participants' video, identify the active speaker, and associate names with faces. Lync supports up to 250 attendees per meeting. Unlike Skype, Lync meetings can be recorded for replaying at a later time. This enables businesses and schools to schedule meetings or organize online classes using Lync capabilities.

File Sharing

Office 365 includes a team site, which is a password-protected portal that supports sharing of large, difficult-to-email files and provides a single location for the latest versions of documents. In business, for example, colleagues working on common projects can save valuable time by being able to access instantly the latest master copy of each document. Security can be managed through different

Figure 3

levels of user access so that users see only what they are supposed to see. Office 365 provides access to shared files using the cloud, making writing, editing, and sharing documents easier. If a construction company creates a commercial bid for a building project, the customers can be invited to view an Excel spreadsheet bid, construction timetable with a shared calendar, and an Access database of all the materials needed using the file sharing feature online.

Website Creation

Office 365 business plan subscriptions include a built-in hosted public website, where customers and clients can find an online storefront of a company. This public website, called the Website, can be customized to market a company by using various templates within the Office 365 cloud. The website creation tools include those for adding a theme, graphics, fonts, maps, directions, blogs, stock tickers, slide shows, PayPal, weather, and videos to interact with the website's visitors.

Synchronization

Office 365 subscription plans provide a central place to store and access your documents and business information. A feature of Office 365 ensures the original and backup computer files in two or more locations are identical through a process called **Active Directory Synchronization**. For example, if you open a PowerPoint presentation on your smartphone while you are riding a city bus and then add a new slide as you head to school, the PowerPoint presentation automatically is synced with Office 365. When you arrive on campus and open the PowerPoint presentation on a school computer, your new slide already is part of the finished slide show. By storing your files in Office 365, you can access your files on another computer if your home computer fails, with no loss of time or important information. When using your mobile phone's data plan, you do not need to search for a Wi-Fi hot spot to connect to the Office 365 cloud. Computer labs in schools can be configured to synchronize automatically all student files to Office 365 online.

Multiple Device Access to Office 365

With a single sign-in process, Office 365 provides access to multiple computers and mobile devices, including Android smartphones and tablets, Apple iPhones and iPads, Windows phones, and Blackberry phones. After you configure your devices' email settings, you can view your Microsoft account calendar, contacts, and email. Your personalized settings, preferences, and documents can be synchronized among all the different devices included in your Office 365 premium subscription. With the mobility of Office 365, students and employees can work anywhere, accessing information and responding to email requests immediately. If you lose your phone, Office 365 includes a feature that allows you to remotely wipe your phone clean of any data. By wiping your phone's data, you can prevent any unauthorized access to sensitive information, such as your banking information, passwords, and contacts, as well as discourage identity theft. Because your phone contacts and other information are stored on the Microsoft cloud, damaged or lost equipment is never a problem.

A thief can be quite resourceful if he or she steals your phone. Before you can alert your parents or spouse to the theft, they might receive a text from "you" asking for your ATM or credit card PIN number. Your parents or spouse might then reply with the PIN number. Your bank account could be emptied in minutes.

Teams Using Office 365 in Business

In the business world, rarely does an employee work in isolation. Companies need their employees to collaborate, whether they work in the same office or in locations around the world. Telecommuters working from home can communicate as if they were on-site by using a common team website and conferencing software. SharePoint Online and Lync Online provide seamless communication.

Small business subscription plans as low as $6.00 per user per month allow employees to create and store Word documents, Excel spreadsheets, and PowerPoint presentations online and communicate with one another via email, instant messaging, or video chat as they work on projects together. As shown in Figure 4, a team portal page is shown when you subscribe at https://portal.microsoftonline.com. Larger companies and those requiring more features can take advantage of the Office 365 business premium package, which, in addition to the features listed above, provides access to the Office 365 portal website and eliminates the effort and cost of the users maintaining their own costly computer servers.

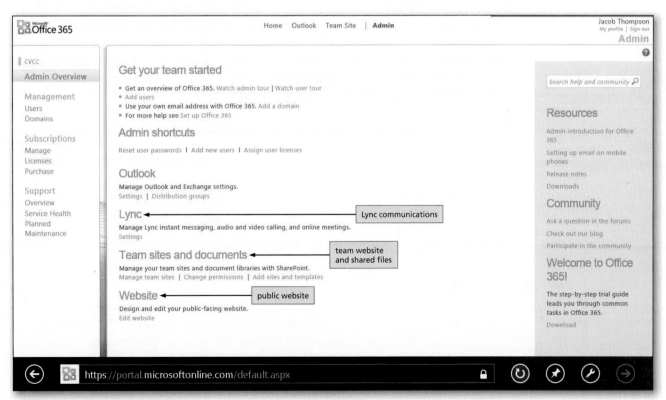

Figure 4

Email Communication Using Exchange

Office 365 includes Exchange Online, an email-based collaborative communications server for business. Exchange enables employees to be more productive by effectively managing email across multiple devices and facilitating teamwork.

Collaboration Using SharePoint

SharePoint Online, a part of Office 365 subscription plans, allows employees to collaborate with one another, share documents, post announcements, and track tasks, as shown in Table 2.

Table 2 Office 365 SharePoint Features	
Team Site Feature	**Description**
Calendar	Track important dates
Shared Document Library	Store related documents according to topic; picture, report, and slide libraries often are included
Task List	Track team tasks according to who is responsible for completion
Team Discussion Board	Discuss the topics at hand in an open forum
Contacts List	Share contact lists of employees, customers, contractors, and suppliers

© 2014 Cengage Learning

Office 365 provides the tools to plan meetings. Users can share calendars side by side, view availability, and suggest meeting times from shared calendars. Typically, a SharePoint team administrator or website owner establishes a folder structure to share and manage documents. The team website is fully searchable online, making locating and sharing data more efficient than using a local server. With a team website, everyone on the team has a central location to store and find all the information for a project, client, or department, as shown in Figure 5.

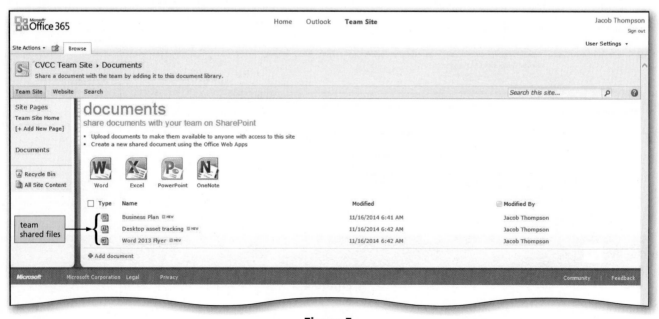

Figure 5

Website Design Using SharePoint

SharePoint provides templates to create a professional looking, public website for an online presence to market your business. As shown in Figure 6, a local pet sitting business is setting up a business website by customizing a SharePoint template. SharePoint Public Website includes features within the Design Manager that you use to customize and design your website by adding your own images, forms, style sheets, maps, themes, and social networking tools. When you finish customizing your business site, you can apply your own domain name to the site. A **domain** is a unique web address that identifies where your website can be found. Office 365 SharePoint hosts your website as part of your subscription. Your customers easily can find your business online and learn about your services.

BTW

Creating SharePoint Intranet Sites
A SharePoint website also can be customized to serve as an internal company website for private communications within the company.

Figure 6

Real-Time Communications Using Lync

Lync Online is Microsoft's server platform for online team communications and comes bundled with Office 365 business subscriptions. As shown in Figure 7, Lync connects in real time to allow instant messaging, videoconferencing, and voice communications; it also integrates with email and Microsoft Office applications.

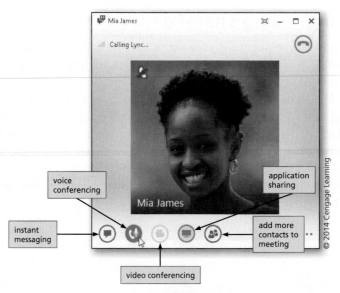

voice conferencing

application sharing

instant messaging

add more contacts to meeting

video conferencing

© 2014 Cengage Learning

Figure 7

Lync allows you to connect with staff at remote locations using instant messaging capabilities, desktop sharing, videoconferencing, and shared agendas or documents. Lync is integrated into Office 365, which allows staff to start communicating from within the applications in which they currently are working. For example, while an employee is creating a PowerPoint presentation for a new product line, as shown in Figure 8, Lync enables him or her to collaborate with the entire team about the details of the product presentation. The team can view the presenter's screen displaying the PowerPoint presentation. The presenter can share control with any member of the team and can share his or her screen at any time during the Lync meeting.

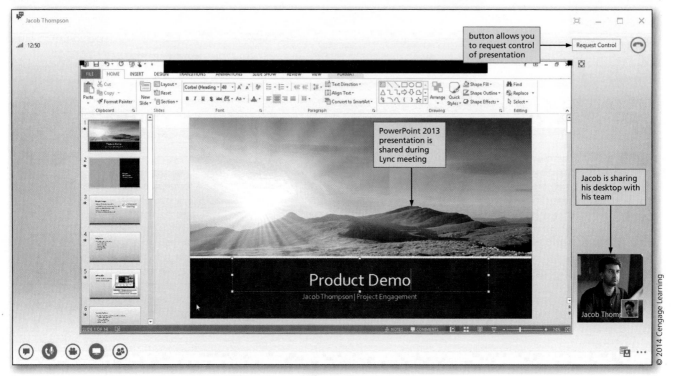

button allows you to request control of presentation

PowerPoint 2013 presentation is shared during Lync meeting

Jacob is sharing his desktop with his team

© 2014 Cengage Learning

Figure 8

Users can send a Lync meeting request to schedule a team meeting, or an impromptu conversation can be started immediately using the Meet Now feature. Participants receive a Lync meeting request link via an email message, and when they click the meeting request link, Lync automatically connects them to the online conference. If the participant does not have Lync installed, the Lync Web App automatically connects to the Lync meeting through the user's PC or Mac OS X browser. If a participant is away from his or her computer, he or she still can participate using the Lync Mobile apps for Windows Phone, iOS, and Android. As shown in Figure 9, Lync utilizes **instant messaging** (IM), allowing two or more people to share text messages. They can communicate in real time, similar to a voice conversation. In addition to a simple instant message, Lync provides a feature called **persistent chat**, which allows end-users to participate in a working session of instant messages that is persistent or sustained over a specified amount of time in a moderated chat room. Consider having an instant messaging session with a group of colleagues in different parts of your organization, regardless of geographic region, where you all are working on the same project. Over the course of the project, different people post questions and concerns, and others are able to respond to all those who have subscribed to your topic or been admitted to the chat room. Instead of a long trail of email messages, a team can keep information in a controlled environment with a full history of the discussion in one location.

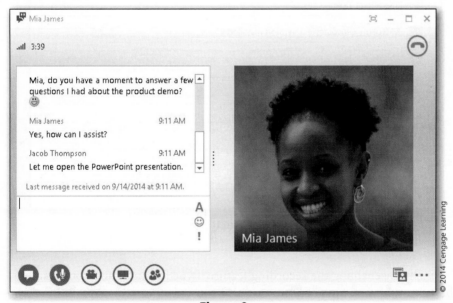

Figure 9

Lync also delivers support for full high-definition (HD) videoconferencing, so that a team can have a clear view of the participants, products, and demos. Before you join the video feed, you can preview your video feed to make sure your video camera is at the correct angle, your image is centered within the video frame, and that your room lighting provides for a clear image. The Lync preview option is important in creating a positive first impression over video. Your audio devices can be tested for clarity to make sure your headset, microphone, and speakers are functioning properly.

Lync provides a polling feature that presenters can use to ask the participants' opinions during a meeting (Figure 10). The poll question can consist of up to seven possible choices. The presenter has the option to view the results privately or share the results with the entire group.

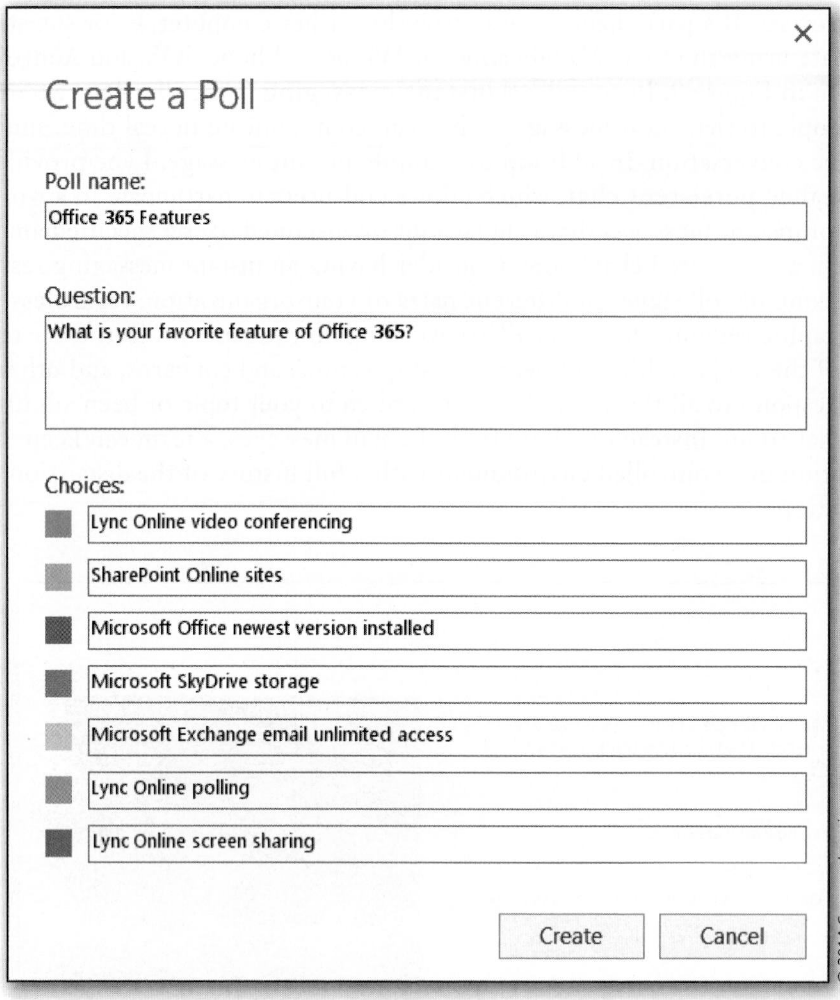

Figure 10

Finally, by enabling the recording feature, Lync meetings and conversations can be captured for viewing at a later time. For instance, you can capture the audio, video, instant messaging (IM), screen sharing, Microsoft PowerPoint presentations, whiteboard, and polling portions of the Lync session and then play them back just as they transpired during the live Lync event. The meeting recordings can be made available to others so that they can view all or part of the Lync event. Instructors can record Lync online class sessions for students who were unable to attend the original presentation. The recording starts in Microsoft Lync; recordings then can be viewed within the Recording Manager feature.

Chapter Summary

In this chapter, you have learned how to subscribe to Office 365, which provides local and online access to Office applications, email, document sharing, web conferencing, and business websites. You also learned how a business can utilize Office 365 features on the cloud to facilitate teamwork. Finally, you learned about the features of SharePoint and Lync, which provide collaboration and communications for business teams using Office 365.

✳ Consider This: Your Turn

Apply your creative thinking and problem solving skills to design and implement a solution.

1: Comparing Office 365 Personal Plans

Personal

Part 1:   You are a freshman in college living at home with your family. You are considering if it would be a better value to subscribe to Office 365 University or Office 365 Home Premium. Write a one-page document comparing the pros and cons of the two subscription plans. Research the different subscriptions in detail at Office365.com. Submit your assignment in the format specified by your instructor.

Part 2:   ✳ Which type of computer and/or devices would you use with your Office 365 subscription? If you are at a friend's home that does not have Office 365, how could you access your Office files if you do not have your computer or mobile device with you?

2: Upgrading a Local Business to Office 365

Professional

Part 1:   You are an employee at Impact Digital Marketing, a small marketing firm with 12 employees. The firm is setting up an Office 365 Small Business subscription next week, and you need to compose an email message with multiple paragraphs to explain the features of this new subscription plan to the members of your firm. Research the Office 365 Small Business subscription plan in detail at Office365.com, and compile your findings in an email message. Submit your assignment in the format specified by your instructor.

Part 2:   ✳ Give three examples of how a marketing firm could use Lync. How could a marketing firm use the SharePoint Websites feature?

3: Conducting a Lync Meeting

Research and Collaboration

* Students need an Office 365 subscription to complete the following assignment.

Part 1:   Using your Office 365 subscription, conduct a meeting using Lync. Working with a partner, use your Office 365 subscription to research how to use Lync. Then, conduct a 15-minute Lync meeting, including instant messaging, to discuss the features of Lync. Use the concepts and techniques presented in this chapter to create the Lync meeting. Submit your assignment in the format specified by your instructor.

Part 2:   ✳ When using Lync in business, when would the video feature best be utilized?

1 Databases and Database Objects: An Introduction

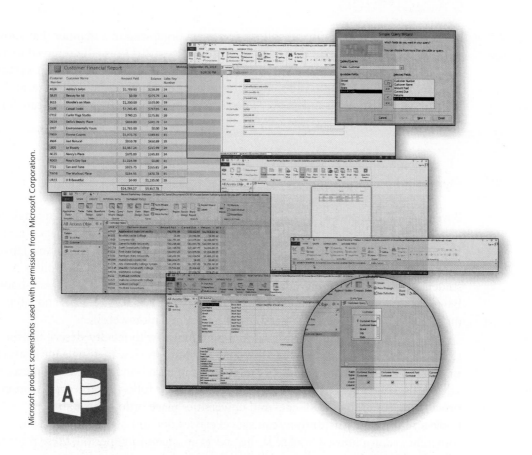

Microsoft product screenshots used with permission from Microsoft Corporation.

Objectives

You will have mastered the material in this chapter when you can:

- Describe the features of the Access window
- Create a database
- Create tables in Datasheet and Design views
- Add records to a table
- Close a database
- Open a database

- Print the contents of a table
- Create and use a query
- Create and use a form
- Create and print custom reports
- Modify a report in Layout view
- Perform special database operations
- Design a database to satisfy a collection of requirements

1 | Databases and Database Objects: An Introduction

Introduction

The term **database** describes a collection of data organized in a manner that allows access, retrieval, and use of that data. Microsoft Access 2013, usually referred to as simply Access, is a database management system. A **database management system** is software that allows you to use a computer to create a database; add, change, and delete data in the database; ask and answer questions concerning the data; and create forms and reports using the data.

Project — Database Creation

Bavant Publishing Inc. is a publishing company that specializes in foreign language textbooks. Bavant sells in both the K-12 and the higher education markets. Recently, Bavant purchased a small, private publisher of Arabic, Russian, Chinese, and Japanese language textbooks. These languages are increasing in popularity with college students. All textbooks are available in hardcover and some are available as e-books. Bavant Publishing also provides ancillary materials, such as workbooks and laboratory manuals, video resources, audio resources, and companion websites.

Bavant representatives visit campuses and meet with faculty, describing the features and strengths of the textbooks and providing review materials for instructors. Bavant pays a base salary to its book reps, who can earn bonus pay based on exceeding sales goals. Customers place orders with the publisher following the organization's procedures; for example, colleges and universities place orders through their bookstores. Because institutions can cancel classes due to low enrollments, customers sometimes return unused books. At the end of an accounting period, these returns are subtracted from the current amount due.

Bavant wants to maintain records on the sales of textbooks from the newly acquired publisher separately from their other foreign language textbooks to better track profitability and market potential. Bavant organizes this data on its customers and book representatives in a database managed by Access. In this way, Bavant keeps its data current and accurate and can analyze it for trends and produce a variety of useful reports.

In a **relational database** such as those maintained by Access, a database consists of a collection of tables, each of which contains information on a specific subject. Figure 1–1 shows the database for Bavant Publishing. It consists of two tables: the Customer table (Figure 1–1a) contains information about Bavant customers, and the Book Rep table (Figure 1–1b) contains information about the book reps to whom these customers are assigned.

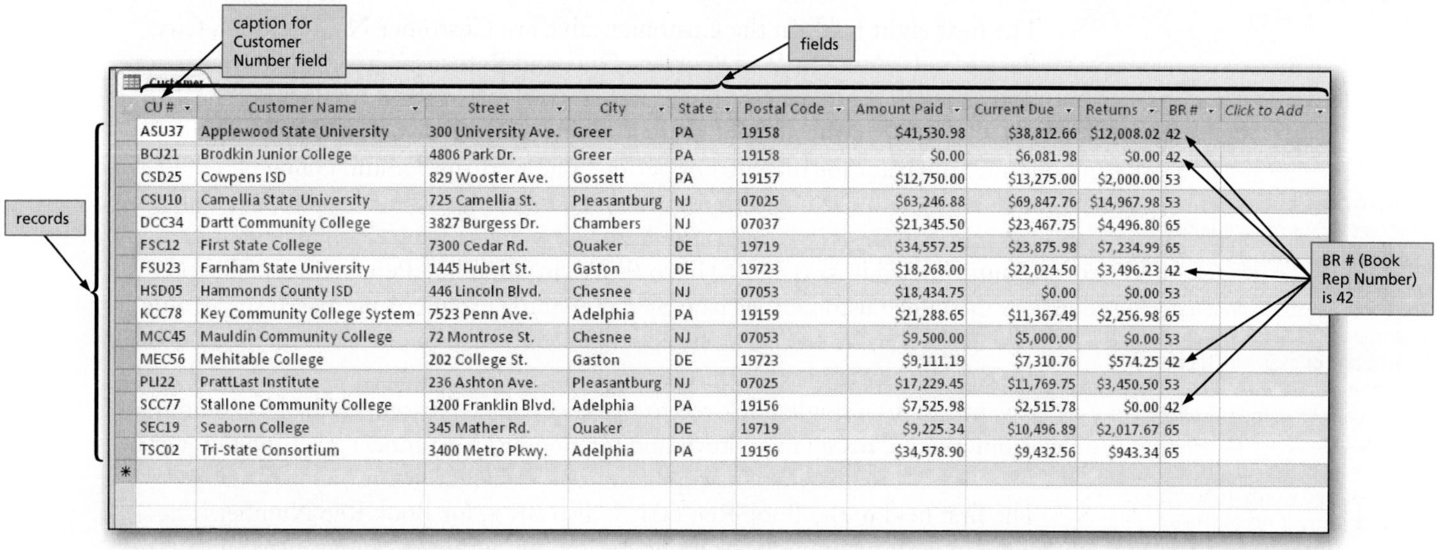

Figure 1–1 (a) Customer Table

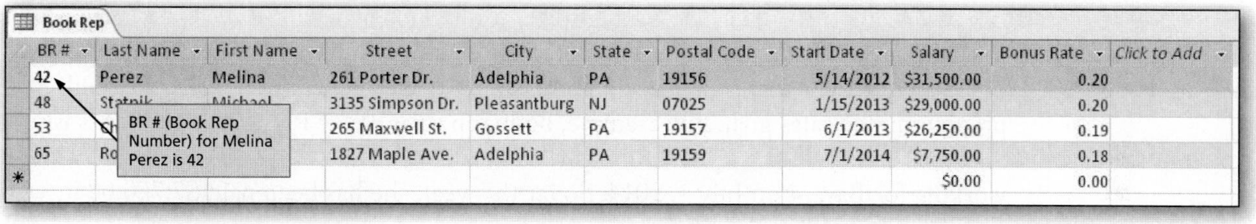

Figure 1–1 (b) Book Rep Table

The rows in the tables are called **records**. A record contains information about a given person, product, or event. A row in the Customer table, for example, contains information about a specific customer, such as the customer's name, address information, and other data.

The columns in the tables are called fields. A **field** contains a specific piece of information within a record. In the Customer table, for example, the fourth field, City, contains the name of the city where the customer is located.

The first field in the Customer table is CU #, which is an abbreviation for Customer Number. Bavant Publishing assigns each customer a number; the Bavant customer numbers consist of three uppercase letters followed by a two-digit number.

The customer numbers are unique; that is, no two customers have the same number. Such a field is a **unique identifier**. A unique identifier, as its name suggests, is a way of uniquely identifying each record in the database. A given customer number will appear only in a single record in the table. Only one record exists, for example, in which the customer number is TSC02. A unique identifier also is called a **primary key**. Thus, the Customer Number field is the primary key for the Customer table.

BTW

BTWs
For a complete list of the BTWs found in the margins of this book, visit the BTW resource on the Student Companion Site located on www.cengagebrain.com. For detailed instructions about accessing available resources, visit www.cengage.com/ct/studentdownload or contact your instructor for information about accessing the required files.

BTW
Naming Fields
Access 2013 has a number
of reserved words, words
that have a special meaning
to Access. You cannot use
these reserved words as field
names. For example, Name
is a reserved word and could
not be used in the Customer
table to describe a customer's
name. For a complete list
of reserved words in Access
2013, consult Access Help.

The next eight fields in the Customer table are Customer Name, Street, City, State, Postal Code, Amount Paid, Current Due, and Returns. The Amount Paid column contains the amount that the customer has paid Bavant Publishing year to date (YTD) prior to the current period. The Current Due column contains the amount due to Bavant for the current period. The Returns column contains the dollar value of the books or other products the customer was unable to sell and has returned to Bavant in the current period. For example, customer TSC02 is Tri-State Consortium. The address is 3400 Metro Pkwy., in Adelphia, Pennsylvania. The postal code is 19156. The customer has paid $34,578.90 for products purchased so far. The amount due for the current period is $9,432.56. The customer has returned products worth $943.34.

Bavant assigns a single book rep to work with each customer. The last column in the Customer table, BR # (an abbreviation for Book Rep Number) gives the number of the customer's book rep. The book rep number for Tri-State Consortium is 65.

The first field in the Book Rep table is also BR #, for Book Rep Number. The book rep numbers are unique, so the Book Rep Number field is the primary key of the Book Rep table.

The other fields in the Book Rep table are Last Name, First Name, Street, City, State, Postal Code, Start Date, Salary, and Bonus Rate. The Start Date field gives the date the rep began working for Bavant. The Salary field gives the salary paid to the rep thus far this year. The Bonus Rate gives the potential bonus percentage based on personal performance. The bonus rate applies when the book rep exceeds a predetermined sales goal. For example, book rep 65 is Tracy Rogers. Her address is 1827 Maple Ave., in Adelphia, Pennsylvania. The postal code is 19159. Tracy started working for Bavant on July 1, 2014. So far this year, she has been paid $7,750.00 in salary. Her bonus rate is 0.18 (18%).

The book rep number appears in both the Customer table and the Book Rep table, and relates customers and book reps. Book rep 48, Michael Statnik, recently transferred from another division of the company and has not yet been assigned any customers. His book rep number, therefore, does not appear on any row in the Customer table.

CONSIDER THIS

How would you find the name of the book rep for Tri-State Consortium?
In the Customer table, you see that the book rep number for customer Tri-State Consortium is 65. To find the name of this book rep, look for the row in the Book Rep table that contains 65 in the BR # column. After you have found it, you know that the book rep for Tri-State Consortium is Tracy Rogers.

CONSIDER THIS

How would you find all the customers assigned to Tracy Rogers?
First, look in the Book Rep table to find that her number is 65. You would then look through the Customer table for all the customers that contain 65 in the BR # column. Tracy's customers are DCC34 (Dartt Community College), FSC12 (First State College), KCC78 (Key Community College System), SEC19 (Seaborn College), and TSC02 (Tri-State Consortium).

Roadmap

In this chapter, you will learn how to create and use the database shown in Figure 1–1 on page AC 3. The following roadmap identifies general activities you will perform as you progress through this chapter:

1. CREATE the FIRST TABLE, Book Rep, using Datasheet view.
2. ADD RECORDS to the Book Rep table.
3. PRINT the CONTENTS of the Book Rep table.
4. IMPORT RECORDS into the second table, Customer.
5. MODIFY the SECOND TABLE using Design view.
6. CREATE a QUERY for the Customer table.
7. CREATE a FORM for the Customer table.
8. CREATE a REPORT for the Customer table.

At the beginning of step instructions throughout the chapter, you will see an abbreviated form of this roadmap. The abbreviated roadmap uses colors to indicate chapter progress: gray means the chapter is beyond that activity, blue means the task being shown is covered in that activity, and black means that activity is yet to be covered. For example, the following abbreviated roadmap indicates the chapter would be showing a task in the 3 PRINT CONTENTS activity.

1 CREATE FIRST TABLE | 2 ADD RECORDS | 3 PRINT CONTENTS | 4 IMPORT RECORDS | 5 MODIFY SECOND TABLE

6 CREATE QUERY | 7 CREATE FORM | 8 CREATE REPORT

Use the abbreviated roadmap as a progress guide while you read or step through the instructions in this chapter.

To Run Access

If you are using a computer to step through the project in this chapter and you want your screens to match the figures in this book, you should change your screen's resolution to 1366 × 768. For information about how to change a computer's resolution, refer to the Office and Windows chapter at the beginning of this book.

The following steps, which assume Windows is running, use the Start screen or the search box to run Access based on a typical installation. You may need to ask your instructor how to run Access on your computer. For a detailed example of the procedure summarized below, refer to the Office and Windows chapter.

1 Scroll the Start screen for an Access 2013 tile. If your Start screen contains an Access 2013 tile, tap or click it to run Access and then proceed to Step 5; if the Start screen does not contain the Access 2013 tile, proceed to the next step to search for the Access app.

2 Swipe in from the right edge of the screen or point to the upper-right corner of the screen to display the Charms bar, and then tap or click the Search charm on the Charms bar to display the Search menu.

3 Type `Access` as the search text in the Search box and watch the search results appear in the Apps list.

4 Tap or click Access 2013 in the search results to run Access.

5 If the Access window is not maximized, tap or click the Maximize button on its title bar to maximize the window.

For an introduction to Windows and instruction about how to perform basic Windows tasks, read the Office and Windows chapter at the beginning of this book, where you can learn how to resize windows, change screen resolution, create folders, move and rename files, use Windows Help, and much more.

For an introduction to Office and instruction about how to perform basic tasks in Office apps, read the Office and Windows chapter at the beginning of this book, where you can learn how to run an application, use the ribbon, save a file, open a file, exit an application, use Help, and much more.

Creating a Database

In Access, all the tables, reports, forms, and queries that you create are stored in a single file called a database. Thus, you first must create the database to hold the tables, reports, forms, and queries. You can use either the Blank desktop database option or a template to create a new database. If you already know the tables and fields you want in your database, you would use the Blank desktop database option. If not, you can use a template. Templates can guide you by suggesting some commonly used databases.

To Create a Database

Because you already know the tables and fields you want in the Bavant Publishing database, you would use the Blank desktop database option rather than using a template. The following steps assume you already have created folders for storing your files, for example, a CIS 101 folder (for your class) that contains an Access folder (for your assignments). Thus, these steps save the database in the Access folder in the CIS 101 folder on your desired save location. For a detailed example of the procedure for saving a file in a folder or saving a file on SkyDrive, refer to the Office and Windows chapter at the beginning of this book.

1 Tap or click the 'Blank desktop database' thumbnail to select the database type.

2 Type Bavant Publishing in the File Name text box to enter the new file name. Do not press the ENTER key after typing the file name because you do not want to create the database at this time.

3 Tap or click the 'Browse for a location to put your database' button to display the File New Database dialog box.

4 Navigate to the location for the database, for example, the Documents library, the My Documents folder, the folder identifying your class (CIS 101, in this case), and then to the Access folder.

5 Tap or click the OK button (File New Database dialog box) to select the location for the database and close the dialog box.

6 Tap or click the Create button to create the database on the selected drive in the selected folder with the file name, Bavant Publishing (Figure 1–2).

Q&A

The title bar for my Navigation Pane contains All Tables rather than All Access Objects, as in the figure. Is that a problem?
It is not a problem. The title bar indicates how the Navigation Pane is organized. You can carry out the steps in the text with either organization. To make your screens match the ones in the text, tap or click the Navigation Pane arrow and then tap or click Object Type.

I do not have the Search bar that appears on the figure. Is that a problem?
It is not a problem. If your Navigation Pane does not display a Search bar and you want your screens to match the ones in the text, press and hold or right-click the Navigation Pane title bar arrow to display a shortcut menu, and then tap or click Search Bar.

One of the few differences between Windows 7 and Windows 8 occurs in the steps to run Access. If you are using Windows 7, click the Start button, type Access in the 'Search programs and files' box, click Access 2013, and then, if necessary, maximize the Access window. For detailed steps to run Access in Windows 7, refer to the Office and Windows chapter at the beginning of this book. For a summary of the steps, refer to the Quick Reference located at the back of this book.

BTW
Organizing Files and Folders
You should organize and store files in folders so that you easily can find the files later. For example, if you are taking an introductory computer class called CIS 101, a good practice would be to save all Access files in an Access folder in a CIS 101 folder. For a discussion of folders and detailed examples of creating folders, refer to the Office and Windows chapter at the beginning of this book.

BTW
Q&As
For a complete list of the Q&As found in many of the step-by-step sequences in this book, visit the Q&A resource on the Student Companion Site located on www.cengagebrain.com. For detailed instructions about accessing available resources, visit www.cengage.com/ct/studentdownload or contact your instructor for information about accessing the required files.

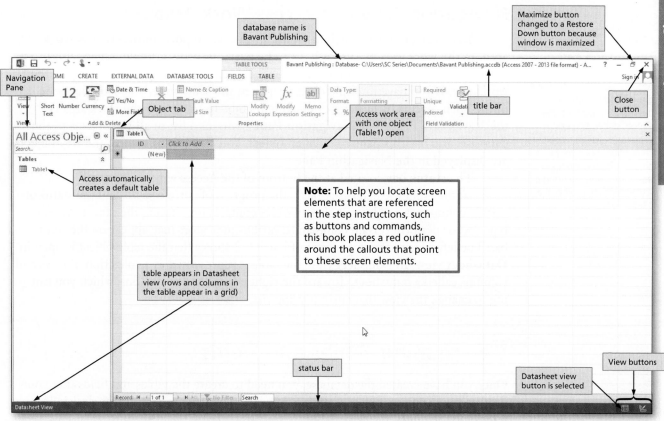

Figure 1–2

TO CREATE A DATABASE USING A TEMPLATE

Ideally, you will design your own database, create a blank database, and then create the tables you have determined that your database should contain. If you are not sure what database design you will need, you could use a template. Templates can guide you by suggesting some commonly used databases. To create a database using a template, you would use the following steps.

1. If you have another database open, close it without exiting Access by tapping or clicking FILE on the ribbon to open the Backstage view and then tapping or clicking Close.

2. If you do not see a template that you want, you can search Microsoft Office online for additional templates.

3. Tap or click the template you want to use. Be sure you have selected one that indicates it is for a desktop database.

4. Enter a file name and select a location for the database.

5. Tap or click the Create button to create the database.

The Access Window

The Access window consists of a variety of components to make your work more efficient. These include the Navigation Pane, Access work area, ribbon, shortcut menus, and Quick Access Toolbar. Some of these components are common to other Microsoft Office apps; others are unique to Access.

Navigation Pane and Access Work Area

You work on objects such as tables, forms, and reports in the **Access work area**. In the work area in Figure 1–2 on the previous page, a single table, Table1, is open in the work area. **Object tabs** for the open objects appear at the top of the work area. If you have multiple objects open at the same time, you can select one of the open objects by tapping or clicking its tab. To the left of the work area is the Navigation Pane. The **Navigation Pane** contains a list of all the objects in the database. You use this pane to open an object. You also can customize the way objects are displayed in the Navigation Pane.

The **status bar**, located at the bottom of the Access window, presents information about the database object, the progress of current tasks, and the status of certain commands and keys; it also provides controls for viewing the object. As you type text or perform certain commands, various indicators may appear on the status bar. The left edge of the status bar in Figure 1–2 shows that the table object is open in **Datasheet view**. In Datasheet view, the table is represented as a collection of rows and columns called a **datasheet**. Toward the right edge are View buttons, which you can use to change the view that currently appears.

Determining Tables and Fields

Once you have created the database, you need to create the tables and fields that your database will contain. Before doing so, however, you need to make some decisions regarding the tables and fields.

Naming Tables and Fields

In creating your database, you must name tables and fields. Before beginning the design process, you must understand the rules Access applies to table and field names. These rules are:

1. Names can be up to 64 characters in length.
2. Names can contain letters, digits, and spaces, as well as most of the punctuation symbols.
3. Names cannot contain periods (.), exclamation points (!), accent graves (`), or square brackets ([ ]).
4. Each field in a table must have a unique name.

The approach to naming tables and fields used in this text is to begin the names with an uppercase letter and to use lowercase for the other letters. In multiple-word names, each word begins with an uppercase letter, and there is a space between words (for example, Customer Number).

Determining the Primary Key

For each table, you need to determine the primary key, the unique identifier. In many cases, you will have obvious choices, such as Customer Number or Book Rep Number. If you do not have an obvious choice, you can use the primary key that Access creates automatically. It is a field called ID. It is an autonumber field, which means that Access will assign the value 1 to the first record, 2 to the second record, and so on.

Determining Data Types for the Fields

For each field in your database, you must determine the field's **data type**, that is, the type of data that can be stored in the field. Four of the most commonly used data types in Access are:

1. **Short Text** — The field can contain any characters. A maximum number of 255 characters is allowed in a field whose data type is Short Text.

2. **Number** — The field can contain only numbers. The numbers can be either positive or negative. Fields assigned this type can be used in arithmetic operations. You usually assign fields that contain numbers but will not be used for arithmetic operations (such as postal codes) a data type of Short Text.

3. **Currency** — The field can contain only monetary data. The values will appear with currency symbols, such as dollar signs, commas, and decimal points, and with two digits following the decimal point. Like numeric fields, you can use currency fields in arithmetic operations. Access assigns a size to currency fields automatically.

4. **Date & Time** — The field can store dates and/or times.

Table 1–1 shows the other data types that are available in Access.

Table 1–1 Additional Data Types

Data Type	Description
Long Text	Field can store a variable amount of text or combinations of text and numbers where the total number of characters may exceed 255.
AutoNumber	Field can store a unique sequential number that Access assigns to a record. Access will increment the number by 1 as each new record is added.
Yes/No	Field can store only one of two values. The choices are Yes/No, True/False, or On/Off.
OLE Object	Field can store an OLE object, which is an object linked to or embedded in the table.
Hyperlink	Field can store text that can be used as a hyperlink address.
Attachment	Field can contain an attached file. Images, spreadsheets, documents, charts, and other elements can be attached to this field in a record in the database. You can view and edit the attached file.
Calculated	Field specified as a calculation based on other fields. The value is not actually stored.

© 2014 Cengage Learning

In the Customer table, because the Customer Number, Customer Name, Street, City, and State all can contain letters, their data types should be Short Text. The data type for Postal Code is Short Text instead of Number because you typically do not use postal codes in arithmetic operations; you do not add postal codes or find an average postal code, for example. The Amount Paid, Current Due, and Returns fields contain monetary data, so their data types should be Currency. The Book Rep Number field contains numbers, but you will not use these numbers in arithmetic operations, so its type should be Short Text.

Similarly, in the Book Rep table, the data type for the Book Rep Number, Last Name, First Name, Street, City, State, and Postal Code fields all should be Short Text. The Start Date field should be Date & Time. The Salary field contains monetary amounts, so its data type should be Currency. The Bonus Rate field contains numbers that are not dollar amounts, so its data type should be Number.

For fields whose type is Short Text, you can change the field size, that is, the maximum number of characters that can be entered in the field. If you set the field size for the State field to 2, for example, Access will not allow the user to enter more than two characters in the field. On the other hand, fields whose data type is Number often

BTW

Text Data Types
Short Text replaces the Text data type in previous editions of Access. Long Text replaces the Memo data type in previous editions.

BTW

Data Types
Different database management systems have different available data types. Even data types that are essentially the same can have different names. The Currency data type in Access, for example, is referred to as Money in SQL Server.

BTW

AutoNumber Fields
AutoNumber fields also are called AutoIncrement fields. In Design view, the New Values field property allows you to increment the field sequentially (Sequential) or randomly (Random). The default is sequential.

require you to change the field size, which is the storage space assigned to the field by Access. Table 1–2 shows the possible field sizes for Number fields.

Field Size	Description
Byte	Integer value in the range of 0 to 255
Integer	Integer value in the range of -32,768 to 32,767
Long Integer	Integer value in the range of -2,147,483,648 to 2,147,483,647
Single	Numeric values with decimal places to seven significant digits — requires 4 bytes of storage
Double	Numeric values with decimal places to more accuracy than Single — requires 8 bytes of storage
Replication ID	Special identifier required for replication
Decimal	Numeric values with decimal places to more accuracy than Single or Double — requires 12 bytes of storage

Table 1–2 Field Sizes for Number Fields

© 2014 Cengage Learning

What is the appropriate size for the Bonus Rate field?
If the size were Byte, Integer, or Long Integer, only integers could be stored. If you try to store a value that has decimal places, such as 0.18, in fields of these sizes, the portion to the right of the decimal point would be removed, giving a result of 0. To address this problem, the bonus rate should have a size of Single, Double, or Decimal. With such small numbers involved, Single, which requires the least storage of the three, is the appropriate choice.

Creating a Table

BTW

On Screen Keyboard
To display the on-screen touch keyboard, tap the Touch Keyboard button on the Windows taskbar. When finished using the touch keyboard, tap the X button on the touch keyboard to close the keyboard.

To create a table in Access, you must define its structure. That is, you must define all the fields that make up the table and their characteristics. You also must indicate the primary key.

In Access, you can use two different views to create a table: Datasheet view and Design view. In **Datasheet view**, the data in the table is presented in rows and columns, similar to a spreadsheet. Although the main reason to use Datasheet view is to add or update records in a table, you also can use it to create a table or to later modify its structure. The other view, **Design view**, is only used to create a table or to modify the structure of a table.

As you might expect, Design view has more functionality for creating a table than Datasheet view. That is, there are certain actions that only can be performed in Design view. One such action is assigning Single as the field size for the Bonus Rate field. In this chapter, you will create the first table, the Book Rep table, in Datasheet view. Once you have created the table in Datasheet view, you will use Design view to change the field size.

Whichever view you choose to use, before creating the table, you need to know the names and data types of the fields that will make up the table. You also can decide to enter a **description** for a particular field to explain important details about the field. When you select this field, this description will appear on the status bar. You also might choose to assign a **caption** to a particular field. If you assign a caption, Access will display the value you assign, rather than the field name, in datasheets and in forms. If you do not assign a caption, Access will display the field name.

When would you want to use a caption?
You would use a caption whenever you want something other than the field name displayed. One common example is when the field name is relatively long and the data in the field is relatively short. In the Book Rep table, the name of the first field is Book Rep Number, but the field contains data that is only two characters long. You will change the caption for this field to BR #, which is much shorter than Book Rep Number yet still describes the field. Doing so will enable you to greatly reduce the width of the column.

The results of these decisions for the fields in the Book Rep table are shown in Table 1–3. The table also shows the data types and field sizes of the fields as well as any special properties that need to be changed. The Book Rep Number field has a caption of BR #, enabling the width of the Book Rep Number column to be reduced in the datasheet.

Table 1–3 Structure of Book Rep Table

Field Name	Data Type	Field Size	Notes
Book Rep Number	Short Text	2	Primary Key **Description:** Unique identifier of book rep **Caption:** BR #
Last Name	Short Text	15	
First Name	Short Text	15	
Street	Short Text	20	
City	Short Text	20	
State	Short Text	2	
Postal Code	Short Text	5	
Start Date	Date/Time		(This appears as Date & Time on the menu of available data types)
Salary	Currency		
Bonus Rate	Number	Single	Format: Fixed Decimal Places: 2

© 2014 Cengage Learning

If you are using your finger on a touch screen and are having difficulty completing the steps in this chapter, consider using a stylus. Many people find it easier to be precise with a stylus than with a finger. In addition, with a stylus you see the pointer. If you still are having trouble completing the steps with a stylus, try using a mouse.

How do you determine the field size?
You need to determine the maximum number of characters that can be entered in the field. In some cases, it is obvious. Field sizes of 2 for the State field and 5 for the Postal Code field are certainly the appropriate choices. In other cases, you need to determine how many characters you wish to allow. In the list shown in Table 1–3, Bavant evidently decided allowing 15 characters was sufficient for last names. This field size can be changed later if it proves to be insufficient.

What is the purpose of the Format and Decimal Places properties?
The format guarantees that bonus rates will be displayed with a fixed number of decimal places. Setting the decimal places property to 2 guarantees that the rates will be displayed with precisely two decimal places. Thus, a bonus rate of 0.2 will be displayed as 0.20.

CONSIDER THIS

CONSIDER THIS

To Modify the Primary Key

1 CREATE FIRST TABLE | 2 ADD RECORDS | 3 PRINT CONTENTS | 4 IMPORT RECORDS | 5 MODIFY SECOND TABLE
6 CREATE QUERY | 7 CREATE FORM | 8 CREATE REPORT

When you first create your database, Access automatically creates a table for you. You can immediately begin defining the fields. If, for any reason, you do not have this table or inadvertently delete it, you can create the table by tapping or clicking CREATE on the ribbon and then tapping or clicking the Table button (CREATE tab | Tables group). In either case, you are ready to define the fields.

The steps on the next page change the name, data type, and other properties of the first field to match the Book Rep Number field in Table 1–3, which is the primary key. *Why? Access has already created the first field as the primary key field, which it has named ID. Book Rep Number is a more appropriate choice.*

1

- Press and hold or right-click the column heading for the ID field to display a shortcut menu (Figure 1–3).

Q&A Why does my shortcut menu look different?
You displayed a shortcut menu for the column instead of the column heading. Be sure you press and hold or right-click the column heading.

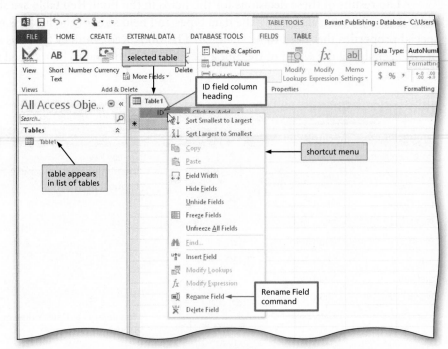

Figure 1–3

2

- Tap or click Rename Field on the shortcut menu to highlight the current name.

- Type `Book Rep Number` to assign a name to the new field.

- Tap or click the white space immediately below the field name to complete the addition of the field (Figure 1–4).

Q&A Why does the full name of the field not appear?
The default column size is not large enough for Book Rep Number to be displayed in its entirety. You will address this issue in later steps.

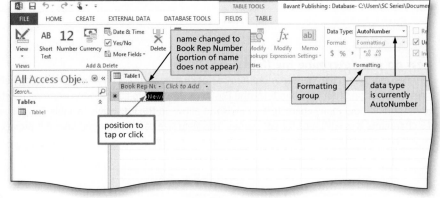

Figure 1–4

3

- Because the data type needs to be changed from AutoNumber to Short Text, tap or click the Data Type arrow (TABLE TOOLS FIELDS tab | Formatting group) to display a menu of available data types (Figure 1–5).

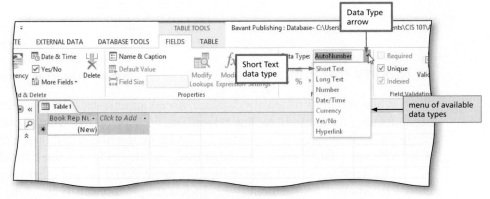

Figure 1–5

- Tap or click Short Text to select the data type for the field (Figure 1–6).

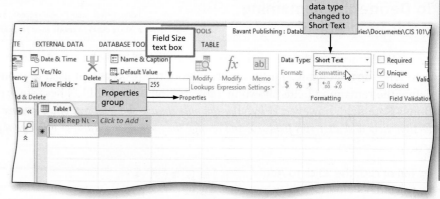

Figure 1–6

- Tap or click the Field Size text box (TABLE TOOLS FIELDS tab | Properties group) to select the current field size, use either the DELETE or BACKSPACE keys to erase the current field size, if necessary, and then type 2 as the new field size.

- Tap or click the Name & Caption button (TABLE TOOLS FIELDS tab | Properties group) to display the Enter Field Properties dialog box.

- Tap or click the Caption text box (Enter Field Properties dialog box), and then type BR # as the caption.

- Tap or click the Description text box, and then type Unique identifier of book rep as the description (Figure 1–7).

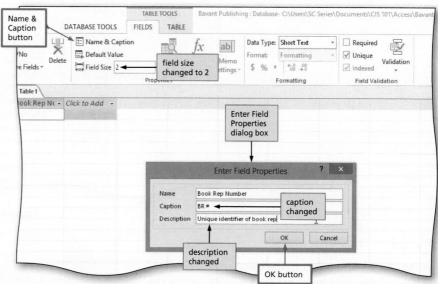

Figure 1–7

- Tap or click the OK button (Enter Field Properties dialog box) to change the caption and description (Figure 1–8).

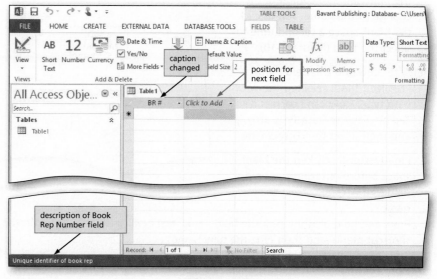

Figure 1–8

To Define the Remaining Fields in a Table

1 CREATE FIRST TABLE | 2 ADD RECORDS | 3 PRINT CONTENTS | 4 IMPORT RECORDS | 5 MODIFY SECOND TABLE
6 CREATE QUERY | 7 CREATE FORM | 8 CREATE REPORT

To define an additional field, you tap or click the Click to Add column heading, select the data type, and then type the field name. This is different from the process you used to modify the ID field. The following steps define the remaining fields shown in Table 1–3 on page AC 11. These steps do not change the field size of the Bonus Rate field, however. *Why? You can only change the field size of a Number field in Design view. Later, you will use Design view to change this field size and change the format and number of decimal places.*

1

- Tap or click the 'Click to Add' column heading to display a menu of available data types (Figure 1–9).

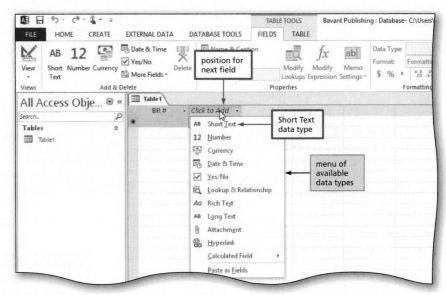

Figure 1–9

2

- Tap or click Short Text in the menu of available data types to select the Short Text data type.

- Type `Last Name` to enter a field name.

- Tap or click the blank space below the field name to complete the change of the name. Tap or click the blank space a second time to select the field (Figure 1–10).

 Q&A

After entering the field name, I realized that I selected the wrong data type. How can I correct it?
Tap or click the Data Type arrow, and then select the correct type.

I inadvertently clicked the blank space before entering the field name. How can I correct the name?
Press and hold or right-click the field name, tap or click Rename Field on the shortcut menu, and then type the new name.

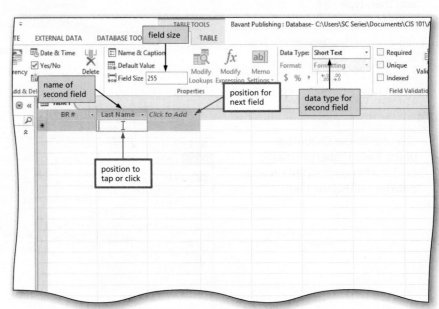

Figure 1–10

- Change the field size to 15 just as you changed the field size of the Book Rep Number field.

- Using the same technique, add the remaining fields in the Book Rep table. For the First Name, Street, City, State, and Postal Code fields, use the Short Text data type, but change the field

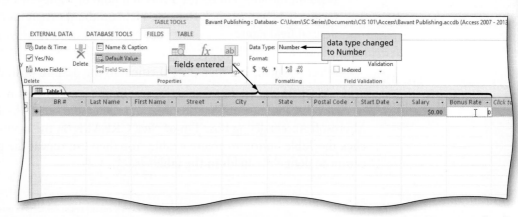

Figure 1–11

sizes to match Table 1–3 on page AC 11. For the Start Date field, change the data type to Date & Time. For the Salary field, change the data type to Currency. For the Bonus Rate field, change the data type to Number (Figure 1–11).

Q&A

I have an extra row between the row containing the field names and the row that begins with the asterisk. What happened? Is this a problem? If so, how do I fix it?
You inadvertently added a record to the table by pressing a key. Even pressing the SPACEBAR would add a record. You now have an unwanted record. To fix it, press the ESC key or tap or click the Undo button to undo the action. You may need to do this more than once.

When I try to move on to specify another field, I get an error message indicating that the primary key cannot contain a null value. How do I correct this?
First, tap or click the OK button to remove the error message. Next, press the ESC key or tap or click the Undo button to undo the action. You may need to do this more than once.

BTW
Currency Symbols
To show the symbol for the Euro (€) instead of the dollar sign, change the Format property for the field whose data type is currency. To change the default symbols for currency, change the settings in Windows.

Making Changes to the Structure

When creating a table, check the entries carefully to ensure they are correct. If you discover a mistake while still typing the entry, you can correct the error by repeatedly pressing the BACKSPACE key until the incorrect characters are removed. Then, type the correct characters. If you do not discover a mistake until later, you can use the following techniques to make the necessary changes to the structure:

- To undo your most recent change, tap or click the Undo button on the Quick Access Toolbar. If there is nothing that Access can undo, this button will be dim, and tapping or clicking it will have no effect.

- To delete a field, press and hold or right-click the column heading for the field (the position containing the field name), and then tap or click Delete Field on the shortcut menu.

- To change the name of a field, press and hold or right-click the column heading for the field, tap or click Rename Field on the shortcut menu, and then type the desired field name.

- To insert a field as the last field, tap or click the 'Click to Add' column heading, tap or click the appropriate data type on the menu of available data types, type the desired field name, and, if necessary, change the field size.

- To insert a field between existing fields, press and hold or right-click the column heading for the field that will follow the new field, and then tap or click Insert

BTW
Touch Screen Differences
The Office and Windows interfaces may vary if you are using a touch screen. For this reason, you might notice that the function or appearance of your touch screen differs slightly from this chapter's presentation.

Field on the shortcut menu. Press and hold or right-click the column heading for the field, tap or click Rename Field on the shortcut menu, and then type the desired field name.

• To move a field, tap or click the column heading for the field to be moved to select the field, and then drag the field to the desired position.

As an alternative to these steps, you might want to start over. To do so, tap or click the Close button for the table, and then tap or click the No button in the Microsoft Access dialog box. Tap or click CREATE on the ribbon, and then tap or click the Table button to create a table. You then can repeat the process you used earlier to define the fields in the table.

To Save a Table

1 CREATE FIRST TABLE | 2 ADD RECORDS | 3 PRINT CONTENTS | 4 IMPORT RECORDS | 5 MODIFY SECOND TABLE
6 CREATE QUERY | 7 CREATE FORM | 8 CREATE REPORT

The Book Rep table structure is complete. The final step is to save the table within the database. As part of the process, you will give the table a name. The following steps save the table, giving it the name Book Rep. *Why? Bavant has decided that Book Rep is an appropriate name for the table.*

1
• Tap or click the Save button on the Quick Access Toolbar to display the Save As dialog box (Figure 1–12).

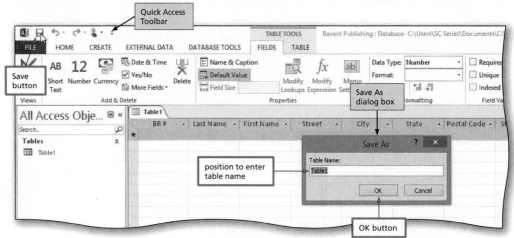

Figure 1–12

2
• Type Book Rep to change the name assigned to the table.

• Tap or click the OK button (Save As dialog box) to save the table (Figure 1–13).

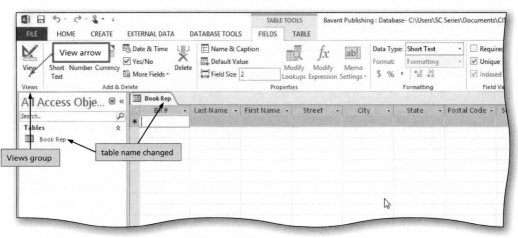

Figure 1–13

Other Ways
1. Tap or click FILE on the ribbon, tap or click Save in the Backstage view	2. Press and hold or right-click tab for table, tap or click Save on shortcut menu	3. Press CTRL+S

To View the Table in Design View

Even when creating a table in Datasheet view, Design view can be helpful. *Why? You easily can view the fields, data types, and properties to ensure you have entered them correctly. It is also easier to determine the primary key in Design view.* The following steps display the structure of the Book Rep table in Design view so that you can verify the design is correct.

- Tap or click the View arrow (TABLE TOOLS FIELDS tab | Views group) to display the View menu (Figure 1–14).

Q&A Could I just tap or click the View button rather than the arrow?
Yes. Tapping or clicking the button is equivalent to tapping or clicking the command represented by the icon currently appearing on the button. Because the icon on the button in Figure 1–14 is for Design view, tapping or clicking the button would display the table in Design view. If you are uncertain, you can always tap or click the arrow and select from the menu.

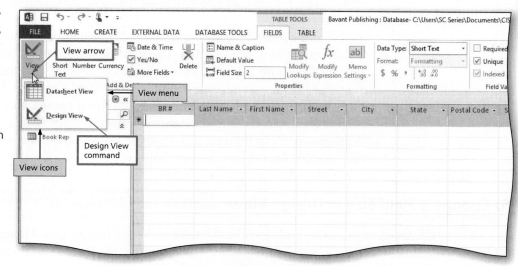

Figure 1–14

2

- Tap or click Design View on the View menu to view the table in Design view (Figure 1–15).

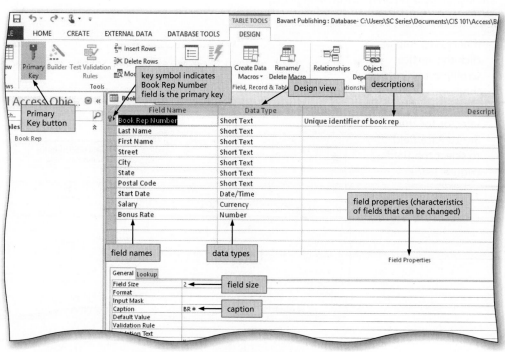

Figure 1–15

Other Ways

1. Tap or click Design View button on status bar

Checking the Structure in Design View

You should use Design view to carefully check the entries you have made. In Figure 1–15 on the previous page, for example, you can see that the Book Rep Number field is the primary key of the Book Rep table by the key symbol in front of the field name. If your table does not have a key symbol, you can tap or click the Primary Key button (TABLE TOOLS DESIGN tab | Tools group) to designate the field as the primary key. You also can check that the data type, description, field size, and caption are all correct.

For the other fields, you can see the field name, data type, and description without taking any special action. To see the field size and/or caption for a field, tap or click the field's **row selector**, the small box that precedes the field. Tapping or clicking the row selector for the Last Name field, for example, displays the properties for the field. You then can check to see that the field size is correct. In addition, if the field has a caption, you can check to see if that is correct. If you find any mistakes, you can make the necessary corrections on this screen. When you have finished, you would tap or click the Save button to save your changes.

To Change a Field Size in Design View

1 CREATE FIRST TABLE | 2 ADD RECORDS | 3 PRINT CONTENTS | 4 IMPORT RECORDS | 5 MODIFY SECOND TABLE
6 CREATE QUERY | 7 CREATE FORM | 8 CREATE REPORT

Most field size changes can be made in either Datasheet view or Design view. However, changing the field size for Number fields, such as the Bonus Rate field, can only be made in Design view. Because the values in the Bonus Rate field have decimal places, only Single, Double, or Decimal would be possible choices for the field size. The difference between these choices concerns the amount of accuracy. Double is more accurate than Single, for example, but requires more storage space. Because the rates are only two decimal places, Single is an acceptable choice.

The following steps change the field size of the Bonus Rate field to Single, the format to Fixed, and the number of decimal places to 2. *Why change the format and number of decimal places? To ensure that each value will appear with precisely two decimal places.*

- If necessary, tap or click the vertical scroll bar to display the Bonus Rate field. Tap or click the row selector for the Bonus Rate field to select the field (Figure 1–16).

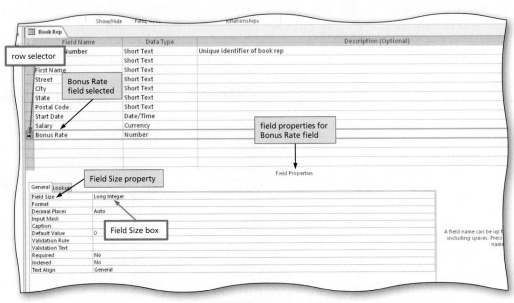

Figure 1–16

2

- Tap or click the Field Size box to display the Field Size arrow.

- Tap or click the Field Size arrow to display the Field Size menu (Figure 1–17).

Figure 1–17

Q&A What would happen if I left the field size set to Long Integer?

If the field size is Long Integer, Integer, or Byte, no decimal places can be stored. For example, a value of .10 would be stored as 0. If you enter rates and the values all appear as 0, chances are you did not change the field size property.

3

- Tap or click Single to select single precision as the field size.

- Tap or click the Format box to display the Format arrow.

- Tap or click the Format arrow to open the Format menu (Figure 1–18).

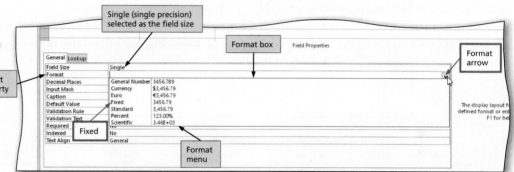

Figure 1–18

4

- Tap or click Fixed to select fixed as the format.

- Tap or click the Decimal Places box to display the Decimal Places arrow.

- Tap or click the Decimal Places arrow to enter the number of decimal places.

- Tap or click 2 to assign the number of decimal places.

- Tap or click the Save button to save your changes (Figure 1–19).

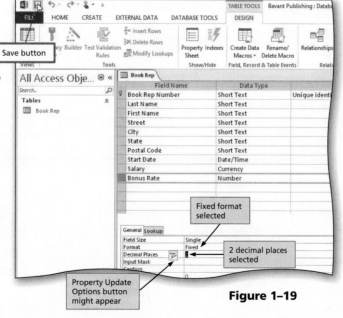

Figure 1–19

Q&A Why did the Property Update Options button appear?

You changed the number of decimal places. The Property Update Options button offers a quick way of making the same change everywhere Bonus Rate appears. So far, you have not added any data or created any forms or reports that use the Bonus Rate field, so no such changes are necessary.

To Close the Table

Once you are sure that your entries are correct and you have saved your changes, you can close the table. The following step closes the table.

1 Tap or click the Close button for the Book Rep table to close the table.

Other Ways

1. Press and hold or right-click tab for table, tap or click Close on shortcut menu

---

To Add Records to a Table

1 CREATE FIRST TABLE | 2 ADD RECORDS | 3 PRINT CONTENTS | 4 IMPORT RECORDS | 5 MODIFY SECOND TABLE
6 CREATE QUERY | 7 CREATE FORM | 8 CREATE REPORT

Creating a table by building the structure and saving the table is the first step in the two-step process of using a table in a database. The second step is to add records to the table. To add records to a table, the table must be open. When making changes to tables, you work in Datasheet view.

You often add records in phases. *Why? You might not have enough time to add all the records in one session, or you might not have all the records currently available.* The following steps open the Book Rep table in Datasheet view and then add the first two records in the Book Rep table (Figure 1–20).

BR #	Last Name	First Name	Street	City	State	Postal Code	Start Date	Salary	Bonus Rate
53	Chin	Robert	265 Maxwell St.	Gossett	PA	19157	6/1/2013	$26,250.00	0.19
42	Perez	Melina	261 Porter Dr.	Adelphia	PA	19156	5/14/2012	$31,500.00	0.20

Figure 1–20

1

- Press and hold or right-click the Book Rep table in the Navigation Pane to display the shortcut menu (Figure 1–21).

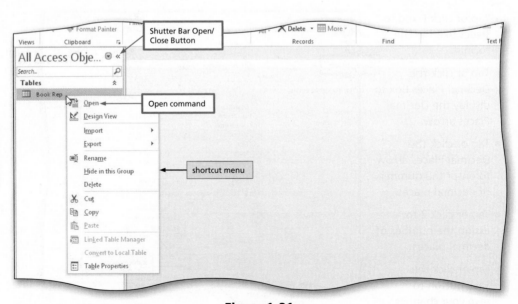

Figure 1–21

2

- Tap or click Open on the shortcut menu to open the table in Datasheet view.
- Tap or click the Shutter Bar Open/Close Button to close the Navigation Pane (Figure 1–22).

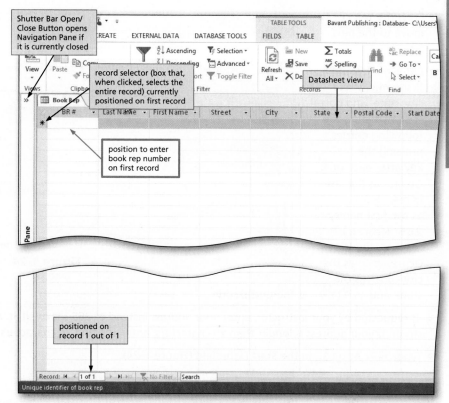

Shutter Bar Open/Close Button opens Navigation Pane if it is currently closed

record selector (box that, when clicked, selects the entire record) currently positioned on first record

Datasheet view

position to enter book rep number on first record

positioned on record 1 out of 1

Unique identifier of book rep

Figure 1–22

3

- Tap or click the first row in the BR # field if necessary to display an insertion point, and type 53 to enter the first book rep number (Figure 1–23).

pencil icon in the record selector column indicates that the record is being edited, but changes to the record are not saved yet

book rep number on first record

Access creates row for a new record

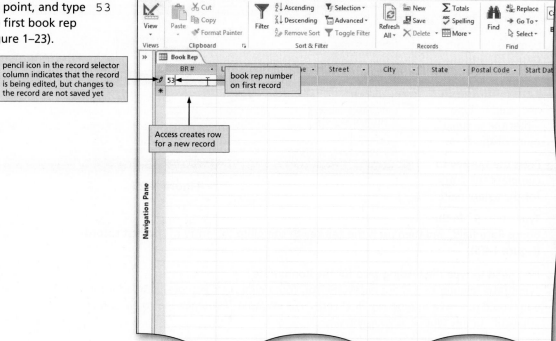

Figure 1–23

4

- Press the TAB key to move to the next field.

- Enter the last name, first name, street, city, state, and postal code by typing the following entries, pressing the TAB key after each one: Chin as the last name, Robert as the first name, 265 Maxwell St. as the street, Gossett as the city, PA as the state, and 19157 as the postal code.

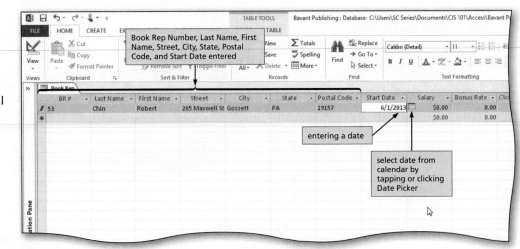

Figure 1–24

- If requested by your instructor, enter your address instead of 265 Maxwell St. as the street. If your address is longer than 20 characters, enter the first 20 characters.

- Type 6/1/2013 in the Start Date field (Figure 1–24).

5

- Press the TAB key and then type 26250 in the Salary field.

Q&A Do I need to type a dollar sign?
You do not need to type dollar signs or commas. In addition, because the digits to the right of the decimal point are both zeros, you do not need to type either the decimal point or the zeros.

- Press the TAB key to complete the entry for the Salary field.

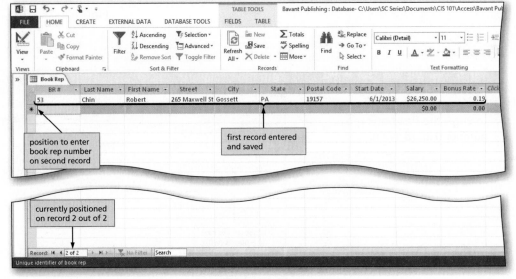

Figure 1–25

- Type 0.19 in the Bonus Rate field, and then press the TAB key to complete the entry of the first record (Figure 1–25).

Q&A Do I need to type the leading zero for the Bonus Rate?
Typing the leading zero is not necessary. You could type .19 if you prefer. In addition, you would not have to type any final zeros. For example, if you needed to enter 0.20, you could simply type .2 as your entry.

How and when do I save the record?
As soon as you have entered or modified a record and moved to another record, Access saves the original record. This is different from other applications. The rows entered in an Excel worksheet, for example, are not saved until the entire worksheet is saved.

6

- Use the techniques shown in Steps 3 through 5 to enter the data for the second record (Figure 1–26).

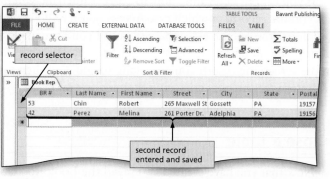

Figure 1–26

Q&A Does it matter that I entered book rep 42 after I entered book rep 53? Should the book rep numbers be in order?

The order in which you enter the records is not important. When you close and later reopen the table, the records will be in book rep number order, because the Book Rep Number field is the primary key.

When I entered the Salary field and changed the data type to Currency, I noticed that the word Currency appeared twice. Why?

The second Currency is the format, which indicates how the data will be displayed. For the Currency data type, Access automatically sets the format to Currency, which is usually what you would want. You could change it to something else, if desired, by tapping or clicking the arrow and selecting the desired format.

⊘ Experiment

- Tap or click the Salary field on either of the records. Be sure the TABLE TOOLS FIELDS tab is selected. Tap or click the Format arrow, and then tap or click each of the formats in the Format box menu to see the effect on the values in the Salary field. When finished, tap or click Currency in the Format box menu.

Making Changes to the Data

As you enter data, check your entries carefully to ensure they are correct. If you make a mistake and discover it before you press the TAB key, correct it by pressing the BACKSPACE key until the incorrect characters are removed, and then type the correct characters. If you do not discover a mistake until later, you can use the following techniques to make the necessary corrections to the data:

- To undo your most recent change, tap or click the Undo button on the Quick Access Toolbar. If there is nothing that Access can undo, this button will be dimmed, and tapping or clicking it will have no effect.

- To add a record, tap or click the New (blank) record button, tap or click the position for the Book Rep Number field on the first open record, and then add the record. Do not worry about it being in the correct position in the table. Access will reposition the record based on the primary key, in this case, the Book Rep Number.

- To delete a record, tap or click the record selector, shown in Figure 1–26, for the record to be deleted. Then press the DELETE key to delete the record, and tap or click the Yes button when Access asks you to verify that you want to delete the record.

- To change the contents of one or more fields in a record, the record must be on the screen. If it is not, use any appropriate technique, such as the UP ARROW and DOWN ARROW keys or the vertical scroll bar, to move to the record. If the field you want to correct is not visible on the screen, use the horizontal scroll bar along the bottom of the screen to shift all the fields until the one you want appears. If the value in the field is currently highlighted, you can simply type the new value. If you would rather edit the existing value, you must have an insertion point in the field. You can place the insertion point by tapping or clicking in the field or by pressing the F2 key. You then can use the arrow keys, the DELETE key, and the BACKSPACE key for making the correction. You also can use the INSERT key to switch between Insert and Overtype mode. When you have made the change, press the TAB key to move to the next field.

BTW

AutoCorrect Feature
The AutoCorrect feature of Access corrects common data entry errors. AutoCorrect corrects two capital letters by changing the second letter to lowercase and capitalizes the first letter in the names of days. It also corrects more than 400 commonly misspelled words.

BTW

Other AutoCorrect Options
Using the Office AutoCorrect feature, you can create entries that will replace abbreviations with spelled-out names and phrases automatically. To specify AutoCorrect rules, tap or click FILE on the ribbon to open the Backstage view, tap or click Options, and then tap or click Proofing in the Access Options dialog box.

If you cannot determine how to correct the data, you may find that you are "stuck" on the record, in which case Access neither allows you to move to another record nor allows you to close the table until you have made the correction. If you encounter this situation, simply press the ESC key. Pressing the ESC key will remove from the screen the record you are trying to add. You then can move to any other record, close the table, or take any other action you desire.

To Close a Table

Now that you have created and saved the Book Rep table, you can close it. The following step closes the table.

1 Tap or click the Close button for the Book Rep table, shown in Figure 1–26 on the previous page, to close the table (Figure 1–27).

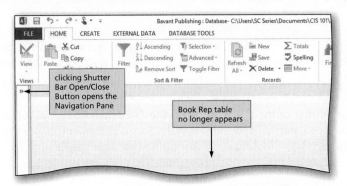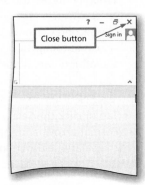

Figure 1–27

To Exit Access

The following steps exit Access. For a detailed example of the procedure summarized below, refer to the Office and Windows chapter at the beginning of this book.

1 Tap or click the Close button on the right side of the title bar to exit Access.

2 If a Microsoft Access dialog box appears, tap or click the Save button to save any changes made to the object since the last save.

Break Point: If you wish to take a break, this is a good place to do so. To resume later, continue following the steps from this location forward.

Starting Access and Opening a Database

Once you have created and later closed a database, you will need to open it in the future in order to use it. Opening a database requires that Access is running on your computer.

To Run Access

1 Scroll the Start screen for an Access 2013 tile. If your Start screen contains an Access 2013 tile, tap or click it to run Access. If the Start screen does not contain the Access 2013 tile, proceed to the next step to search for the Access app.

2 Swipe in from the right edge of the screen or point to the upper-right corner of the screen to display the Charms bar, and then tap or click the Search charm on the Charms bar to display the Search menu.

3 Type Access as the search text in the Search text box and watch the search results appear in the Apps list.

4 Tap or click Access 2013 in the search results to run Access.

To Open a Database from Access

Earlier in this chapter, you created the Bavant Publishing database in an appropriate storage location. The following steps open the database from the location you specified when you first created it (for example, the Access folder in the CIS 101 folder). For a detailed example of the procedure summarized below, refer to the Office 2013 and Windows chapter at the beginning of this book.

1 Tap or click FILE on the ribbon to open the Backstage view, if necessary.

2 If the database you want to open is displayed in the Recent list, tap or click the file name to open the database and display the opened database in the Access window; then skip to Step 7. If the database you want to open is not displayed in the Recent list or if the Recent list does not appear, tap or click 'Open Other Files' to display the Open Gallery.

3 If the database you want to open is displayed in the Recent list in the Open gallery, tap or click the file name to open the database and display the opened database in the Access window; then skip to Step 7.

4 Tap or click Computer, SkyDrive, or another location in the left pane and then navigate to the location of the database to be opened (for example, the Access folder in the CIS 101 folder).

5 Tap or click Bavant Publishing to select the database to be opened.

6 Tap or click the Open button (Open dialog box) to open the selected file and display the opened database in the Access window (Figure 1–28).

7 If a Security Warning appears, tap or click the Enable Content button.

BTW
Enabling Content
If the database is one that you created, or if it comes from a trusted source, you can enable the content. You should disable the content of a database if you suspect that your database might contain harmful content or damaging macros.

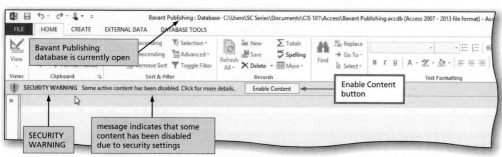

Figure 1–28

To Add Records to a Table that Contains Data

1 CREATE FIRST TABLE | 2 ADD RECORDS | 3 PRINT CONTENTS | 4 IMPORT RECORDS | 5 MODIFY SECOND TABLE
6 CREATE QUERY | 7 CREATE FORM | 8 CREATE REPORT

You can add records to a table that already contains data using a process almost identical to that used to add records to an empty table. The only difference is that you place the insertion point after the last record before you enter the additional data. To position the insertion point after the last record, you can use the **Navigation buttons**, which are buttons used to move within a table, found near the lower-left corner of the screen when a table is open. *Why not just tap or click the Book Rep Number (BR #) on the first open record? You could do this, but it is a good habit to use the New (blank) record button. Once a table contains more records than will fit on the screen, it is easier to tap or click the New (blank) record button.* The purpose of each Navigation button is described in Table 1–4.

Table 1–4 Navigation Buttons in Datasheet View	
Button	**Purpose**
First record	Moves to the first record in the table
Previous record	Moves to the previous record
Next record	Moves to the next record
Last record	Moves to the last record in the table
New (blank) record	Moves to the end of the table to a position for entering a new record

The following steps add the remaining records (Figure 1–29) to the Book Rep table.

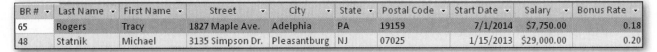

BR # ▾	Last Name ▾	First Name ▾	Street ▾	City ▾	State ▾	Postal Code ▾	Start Date ▾	Salary ▾	Bonus Rate ▾
65	Rogers	Tracy	1827 Maple Ave.	Adelphia	PA	19159	7/1/2014	$7,750.00	0.18
48	Statnik	Michael	3135 Simpson Dr.	Pleasantburg	NJ	07025	1/15/2013	$29,000.00	0.20

Figure 1–29

- If the Navigation Pane is closed, tap or click the Shutter Bar Open/Close Button, shown in Figure 1–27 on page AC 24, to open the Navigation Pane (Figure 1–30).

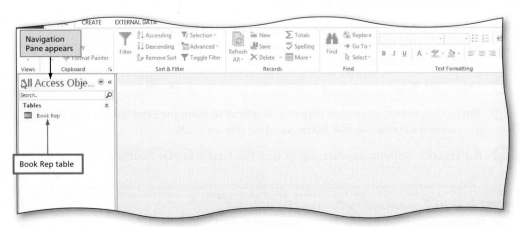

Figure 1–30

2

- Press and hold or right-click the Book Rep table in the Navigation Pane to display a shortcut menu.

- Tap or click Open on the shortcut menu to open the table in Datasheet view.

Q&A Why do the records appear in a different order than the order in which I entered them?
When you open the table, they are sorted in the order of the primary key. In this case, that means they will appear in Book Rep Number order.

- Close the Navigation Pane by tapping or clicking the Shutter Bar Open/Close Button (Figure 1–31).

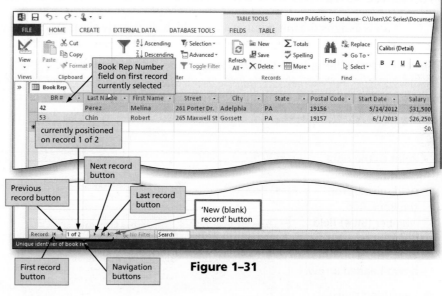

Figure 1–31

3

- Tap or click the 'New (blank) record' button to move to a position to enter a new record (Figure 1–32).

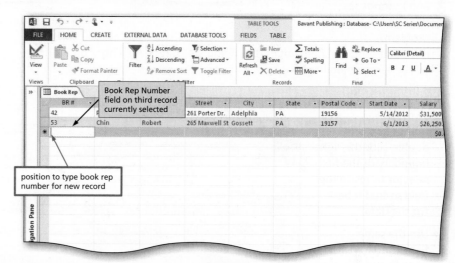

Figure 1–32

4

- Add the records shown in Figure 1–29 using the same techniques you used to add the first two records (Figure 1–33).

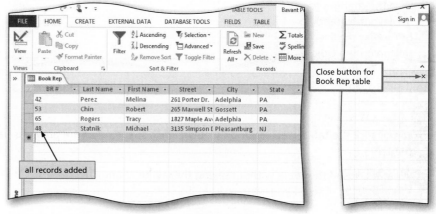

Figure 1–33

Other Ways

1. Tap or click New button (HOME tab | Records group)   2. Press CTRL+PLUS SIGN (+)

To Resize Columns in a Datasheet

Access assigns default column sizes, which do not always provide space to display all the data in the field. In some cases, the data might appear but the entire field name will not. You can correct this problem by **resizing** the column (changing its size) in the datasheet. In some instances, you may want to reduce the size of a column. *Why? Some fields, such as the State field, are short enough that they do not require all the space on the screen that is allotted to them.* Changing a column width changes the **layout**, or design, of a table. The following steps resize the columns in the Book Rep table and save the changes to the layout.

- Point to the right boundary of the field selector for the Book Rep Number (BR #) field (Figure 1–34) so that the pointer becomes a two-headed arrow.

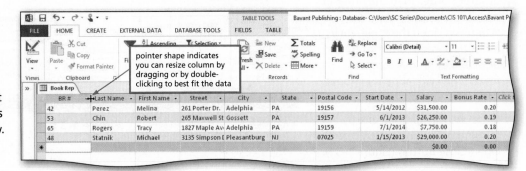

Figure 1–34

Q&A I am using touch and I cannot see the pointer. Is this a problem?

It is not a problem. Remember that if you are using your finger on a touch screen, you will not see the pointer.

- Double-tap or double-click the right boundary of the field selector to resize the field so that it best fits the data.

- Use the same technique to resize all the other fields to best fit the data.

- Save the changes to the layout by tapping or clicking the Save button on the Quick Access Toolbar (Figure 1–35).

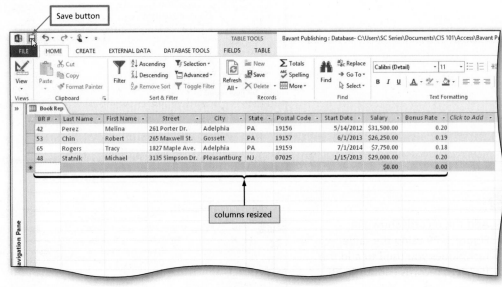

Figure 1–35

- Tap or click the table's Close button (shown in Figure 1–33 on the previous page) to close the table.

Q&A What if I closed the table without saving the layout changes?

You would be asked if you want to save the changes.

Other Ways

1. Press and hold or right-click field name, tap or click Field Width

What is the best method for distributing database objects?

The traditional method of distributing database objects such as tables, reports, and forms uses a printer to produce a hard copy. A **hard copy** or **printout** is information that exists on a physical medium such as paper. Hard copies can be useful for the following reasons:

• Some people prefer proofreading a hard copy of a document rather than viewing it on the screen to check for errors and readability.

• Hard copies can serve as a backup reference if your storage medium is lost or becomes corrupted and you need to recreate the document.

Instead of distributing a hard copy, users can distribute the document as an electronic image that mirrors the original document's appearance. The electronic image of the document can be emailed, posted on a website, or copied to a portable storage medium such as a USB flash drive. Two popular electronic image formats, sometimes called fixed formats, are PDF by Adobe Systems and XPS by Microsoft. In Access, you can create electronic image files through the EXTERNAL DATA tab on the ribbon. Electronic images of documents, such as PDF and XPS, can be useful for the following reasons:

• Users can view electronic images of documents without the software that created the original document (e.g., Access). Specifically, to view a PDF file, you use a program called Adobe Reader, which can be downloaded free from Adobe's website. Similarly, to view an XPS file, you use a program called XPS Viewer, which is included in the latest versions of Windows and Internet Explorer.

• Sending electronic documents saves paper and printer supplies. Society encourages users to contribute to **green computing,** which involves reducing the electricity consumed and environmental waste generated when using computers, mobile devices, and related technologies.

Previewing and Printing the Contents of a Table

When working with a database, you often will need to print a copy of the table contents. Figure 1–36 shows a printed copy of the contents of the Book Rep table. (Yours may look slightly different, depending on your printer.) Because the Book Rep table is substantially wider than the screen, it also will be wider than the normal printed page in portrait orientation. **Portrait orientation** means the printout is across the width of the page. **Landscape orientation** means the printout is across the height of the page. To print the wide database table, you might prefer to use landscape orientation. A convenient way to change to landscape orientation is to preview what the printed copy will look like by using Print Preview. This allows you to determine whether landscape orientation is necessary and, if it is, to change the orientation easily to landscape. In addition, you also can use Print Preview to determine whether any adjustments are necessary to the page margins.

BTW

Changing Printers
To change the default printer that appears in the Print dialog box, tap or click FILE on the ribbon, tap or click the Print tab in the Backstage view, tap or click Print in the Print gallery, then tap or click the Name arrow and select the desired printer.

		Book Rep							9/15/2014

BR #	Last Name	First Name	Street	City	State	Postal Code	Start Date	Salary	Bonus Rate
42	Perez	Melina	261 Porter Dr.	Adelphia	PA	19156	5/14/2012	$31,500.00	0.20
48	Statnik	Michael	3135 Simpson Dr.	Pleasantburg	NJ	07025	1/15/2013	$29,000.00	0.20
53	Chin	Robert	265 Maxwell St.	Gossett	PA	19157	6/1/2013	$26,250.00	0.19
65	Rogers	Tracy	1827 Maple Ave.	Adelphia	PA	19159	7/1/2014	$7,750.00	0.18

Figure 1–36

To Preview and Print the Contents of a Table

The following steps use Print Preview to preview and then print the contents of the Book Rep table. *Why? By previewing the contents of the table in Print Preview, you can make any necessary adjustments to the orientation or to the margins before printing the contents.*

1

- If the Navigation Pane is closed, open the Navigation Pane by tapping or clicking the Shutter Bar Open/Close Button.

- Be sure the Book Rep table is selected.

Q&A Why do I have to be sure the Book Rep table is selected? It is the only object in the database. When the database contains only one object, you do not have to worry about selecting the object. Ensuring that the correct object is selected is a good habit to form, however, to make sure that the object you print is the one you want.

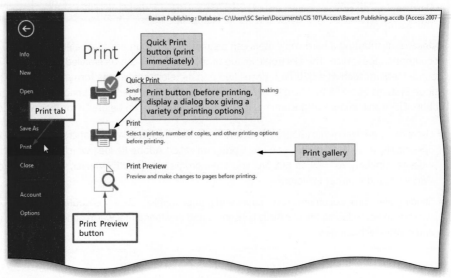

Figure 1–37

- Tap or click FILE on the ribbon to open the Backstage view.

- Tap or click the Print tab in the Backstage view to display the Print gallery (Figure 1–37).

2

- Tap or click the Print Preview button in the Print gallery to display a preview of what the table will look like when printed (Figure 1–38).

Q&A I cannot read the table. Can I magnify a portion of the table?
Yes. Point the pointer, whose shape will change to a magnifying glass, at the portion of the table that you want to magnify, and then tap or click. You can return to the original view of the table by tapping or clicking a second time.

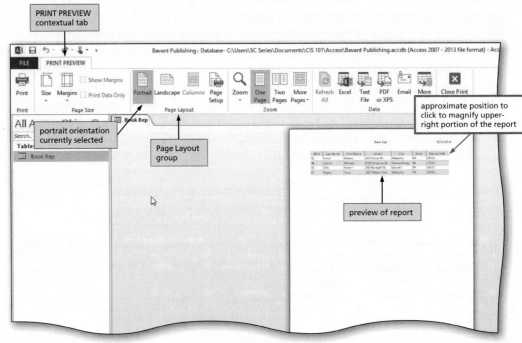

Figure 1–38

3

- Tap or click the pointer in the position shown in Figure 1–38 to magnify the upper-right section of the table (Figure 1–39).

Q&A My table was already magnified in a different area. How can I see the area shown in the figure? One way is to use the scroll bars to move to the desired portion of the table. You also can tap or click the pointer anywhere in the table to produce a screen like the one shown in Figure 1–38, and then tap or click in the location shown in the figure.

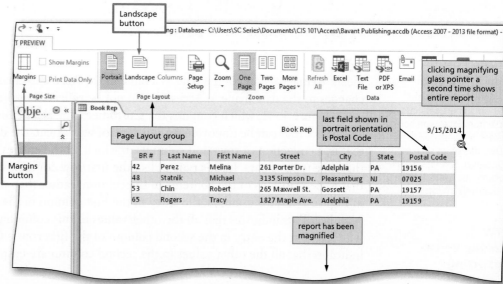

Figure 1–39

4

- Tap or click the Landscape button (PRINT PREVIEW tab | Page Layout group) to change to landscape orientation.

- Tap or click the Margins button (PRINT PREVIEW tab | Page Size group) and then click Normal if necessary to display all the fields (Figure 1–40).

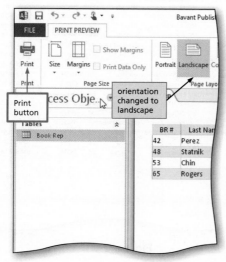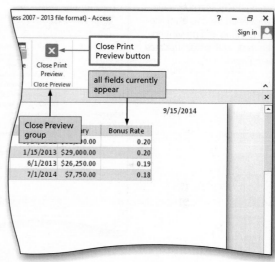

Figure 1–40

5

- Tap or click the Print button (PRINT PREVIEW tab | Print group) to display the Print dialog box.

- Tap or click the OK button (Print dialog box) to print the table.

- When the printer stops, retrieve the hard copy of the Book Rep table.

- Tap or click the Close Print Preview button (PRINT PREVIEW tab | Close Preview group) to close the Print Preview window.

Q&A Do I have to select Print Preview before printing the table?
No. If you wish to print without previewing, you would select either Print or Quick Print rather than Print Preview.

Other Ways

1. Press CTRL+P, tap or click OK button in Print dialog box

Importing or Linking Data from Other Applications to Access

BTW

Importing Data in Other Formats

You can import data into a table from Excel workbooks, Access databases, XML files, ODBC databases such as SQL Server, text files, HTML documents, Outlook folders, and SharePoint lists.

BTW

Linking Versus Importing

When you link to the data in the worksheet, the data appears as a table in the Access database but it is maintained in its original form in Excel. Any changes to the Excel data are reflected when the linked table is viewed in Access. In this arrangement, Access would typically be used as a vehicle for querying and presenting the data, with actual updates being made in Excel.

If your data for a table is stored in an Excel worksheet, you can **import** the data, which means to make a copy of the data as a table in the Access database. In this case, any changes to the data made in Access would not be reflected in the Excel worksheet.

Figure 1–41, which contains the Customer data, is an example of the type of worksheet that can be imported. In this type of worksheet, the data is stored as a **list**, that is, a collection of rows and columns in which all the entries in a column represent the same type of data. In this type of list, the first row contains **column headings**, that is, descriptions of the contents of the column, rather than data. In the worksheet in Figure 1–41, for example, the entry in the first column of the first row is Customer Number. This indicates that all the other values in this column are customer numbers. The fact that the entry in the second column of the first row is Customer Name indicates that all the other values in the second column are customer names.

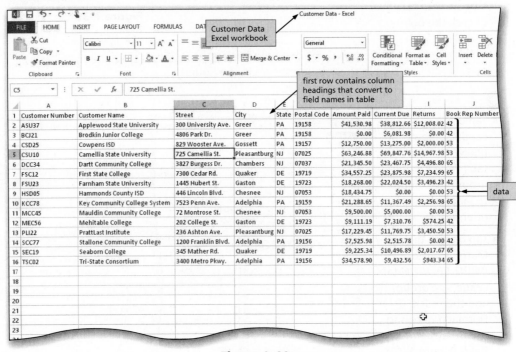

Figure 1–41

Does it matter how the data in the Excel workbook is formatted? If so, how can you be sure the Excel data is formatted in such a way you can import it?

The format of data in an Excel workbook is important when you want to import it into Access. To ensure the data is in an appropriate format:

1. Make sure the data is in the form of a list, a collection of rows and columns in which all the entries in a column represent the same type of data.

2. Make sure there are no blank rows within the list. If there are, remove them prior to importing or linking.

3. Make sure there are no blank columns within the list. If there are, remove them prior to importing or linking.

4. Determine whether the first row contains column headings that will make appropriate field names in the resulting table. If not, you might consider adding such a row. In general, the process is simpler if the first row in the worksheet contains appropriate column headings.

The Import process will create a table. In this table, the column headings in the first row of the worksheet become the field names. The rows of the worksheet, other than the first row, become the records in the table. In the process, each field will be assigned the data type that seems the most reasonable, given the data currently in the worksheet. When the Import process is finished, you can use Datasheet or Design view to modify these data types or to make any other changes to the structure you feel are necessary.

To Import an Excel Worksheet

1 CREATE FIRST TABLE | 2 ADD RECORDS | 3 PRINT CONTENTS | 4 IMPORT RECORDS | 5 MODIFY SECOND TABLE
6 CREATE QUERY | 7 CREATE FORM | 8 CREATE REPORT

You import a worksheet by using the Import Spreadsheet Wizard. In the process, you will indicate that the first row in the worksheet contains the column headings. *Why? You are indicating that Access is to use those column headings as the field names in the Access table.* In addition, you will indicate the primary key for the table. As part of the process, you could, if appropriate, choose not to include all the fields from the worksheet in the resulting table.

The following steps import the Customer worksheet.

- Tap or click EXTERNAL DATA on the ribbon to display the EXTERNAL DATA tab (Figure 1–42).

Figure 1–42

2

- Tap or click the Excel button (EXTERNAL DATA tab | Import & Link group) to display the Get External Data - Excel Spreadsheet dialog box.

- Tap or click the Browse button in the Get External Data - Excel Spreadsheet dialog box.

- Navigate to the location containing the workbook (for example, the Access folder in the CIS 101 folder). For a detailed example of this procedure, refer to Steps 4a – 4b in the To Save a File in a Folder section in the Office and Windows chapter at the beginning of this book.

- Tap or click the Customer Data workbook, and then tap or click the Open button to select the workbook (Figure 1–43).

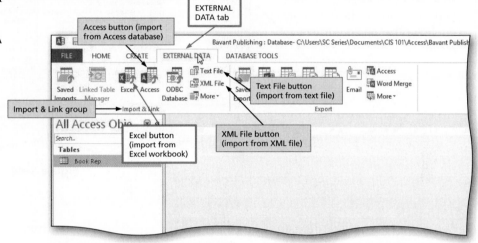

Figure 1–43

3

- With the option button to import the data to a new table selected, tap or click the OK button to display the Import Spreadsheet Wizard dialog box (Figure 1–44).

Q&A
What happens if I select the option button to append records to an existing table?

Instead of the records being placed in a new table, they will be added to an existing table that you specify, provided the value in the primary key field does not duplicate that on an existing record.

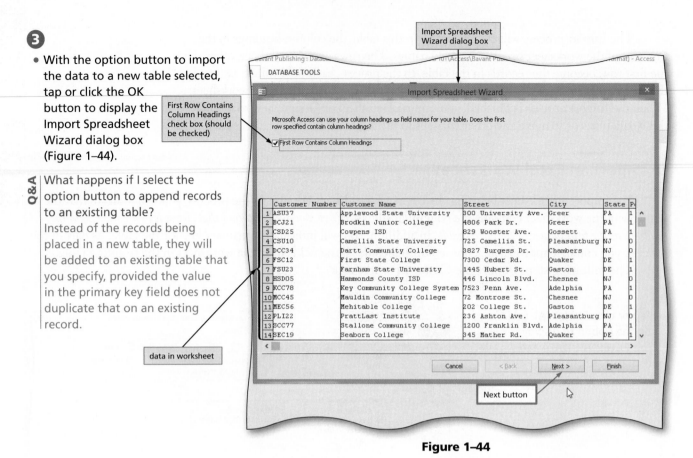

Figure 1–44

4

- If necessary, tap or click First Row Contains Column Headings to select it.

- Tap or click the Next button (Figure 1–45).

Q&A
When would I use the Field Options on the Import Spreadsheet Wizard?

You would use these options if you wanted to change properties for one or more fields. You can change the name, the data type, and whether the field is indexed. You also can indicate that some fields should not be imported.

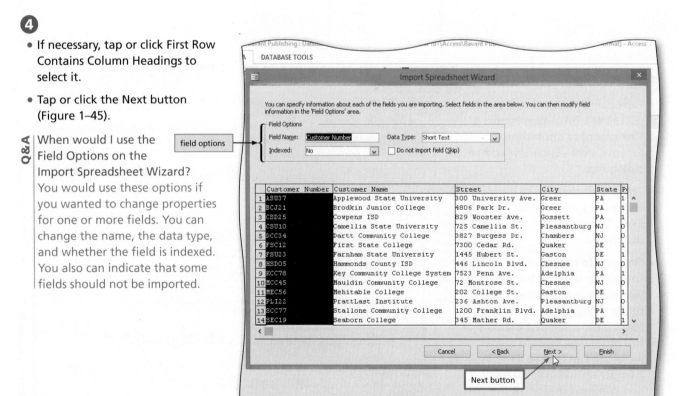

Figure 1–45

5

- Because the Field Options need not be specified, tap or click the Next button (Figure 1–46).

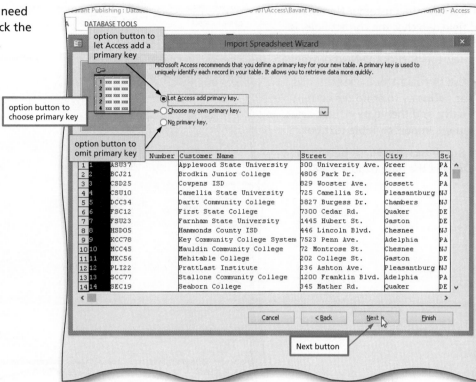

Figure 1–46

6

- Tap or click the 'Choose my own primary key' option button (Figure 1–47).

Q&A How do I decide which option button to select?
If one of the fields is an appropriate primary key, choose your own primary key from the list of fields. If you are sure you do not want a primary key, choose No primary key. Otherwise, let Access add the primary key.

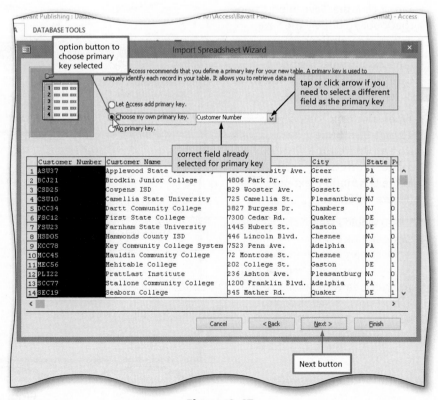

Figure 1–47

- Because the Customer Number field, which is the correct field, is already selected as the primary key, tap or click the Next button.

- Use the DELETE or BACKSPACE keys as necessary to erase the current entry, and then type Customer in the Import to Table text box.

- Tap or click the Finish button to import the data (Figure 1–48).

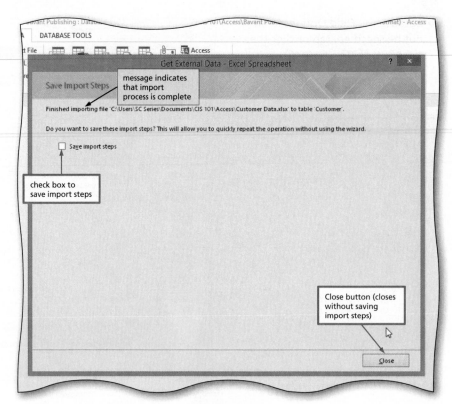

Figure 1–48

- Tap or click the 'Save import steps' check box to display the Save import steps options.

- If necessary, type Import-Customer Data in the Save as text box.

- Type Import data from Customer Data workbook into Customer table in the Description text box (Figure 1–49).

Q&A When would I create an Outlook task?

If the import operation is one you will repeat on a regular basis, you can create and schedule the import process just as you can schedule any other Outlook task.

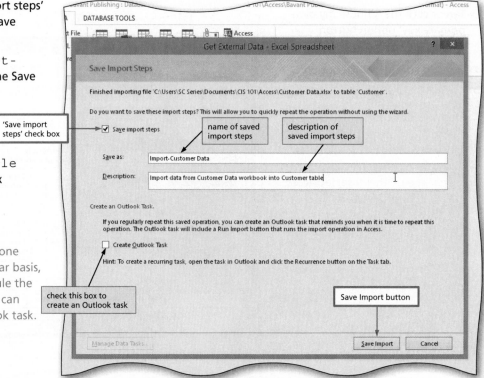

Figure 1–49

9

- Tap or click the Save Import button to save the import steps (Figure 1–50).

Q&A

I saved the table as Customer Data. How can I change the name?

Press and hold or right-click the table name in the Navigation Pane. Click Rename on the shortcut menu and change the table name to Customer.

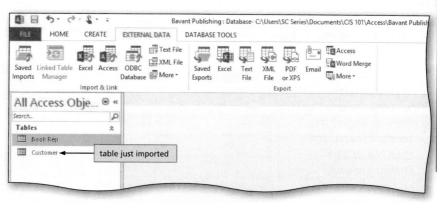

Figure 1–50

Modifying the Table

The import process has created the Customer table. The table has the correct fields and records. There are some details the process cannot handle, however. These include field sizes, descriptions, and captions. You will use Design view to make the necessary changes. The information you need is shown in Table 1–5.

BTW

Creating a Table in Design View

To create a table in Design view, display the CREATE tab, and then tap or click the Table Design button (CREATE tab | Tables group). You will then see the same screen as in Figure 1–51 on the following page, except that there will be no entries. Make all the necessary entries for the fields in your table, save the table, and assign the table a name.

Field Name	Data Type	Field Size	Notes
Table 1–5 Structure of Customer Table			
Customer Number	Short Text	5	Primary Key **Description:** Customer Number (three uppercase letters followed by 2-digit number) **Caption:** CU #
Customer Name	Short Text	30	
Street	Short Text	20	
City	Short Text	20	
State	Short Text	2	
Postal Code	Short Text	5	
Amount Paid	Currency		
Current Due	Currency		
Returns	Currency		
Book Rep Number	Short Text	2	**Description:** Book Rep Number (number of book rep for customer) **Caption:** BR #

© 2014 Cengage Learning

To Modify a Table in Design View

1 CREATE FIRST TABLE | 2 ADD RECORDS | 3 PRINT CONTENTS | 4 IMPORT RECORDS | **5 MODIFY SECOND TABLE**
6 CREATE QUERY | 7 CREATE FORM | 8 CREATE REPORT

You will usually need to modify the design of a table created during the import process. *Why? Some properties of a table are not specified during the import process, such as descriptions, captions, and field sizes. You also might need to change a data type.* The steps on the next page make the necessary modifications to the design of the Customer table.

1

- Open the Navigation Pane, if necessary.

- Press and hold or right-click the Customer table in the Navigation Pane to display the shortcut menu, and then tap or click Design View on the shortcut menu to open the table in Design view (Figure 1–51).

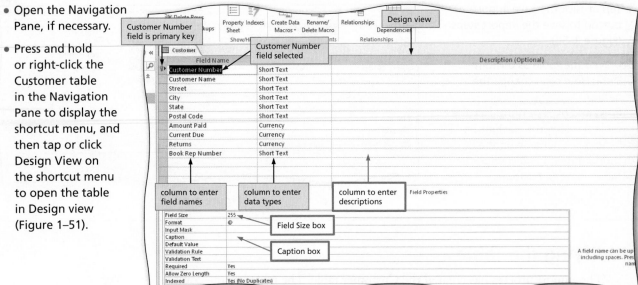

Figure 1–51

2

- Tap or click the Description (Optional) box for the Customer Number field, and then type Customer Number (three uppercase letters followed by 2-digit number) as the description.

- With the Customer Number field selected, tap or click the Field Size box, erase the current field size, and type 5 as the new field size.

- Tap or click the Caption box, and type CU # as the caption (Figure 1–52).

Figure 1–52

3

- Make the other changes shown in Table 1–5 on the previous page. To select a field to be changed, tap or click the field's row selector. For most fields, you only need to change the field size. For the Book Rep Number field, you also need to change the description and caption.

- Tap or click the Save button on the Quick Access Toolbar to save your changes.

- Because you know the data will satisfy the new field sizes, click the Yes button when given a message about the possibility of data loss.

Other Ways

1. Press F6 to move between upper and lower panes in Table Design window

Correcting Errors in the Structure

Whenever you create or modify a table in Design view, you should check the entries carefully to ensure they are correct. If you make a mistake and discover it before you press the TAB key, you can correct the error by repeatedly pressing the BACKSPACE key until the incorrect characters are removed. Then, type the correct characters. If you do not discover a mistake until later, you can tap or click the entry, type the correct value, and then press the ENTER key. You can use the following techniques to make changes to the structure:

- If you accidentally add an extra field to the structure, select the field by tapping or clicking the row selector (the leftmost column on the row that contains the field to be deleted). Once you have selected the field, press the DELETE key. This will remove the field from the structure.

- If you forget to include a field, select the field that will follow the one you want to add by tapping or clicking the row selector, and then press the INSERT key. The remaining fields move down one row, making room for the missing field. Make the entries for the new field in the usual manner.

- If you made the wrong field a primary key field, tap or click the correct primary key entry for the field and then tap or click the Primary Key button (TABLE TOOLS DESIGN tab | Tools group).

- To move a field, tap or click the row selector for the field to be moved to select the field, and then drag the field to the desired position.

As an alternative to these steps, you may want to start over. To do so, tap or click the Close button for the window containing the table, and then tap or click the No button in the Microsoft Access dialog box. You then can repeat the process you used earlier to define the fields in the table.

BTW

Importing Data to an Existing Table
When you create a new table in Design view, you can import data from other sources into the table using the EXTERNAL DATA tab.

To Close the Table

Now that you have completed and saved the Customer table, you can close it. The following step closes the table.

1 Tap or click the Close button for the Customer table (see Figure 1–52) to close the table.

To Resize Columns in a Datasheet

You can resize the columns in the datasheet for the Customer table just as you resized the columns in the datasheet for the Book Rep table. The following steps resize the columns in the Customer table to best fit the data.

1 Open the Customer table in Datasheet view.

2 Double-tap or double-click the right boundary of the field selectors of each of the fields to resize the columns so that they best fit the data.

3 Save the changes to the layout by tapping or clicking the Save button on the Quick Access Toolbar.

4 Close the table.

BTW

Resizing Columns
To resize all columns in a datasheet to best fit simultaneously, select the column heading for the first column, hold down the SHIFT key and select the last column in the datasheet. Then, double-tap or double-click the right boundary of any field selector.

Break Point: If you wish to take a break, this is a good place to do so. You can exit Access now. To resume at a later time, run Access, open the database called Bavant Publishing, and continue following the steps from this location forward.

Additional Database Objects

A database contains many types of objects. Tables are the objects you use to store and manipulate data. Access supports other important types of objects as well; each object has a specific purpose that helps maximize the benefits of a database. Through queries (questions), Access makes it possible to ask complex questions concerning the data in the database and then receive instant answers. Access also allows the user to produce attractive and useful forms for viewing and updating data. Additionally, Access includes report creation tools that make it easy to produce sophisticated reports for presenting data.

Creating Queries

Queries are simply questions, the answers to which are in the database. Access contains a powerful query feature that helps you find the answers to a wide variety of questions. Once you have examined the question you want to ask to determine the fields involved in the question, you can begin creating the query. If the query involves no special sort order, restrictions, or calculations, you can use the Simple Query Wizard.

To Use the Simple Query Wizard to Create a Query

1 CREATE FIRST TABLE | 2 ADD RECORDS | 3 PRINT CONTENTS | 4 IMPORT RECORDS | 5 MODIFY SECOND TABLE
6 CREATE QUERY | 7 CREATE FORM | 8 CREATE REPORT

The following steps use the Simple Query Wizard to create a query that Bavant Publishing might use to obtain financial information on its customers. *Why? The Simple Query Wizard is the quickest and easiest way to create a query.* This query displays the number, name, amount paid, current due, returns, and book rep number of all customers.

- If the Navigation Pane is closed, tap or click the Shutter Bar Open/Close Button to open the Navigation Pane.

- Be sure the Customer table is selected.

- Tap or click CREATE on the ribbon to display the CREATE tab.

- Tap or click the Query Wizard button (CREATE tab | Queries group) to display the New Query dialog box (Figure 1–53).

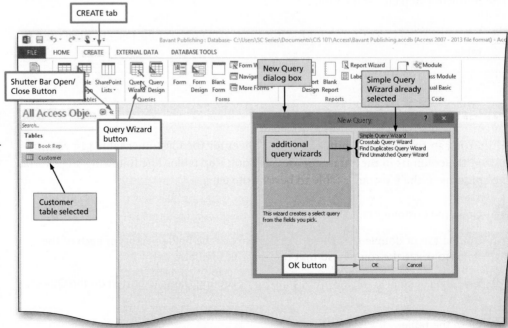

Figure 1–53

2

● Be sure Simple Query Wizard is selected, and then tap or click the OK button (New Query dialog box) to display the Simple Query Wizard dialog box (Figure 1–54).

Q&A What would happen if the Book Rep table were selected instead of the Customer table?
The list of available fields would contain fields from the Book Rep table rather than the Customer table.

If the list contained Book Rep table fields, how could I make it contain Customer table fields?
Tap or click the arrow in the Tables / Queries box, and then tap or click the Customer table in the list that appears.

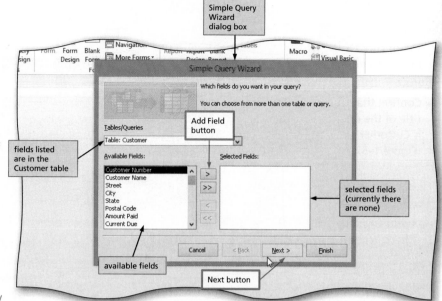

Figure 1–54

3

● With the Customer Number field selected, tap or click the Add Field button to add the field to the query.

● With the Customer Name field selected, tap or click the Add Field button a second time to add the field.

● Tap or click the Amount Paid field, and then tap or click the Add Field button to add the field.

● In a similar fashion, add the Current Due, Returns, and Book Rep Number fields (Figure 1–55).

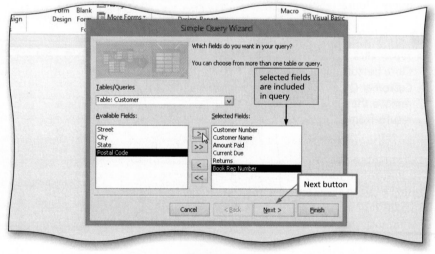

Figure 1–55

4

● Tap or click the Next button to move to the next screen.

● Ensure that the Detail (shows every field of every record) option button is selected (Figure 1–56).

Q&A What is the difference between Detail and Summary?
Detail shows all the records and fields. Summary only shows computations (for example, the total amount paid).

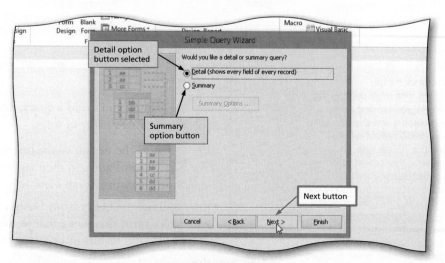

Figure 1–56

5

• Tap or click the Next button to move to the next screen.

• Confirm that the title of the query is Customer Query (Figure 1–57).

Q&A What should I do if the title is incorrect? Click the box containing the title to produce an insertion point. Erase the current title and then type Customer Query.

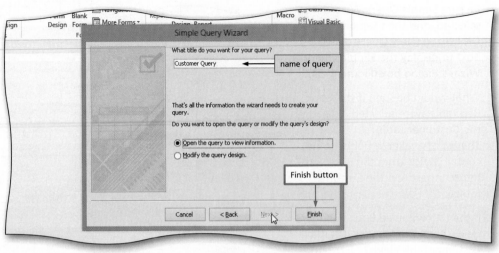

Figure 1–57

6

• Tap or click the Finish button to create the query (Figure 1–58).

7

• Tap or click the Close button for the Customer Query to remove the query results from the screen.

Q&A If I want to use this query in the future, do I need to save the query? Normally you would. The one exception is a query created by the wizard. The wizard automatically saves the query it creates.

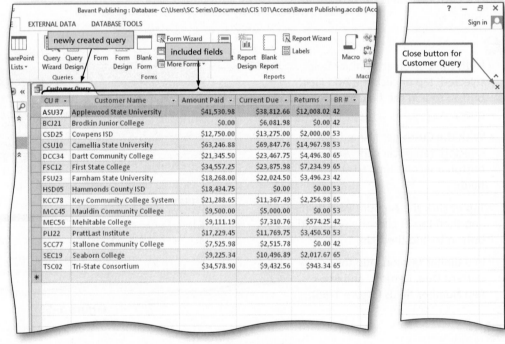

Figure 1–58

BTW

Access Help
At any time while using Access, you can find answers to questions and display information about various topics through Access Help. Used properly, this form of assistance can increase your productivity and reduce your frustrations by minimizing the time you spend learning how to use Access. For instruction about Access Help and exercises that will help you gain confidence in using it, read the Office and Windows chapter at the beginning of this book.

Using Queries

After you have created and saved a query, Access stores it as a database object and makes it available for use in a variety of ways:

• If you want to change the design of the query, press and hold or right-click the query in the Navigation Pane and then tap or click Design View on the shortcut menu to open the query in Design view.

• To view the results of the query from Design view, tap or click the Run button to instruct Access to **run** the query, that is, to perform the necessary actions to produce and display the results in Datasheet view.

• To view the results of the query from the Navigation Pane, open it by pressing and holding or right-clicking the query and tapping or clicking Open on the shortcut menu. Access automatically runs the query and displays the results in Datasheet view.

- To print the results with the query open in either Design view or Datasheet view, tap or click FILE on the ribbon, tap or click the Print tab, and then tap or click either Print or Quick Print.

- To print the query without first opening it, be sure the query is selected in the Navigation Pane and tap or click FILE on the ribbon, tap or click the Print tab, and then tap or click either Print or Quick Print.

You can switch between views of a query using the View button (HOME tab | Views group). Tapping or clicking the arrow in the bottom of the button produces the View button menu. You then tap or click the desired view in the menu. The two query views you will use in this chapter are Datasheet view (which displays the query results) and Design view (for changing the query design). You also can tap or click the top part of the View button, in which case, you will switch to the view identified by the icon on the button. In the figure, the button contains the icon for Design view, so tapping or clicking the button would change to Design view. For the most part, the icon on the button represents the view you want, so you can usually simply tap or click the button.

BTW
Creating Queries
Although the Simple Query Wizard is a convenient way to create straightforward queries, you will find that many of the queries you create require more control than the wizard provides. In Chapter 2, you will use Design view to create customized queries.

To Use a Criterion in a Query

1 CREATE FIRST TABLE | 2 ADD RECORDS | 3 PRINT CONTENTS | 4 IMPORT RECORDS | 5 MODIFY SECOND TABLE
6 CREATE QUERY | 7 CREATE FORM | 8 CREATE REPORT

After you have determined the fields to be included in a query, you will determine whether you need to further restrict the results of the query. For example, you might want to include only those customers whose book rep number is 53. In such a case, you need to enter the number 53 as a criterion for the book rep field. **Why?** *A criterion is a condition that the records must satisfy in order to be included in the query results.* To do so, you will open the query in Design view, enter the criterion below the appropriate field, and then view the results of the query. The following steps enter a criterion to include only the customers of book rep 53 and then view the query results.

- Press and hold or right-click the Customer Query in the Navigation Pane to produce a shortcut menu (Figure 1–59).

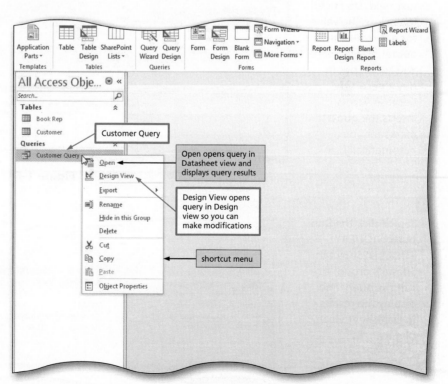

Figure 1–59

2

● Tap or click Design View on the shortcut menu to open the query in Design view (Figure 1–60).

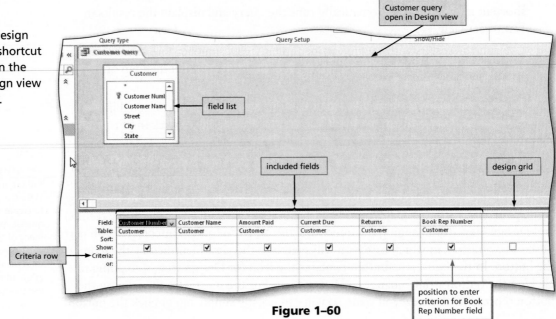

Figure 1–60

3

● Tap or click the Criteria row in the Book Rep Number column of the grid, and then type 53 as the criterion (Figure 1–61).

The Book Rep Number field is a text field. Do I need to enclose the value for a text field in quotation marks? You could, but it is not necessary, because Access inserts the quotation marks for you automatically.

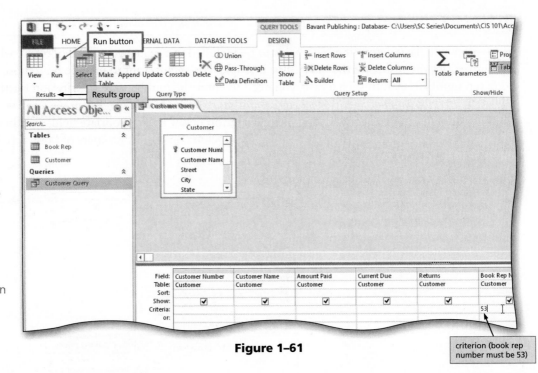

Figure 1–61

4

● Tap or click the Run button (QUERY TOOLS DESIGN tab | Results group) to run the query and display the results in Datasheet view (Figure 1–62).

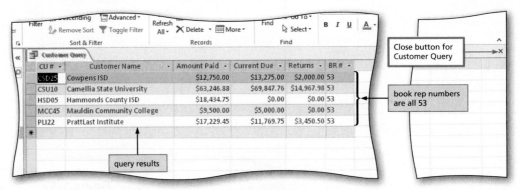

Figure 1–62

5

- Tap or click the Close button for the Customer Query to close the query.

- When asked if you want to save your changes, tap or click the No button.

Q&A

If I saved the query, what would happen the next time I ran the query?
You would see only customers of book rep 53.

Could I save a query with another name?
Yes. To save a query with a different name, tap or click FILE on the ribbon, tap or click the Save As tab, tap or click Save Object As, tap or click the Save As button, enter a new file name in the Save As dialog box, and then tap or click the OK button (Save As dialog box).

Other Ways

1. Tap or click View button (QUERY TOOLS DESIGN tab | Results group)   2. Tap or click Datasheet View button on status bar

To Print the Results of a Query

The following steps print the results of a saved query.

1 With the Customer Query selected in the Navigation Pane, tap or click FILE on the ribbon to open the Backstage view.

2 Tap or click the Print tab in the Backstage view to display the Print gallery.

3 Tap or click the Quick Print button to print the query.

Creating and Using Forms

In Datasheet view, you can view many records at once. If there are many fields, however, only some of the fields in each record might be visible at a time. In **Form view**, where data is displayed in a form on the screen, you usually can see all the fields, but only for one record.

To Create a Form

1 CREATE FIRST TABLE | 2 ADD RECORDS | 3 PRINT CONTENTS | 4 IMPORT RECORDS | 5 MODIFY SECOND TABLE
6 CREATE QUERY | **7 CREATE FORM** | **8 CREATE REPORT**

Like a paper form, a **form** in a database is a formatted document with fields that contain data. Forms allow you to view and maintain data. Forms also can be used to print data, but reports are more commonly used for that purpose. The simplest type of form in Access is one that includes all the fields in a table stacked one above the other. The following steps use the Form button to create a form. *Why? Using the Form button is the simplest way to create this type of form.* The steps then use the form to view records and then save the form.

1

- Select the Customer table in the Navigation Pane.

- If necessary, tap or click CREATE on the ribbon to display the CREATE tab (Figure 1–63).

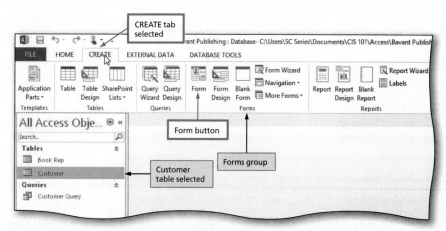

Figure 1–63

2

- Tap or click the Form button (CREATE tab | Forms group) to create a simple form (Figure 1–64).

Q&A | A Field list appeared on my screen. What should I do?
Tap or click the Add Existing Fields button (FORM LAYOUT TOOLS DESIGN tab | Tools group) to remove the Field list from the screen.

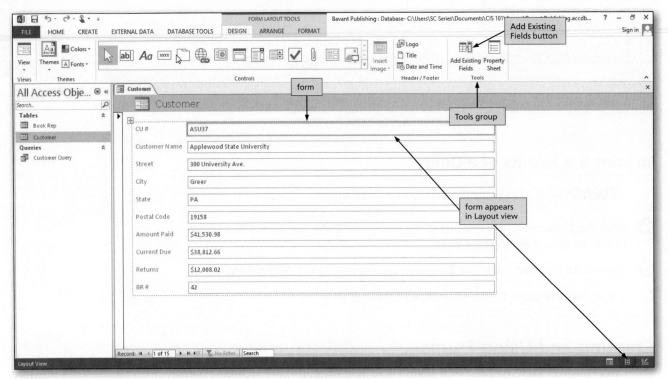

Figure 1–64

3

- Tap or click the Form View button on the Access status bar to display the form in Form view rather than Layout view.

Q&A | What is the difference between Layout view and Form view?
Layout view allows you to make changes to the look of the form. Form view is the view you use to examine or make changes to the data.

How can I tell when I am in Layout view?
Access identifies Layout view in three ways. The left side of the status bar will contain the words Layout View; shading will appear around the outside of the selected field in the form; and the Layout View button will be selected on the right side of the status bar.

- Tap or click the Next record button three times to move to record 4 (Figure 1–65).

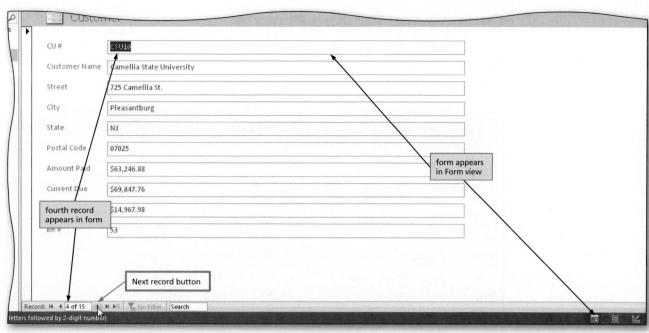

Figure 1–65

4

- Tap or click the Save button on the Quick Access Toolbar to display the Save As dialog box (Figure 1–66).

Q&A Do I have to tap or click the Next record button before saving?
No. The only reason you were asked to tap or click the button was so that you could experience navigation within the form.

5

- Type `Customer Form` as the form name, and then tap or click the OK button to save the form.

- Tap or click the Close button for the form to close the form.

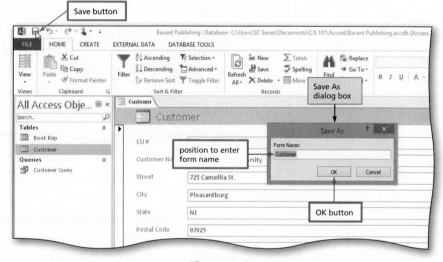

Figure 1–66

Other Ways

1. Tap or click View button (FORM LAYOUT TOOLS DESIGN tab | Views group)

Using a Form

After you have saved a form, you can use it at any time by pressing and holding or right-clicking the form in the Navigation Pane and then tapping or clicking Open on the shortcut menu. In addition to viewing data in the form, you also can use it to enter or update data, a process that is very similar to updating data using a datasheet. If you plan to use the form to enter or revise data, you must ensure you are viewing the form in Form view.

Break Point: If you wish to take a break, this is a good place to do so. You can exit Access now. To resume at a later time, run Access, open the database called Bavant Publishing, and continue following the steps from this location forward.

Creating and Printing Reports

Bavant Publishing wants to create the Customer Financial Report shown in Figure 1–67. To create this report, you will first create a simple report containing all records. Then, you will modify the report to match the one shown in Figure 1–67.

Customer Financial Report					Monday, September 15, 2014 2:23:09 PM	
Customer Number	Customer Name	Amount Paid	Current Due	Returns	Book Rep Number	
ASU37	Applewood State University	$41,530.98	$38,812.66	$12,008.02	42	
BCJ21	Brodkin Junior College	$0.00	$6,081.98	$0.00	42	
CSD25	Cowpens ISD	$12,750.00	$13,275.00	$2,000.00	53	
CSU10	Camellia State University	$63,246.88	$69,847.76	$14,967.98	53	
DCC34	Dartt Community College	$21,345.50	$23,467.75	$4,496.80	65	
FSC12	First State College	$34,557.25	$23,875.98	$7,234.99	65	
FSU23	Farnham State University	$18,268.00	$22,024.50	$3,496.23	42	
HSD05	Hammonds County ISD	$18,434.75	$0.00	$0.00	53	
KCC78	Key Community College System	$21,288.65	$11,367.49	$2,256.98	65	
MCC45	Mauldin Community College	$9,500.00	$5,000.00	$0.00	53	
MEC56	Mehitable College	$9,111.19	$7,310.76	$574.25	42	
PLI22	PrattLast Institute	$17,229.45	$11,769.75	$3,450.50	53	
SCC77	Stallone Community College	$7,525.98	$2,515.78	$0.00	42	
SEC19	Seaborn College	$9,225.34	$10,496.89	$2,017.67	65	
TSC02	Tri-State Consortium	$34,578.90	$9,432.56	$943.34	65	
		$318,592.87	$255,278.86	$53,446.76		

Figure 1–67

To Create a Report

1 CREATE FIRST TABLE | 2 ADD RECORDS | 3 PRINT CONTENTS | 4 IMPORT RECORDS | 5 MODIFY SECOND TABLE
6 CREATE QUERY | 7 CREATE FORM | 8 CREATE REPORT

You will first create a report containing all fields. *Why? It is easiest to create a report with all the fields and then delete the fields you do not want.* The following steps create and save the initial report. They also modify the report title.

- Be sure the Customer table is selected in the Navigation Pane.

- Tap or click CREATE on the ribbon to display the CREATE tab (Figure 1–68).

Q&A Do I need to select the Customer table prior to tapping or clicking CREATE on the ribbon?
You do not need to select the table at that point. You do need to select a table prior to tapping or clicking the Report button, because Access will include all the fields in whichever table or query is currently selected.

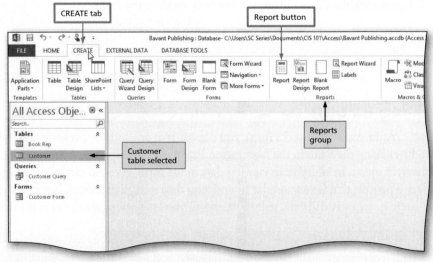

Figure 1–68

2

- Tap or click the Report button (CREATE tab | Reports group) to create the report (Figure 1–69).

Q&A Why is the report title Customer? Access automatically assigns the name of the table or query as the title of the report. It also automatically includes the date. You can change either of these later.

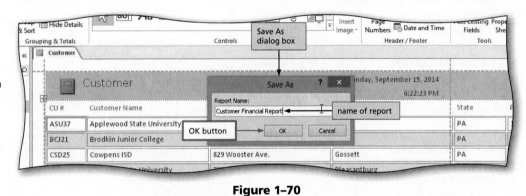

Figure 1–69

3

- Tap or click the Save button on the Quick Access Toolbar to display the Save As dialog box, and then type `Customer Financial Report` as the name of the report (Figure 1–70).

Figure 1–70

4

- Tap or click the OK button (Save As dialog box) to save the report (Figure 1–71).

Q&A The name of the report changed. Why did the report title not change? The report title is assigned the same name as the report by default. Changing the name of the report does not change the report title. You can change the title at any time to anything you like.

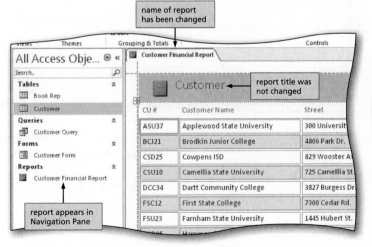

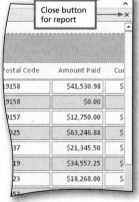

Figure 1–71

5

- Close the report by tapping or clicking its Close button.

Using Layout View in a Report

Access has four different ways to view reports: Report view, Print Preview, Layout view, and Design view. Report view shows the report on the screen. Print Preview shows the report as it will appear when printed. Layout view is similar to Report view in that it shows the report on the screen, but also allows you to make changes to the report. Layout view is usually the easiest way to make such changes. Design view also allows you to make changes, but does not show you the actual report. Design view is most useful when the changes you need to make are especially complex. In this chapter, you will use Layout view to modify the report.

To Modify Report Column Headings and Resize Columns

1 CREATE FIRST TABLE | 2 ADD RECORDS | 3 PRINT CONTENTS | 4 IMPORT RECORDS | 5 MODIFY SECOND TABLE

6 CREATE QUERY | 7 CREATE FORM | **8 CREATE REPORT**

To make the report match the one shown in Figure 1–67 on page AC 48, you need to change the title, remove some columns, modify the column headings, and also resize the columns. The following steps use Layout view to make the necessary modifications to the report. *Why? Working in Layout view gives you all the tools you need to make the desired modifications. You can view the results of the modifications immediately.*

- Press and hold or right-click Customer Financial Report in the Navigation Pane, and then tap or click Layout View on the shortcut menu to open the report in Layout view.

- If a Field list appears, tap or click the Add Existing Fields button (REPORT LAYOUT TOOLS DESIGN tab | Tools group) to remove the Field list from the screen.

- Close the Navigation Pane.

- Tap or click the report title once to select it.

- Tap or click the report title a second time to produce an insertion point (Figure 1–72).

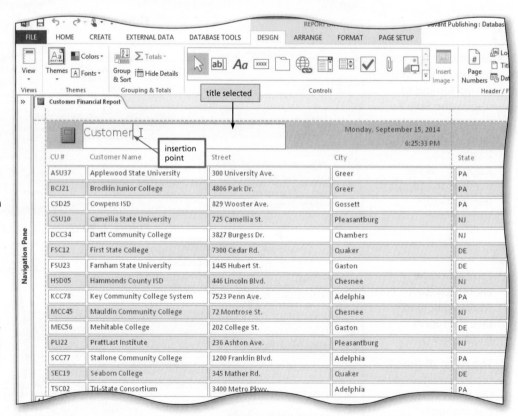

Figure 1–72

Q&A | My insertion point is in the middle of Customer. How do I produce an insertion point at the position shown in the figure?

You can use the RIGHT ARROW key to move the insertion point to the position in the figure, or you can tap or click the desired position.

2

- Press the SPACEBAR to insert a space, and then type Financial Report to complete the title.

- Tap or click the column heading for the Street field to select it.

- Hold the SHIFT key down and then tap or click the column headings for the City, State, and Postal Code fields to select multiple column headings.

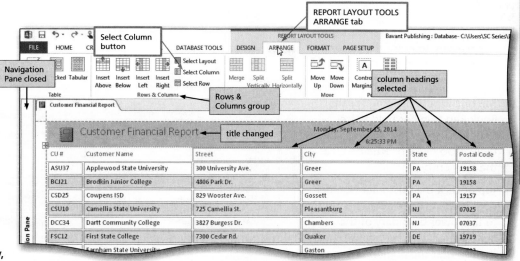

Figure 1–73

Q&A What happens if I do not hold down the SHIFT key?

When you tap or click another column heading, it will be the only one that is selected. To select multiple objects, you need to hold the SHIFT key down for every object after the first selection.

I selected the wrong collection of objects. What should I do?

You can tap or click somewhere else on the report so that the objects you want are not selected, and then begin the process again. Alternatively, you can repeatedly tap or click the Undo button on the Quick Access Toolbar to undo your selections. Once you have done so, you can select the objects you want.

- Tap or click ARRANGE on the ribbon to display the REPORT LAYOUT TOOLS ARRANGE tab (Figure 1–73).

3

- Tap or click the Select Column button (REPORT LAYOUT TOOLS ARRANGE tab | Rows & Columns group) to select the entire columns corresponding to the column headings you selected in the previous step.

- Press the DELETE key to delete the selected columns.

- Tap or click the column heading for the Customer Number field twice, once to select it and the second time to produce an insertion point (Figure 1–74).

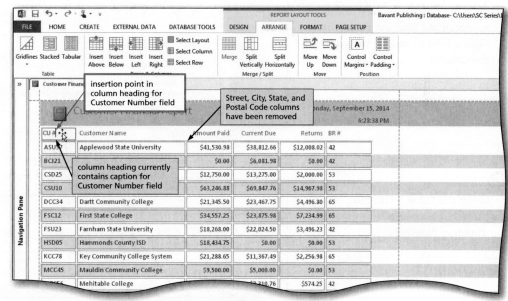

Figure 1–74

Q&A I selected the wrong field. What should I do?

Tap or click somewhere outside the various fields to deselect the one you have selected. Then, tap or click the Customer Number field twice.

4

- Use the DELETE or BACKSPACE keys as necessary to erase the current entry, and then type `Customer Number` as the new entry.

- Tap or click the heading for the Book Rep Number field twice, erase the current entry, and then type `Book Rep Number` as the new entry.

- Tap or click the Customer Number field heading to select it, point to the lower boundary of the heading for the Customer Number field so that the pointer changes to a two-headed arrow, and then drag the lower boundary to the approximate position shown in Figure 1–75 to expand the column headings.

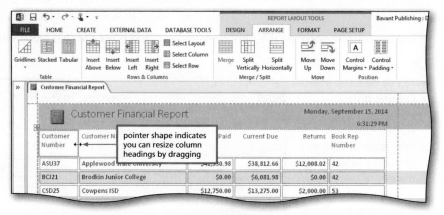

Figure 1–75

Q&A I did something wrong when I dragged and now my report looks strange. What should I do?
Tap or click the Undo button on the Quick Access Toolbar to undo the change. Depending on the specific action you took, you may need to tap or click it more than once.

My screen displays Book Rep Number on one line not two. Is this a problem?
No. You will adjust the column heading in a later step.

5

- Point to the right boundary of the heading for the Customer Number field so that the pointer changes to a two-headed arrow, and then drag the right boundary to the approximate position shown in Figure 1–76 to reduce the width of the column.

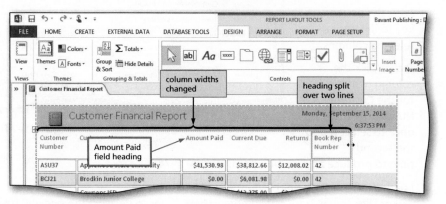

Figure 1–76

6

- Using the same technique, resize the other columns to the sizes shown in Figure 1–77.

Figure 1–77

To Add Totals to a Report

The report in Figure 1–67 contains totals for the Amount Paid, Current Due, and Returns columns. You can use Layout view to add these totals. The following steps use Layout view to include totals for these three columns. *Why? In Layout view you can tap or click a single button to add totals. This button sums all the values in the field.*

1

- Tap or click the Amount Paid field heading (shown in Figure 1–77) to select the field.

Q&A Do I have to tap or click the heading? Could I tap or click the field on one of the records?
You do not have to tap or click the heading. You also could tap or click the Amount Paid field on any record.

- Tap or click DESIGN on the ribbon to display the DESIGN tab.

- Tap or click the Totals button (REPORT LAYOUT TOOLS DESIGN

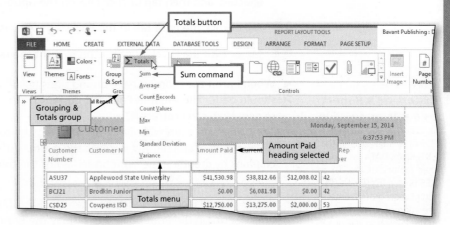

Figure 1–78

tab | Grouping & Totals group) to display the Totals menu containing a list of available calculations (Figure 1–78).

2

- Tap or click Sum to calculate the sum of the amount of paid values.

- Using the same technique, add totals for the Current Due and Returns columns.

Q&A When I clicked the Totals button after selecting the Returns field heading, Sum was already checked. Do I still need to tap or click Sum?
No. In fact, if you do tap or click it, you will remove the check mark, which will remove the total from the column.

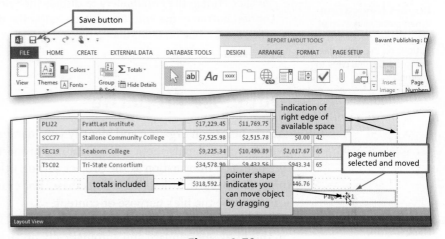

Figure 1–79

- Scroll down to the bottom of the report to verify that the totals are included. If necessary, expand the size of the total controls so they appear completely by dragging the lower boundary of the controls to the approximate position shown in Figure 1–79.

- Tap or click the page number to select it, and then drag it to the approximate position shown in Figure 1–79.

Q&A Why did I need to move the page number?
The dotted line near the right-hand edge of the screen indicates the right-hand border of the available space on the printed page, based on whatever margins and orientation are currently selected. A portion of the page number extends beyond this border. By moving the page number, it no longer extends beyond the border.

3

- Tap or click the Save button on the Quick Access Toolbar to save your changes to the report layout.

- Close the report.

To Print a Report

The following steps print the report.

1 Open the Navigation Pane if necessary, confirm that the Customer Financial Report is selected, and then tap or click FILE on the ribbon to open the Backstage view.

2 Tap or click the Print tab in the Backstage view to display the Print gallery.

3 Tap or click the Quick Print button to print the report.

Q&A

When I print the report, I have pound signs (####) rather than numbers where the totals should be for the Amount Paid and Current Due columns. The report looked fine on the screen. How can I correct it?

The columns are not wide enough to display the complete number. Open the report in Layout view and slightly increase the width of the Amount Paid and Current Due columns by dragging the right boundary of the column headings.

How can I print multiple copies of my report?

Tap or click FILE on the ribbon to open the Backstage view. Tap or click the Print tab, tap or click Print in the Print gallery to display the Print dialog box, increase the number in the Number of Copies box, and then tap or click the OK button (Print dialog box).

How can I print a range of pages rather than printing the whole report?

Tap or click FILE on the ribbon to open the Backstage view. Tap or click the Print tab, tap or click Print in the Print gallery to display the Print dialog box, tap or click the Pages option button in the Print Range area, enter the desired page range, and then tap or click the OK button (Print dialog box).

BTW

Exporting a Report as a PDF or XPS File
To export a report as a PDF or XPS file, display the EXTERNAL DATA tab, and then tap or click the PDF or XPS button (EXTERNAL DATA tab | Export group). Enter the appropriate information in the Publish to PDF or XPS dialog box and tap or click the Publish button.

BTW

Report Navigation
When previewing a report, you can use the Navigation buttons on the status bar to move from one page to another.

Database Properties

Access helps you organize and identify your databases by using **database properties,** which are the details about a file. Database properties, also known as **metadata,** can include such information as the project author, title, or subject. **Keywords** are words or phrases that further describe the database. For example, a class name or database topic can describe the file's purpose or content.

Five different types of database properties exist, but the more common ones used in this book are standard and automatically updated properties. **Standard properties** are associated with all Microsoft Office documents and include author, title, and subject. **Automatically updated properties** include file system properties, such as the date you create or change a file, and statistics, such as the file size.

CONSIDER THIS

Why would you want to assign database properties to a database?
Database properties are valuable for a variety of reasons:

- Users can save time locating a particular file because they can view a file's database properties without opening the database.

- By creating consistent properties for files having similar content, users can better organize their databases.

- Some organizations require Access users to add database properties so that other employees can view details about these files.

To Change Database Properties

To change database properties, you would follow these steps.

1. Tap or click FILE on the ribbon to open the Backstage view and then, if necessary, tap or click the Info tab in the Backstage view to display the Info gallery.

2. Click the 'View and edit database properties' link in the right pane of the Info gallery to display the Bavant Publishing Properties dialog box.

Q&A | Why are some of the database properties already filled in?
The person who installed Office 2013 on your computer or network might have set or customized the properties.

3. If the property you want to change is displayed in the Properties dialog box, click the text box for the property and make the desired change. Skip the remaining steps.

4. If the property you want to change is not displayed in the Properties dialog box, click the appropriate tab so the property is displayed and then make the desired change.

5. Click the OK button in the Properties dialog box to save your changes and remove the dialog box from the screen.

To Sign Out of a Microsoft Account

If you are signed in to a Microsoft account and are using a public computer or otherwise wish to sign out of your Microsoft account, you should sign out of the account from the Account gallery in the Backstage view before exiting Access. Signing out of the account is the safest way to make sure that nobody else can access SkyDrive files or settings stored in your Microsoft account. The following steps sign out of a Microsoft account from Access. For a detailed example of the procedure summarized below, refer to the Office and Windows chapter at the beginning of this book.

1 If you wish to sign out of your Microsoft account, tap or click FILE on the ribbon to open the Backstage view and then tap or click the Account tab to display the Account gallery.

2 Tap or click the Sign out link, which displays the Remove Account dialog box. If a Can't remove Windows accounts dialog box appears instead of the Remove Account dialog box, click the OK button and skip the remaining steps.

Q&A | Why does a Can't remove Windows accounts dialog box appear?
If you signed in to Windows using your Microsoft account, then you also must sign out from Windows, rather than signing out from within Access. When you are finished using Windows, be sure to sign out at that time.

3 Tap or click the Yes button (Remove Account dialog box) to sign out of your Microsoft account on this computer.

Q&A | Should I sign out of Windows after signing out of my Microsoft account? [End Q]
When you are finished using the computer, you should sign out of your account for maximum security.

4 Tap or click the Back button in the upper-left corner of the Backstage view to return to the database.

To Exit Access

The following steps exit Access.

1 Tap or click the Close button on the right side of the title bar to close the open database, if there is one, and exit Access.

2 If a Microsoft Access dialog box appears, tap or click the Save button to save any changes made to the database since the last save.

Special Database Operations

Additional operations involved in maintaining a database are backup, recovery, compacting, and repairing.

Backup and Recovery

It is possible to damage or destroy a database. Users can enter data that is incorrect; programs that are updating the database can end abnormally during an update; a hardware problem can occur; and so on. After any such event has occurred, the database may contain invalid data or it might be totally destroyed.

Obviously, you cannot allow a situation in which data has been damaged or destroyed to go uncorrected. You must somehow return the database to a correct state. This process is called recovery; that is, you **recover** the database.

The simplest approach to recovery involves periodically making a copy of the database (called a **backup copy** or a **save copy**). This is referred to as **backing up** the database. If a problem occurs, you correct the problem by overwriting the actual database — often referred to as the **live database** — with the backup copy.

To back up the database that is currently open, you use the Back Up Database command on the Save As tab in the Backstage view. In the process, Access suggests a name that is a combination of the database name and the current date. For example, if you back up the Bavant Publishing database on October 20, 2014, Access will suggest the name, Bavant Publishing_2014-10-20. You can change this name if you desire, although it is a good idea to use this name. By doing so, it will be easy to distinguish between all the backup copies you have made to determine which is the most recent. In addition, if you discover that a critical problem occurred on October 18, 2014, you may want to go back to the most recent backup before October 18. If, for example, the database was not backed up on October 17 but was backed up on October 16, you would use Bavant Publishing_2014-10-16.

To Back Up a Database

You would use the following steps to back up a database to a file on a hard disk or high-capacity removable disk.

1. Open the database to be backed up.

2. Tap or click FILE on the ribbon to open the Backstage view, and then tap or click the Save As tab.

3. With Save Database As selected in the File Types area, tap or click 'Back Up Database' in the Save Database As area, and then tap or click the Save As button.

4. Navigate to the desired location in the Save As box. If you do not want the name Access has suggested, enter the desired name in the File name text box.

5. Tap or click the Save button to back up the database.

Access creates a backup copy with the desired name in the desired location. Should you ever need to recover the database using this backup copy, you can simply copy it over the live version.

Compacting and Repairing a Database

As you add more data to a database, it naturally grows larger. When you delete an object (records, tables, forms, or queries), the space previously occupied by the object does not become available for additional objects. Instead, the additional objects are given new space; that is, space that was not already allocated. To remove this empty space from the database, you must **compact** the database. The same option that compacts the database also repairs problems that might have occurred in the database.

TO COMPACT AND REPAIR A DATABASE

You would use the following steps to compact and repair a database.

1. Open the database to be compacted.
2. Tap or click FILE on the ribbon to open the Backstage view, and then, if necessary, select the Info tab.
3. Tap or click the Compact & Repair Database button in the Info gallery to compact and repair the database.
    The database now is the compacted form of the original.

Additional Operations

Additional special operations include opening another database, closing a database without exiting Access, and saving a database with another name. They also include deleting a table (or other object) as well as renaming an object.

When you open another database, Access will automatically close the database that previously was open. Before deleting or renaming an object, you should ensure that the object has no dependent objects; that is, other objects that depend on the object you want to delete.

TO CLOSE A DATABASE WITHOUT EXITING ACCESS

You would use the following steps to close a database without exiting Access.

1. Tap or click FILE on the ribbon to open the Backstage view.
2. Tap or click Close.

TO SAVE A DATABASE WITH ANOTHER NAME

To save a database with another name, you would use the following steps.

1. Tap or click FILE on the ribbon to open the Backstage view, and then select the Save As tab.
2. With Save Database As selected in the Database File Types area and Access Database selected in the Save Database As area, tap or click the Save As button.
3. Enter a name and select a location for the new version.
4. Tap or click the Save button.

If you want to make a backup, could you just save the database with another name?

You could certainly do that. Using the backup procedure discussed earlier has the advantage that it automatically includes the current database name and the date in the name of the file it creates.

TO DELETE A TABLE OR OTHER OBJECT IN THE DATABASE

You would use the following steps to delete a database object.

1. Press and hold or right-click the object in the Navigation Pane.
2. Tap or click Delete on the shortcut menu.
3. Tap or click the Yes button in the Microsoft Access dialog box.

TO RENAME AN OBJECT IN THE DATABASE

You would use the following steps to rename a database object.

1. Press and hold or right-click the object in the Navigation Pane.
2. Tap or click Rename on the shortcut menu.
3. Type the new name and press the ENTER key.

Database Design

BTW

Database Design Language (DBDL)
Database Design Language (DBDL) is a commonly accepted shorthand representation for showing the structure of a relational database. You write the name of the table and then within parentheses you list all the columns in the table. If the columns continue beyond one line, indent the subsequent lines.

This section illustrates the **database design** process, that is, the process of determining the tables and fields that make up the database. It does so by showing how you would design the database for Bavant Publishing from a set of requirements. In this section, you will use commonly accepted shorthand to represent the tables and fields that make up the database as well as the primary keys for the tables. For each table, you give the name of the table followed by a set of parentheses. Within the parentheses is a list of the fields in the table separated by commas. You underline the primary key. For example,

Product (<u>Product Code</u>, Description, On Hand, Price) represents a table called Product. The Product table contains four fields: Product Code, Description, On Hand, and Price. The Product Code field is the primary key.

Database Requirements

BTW

Determining Database Requirements
The determination of database requirements is part of a process known as systems analysis. A systems analyst examines existing and proposed documents, and examines organizational policies to determine exactly the type of data needs the database must support.

The Bavant Publishing database must maintain information on both customers and book reps. The business currently keeps this data in two Word tables and two Excel workbooks, as shown in Figure 1–80. They use Word tables for address information and Excel workbooks for financial information.

- For customers, Bavant needs to maintain address data. It currently keeps this data in a Word table (Figure 1–80a).
- Bavant also maintains financial data for each customer. This includes the amount paid, current amount due, and return amount for the customer. It keeps these amounts, along with the customer name and number, in the Excel worksheet shown in Figure 1–80b.
- Bavant keeps book rep address data in a Word table, as shown in Figure 1–80c.
- Just as with customers, it keeps financial data for book reps, including their start date, salary, and bonus rate, in a separate Excel worksheet, as shown in Figure 1–80d.

Customer Number	Customer Name	Street	City	State	Postal Code
ASU37	Applewood State University	300 University Ave.	Greer	PA	19158
BCJ21	Brodkin Junior College	4806 Park Dr.	Greer	PA	19158
CSD25	Cowpens ISD	829 Wooster Ave.	Gossett	PA	19157
CSU10	Camellia State University	725 Camellia St.	Pleasantburg	NJ	07025
DCC34	Dartt Community College	3827 Burgess Dr.	Chambers	NJ	07037
FSC12	First State College	7300 Cedar Rd.	Quaker	DE	19719
FSU23	Farnham State University	1445 Hubert St.	Gaston	DE	19723
HSD05	Hammonds County ISD	446 Lincoln Blvd.	Chesnee	NJ	07053
KCC78	Key Community College System	7523 Penn Ave.	Adelphia	PA	19159
MCC45	Mauldin Community College	72 Montrose St.	Chesnee	NJ	07053
MEC56	Mehitable College	202 College St.	Gaston	DE	19723
PLI22	PrattLast Institute	236 Ashton Ave.	Pleasantburg	NJ	07025
SCC77	Stallone Community College	1200 Franklin Blvd.	Adelphia	PA	19156
SEC19	Seaborn College	345 Mather Rd.	Quaker	DE	19719
TSC02	Tri-State Consortium	3400 Metro Pkwy.	Adelphia	PA	19156

© 2014 Cengage Learning

Figure 1–80 (a) Customer Address Information (Word Table)

Figure 1–80 (b) Customer Financial Information (Excel Worksheet)

Book Rep Number	Last Name	First Name	Street	City	State	Postal Code
42	Perez	Melina	261 Porter Dr.	Adelphia	PA	19156
48	Statnik	Michael	3135 Simpson Dr.	Pleasantburg	NJ	07025
53	Chin	Robert	265 Maxwell St.	Gossett	PA	19157
65	Rogers	Tracy	1827 Maple Ave.	Adelphia	PA	19159

© 2014 Cengage Learning

Figure 1–80 (c) Book Rep Address Information (Word Table)

Figure 1–80 (d) Book Rep Financial Information (Excel Worksheet)

• Finally, Bavant keeps track of which customers are assigned to which book reps. Each customer is assigned to a single book rep, but each book rep might be assigned many customers. Currently, for example, customers ASU37 (Applewood State University), BCJ21 (Brodkin Junior College), FSU23 (Farnham State University), MEC56 (Mehitable College), and SCC77 (Stallone Community College) are assigned to book rep 42 (Melina Perez). Customers CSD25 (Cowpens ISD), CSU10 (Camellia State University), HSD05 (Hammonds County ISD), MCC45 (Mauldin Community College), and PLI22 (PrattLast Institute) are assigned to book rep 53 (Robert Chin). Customers DCC34 (Dartt Community College), FSC12 (First State College), KCC78 (Key Community College System), SEC19 (Seaborn College), and TSC02 (Tri-State Consortium) are assigned to book rep 65 (Tracy Rogers). Bavant has an additional book rep, Michael Statnik, whose number has been assigned as 48, but who has not yet been assigned any customers.

Database Design Process

The database design process involves several steps.

CONSIDER THIS

What is the first step in the process?
Identify the tables. Examine the requirements for the database to identify the main objects that are involved. There will be a table for each object you identify.

In a database for one organization, for example, the main objects might be departments and employees. This would require two tables: one for departments and the other for employees. In the database for another organization, the main objects might be customers and book reps. In this case, there also would be two tables: one for customers and the other for book reps. In still another organization's database, the main objects might be books, publishers, and authors. This database would require three tables: one for books, a second for publishers, and a third for authors.

Identifying the Tables

For the Bavant Publishing database, the main objects are customers and book reps. This leads to two tables, which you must name. Reasonable names for these two tables are:

Customer
Book Rep

CONSIDER THIS

After identifying the tables, what is the second step in the database design process?
Determine the primary keys. Recall that the primary key is the unique identifier for records in the table. For each table, determine the unique identifier. In a Department table, for example, the unique identifier might be the Department Code. For a Book table, the unique identifier might be the ISBN (International Standard Book Number).

Determining the Primary Keys

The next step is to identify the fields that will be the unique identifiers, or primary keys. Customer numbers uniquely identify customers, and book rep numbers uniquely identify book reps. Thus, the primary key for the Customer table is the customer number, and the primary key for the Book Rep table is the book rep number. Reasonable names for these fields would be Customer Number and Book Rep Number, respectively. Adding these primary keys to the tables gives:

Customer (<u>Customer Number</u>)
Book Rep (<u>Book Rep Number</u>)

What is the third step in the database design process after determining the primary keys?
Determine the additional fields. The primary key will be a field or combination of fields in a table. A table typically will contain many additional fields, each of which contains a type of data. Examine the project requirements to determine these additional fields. For example, in an Employee table, additional fields might include Employee Name, Street Address, City, State, Postal Code, Date Hired, and Salary.

Determining Additional Fields

After identifying the primary keys, you need to determine and name the additional fields. In addition to the customer number, the Customer Address Information shown in Figure 1–80a on page AC 59 contains the customer name, street, city, state, and postal code. These would be fields in the Customer table. The Customer Financial Information shown in Figure 1–80b on page AC 59 also contains the customer number and customer name, which are already included in the Customer table. The financial information also contains the amount paid, current due, and returns. Adding the amount paid, current due, and returns fields to those already identified in the Customer table and assigning reasonable names gives:

> Customer (<u>Customer Number</u>, Customer Name, Street, City, State, Postal Code, Amount Paid, Current Due, Returns)

Similarly, examining the Book Rep Address Information in Figure 1–80c on page AC 59 adds the last name, first name, street, city, state, and postal code fields to the Book Rep table. In addition to the book rep number, last name, and first name, the Book Rep Financial Information in Figure 1–80d on page AC 59 would add the start date, salary, and bonus rate. Adding these fields to the Book Rep table and assigning reasonable names gives:

> Book Rep (<u>Book Rep Number</u>, Last Name, First Name, Street, City, State, Postal Code, Start Date, Salary, Bonus Rate)

BTW
Additional Data for Bavant Publishing
Bavant could include other types of data in the database. The Customer table could include data on a contact person at each organization, such as, name, telephone number, and email address. The Book Rep table could include the mobile telephone number, email address, and emergency contact information for the book rep.

What happens as the fourth step, after determining additional fields?
Determine relationships between the tables. A relationship is an association between objects. In a database containing information about departments and employees, there is an association between the departments and the employees. A department is associated with all the employees in the department, and an employee is associated with the department to which he or she is assigned. Technically, you say that a department is related to all the employees in the department, and an employee is related to his or her department.

The relationship between department and employees is an example of a **one-to-many relationship** because one employee is associated with one department, but each department can be associated with many employees. The Department table would be the "one" table in the relationship. The Employee table would be the "many" table in the relationship.

When you have determined that two tables are related, follow these general guidelines:

Identify the "one" table.

Identify the "many" table.

Include the primary key from the "one" table as a field in the "many" table.

Determining and Implementing Relationships Between the Tables

According to the requirements, each customer has one book rep, but each book rep can have many customers. Thus, the Book Rep table is the "one" table, and the Customer table is the "many" table. To implement this one-to-many relationship between book reps and customers, add the Book Rep Number field (the primary key of the Book Rep table) to the Customer table. This produces:

Customer (<u>Customer Number</u>, Customer Name, Street, City, State, Postal Code, Amount Paid, Current Due, Returns, Book Rep Number)
Book Rep (<u>Book Rep Number</u>, Last Name, First Name, Street, City, State, Postal Code, Start Date, Salary, Bonus Rate)

CONSIDER THIS

After creating relationships between tables, what is the fifth step in the database design process?
Determine data types for the fields, that is, the type of data that can be stored in the field.

Determining Data Types for the Fields

See Pages AC 9 through AC 10 for a discussion of the available data types and their use in the Bavant Publishing database. That section also discusses other properties that can be assigned, such as captions, field size, and the number of decimal places.

Identifying and Removing Redundancy

Redundancy means storing the same fact in more than one place. It usually results from placing too many fields in a table — fields that really belong in separate tables — and often causes serious problems. If you had not realized there were two objects, such as customers and book reps, you might have placed all the data in a single Customer table. Figure 1–81 shows an example of a table that includes both customer and book rep information. Notice that the data for a given book rep (number, name, address, and so on) occurs on more than one record. The data for rep 42, Melina Perez, is repeated in the figure. Storing this data on multiple records is an example of redundancy.

name of Book Rep 42 appears more than once

Customer Number	Customer Name	Street	...	Book Rep Number	Last Name	First Name
ASU37	Applewood State University	300 University Ave.	...	42	Perez	Melina
BCJ21	Brodkin Junior College	4806 Park Dr.	...	42	Perez	Melina
CSD25	Cowpens ISD	829 Wooster Ave.	...	53	Chin	Robert
CSU10	Camellia State University	725 Camellia St.	...	53	Chin	Robert
DCC34	Dartt Community College	3827 Burgess Dr.	...	65	Rogers	Tracy
...	...	...	...	...	...	...

Book Rep numbers are 42

© 2014 Cengage Learning

Figure 1–81

What problems does this redundancy cause?

Redundancy results in several problems, including:

1. Wasted storage space. The name of book rep 42, Melina Perez, for example, should be stored only once. Storing this fact several times is wasteful.

2. More complex database updates. If, for example, Melina Perez's name is spelled incorrectly and needs to be changed in the database, her name would need to be changed in several different places.

3. Possible inconsistent data. Nothing prohibits the book rep's last name from being Perez on customer ASU37's record and Perret on customer BCJ21's record. The data would be inconsistent. In both cases, the book rep number is 42, but the last names are different.

How do you eliminate redundancy?

The solution to the problem is to place the redundant data in a separate table, one in which the data no longer will be redundant. If, for example, you place the data for book reps in a separate table (Figure 1–82), the data for each book rep will appear only once.

Customer Number	Customer Name	Street	...	Book Rep Number
ASU37	Applewood State University	300 University Ave.	...	42
BCJ21	Brodkin Junior College	4806 Park Dr.	...	42
CSD25	Cowpens ISD	829 Wooster Ave.	...	53
CSU10	Camellia State University	725 Camellia St.	...	53
DCC34	Dartt Community College	3827 Burgess Dr.	...	65

Book Rep numbers are 42

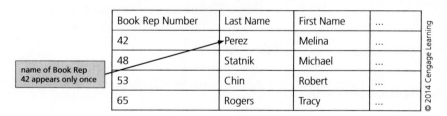

Book Rep Number	Last Name	First Name	...
42	Perez	Melina	...
48	Statnik	Michael	...
53	Chin	Robert	...
65	Rogers	Tracy	...

name of Book Rep 42 appears only once

© 2014 Cengage Learning

Figure 1–82

Notice that you need to have the book rep number in both tables. Without it, there would be no way to tell which book rep is associated with which customer. The remaining book rep data, however, was removed from the Customer table and placed in the Book Rep table. This new arrangement corrects the problems of redundancy in the following ways:

1. Because the data for each book rep is stored only once, space is not wasted.

2. Changing the name of a book rep is easy. You need to change only one row in the Book Rep table.

3. Because the data for a book rep is stored only once, inconsistent data cannot occur.

Designing to omit redundancy will help you to produce good and valid database designs. You should always examine your design to see if it contains redundancy. If it does, you should decide whether you need to remove the redundancy by creating a separate table.

If you examine your design, you will see that there is one area of redundancy (see the data in Figure 1–1 on page AC 3). Cities and states are both repeated. Every customer whose postal code is 19158, for example, has Greer as the city and PA as the state. To remove this redundancy, you would create a table with the primary key Postal Code and City and State as additional fields. City and State would be removed from the Customer table. Having City, State, and Postal Code in a table is very common, however, and usually you would not take such action. No other redundancy exists in your tables.

BTW

Postal Codes
Some organizations with customers throughout the country have a separate table of postal codes, cities, and states. When placing an order, you typically are asked for your postal code (or ZIP code), rather than city, state, and postal code. You then are asked to confirm that the city and state correspond to that postal code.

Chapter Summary

In this chapter you have learned to create an Access database, create tables and add records to a database, print the contents of tables, import data, create queries, create forms, create reports, and change database properties. You also have learned how to design a database. The items listed below include all the new Access skills you have learned in this chapter, with tasks grouped by activity.

Database Object Management
Delete a Table or Other Object in the Database (AC 58)
Rename an Object in the Database (AC 58)

Database Properties
Change Database Properties (AC 55)

File Management
Run Access (AC 5)
Create a Database (AC 6)
Create a Database Using a Template (AC 7)
Exit Access (AC 24)
Open a Database from Access (AC 25)
Back Up a Database (AC 56)
Compact and Repair a Database (AC 57)
Close a Database without Exiting Access (AC 57)
Save a Database with Another Name (AC 57)

Form Creation
Create a Form (AC 45)

Import Data
Import an Excel Worksheet (AC 33)

Print Objects
Preview and Print the Contents of a Table (AC 30)

Print the Results of a Query (AC 45)
Print a Report (AC 54)

Query Creation
Use the Simple Query Wizard to Create a Query (AC 40)
Use a Criterion in a Query (AC 43)

Report Creation
Create a Report (AC 48)
Modify Report Column Headings and Resize Columns (AC 50)
Add Totals to a Report (AC 53)

Table Creation
Modify the Primary Key (AC 11)
Define the Remaining Fields in a Table (AC 14)
Save a Table (AC 16)
View the Table in Design View (AC 17)
Change a Field Size in Design View (AC 18)
Close the Table (AC 20)
Resize Columns in a Datasheet (AC 28)
Modify a Table in Design View (AC 37)

Table Update
Add Records to a Table (AC 20)
Add Records to a Table that Contains Data (AC 26)

CONSIDER THIS

What decisions will you need to make when creating your next database?
Use these guidelines as you complete the assignments in this chapter and create your own databases outside of this class.

1. Identify the tables that will be included in the database.

2. Determine the primary keys for each of the tables.

3. Determine the additional fields that should be included in each of the tables.

4. Determine relationships between the tables.

   a) Identify the "one" table.
   b) Identify the "many" table.
   c) Include the primary key of the "one" table as a field in the "many" table.

5. Determine data types for the fields in the tables.

6. Determine additional properties for fields.

   a) Determine if a special caption is warranted.
   b) Determine if a special description is warranted.
   c) Determine field sizes.
   d) Determine formats.

7. Identify and remove any unwanted redundancy.

8. Determine a storage location for the database.

9. Determine the best method for distributing the database objects.

How should you submit solutions to questions in the assignments identified with a ✴ symbol?

Every assignment in this book contains one or more questions identified with a ✴ symbol. These questions require you to think beyond the assigned database. Present your solutions to the questions in the format required by your instructor. Possible formats may include one or more of these options: write the answer; create a document that contains the answer; present your answer to the class; discuss your answer in a group; record the answer as audio or video using a webcam, smartphone, or portable media player; or post answers on a blog, wiki, or website.

CONSIDER THIS

Apply Your Knowledge

Reinforce the skills and apply the concepts you learned in this chapter.

Adding a Caption, Changing a Data Type, Creating a Query, a Form, and a Report

Note: To complete this assignment, you will be required to use the Data Files for Students. Visit www.cengage.com/ct/studentdownload for detailed instructions or contact your instructor for information about accessing the required files.

Instructions: Cosmetics Naturally Inc. manufactures and sells beauty and skin care products made with only natural ingredients. The company's products do not contain any synthetic chemicals, artificial fragrances, or chemical preservatives. Cosmetics Naturally has a database that keeps track of its sales representatives and customers. Each customer is assigned to a single sales rep, but each sales rep may be assigned to many customers. The database has two tables. The Customer table contains data on the customers who purchase Cosmetics Naturally products. The Sales Rep table contains data on the sales reps. You will add a caption, change a data type, create two queries, a form, and a report, as shown in Figure 1–83 on the next page.

Perform the following tasks:

1. Start Access, open the Apply Cosmetics Naturally database from the Data Files for Students, and enable the content.

2. Open the Sales Rep table in Datasheet view, add SR # as the caption for the Sales Rep Number field, and resize all columns to best fit the data. Save the changes to the layout of the table and close the table.

3. Open the Customer table in Design view and change the data type for the Postal Code field to Short Text. Change the field size for the field to 5. Save the changes to the table and close the table.

4. Use the Simple Query Wizard to create a query for the Customer table that contains the Customer Number, Customer Name, Amount Paid, Balance, and Sales Rep Number. The query is a detail query. Use the name Customer Query for the query and close the query.

5. Create a simple form for the Sales Rep table. Save the form and use the name Sales Rep for the form. Close the form.

6. Create the report shown in Figure 1–83 for the Customer table. The report includes totals for both the Amount Paid and Balance fields. Be sure the totals appear completely. You might need to expand the size of the total controls. Move the page number so that it is within the margins. Save the report as Customer Financial Report.

7. If requested by your instructor, add your last name to the title of the report, that is, change the title to Customer Financial Report LastName where LastName is your actual last name.

8. Compact and repair the database.

9. Submit the revised database in the format specified by your instructor.

10. ✴ How would you change the field name of the Balance field in the Customer table to Current Balance?

Continued >

Apply Your Knowledge *continued*

Figure 1–83

Extend Your Knowledge

Extend the skills you learned in this chapter and experiment with new skills. You may need to use Help to complete the assignment.

Using a Database Template to Create a Contacts Database

Note: To complete this assignment, you will be required to use the Data Files for Students. Visit www.cengage.com/ct/studentdownload for detailed instructions or contact your instructor for information about accessing the required files.

Instructions: Access includes both desktop database templates and web-based templates. You can use a template to create a beginning database that can be modified to meet your specific needs. You will use a template to create a Contacts database. The database template includes sample tables, queries, forms, and reports. You will modify the database and create the Contacts Query shown in Figure 1–84.

Perform the following tasks:
1. Start Access.
2. Select the Desktop contacts template in the template gallery and create a new database with the file name Extend Contacts.
3. Enable the content. If requested to do so by your instructor, watch the videos in the Getting Started with Contacts dialog box. Close the Getting Started with Contacts dialog box.
4. Close the Contact List form.
5. Open the Contacts table in Datasheet view and delete the Fax Number field and the Attachments field in the table. The Attachments field has a paperclip as the column heading.
6. Change the data type for the ID field to Short Text, change the field name to Contact ID, and change the field size to 4. Change the column width so that the complete field name is displayed.
7. Save the changes to the Contacts table and close the table.
8. Use the Simple Query Wizard to create the Contacts Query shown in Figure 1–84. Close the query.

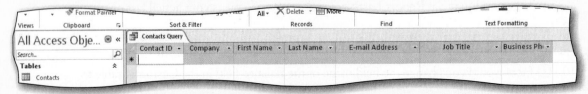

Figure 1–84

9. Open the Phone Book report in Layout view. Delete the control containing the date. Change the title of the report to Contact Phone List.

10. Save the changes to the report.

11. If requested to do so by your instructor, add your first and last names to the end of the title and save the changes to the report.

12. Submit the revised database in the format specified by your instructor.

13. ✴ a. Why would you use a template instead of creating a database from scratch with just the fields you need?

   b. The Attachment data type allows you to attach files to a database record. If you were using this database for a job search, what specific documents might you attach to a Contacts record?

Analyze, Correct, Improve

Analyze a database, correct all errors, and improve the design.

Correcting Errors in the Table Structure

Note: To complete this assignment, you will be required to use the Data Files for Students. Visit www.cengage.com/ct/studentdownload for detailed instructions or contact your instructor for information about accessing the required files.

Instructions: Analyze SciFi Movies is a database containing information on classic science fiction movies that your film professor would like to use for teaching. The Movie table shown in Figure 1–85 contains errors to the table structure. Your professor has asked you to correct the errors and make some improvements to the database. Start Access and open the Analyze SciFi Movies database from the Data Files for Students.

Figure 1–85

1. Correct Movie Number should be the primary key for the Movie table. The ID field should not be a field in the table. The Rating field represents a numerical rating system of one to four to indicate the quality of the movie. Your instructor wants to be able to find the average rating for films directed by a particular director. Only integers should be stored in both the Rating and the Length (Minutes) fields.

2. Improve The default field size for Short Text fields is 255. Changing the field size to more accurately represent the maximum number of characters that can be stored in a field is one way to improve the accuracy of the data. The Movie Number, Director Number, and Awards fields should have a maximum size of 3 characters. The Year Made field should have a maximum field size of 4. The Movie Name and Studio fields should have a maximum field size of 50. If instructed to do so by your instructor, rename the Movie table as Movie Last Name where Last Name is your last name. Submit the revised database in the format specified by your instructor.

3. ✴ The Awards field currently has a data type of Short Text, but the only values that will be stored in that field are Yes and No to indicate whether the movie won any awards. What would be a more appropriate data type for this field?

In the Labs

Design, create, modify, and/or use a database following the guidelines, concepts, and skills presented in this chapter. Labs are listed in order of increasing difficulty. Labs 1 and 2, which increase in difficulty, require you to create solutions based on what you learned in the chapter; Lab 3 requires you to create a solution, which uses cloud and web technologies, by learning and investigating on your own from general guidance.

Lab 1: Creating Objects for the Dartt Offsite Services Database

Problem: Dartt Offsite Services is a local company that provides offsite data services and solutions. The company provides remote data backup, disaster recovery planning and services, website backup, and offsite storage of paper documents for small businesses and nonprofit organizations. Service representatives are responsible for communicating data solutions to the client, scheduling backups and other tasks, and resolving any conflicts. The company recently decided to store its client and service rep data in a database. Each client is assigned to a single service rep, but each service rep may be assigned many clients. The database and the Service Rep table have been created, but the Monthly Salary field needs to be added to the table. The records shown in Table 1–6 must be added to the Service Rep table. The company plans to import the Client table from the Excel worksheet shown in Figure 1–86. Dartt would like to finish storing this data in a database and has asked you to help.

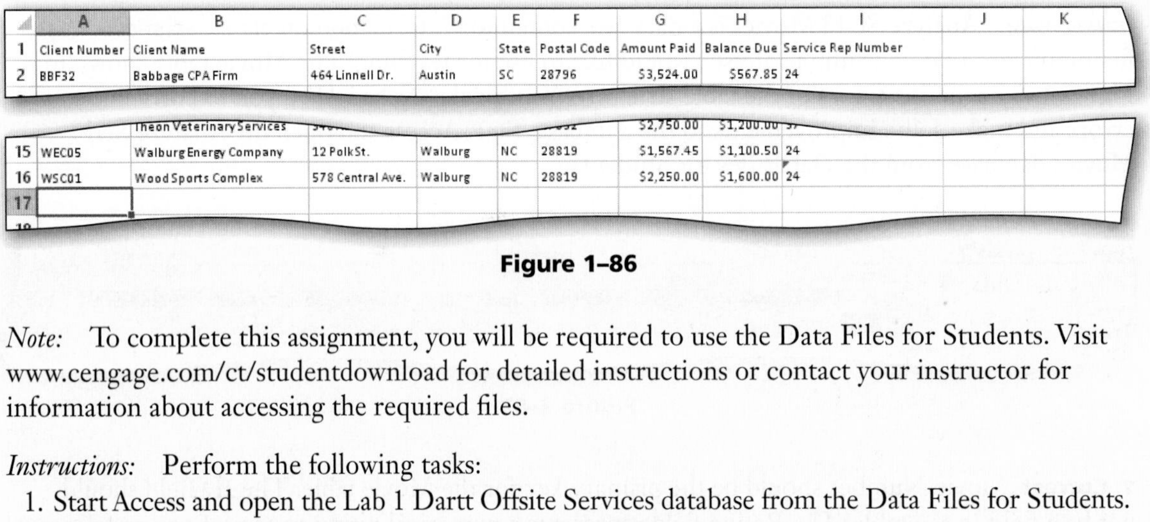

Figure 1–86

Note: To complete this assignment, you will be required to use the Data Files for Students. Visit www.cengage.com/ct/studentdownload for detailed instructions or contact your instructor for information about accessing the required files.

Instructions: Perform the following tasks:

1. Start Access and open the Lab 1 Dartt Offsite Services database from the Data Files for Students.

2. Open the Service Rep table in Datasheet view and add the Monthly Salary field to the end of the table. The field has the Currency data type. Assign the caption SR # to the Service Rep Number field.

3. Add the records shown in Table 1–6.

4. Resize the columns to best fit the data. Save the changes to the layout of the table.

Table 1–6 Data for Service Rep Table								
Service Rep Number	Last Name	First Name	Street	City	State	Postal Code	Start Date	Monthly Salary
21	Kelly	Jenna	25 Paint St.	Kyle	SC	28797	5/14/2012	$3,862.45
45	Scott	Josh	1925 Pine Rd.	Byron	SC	28795	4/28/2014	$3,062.08
24	Liu	Mia	265 Marble Dr.	Kyle	SC	28797	1/7/2013	$3,666.67
37	Martinez	Mike	31 Steel St.	Georgetown	SC	28794	5/13/2013	$3,285.00

5. Import the Lab 1–1 Client Data workbook shown in Figure 1–86 into the database. The first row of the workbook contains the column headings. Client Number is the primary key for the new table. Assign the name Client to the table. Save the Import steps, and assign the name Import-Client Data to the steps. Assign Import Client Data as the description.
6. Open the Client table in Design view and make the following changes:
   a. Change the field size for the Client Number field to 5. Change the field size for the Client Name field to 30. Change the field size for the Street and City fields to 20. Change the field size for the State field to 2 and the field size for the Postal Code field to 5. Change the field size for the Service Rep Number field to 2.
   b. Add the caption CL # to the Client Number field.
   c. Add the caption SR # to the Service Rep Number field.
7. Save the changes to the Client table. If a Microsoft Access dialog box appears with the 'Some data may be lost' message, click the Yes button.
8. Open the Client table in Datasheet view and resize all columns to best fit the data. Save the changes to the layout of the table.
9. Create a query using the Simple Query Wizard for the Client table that displays the Client Number, Client Name, Amount Paid, Balance Due, and Service Rep Number. Save the query as Client Query.
10. Create the report shown in Figure 1–87 for the Client table. The report should include the Client Number, Client Name, Amount Paid, Balance Due, and Service Rep Number fields. Include totals for the Amount Paid and Balance Due fields. Be sure to change the column headings to those shown in Figure 1–87. Save the report as Client Financial Report.
11. If requested to do so by your instructor, change the address for Jenna Kelly in the Service Rep table to your address. If your address is longer than 20 characters, simply enter as much as you can.
12. Submit the revised database in the format specified by your instructor.
13. You entered the records for the Service Rep table in the order shown in Table 1–6 on the previous page, that is service reps 21, 45, 24, 37. What order will the records be in after you close and reopen the Service Rep table? Why?

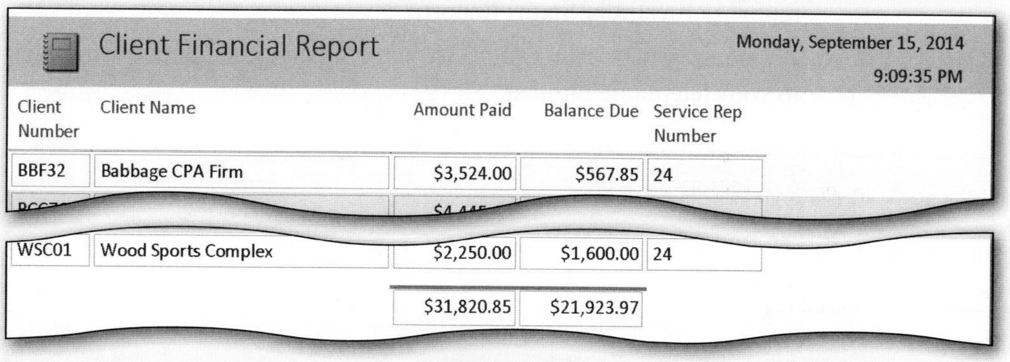

Client Financial Report — Monday, September 15, 2014 — 9:09:35 PM

Client Number	Client Name	Amount Paid	Balance Due	Service Rep Number
BBF32	Babbage CPA Firm	$3,524.00	$567.85	24
WSC01	Wood Sports Complex	$2,250.00	$1,600.00	24
		$31,820.85	$21,923.97	

Figure 1–87

Lab 2: Creating the Tennis Logos Database

Problem: Tennis Logos supplies customized tennis clothing and accessories for clubs and tournaments. The company purchases these items from suppliers at wholesale prices and adds the customer's logo. The final item price is determined by marking up the wholesale price and adding a fee that is based on the complexity of the logo. Tennis Logos also does graphic design work for customers. Currently, the information about the items and the suppliers is stored in two Excel workbooks. Each item is assigned to a single supplier, but each supplier may be assigned many items. You are to create a database that will store the item and supplier information. You already have determined that you need two tables, a Supplier table and an Item table, in which to store the information.

Note: To complete this assignment, you will be required to use the Data Files for Students. Visit www.cengage.com/ct/studentdownload for detailed instructions or contact your instructor for information about accessing the required files.

Continued >

In the Labs *continued*

Instructions: Perform the following tasks:

1. Use the Blank desktop database option to create a new database in which to store all objects related to the items for sale. Call the database Lab 2 Tennis Logos.

2. Import the Lab 1–2 Supplier Data Excel workbook into the database. The first row of the workbook contains the column headings. Supplier Code is the primary key for the new table. Assign the name Supplier to the table. Do not save the Import steps.

3. Open the Supplier table in Datasheet view. Change the field size for the Supplier Code field to 2; the field size for the Supplier Name field to 30; and the field size for the Telephone Number field to 12.

4. Import the Lab 1–2 Item Data Excel workbook into the database. The first row of the workbook contains the column headings. Item Number is the primary key for this table. Assign the name Item to the table. Save the Import steps, and assign the name Import-Item Data to the steps. You do not need a description.

5. Open the Item table in Design view. Change the field size for the Item Number field to 4. Change the field size for the Description field to 30. Add the caption Wholesale for the Wholesale Price field. The On Hand field should be an Integer field. Be sure that the field size for the Supplier Code in the Item table is identical to the field size for the Supplier Code in the Supplier table. Save the changes to the table and close the table.

6. Open the Item table in Datasheet view and resize the columns to best fit the data. Save the changes to the layout of the table and close the table.

7. Create a query for the Item table. Include the Item Number, Description, Wholesale Price, Base Cost, and Supplier Code. Save the query as Item Query.

8. Create a simple form for the Item table. Use the name Item for the form.

9. Create the report shown in Figure 1–88 for the Item table. Do not add any totals. Save the report as Inventory Status Report.

10. If requested to do so by your instructor, change the telephone number for Last Merchandisers to your telephone number.

11. Submit the database in the format specified by your instructor.

12. ✸ If you had designed this database, could you have used the field name, Name, for the Supplier Name? If not, why not?

| Inventory Status Report | | | Monday, September 15, 2014 |
| | | | 9:37:32 PM |

Item Number	Description	On Hand	Wholesale Price
3363	Baseball Cap	110	$4.87
3673	Cotton Visor	150	$4.59
4543	Crew Sweatshirt	75	$7.29
4583			

Figure 1–88

Lab 3: Expand Your World: Cloud and Web Technologies
Exporting Query Results and Reports

Problem: You and two of your friends have started a pet sitting business. You want to be able to share query results and reports, so you have decided to store the items on the SkyDrive. You are still learning Access, so you are going to create a sample query and the report shown in Figure 1–89, export the results, and save to the SkyDrive.

Note: To complete this assignment, you will be required to use the Data Files for Students. Visit www.cengage.com/ct/studentdownload for detailed instructions or contact your instructor for information about accessing the required files.

| Customer Balance Report | | | Monday, September 15, 2014 | |
| | | | 9:39:02 PM | |

Customer Number	Last Name	First Name	Balance	Sitter Number
AB10	Alvarez	Frances	$45.00	103
BR16	B	Alex	$80.00	
	Santoro	Maria	$0.00	107
TR35	Trent	Gerry	$40.00	105
			$419.00	

Figure 1–89

Instructions:

1. Open the Lab 3 Pet Sitters database from the Data Files for Students.

2. Use the Simple Query Wizard to create a query that includes the Customer Number, First Name, Last Name, Balance, and Sitter Number. Save the query as Customer Query.

3. Export the Customer Query as an XPS document to your SkyDrive in the Access folder.

4. Create the report shown in Figure 1–89. Save the report as Customer Balance Report.

5. Export the Customer Balance Report as a PDF document to your Sky Drive in the Access folder. For information about how to use the Sky Drive, refer to the Office and Windows chapter at the beginning of this book.

6. If requested to do so by your instructor, open the Sitter table and change the last name and first name for sitter 103 to your last name and your first name.

7. Submit the assignment in the format specified by your instructor.

8. ✺ Based on your current knowledge of XPS and PDF documents, which one do you think you would use most frequently? Why?

✺ Consider This: Your Turn

Apply your creative thinking and problem solving skills to design and implement a solution.

1. Creating the Craft Database

Note: To complete this assignment, you will be required to use the Data Files for Students. Visit www.cengage.com/ct/studentdownload for detailed instructions or contact your instructor for information about accessing the required files.

Personal/Academic

Part 1: You attend a college that is renowned for its school of arts and crafts. Students who major in arts and crafts can sell their designs online through the college bookstore. The bookstore has used an Excel workbook to store data on wood-crafted items as well as the students who created the items. Because you are a major in computer science and also are studying woodworking, your senior project is to create a database of these wood-crafted items. The database must keep track of the wood-crafted items for sale and maintain data on the students who created the items. Each item is created by a single student, but each student may have created several items.

Based on the information in the Your Turn 1–1 Craft workbook, use the concepts and techniques presented in this chapter to design and create a database to store the craft data. Create a Wood Crafts for Sale report that lists the item number, description, price, and student code. Submit your assignment in the format specified by your instructor.

Part 2: ✺ You made several decisions while determining the table structures and adding data to the tables in this assignment. What method did you use to add the data to each table? Are there any other methods that also would have worked?

Continued >

STUDENT ASSIGNMENTS

Consider This: Your Turn *continued*

2. Creating the Mums Landscaping Database
Professional

Part 1: Mums Landscaping is a local company that provides landscaping and lawn maintenance services to commercial customers, such as businesses, housing subdivisions, and schools. You worked for Mums part-time in both high school and in college. Mums has used an Excel workbook to store financial data on its customers but now would like to create a database that includes information on its customers and crew supervisors. Each customer is assigned to a single crew supervisor, but each supervisor may be assigned many customers.

Based on the information in the Your Turn 1–2 Mums Landscaping workbook, use the concepts and techniques presented in this chapter to design and create a database to store the data that Mums needs. Submit your assignment in the format specified by your instructor.

Part 2: ☀ You made several decisions while creating the Mums Landscaping database in this assignment. What did you decide to use as the primary key for each table? Why?

3. Creating an Electronic Assets Database
Research and Collaboration

Part 1: In today's world, most college students will own at least one electronic device, such as a cell phone. Many students have multiple electronic devices. Microsoft Access includes a desktop Asset tracking template that you can modify to keep track of your electronic devices, such as cell phone, MP3 player, and computer. Get together with your group and make a list of the electronic devices that each of you own. Use the desktop Asset tracking template to create an Electronic Assets database. Watch the video to learn how the database works. As a team, review the fields in the Assets table and decide which fields to include in the database. Delete any unwanted fields. Decide how you will describe each device, for example, will you use the term cell phone, smartphone, or mobile phone? Have each team member enter at least two devices. Create a query to find one type of device, such as cell phone. Submit your assignment in the format specified by your instructor.

Part 2: ☀ You made several decisions while creating the Electronic Assets database. Which fields did you decide to delete from the Assets table? What terms did you use to describe each device? What was the rationale for these decisions?

Learn Online

Reinforce what you learned in this chapter with games, exercises, training, and many other online activities and resources.

Student Companion Site Reinforcement activities and resources are available at no additional cost on www.cengagebrain.com. Visit www.cengage.com/ct/studentdownload for detailed instructions about accessing the resources available at the Student Companion Site.

SAM Put your skills into practice with SAM! If you have a SAM account, go to www.cengage.com/sam2013 to access SAM assignments for this chapter.

2 | Querying a Database

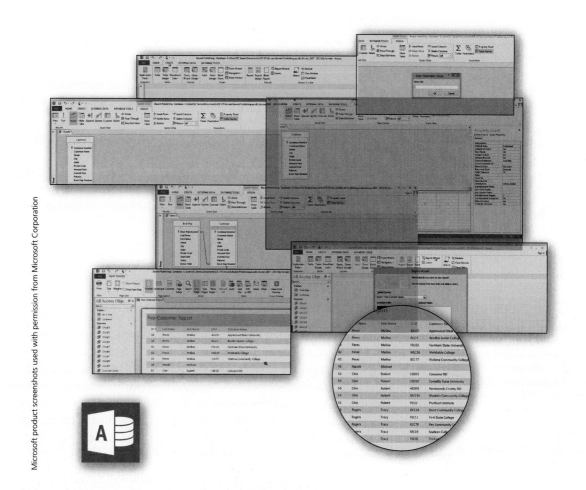

Microsoft product screenshots used with permission from Microsoft Corporation

Objectives

You will have mastered the material in this chapter when you can:

- Create queries using Design view
- Include fields in the design grid
- Use text and numeric data in criteria
- Save a query and use the saved query
- Create and use parameter queries
- Use compound criteria in queries
- Sort data in queries

- Join tables in queries
- Create a report and a form from a query
- Export data from a query to another application
- Perform calculations and calculate statistics in queries
- Create crosstab queries
- Customize the Navigation Pane

2 | Querying a Database

Introduction

BTW

Select Queries
The queries you create in this chapter are select queries. In a select query, you retrieve data from one or more tables using criteria that you specify and display the data in a datasheet.

One of the primary benefits of using a database management system such as Access is having the ability to find answers to questions related to data stored in the database. When you pose a question to Access, or any other database management system, the question is called a query. A **query** is simply a question presented in a way that Access can process.

To find the answer to a question, you first create a corresponding query using the techniques illustrated in this chapter. After you have created the query, you instruct Access to run the query, that is, to perform the steps necessary to obtain the answer. Access then displays the answer in Datasheet view.

BTW

BTWs
For a complete list of the BTWs found in the margins of this book, visit the BTW resource on the Student Companion Site located on www.cengagebrain.com. For detailed instructions about accessing available resources, visit www.cengage.com/ct/studentdownload or contact your instructor for information about accessing the required files.

Project — Querying a Database

One of the most important benefits of using Access to manage a database is easily finding the answers to questions and requests. Figure 2–1 presents examples of such queries, which concern the data in the Bavant Publishing database.

In addition to these questions, Bavant Publishing managers need to find information about customers located in a specific city, but they want to enter a different city each time they ask the question. The company can use a parameter query to accomplish this task. Bavant Publishing managers also want to summarize data in a specific way, which might involve performing calculations, and they can use a crosstab query to present the data in the desired form.

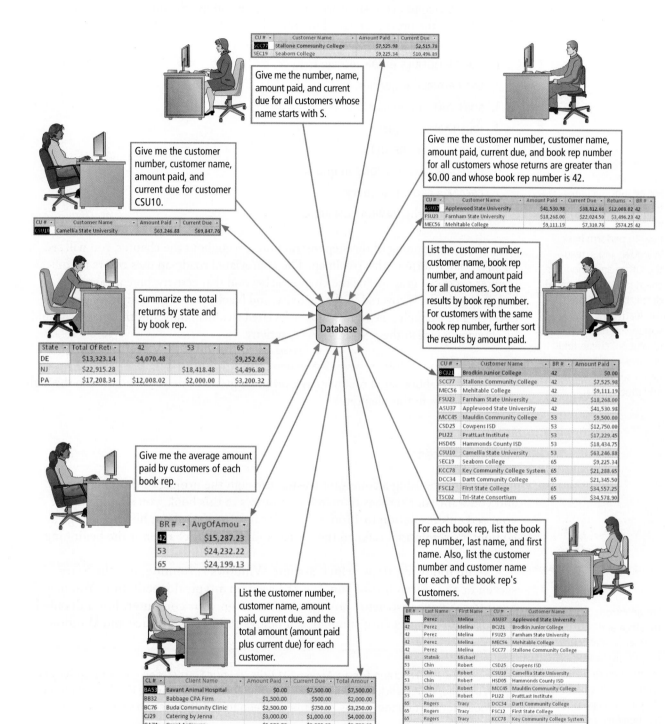

Figure 2–1

Roadmap

In this chapter, you will learn how to create and use the queries shown in Figure 2–1 on the previous page. The following roadmap identifies general activities you will perform as you progress through this chapter:

1. CREATE QUERIES in Design view.
2. USE CRITERIA in queries.
3. SORT DATA in queries.
4. JOIN TABLES in queries.
5. EXPORT query RESULTS.
6. PERFORM CALCULATIONS in queries.
7. CREATE a CROSSTAB query.
8. CUSTOMIZE the NAVIGATION PANE.

For an introduction to Windows and instruction about how to perform basic Windows tasks, read the Office and Windows chapter at the beginning of this book, where you can learn how to resize windows, change screen resolution, create folders, move and rename files, use Windows Help, and much more.

At the beginning of the step instructions throughout the chapter, you will see an abbreviated form of this roadmap. The abbreviated roadmap uses colors to indicate chapter progress: gray means the chapter is beyond that activity, blue means the task being shown is covered in that activity, and black means that activity is yet to be covered. For example, the following abbreviated roadmap indicates the chapter would be showing a task in the 3 SORT DATA activity.

1 CREATE QUERIES | 2 USE CRITERIA | 3 SORT DATA | 4 JOIN TABLES | 5 EXPORT RESULTS
6 PERFORM CALCULATIONS | 7 CREATE CROSSTAB | 8 CUSTOMIZE NAVIGATION PANE

Use the abbreviated roadmap as a progress guide while you read or step through the instructions in this chapter.

To Run Access

If you are using a computer to step through the project in this chapter and you want your screens to match the figures in this book, you should change your screen's resolution to 1366 × 768. For information about how to change a computer's resolution, refer to the Office and Windows chapter at the beginning of this book.

The following steps, which assume Windows is running, use the Start screen or the search box to run Access based on a typical installation. You may need to ask your instructor how to run Access on your computer. For a detailed example of the procedure summarized below, refer to the Office and Windows chapter.

For an introduction to Office and instruction about how to perform basic tasks in Office programs, read the Office and Windows chapter at the beginning of this book, where you can learn how to run an app, use the ribbon, save a file, open a file, exit an app, use Help, and much more.

1 Scroll the Start screen for an Access 2013 tile. If your Start screen contains an Access 2013 tile, tap or click it to run Access and then proceed to Step 5; if the Start screen does not contain the Access 2013 tile, proceed to the next step to search for the Access app.

2 Swipe in from the right edge of the screen or point to the upper-right corner of the screen to display the Charms bar, and then tap or click the Search charm on the Charms bar to display the Search menu.

3 Type `Access` as the search text in the Search text box and watch the search results appear in the Apps list.

4 Tap or click Access 2013 in the search results to run Access.

5 If the Access window is not maximized, tap or click the Maximize button on its title bar to maximize the window.

To Open a Database from Access

In the previous chapter, you created the Bavant Publishing database in an appropriate storage location. The following steps open the database from the location you specified when you first created it (for example, the Access folder in the CIS 101 folder). For a detailed example of the procedure summarized below, refer to the Office and Windows chapter at the beginning of this book.

1 Tap or click FILE on the ribbon to open the Backstage view, if necessary.

2 If the database you want to open is displayed in the Recent list, tap or click the file name to open the database and display the opened database in the Access window; then skip to Step 7. If the database you want to open is not displayed in the Recent list or if the Recent list does not appear, tap or click 'Open Other Files' to display the Open Gallery.

3 If the database you want to open is displayed in the Recent list in the Open gallery, tap or click the file name to open the database and display the opened database in the Access window; then skip to Step 7.

4 Tap or click Computer, SkyDrive, or another location in the left pane and then navigate to the location of the database to be opened (for example, the Access folder in the CIS 101 folder).

5 Tap or click Bavant Publishing to select the database to be opened.

6 Tap or click the Open button (Open dialog box) to open the selected file and display the opened database in the Access window.

7 If a Security Warning appears, tap or click the Enable Content button.

One of the few differences between Windows 7 and Windows 8 occurs in the steps to run Access. If you are using Windows 7, click the Start button, type `Access` in the 'Search programs and files' box, click Access 2013, and then, if necessary, maximize the Access window. For detailed steps to run Access in Windows 7, refer to the Office and Windows chapter at the beginning of this book. For a summary of the steps, refer to the Quick Reference located at the back of this book.

Creating Queries

As you learned in Chapter 1, you can use queries in Access to find answers to questions about the data contained in the database. *Note:* In this chapter, you will save each query example. When you use a query for another task, such as to create a form or report, you will assign a specific name to a query, for example, Rep-Customer Query. In situations in which you will not use the query again, you will assign a name using a convention that includes the chapter number and a query number, for example, Ch2q01. Queries are numbered consecutively.

To Create a Query in Design View

In Chapter 1, you used the Simple Query Wizard to create a query. Most of the time, however, you will use Design view, which is the primary option for creating queries. *Why? Once you have created a new query in Design view, you have more options than with the wizard and can specify fields, criteria, sorting, calculations, and so on.* The following steps create a new query in Design view.

- Tap or click the 'Shutter Bar Open/Close Button' to close the Navigation Pane.

- Tap or click CREATE on the ribbon to display the CREATE tab (Figure 2–2).

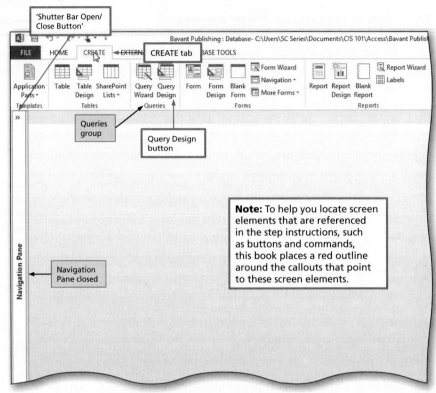

Figure 2–2

- Tap or click the Query Design button (CREATE tab | Queries group) to create a new query (Figure 2–3).

Q&A
Is it necessary to close the Navigation Pane?
No. Closing the pane gives you more room for the query, however, so it is usually a good practice.

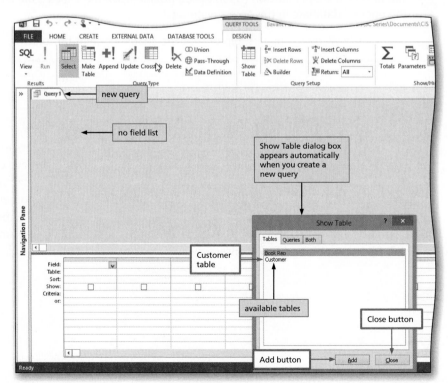

Figure 2–3

3

- Tap or click the Customer table (Show Table dialog box) to select the table.

- Tap or click the Add button to add the selected table to the query.

- Tap or click the Close button to remove the dialog box from the screen.

Q&A What if I inadvertently add the wrong table? Press and hold or right-click the table that you added in error and tap or click Remove Table on the shortcut menu. You also can just close the query, indicate that you do not want to save it, and then start over.

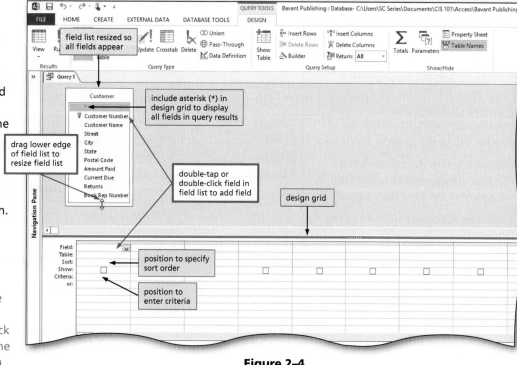

Figure 2–4

- Drag the lower edge of the field list down far enough so all fields in the table appear (Figure 2–4).

Q&A Is it essential that I resize the field list?
No. You can always scroll through the list of fields using the scroll bar. Resizing the field list so that all fields appear is usually more convenient.

To Add Fields to the Design Grid

1 CREATE QUERIES | 2 USE CRITERIA | 3 SORT DATA | 4 JOIN TABLES | 5 EXPORT RESULTS
6 PERFORM CALCULATIONS | 7 CREATE CROSSTAB | 8 CUSTOMIZE NAVIGATION PANE

Once you have a new query displayed in Design view, you are ready to make entries in the **design grid**, the portion of the window where you specify fields and criteria for the query. The design grid is located in the lower pane of the window. You add the fields you want included in the query to the Field row in the grid. *Why add fields to the grid? Only the fields that appear in the design grid will be included in the query results.* The following step begins creating a query that Bavant Publishing might use to obtain the customer number, customer name, amount paid, and current due for a particular customer.

1

- Double-tap or double-click the Customer Number field in the field list to add the field to the query.

Q&A What if I add the wrong field?
Tap or click just above the field name in the design grid to select the column and then press the DELETE key to remove the field.

- Double-tap or double-click the Customer Name field in the field list to add the field to the query.

- Add the Amount Paid field to the query.

- Add the Current Due field to the query (Figure 2–5).

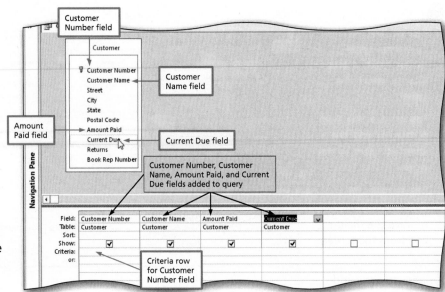

Figure 2–5

Q&A What if I want to include all fields?
Do I have to add each field individually?
No. Instead of adding individual fields, you can double-tap or double-click the asterisk (*) to add the asterisk to the design grid. The asterisk is a shortcut indicating all fields are to be included.

Determining Criteria

When you use queries, usually you are looking for those records that satisfy some criterion. In the simple query you created in the previous chapter, for example, you entered a criterion to restrict the records to those with the book rep number 53. In another query, you might want the name, amount paid, and current due amounts for the customer whose number is CSU10, for example, or for those customers whose names start with the letters, Gr. You enter criteria in the Criteria row in the design grid below the field name to which the criterion applies. For example, to indicate that the customer number must be CSU10, you first must add the Customer Number field to the design grid. You then would type CSU10 in the Criteria row below the Customer Number field.

Running the Query

After adding the appropriate fields and defining the query's criteria, you must run the query to get the results. To view the results of the query from Design view, tap or click the Run button to instruct Access to run the query, that is, to perform the necessary actions to produce and display the results in Datasheet view.

To Use Text Data in a Criterion

To use **text data** (data in a field whose data type is Short Text) in criteria, simply type the text in the Criteria row below the corresponding field name, just as you did in Chapter 1. In Access, you do not need to enclose text data in quotation marks as you do in many other database management systems. *Why? Access will enter the quotation marks automatically, so you can simply type the desired text.* The following steps finish creating a query that Bavant Publishing might use to obtain the customer number, customer name, amount paid, and current due amount of customer CSU10. These steps add the appropriate criterion so that only the desired customer will appear in the results. The steps also save the query.

1

- Tap or click the Criteria row for the Customer Number field to produce an insertion point.

- Type CSU10 as the criterion (Figure 2–6).

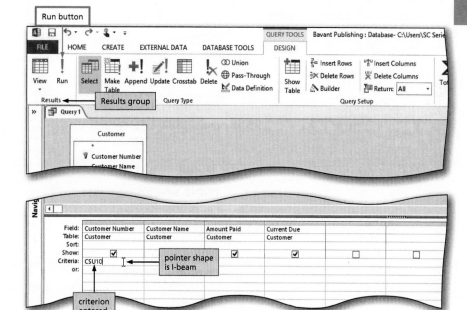

Figure 2–6

2

- Tap or click the Run button (QUERY TOOLS DESIGN tab | Results group) to run the query (Figure 2–7).

Q&A Can I also use the View button in the Results group to run the query?
Yes. You can tap or click the View button to view the query results in Datasheet view.

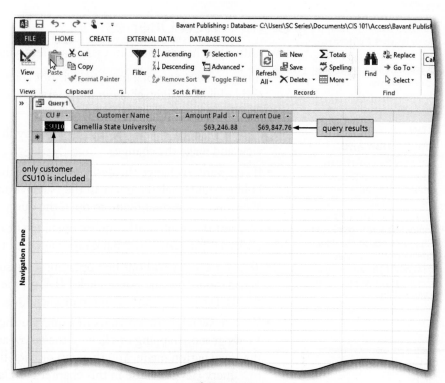

Figure 2–7

3

• Tap or click the Save button on the Quick Access Toolbar to display the Save As dialog box.

• Type `Ch2q01` as the name of the query (Figure 2–8).

Q&A

Can I also save from Design view? Yes. You can save the query when you view it in Design view just as you can save it when you view query results in Datasheet view.

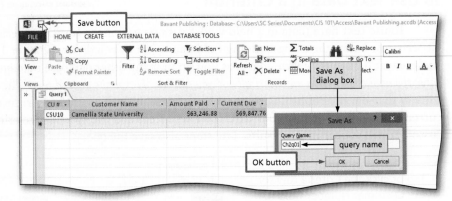

Figure 2–8

4

• Tap or click the OK button (Save As dialog box) to save the query (Figure 2–9).

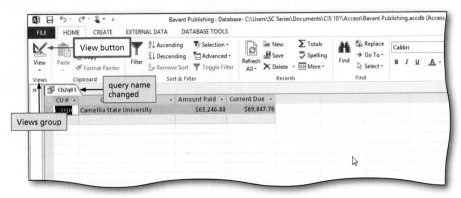

Figure 2–9

Other Ways

1. Press and hold or right-click query tab, tap or click Save on shortcut menu   2. Press CTRL + S

Using Saved Queries

After you have created and saved a query, you can use it in a variety of ways:

• To view the results of a query that is not currently open, open it by pressing and holding or right-clicking the query in the Navigation Pane and tapping or clicking Open on the shortcut menu.

• If you want to change the design of a query that is already open, return to Design view and make the changes.

• If you want to change the design of a query that is not currently open, press and hold or right-click the query in the Navigation Pane and then tap or click Design View on the shortcut menu to open the query in Design view.

• To print the results with a query open, tap or click FILE on the ribbon, tap or click the Print tab in the Backstage view, and then tap or click Quick Print.

• To print a query without first opening it, be sure the query is selected in the Navigation Pane and tap or click FILE on the ribbon, tap or click the Print tab in the Backstage view, and then tap or click Quick Print.

• You can switch between views of a query using the View button (HOME tab | Views group). Tapping or clicking the arrow at the bottom of the button produces the View button menu. You then tap or click the desired view in the menu. The two query views you use in this chapter are Datasheet view (to see the results) and Design view (to change the design). You can tap or click the top part of the

View button, in which case you will switch to the view identified by the icon on the button. In Figure 2–9, the View button displays the icon for Design view, so tapping or clicking the button would change to Design view. For the most part, the icon on the button represents the view you want, so you can usually simply tap or click the button.

BTW
On Screen Keyboard
To display the on-screen touch keyboard, tap the Touch Keyboard button on the Windows taskbar. When finished using the touch keyboard, tap the X button on the touch keyboard to close the keyboard

Wildcards

Microsoft Access supports wildcards. **Wildcards** are symbols that represent any character or combination of characters. One common wildcard, the **asterisk (*)**, represents any collection of characters. Another wildcard symbol is the **question mark (?)**, which represents any individual character.

What does S* represent? What does T?m represent?
S* represents the letter, S, followed by any collection of characters. T?m represents the letter, T, followed by any single character, followed by the letter, m. A search for T?m might return the names Tim or Tom.

CONSIDER THIS

To Use a Wildcard

1 CREATE QUERIES | 2 USE CRITERIA | 3 SORT DATA | 4 JOIN TABLES | 5 EXPORT RESULTS
6 PERFORM CALCULATIONS | 7 CREATE CROSSTAB | 8 CUSTOMIZE NAVIGATION PANE

The following steps modify the previous query to use the asterisk wildcard so that Bavant Publishing can select only those customers whose names begin with S. *Why? Because you do not know how many characters will follow the S, the asterisk wildcard symbol is appropriate.* The steps also save the query with a new name using the Save As command.

- Tap or click the View button (HOME tab | Views group), shown in Figure 2–9 on page AC 82, to return to Design view.

- If necessary, tap or click the Criteria row below the Customer Number field to produce an insertion point.

Q&A The text I entered now has quotation marks surrounding it. What happened?
Criteria for text data needs to be enclosed in quotation marks. You do not have to type the quotation marks; Access adds them automatically.

- Use the DELETE or BACKSPACE key as necessary to delete the current entry.

- Tap or click the Criteria row below the Customer Name field to produce an insertion point.

- Type S* as the criterion (Figure 2–10).

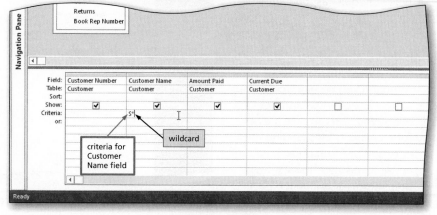
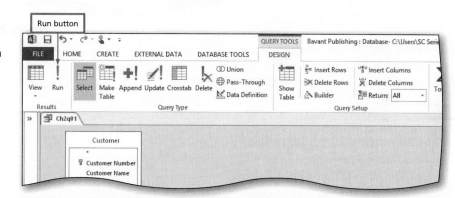

Figure 2–10

2

- Run the query by tapping or clicking the Run button (QUERY TOOLS DESIGN tab | Results group) (Figure 2–11).

🔍 **Experiment**

- Change the letter S to lowercase in the criteria and run the query to determine whether case makes a difference when entering a wildcard.

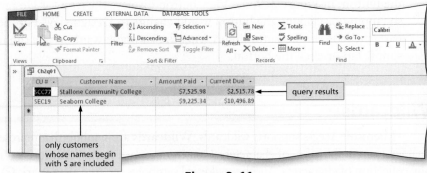

Figure 2–11

3

- Tap or click FILE on the ribbon to open the Backstage view.

- Tap or click the Save As tab in the Backstage view to display the Save As gallery.

- Tap or click Save Object As in the File Types area (Figure 2–12).

Q&A Can I just tap or click the Save button on the Quick Access Toolbar as I did when saving the previous query?
If you tapped or clicked the Save button, you would replace the previous query with the version you just created. Because you want to save both the previous query and the new one, you need to save the new version with a different name. To do so, you must use Save Object As, which is available through the Backstage view.

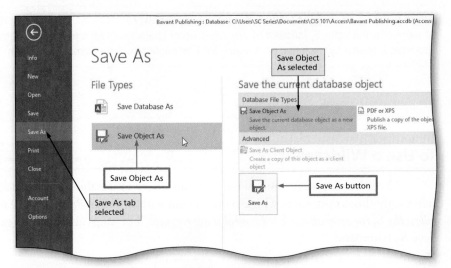

Figure 2–12

4

- With Save Object As selected in the File Types gallery, tap or click the Save As button to display the Save As dialog box.

- Type `Ch2q02` as the name for the saved query (Figure 2–13).

Q&A The current entry in the As text box is Query. Could I save the query as some other type of object?
Although you usually would want to save the query as another query, you also can save it as a form or report by changing the entry in the As text box. If you do, Access would create either a simple form or a simple report for the query.

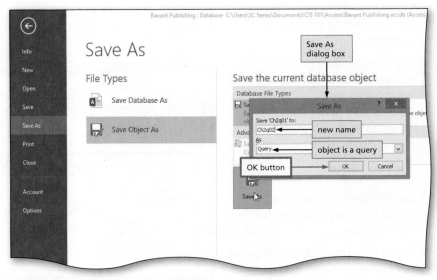

Figure 2–13

5

- Tap or click the OK button (Save As dialog box) to save the query with the new name and close the Backstage view (Figure 2–14).

Q&A How can I tell that the query was saved with the new name?
The new name will appear on the tab.

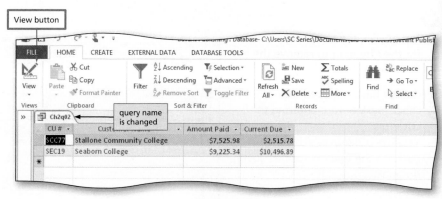

Figure 2–14

Other Ways

1. Tap or click Design View button on status bar

To Use Criteria for a Field Not Included in the Results

1 CREATE QUERIES | 2 USE CRITERIA | 3 SORT DATA | 4 JOIN TABLES | 5 EXPORT RESULTS
6 PERFORM CALCULATIONS | 7 CREATE CROSSTAB | 8 CUSTOMIZE NAVIGATION PANE

In some cases, you might require criteria for a particular field that should not appear in the results of the query. For example, you may want to see the customer number, customer name, address, and amount paid for all customers located in Gaston. The criteria involve the City field, but you do not want to include the City field in the results.

To enter a criterion for the City field, it must be included in the design grid. Normally, it would then appear in the results. To prevent this from happening, remove the check mark from its Show check box in the Show row of the grid. *Why? A check mark in the Show Check box instructs Access to show the field in the result. If you remove the check mark, you can use the field in the query but not display it in the query results.*

The following steps modify the previous query so that Bavant Publishing can select only those customers located in Gaston. Bavant does not want the city to appear in the results, however. The steps also save the query with a new name.

1

- Tap or click the View button (HOME tab | Views group), shown in Figure 2–14, to return to Design view.

Q&A The text I entered is now preceded by the word, Like. What happened?
Criteria including wildcards need to be preceded by the word, Like. However, you do not have to type it; Access adds the word automatically to any criterion involving a wildcard.

- Erase the criterion in the Criteria row of the Customer Name field.

- Add the City field to the query.

- Type Gaston as the criterion for the City field (Figure 2–15).

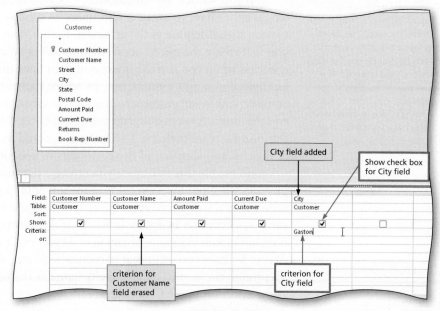

Figure 2–15

2

- Tap or click the Show check box for the City field to remove the check mark (Figure 2–16).

Q&A

Could I have removed the check mark before entering the criterion?
Yes. The order in which you perform the two operations does not matter.

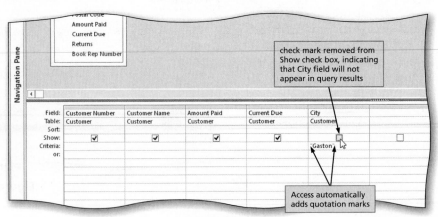

Figure 2–16

3

- Run the query (Figure 2–17).

🔍 **Experiment**

- Tap or click the View button to return to Design view, enter a different city name as the criterion, and run the query. Repeat this process with additional city names, including at least one city name that is not in the database. When finished, change the criterion back to Gaston.

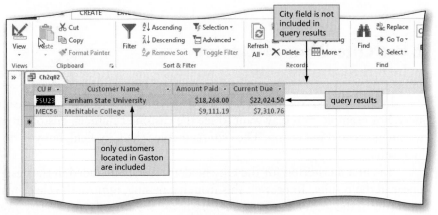

Figure 2–17

BTW

Designing Queries
Before creating queries, examine the contents of the tables involved. You need to know the data type for each field and how the data for the field is stored. If a query includes a state, for example, you need to know whether state is stored as the two-character abbreviation or as the full state name.

Creating a Parameter Query

If you wanted to find customers located in Adelphia instead of Gaston, you would either have to create a new query or modify the existing query by replacing Gaston with Adelphia as the criterion. Rather than giving a specific criterion when you first create the query, occasionally you may want to be able to enter part of the criterion when you run the query and then have the appropriate results appear. For example, you might want a query to return the customer number, customer name, and amount paid for all customers in a specific city, specifying a different city each time you run the query. A user could run the query, enter Adelphia as the city, and then see all the customers in Adelphia. Later, the user could use the same query but enter Gaston as the city, and then see all the customers in Gaston.

To enable this flexibility, you create a **parameter query**, which is a query that prompts for input whenever it is used. You enter a parameter (the prompt for the user), rather than a specific value as the criterion. You create the parameter by enclosing a value in a criterion in square brackets. It is important that the value in the brackets does not match the name of any field. If you enter a field name in square brackets, Access assumes you want that particular field and does not prompt the user for input. To prompt the user to enter the city name as the input, you could place [Enter City] as the criterion in the City field.

To Create and View a Parameter Query

The following steps create a parameter query. ***Why?*** *The parameter query will give users at Bavant the ability to enter a different city when they run the query rather than having a specific city as part of the criterion in the query. The steps also save the query with a new name.*

1

- Return to Design view.

- Erase the current criterion in the City column, and then type [Enter City] as the new criterion (Figure 2–18).

Q&A

What is the purpose of the square brackets?

The square brackets indicate that the text entered is not text that the value in the column must match. Without the brackets, Access would search for records on which the city is Enter City.

What if I typed a field name in the square brackets?

Access would simply use the value in that field. To create a parameter query, you must not use a field name in the square brackets.

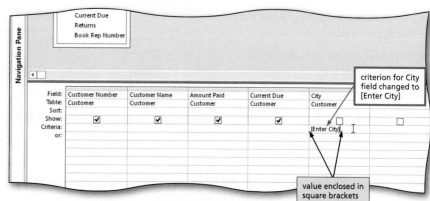

Figure 2–18

2

- Tap or click the Run button (QUERY TOOLS DESIGN tab | Results group) to display the Enter Parameter Value dialog box (Figure 2–19).

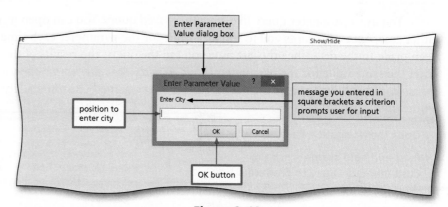

Figure 2–19

3

- Type Adelphia as the parameter value in the Enter City text box, and then tap or click the OK button (Enter Parameter Value dialog box) to close the dialog box and view the query (Figure 2–20).

Experiment

- Try using other characters between the square brackets. In each case, run the query. When finished, change the characters between the square brackets back to Enter City.

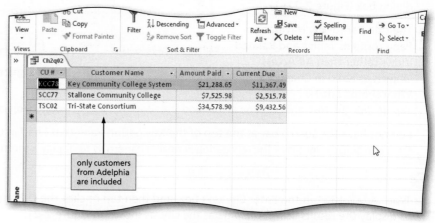

Figure 2–20

- Tap or click FILE on the ribbon to open the Backstage view.

- Tap or click the Save As tab in the Backstage view to display the Save As gallery.

- Tap or click Save Object As in the File Types area.

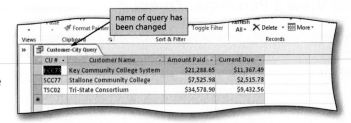

Figure 2–21

- With Save Object As selected in the File Types area, click the Save As button to display the Save As dialog box.

- Type `Customer-City Query` as the name for the saved query.

- Tap or click the OK button (Save As dialog box) to save the query with the new name and close the Backstage view (Figure 2–21).

- Tap or click the Close button for the Customer-City query to close the query.

Break Point: If you wish to take a break, this is a good place to do so. You can exit Access now. To resume later, run Access, open the database called Bavant Publishing, and continue following the steps from this location forward.

To Use a Parameter Query

1 CREATE QUERIES | 2 USE CRITERIA | 3 SORT DATA | 4 JOIN TABLES | 5 EXPORT RESULTS
6 PERFORM CALCULATIONS | 7 CREATE CROSSTAB | 8 CUSTOMIZE NAVIGATION PANE

You use a parameter query like any other saved query. You can open it or you can print the query results. In either case, Access prompts you to supply a value for the parameter each time you use the query. If changes have been made to the data since the last time you ran the query, the results of the query may be different, even if you enter the same value for the parameter. *Why? As with other queries, the query always uses the data that is currently in the table.* The following steps use the parameter query named Customer-City Query.

- Open the Navigation Pane.

- Press and hold or right-click the Customer-City Query to produce a shortcut menu.

- Tap or click Open on the shortcut menu to open the query and display the Enter Parameter Value dialog box (Figure 2–22).

Q&A The title bar for my Navigation Pane contains Tables and Related Views rather than All Access Objects as it did in Chapter 1. What should I do?
Tap or click the Navigation Pane arrow and then tap or click All Access Objects.

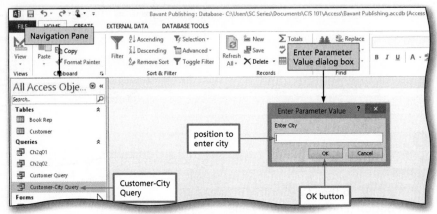

Figure 2–22

I do not have the Search bar at the top of the Navigation Pane that I had in Chapter 1. What should I do?
Press and hold or right-click the Navigation Pane title bar arrow to display a shortcut menu, and then tap or click Search Bar.

- Type `Adelphia` in the Enter City text box, and then tap or click the OK button (Enter Parameter Value dialog box) to display the results using Adelphia as the city, as shown in Figure 2–21.

- Close the query.

To Use a Number in a Criterion

To enter a number in a criterion, type the number without any dollar signs or commas. *Why? If you enter a dollar sign, Access assumes you are entering text. If you enter a comma, Access considers the criterion invalid.* The following steps create a query that Bavant Publishing might use to display all customers whose current due amount is $0. The steps also save the query with a new name.

- Close the Navigation Pane.

- Tap or click CREATE on the ribbon to display the CREATE tab.

- Tap or click the Query Design button (CREATE tab | Queries group) to create a new query.

- Tap or click the Customer table (Show Table dialog box) to select the table.

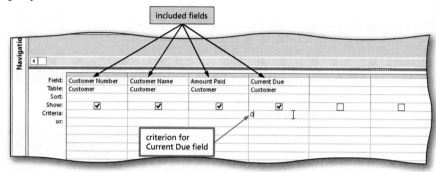

Figure 2–23

- Tap or click the Add button to add the selected table to the query.

- Tap or click the Close button to remove the dialog box from the screen.

- Drag the lower edge of the field list down far enough so all fields in the list are displayed.

- Include the Customer Number, Customer Name, Amount Paid, and Current Due fields in the query.

- Type 0 as the criterion for the Current Due field (Figure 2–23).

Q&A Do I need to enter a dollar sign and decimal point?
No. Access will interpret 0 as $0 because the data type for the Current Due field is currency.

- Run the query (Figure 2–24).

Q&A Why did Access display the results as $0.00 when I only entered 0? Access uses the format for the field to determine how to display the result. In this case, the format indicated that Access should include the dollar sign, decimal point, and two decimal places.

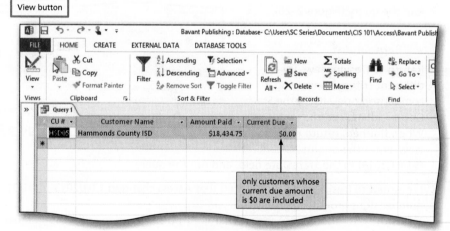

Figure 2–24

- Save the query as Ch2q03.

Q&A How do I know when to use the Save button to save a query or use the Backstage view to perform a Save As?
If you are saving a new query, the simplest way is to use the Save button on the Quick Access Toolbar. If you are saving changes to a previously saved query but do not want to change the name, use the Save button. If you want to save a previously saved query with a new name, you must use the Backstage view and perform a Save Object As.

- Close the query.

Comparison Operators

Unless you specify otherwise, Access assumes that the criteria you enter involve equality (exact matches). In the last query, for example, you were requesting those customers whose current due amount is equal to 0 (zero). In other situations, you might want to find a range of results; for example, you could request customers whose current due is greater than $1,000.00. If you want a query to return something other than an exact match, you must enter the appropriate **comparison operator**. The comparison operators are > (greater than), < (less than), >= (greater than or equal to), <= (less than or equal to), and NOT (not equal to).

To Use a Comparison Operator in a Criterion

1 CREATE QUERIES | 2 USE CRITERIA | 3 SORT DATA | 4 JOIN TABLES | 5 EXPORT RESULTS
6 PERFORM CALCULATIONS | 7 CREATE CROSSTAB | 8 CUSTOMIZE NAVIGATION PANE

The following steps use the > operator to create a query that Bavant Publishing might use to find all book reps whose start date is after 1/1/2013. *Why? A date greater than 1/1/2013 means the date comes after 1/1/2013.* The steps also save the query with a new name.

1

- Start a new query using the Book Rep table.

- Include the Book Rep Number, Last Name, First Name, and Start Date fields.

- Type >1/01/2013 as the criterion for the Start Date field (Figure 2–25).

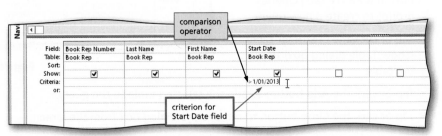

Figure 2–25

 Did I have to type the leading zero in the Day portion of the date?
No. You could have typed 1/1/2013. Some people often type the day using two digits, such as 1/01/2013. You also could have typed a leading zero in the month, 01/01/2013.

2

- Run the query (Figure 2–26).

Experiment

- Return to Design view. Try a different criterion involving a comparison operator in the Start Date field and run the query. When finished, return to Design view, enter the original criterion (>1/01/2013) in the Start Date field, and run the query.

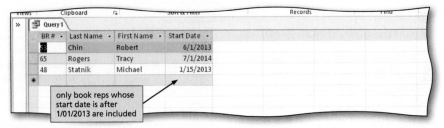

Figure 2–26

I returned to Design view and noticed that Access changed 1/01/2013 to #1/01/2013#. Why does the date now have number signs around it?
This is the date format in Access. You usually do not have to enter the number signs because in most cases Access will insert them automatically.

My records are in a different order. Is this a problem?
No. The important thing is which records are included in the results. You will see later in this chapter how you can specify the specific order you want for cases when the order is important.

Can I use the same comparison operators with text data?
Yes. Comparison operators function the same whether you use them with number fields, currency fields, date fields, or text fields.

3

- Save the query as Ch2q04.

- Close the query.

Using Compound Criteria

Often your search data must satisfy more than one criterion. This type of criterion is called a **compound criterion** and is created using the words AND or OR.

In an **AND criterion**, each individual criterion must be true in order for the compound criterion to be true. For example, an AND criterion would allow you to find customers that have returns greater than $0.00 and whose book rep is book rep 42.

An **OR criterion** is true if either individual criterion is true. An OR criterion would allow you to find customers that have returns greater than $0.00 as well as customers whose book rep is book rep 42. In this case, any customer who has returns greater than $0.00 would be included in the answer, regardless of whether the customer's book rep is book rep 42. Likewise, any customer whose book rep is book rep 42 would be included, regardless of whether the customer has returns greater than $0.00.

BTW

Queries: Query-by-Example
Query-By-Example, often referred to as QBE, was a query language first proposed in the mid-1970s. In this approach, users asked questions by filling in a table on the screen. The Access approach to queries is based on Query-By-Example.

To Use a Compound Criterion Involving AND

1 CREATE QUERIES | 2 USE CRITERIA | 3 SORT DATA | 4 JOIN TABLES | 5 EXPORT RESULTS
6 PERFORM CALCULATIONS | 7 CREATE CROSSTAB | 8 CUSTOMIZE NAVIGATION PANE

To combine criteria with AND, place the criteria on the same row of the design grid. *Why? Placing the criteria in the same row indicates that both criteria must be true in Access.* The following steps use an AND criterion to enable Bavant to find those customers who have returns greater than $0.00 and whose book rep is rep 42. The steps also save the query.

1

- Start a new query using the Customer table.

- Include the Customer Number, Customer Name, Amount Paid, Current Due, Returns, and Book Rep Number fields.

- Type >0 as the criterion for the Returns field.

- Type 42 as the criterion for the Book Rep Number field (Figure 2–27).

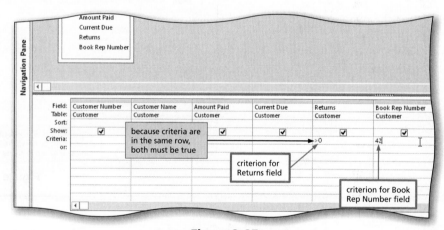

Figure 2–27

2

- Run the query (Figure 2–28).

3

- Save the query as Ch2q05.

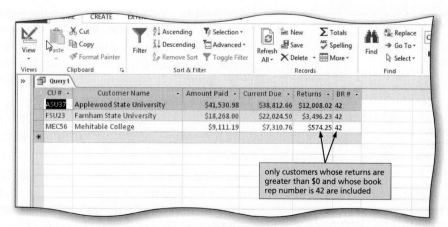

Figure 2–28

To Use a Compound Criterion Involving OR

To combine criteria with OR, each criterion must go on separate rows in the Criteria area of the grid. *Why? Placing criteria on separate rows indicates at least one criterion must be true in Access.* The following steps use an OR criterion to enable Bavant to find those customers who have returns greater than $0.00 or whose book rep is rep 42 (or both). The steps also save the query with a new name.

- Return to Design view.

- If necessary, tap or click the Criteria entry for the Book Rep Number field and then use the BACKSPACE key or the DELETE key to erase the entry ("42").

- Tap or click the or row (the row below the Criteria row) for the Book Rep Number field, and then type 42 as the entry (Figure 2–29).

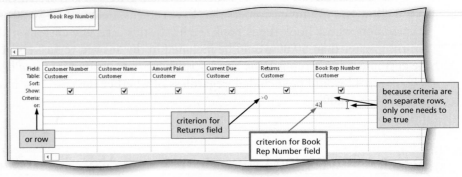

Figure 2–29

- Run the query (Figure 2–30).

- Save the query as Ch2q06.

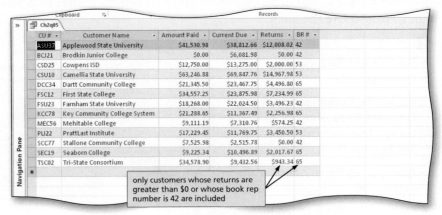

Figure 2–30

BTW

Rearranging Fields in a Query

To move a field in the design grid, tap or click the column selector for the field to select the field and drag it to the appropriate location.

BTW

Q&As

For a complete list of the Q&As found in many of the step-by-step sequences in this book, visit the Q&A resource on the Student Companion Site located on www.cengagebrain.com. For detailed instructions about accessing available resources, visit www.cengage.com/ct/studentdownload or contact your instructor for information about accessing the required files.

Special Criteria

You can use three special criteria in queries:

1. If you want to create a criterion involving a range of values in a single field, you can use the **AND operator**. You place the word AND between the individual conditions. For example, if you wanted to find all customers whose amount paid is greater than or equal to $20,000.00 and less than or equal to $40,000.00, you would enter >= 20000 AND <= 40000 as the criterion in the Amount Paid column.

2. You can select values in a given range by using the **BETWEEN operator**. This is often an alternative to the AND operator. For example, to find all customers whose amount paid is between $20,000.00 and $40,000.00, inclusive, you would enter BETWEEN 20000 AND 40000 as the criterion in the Amount Paid column.

3. You can select a list of values by using the **IN operator**. You follow the word IN with the list of values in parentheses. For example, to find customers whose book rep number is 42 and customers whose book rep is 65 using the IN operator, you would enter IN ("42","65") on the Criteria row in the Book Rep Number column. Unlike when you enter a simple criterion, you must enclose text values in quotation marks.

How would you find customers whose book rep number is 42 or 65 without using the IN operator?
Place the number 42 in the Criteria row of the Book Rep Number column. Place the number 65 in the or row of the Book Rep Number column.

Sorting

In some queries, the order in which the records appear is irrelevant. All you need to be concerned about are the records that appear in the results. It does not matter which one is first or which one is last.

In other queries, however, the order can be very important. You may want to see the cities in which customers are located and would like them arranged alphabetically. Perhaps you want to see the customers listed by book rep number. Further, within all the customers of any given book rep, you might want them to be listed by amount paid from largest amount to smallest.

To order the records in a query result in a particular way, you **sort** the records. The field or fields on which the records are sorted is called the **sort key**. If you are sorting on more than one field (such as sorting by amount paid within book rep number), the more important field (Book Rep Number) is called the **major key** (also called the **primary sort key**) and the less important field (Amount Paid) is called the **minor key** (also called the **secondary sort key**).

To sort in Microsoft Access, specify the sort order in the Sort row of the design grid below the field that is the sort key. If you specify more than one sort key, the sort key on the left will be the major sort key, and the one on the right will be the minor key.

BTW

Sorting Data in a Query
When sorting data in a query, the records in the underlying tables (the tables on which the query is based) are not actually rearranged. Instead, the DBMS determines the most efficient method of simply displaying the records in the requested order. The records in the underlying tables remain in their original order.

BTW

Clearing the Design Grid
You also can clear the design grid using the ribbon. To do so, tap or click the HOME tab, tap or click the Advanced button to display the Advanced menu, and then tap or click Clear Grid on the Advanced menu.

To Clear the Design Grid

1 CREATE QUERIES | 2 USE CRITERIA | 3 SORT DATA | 4 JOIN TABLES | 5 EXPORT RESULTS
6 PERFORM CALCULATIONS | 7 CREATE CROSSTAB | 8 CUSTOMIZE NAVIGATION PANE

Why? If the fields you want to include in the next query are different from those in the previous query, it is usually simpler to start with a clear grid, that is, one with no fields already in the design grid. You always can clear the entries in the design grid by closing the query and then starting over. A simpler approach to clearing the entries is to select all the entries and then press the DELETE key. The following steps return to Design view and clear the design grid.

- Return to Design view.

- Tap or click just above the Customer Number column heading in the grid to select the column.

Q&A
I clicked above the column heading, but the column is not selected. What should I do?
You did not point to the correct location. Be sure the pointer changes into a down-pointing arrow and then tap or click again.

- Hold the SHIFT key down and tap or click just above the Book Rep Number column heading to select all the columns (Figure 2–31).

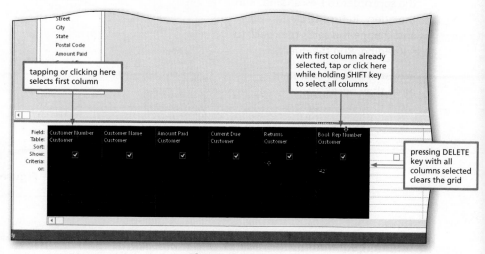

Figure 2–31

- Press the DELETE key to clear the design grid.

To Sort Data in a Query

If you determine that the query results should be sorted, you will need to specify the sort key. The following steps sort the cities in the Customer table by indicating that the City field is to be sorted. The steps specify Ascending sort order. **Why?** *When sorting text data, Ascending sort order arranges the results in alphabetical order.*

①

- Include the City field in the design grid.
- Tap or click the Sort row below the City field, and then tap or click the Sort arrow to display a menu of possible sort orders (Figure 2–32).

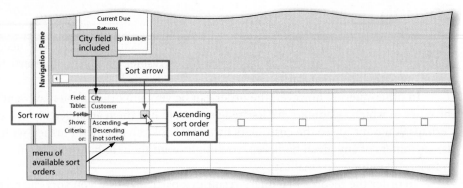

Figure 2–32

②

- Tap or click Ascending to select the sort order (Figure 2–33).

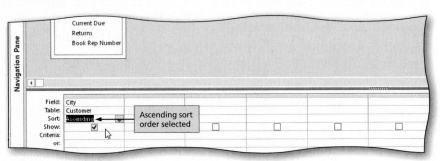

Figure 2–33

③

- Run the query (Figure 2–34).

 Experiment

- Return to Design view and change the sort order to Descending. Run the query. Return to Design view and change the sort order back to Ascending. Run the query.

Q&A | Why do some cities appear more than once?
More than one customer is located in those cities.

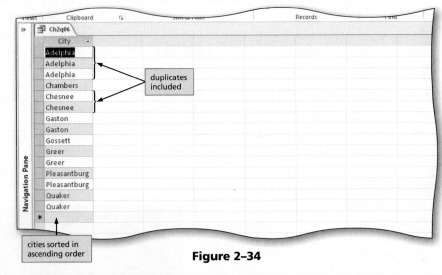

Figure 2–34

To Omit Duplicates

When you sort data, duplicates normally are included. In the query shown in Figure 2–34, for example, Adelphia appears three times. Several other cities appear twice. You eliminate duplicates using the query's property sheet. A **property sheet** is a window containing the various properties of the object. To omit duplicates, you will use the property sheet to change the Unique Values property from No to Yes.

The following steps create a query that Bavant Publishing might use to obtain a sorted list of the cities in the Customer table in which each city is listed only once. *Why? Unless you wanted to know how many customers were located in each city, the duplicates typically do not add any value.* The steps also save the query with a new name.

1

- Return to Design view.

- Tap or click the second field (the empty field to the right of City) in the design grid to produce an insertion point.

- If necessary, tap or click DESIGN on the ribbon to display the DESIGN tab.

- Tap or click the Property Sheet button (QUERY TOOLS DESIGN tab | Show/Hide group) to display the property sheet (Figure 2–35).

Q&A | My property sheet looks different. What should I do?
If your sheet looks different, close the property sheet and repeat this step.

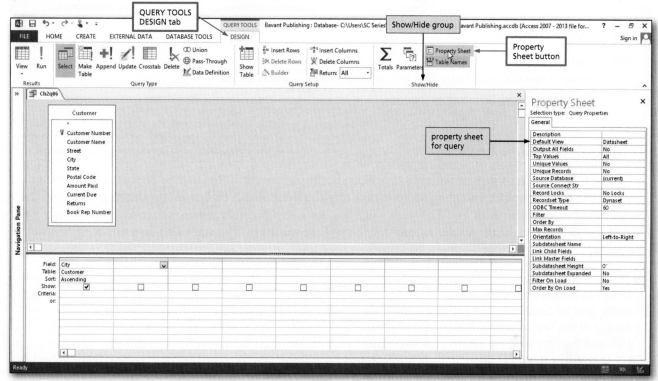

Figure 2–35

2

- Tap or click the Unique Values property box, and then tap or click the arrow that appears to display a list of available choices (Figure 2–36).

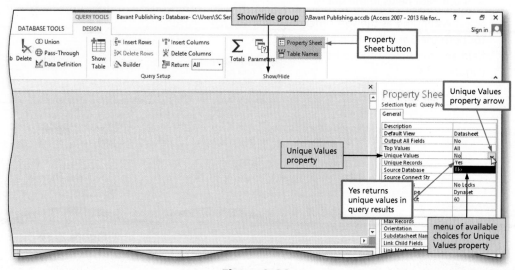

Figure 2–36

- Tap or click Yes to indicate that the query will return unique values, which means that each value will appear only once in the query results.

- Close the Query Properties property sheet by tapping or clicking the Property Sheet button (QUERY TOOLS DESIGN tab | Show/Hide group) a second time.

- Run the query (Figure 2–37).

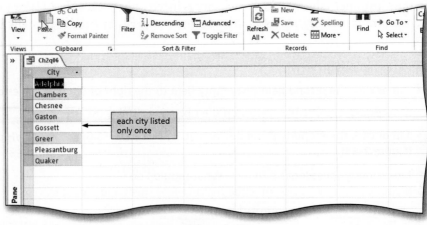

Figure 2–37

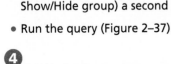

- Save the query as Ch2q07.

Other Ways

1. Press and hold or right-click second field in design grid, tap or click Properties on shortcut menu

To Sort on Multiple Keys

1 CREATE QUERIES | 2 USE CRITERIA | 3 SORT DATA | 4 JOIN TABLES | 5 EXPORT RESULTS
6 PERFORM CALCULATIONS | 7 CREATE CROSSTAB | 8 CUSTOMIZE NAVIGATION PANE

The following steps sort on multiple keys. Specifically, Bavant needs the data to be sorted by amount paid (low to high) within book rep number, which means that the Book Rep Number field is the major key and the Amount Paid field is the minor key. The steps place the Book Rep Number field to the left of the Amount Paid field. *Why? In Access, the major key must appear to the left of the minor key.* The steps also save the query with a new name.

- Return to Design view. Clear the design grid by tapping or clicking the top of the first column in the grid, and then pressing the DELETE key to clear the design grid.

- In the following order, include the Customer Number, Customer Name, Book Rep Number, and Amount Paid fields in the query.

- Select Ascending as the sort order for both the Book Rep Number field and the Amount Paid field (Figure 2–38).

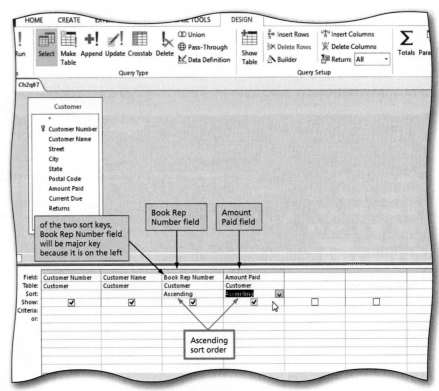

Figure 2–38

2

- Run the query (Figure 2–39).

 Experiment

- Return to Design view and try other sort combinations for the Book Rep Number and Amount Paid fields, such as Ascending for Book Rep Number and Descending for Amount Paid. In each case, run the query to see the effect of the changes. When finished, select Ascending as the sort order for both fields.

Q&A What if the Amount Paid field is to the left of the Book Rep Number field?

It is important to remember that the major sort key must appear to the left of the minor sort key in the design grid. If you attempted to sort by amount paid within book rep number, but placed the Amount Paid field to the left of the Book Rep Number field, your results would be incorrect.

CU #	Customer Name	BR #	Amount Paid
BCJ21	Brodkin Junior College	42	$0.00
SCC77	Stallone Community College	42	$7,525.98
MEC56	Mehitable College	42	$9,111.19
FSU23	Farnham State University	42	$18,268.00
ASU37	Applewood State University	42	$41,530.98
MCC45	Mauldin Community College	53	$9,500.00
CSD25	Cowpens ISD	53	$12,750.00
PLI22	PrattLast Institute	53	$17,229.45
HSD05	Hammonds County ISD	53	$18,434.75
CSU10	Camellia State University	53	$63,246.88
SEC19	Seaborn College	65	$9,225.34
KCC78	Key Community College System	65	$21,288.65
DCC34	Dartt Community College	65	$21,345.50
FSC12	First State College	65	$34,557.25
TSC02	Tri-State Consortium	65	$34,578.90

within group of customers with the same book rep number, rows are sorted by amount paid in ascending order

overall order is by book rep number in ascending order

Figure 2–39

3

- Save the query as Ch2q08.

Is there any way to sort the records in this same order, but have the Amount Paid field appear to the left of the Book Rep Number field in the query results?

Yes. Remove the check mark from the Book Rep Number field, and then add an additional Book Rep Number field at the end of the query. The first Book Rep Number field will be used for sorting but will not appear in the results. The second will appear in the results, but will not be involved in the sorting process.

How do you approach the creation of a query that might involve sorting?

Examine the query or request to see if it contains words such as *order* or *sort*. Such words imply that the order of the query results is important. If so, you need to sort the query.

If sorting is required, identify the field or fields on which the results are to be sorted. In the request, look for language such as *ordered by* or *sort the results by*, both of which would indicate that the specified field is a sort key.

If using multiple sort keys, determine the major and minor keys. If you are using two sort keys, determine which one is the more important, or the major key. Look for language such as *sort by amount paid within book rep number*, which implies that the overall order is by book rep number. In this case, the Book Rep Number field would be the major sort key and the Amount Paid field would be the minor sort key.

Determine sort order. Words such as *increasing*, *ascending*, or *low-to-high* imply Ascending order. Words such as *decreasing*, *descending*, or *high-to-low* imply Descending order. Sorting in *alphabetical order* implies Ascending order. If there were no words to imply a particular order, you would typically use Ascending.

Examine the query or request to see if there are any special restrictions. One common restriction is to exclude duplicates. Another common restriction is to list only a certain number of records, such as the first five records.

To Create a Top-Values Query

Rather than show all the results of a query, you may want to show only a specified number of records or a percentage of records. **Why?** *You might not need to see all the records, just enough to get a general idea of the results.* Creating a **top-values query** allows you to restrict the number of records that appear. When you sort records, you can limit results to those records having the highest (descending sort) or lowest (ascending sort) values. To do so, first create a query that sorts the data in the desired order. Next, use the Return box on the DESIGN tab to change the number of records to be included from All to the desired number or percentage.

The following steps create a query for Bavant Publishing that shows only the first five records that were included in the results of the previous query. The steps also save the resulting query with a new name.

1

- Return to Design view.

- If necessary, tap or click DESIGN on the ribbon to display the Design tab.

- Tap or click the Return arrow (QUERY TOOLS DESIGN tab | Query Setup group) to display the Return menu (Figure 2–40).

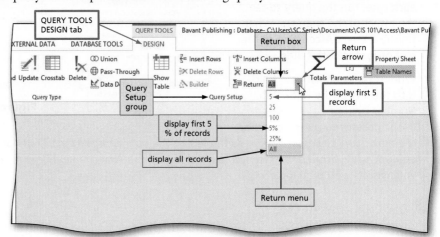

Figure 2–40

2

- Tap or click 5 in the Return menu to specify that the query results should contain the first five rows.

Q&A Could I have typed the 5? What about other numbers that do not appear in the list?
Yes, you could have typed the 5. For numbers not appearing in the list, you must type the number.

- Run the query (Figure 2–41).

3

- Save the query as Ch2q09.

- Close the query.

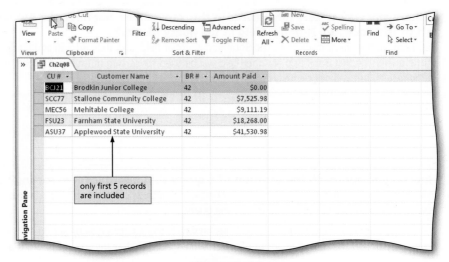

Figure 2–41

Q&A Do I need to close the query before creating my next query?
Not necessarily. When you use a top-values query, however, it is important to change the value in the Return box back to All. If you do not change the Return value back to All, the previous value will remain in effect. Consequently, you might not get all the records you should in the next query. A good practice whenever you use a top-values query is to close the query as soon as you are done. That way, you will begin your next query from scratch, which guarantees that the value is reset to All.

Break Point: If you wish to take a break, this is a good place to do so. You can exit Access now. To resume later, run Access, open the database called Bavant Publishing, and continue following the steps from this location forward.

Joining Tables

In designing a query, you need to determine whether more than one table is required. For example, if the question being asked involves data from both the Customer and Book Rep tables, then both tables are required for the query. A query might require listing the number and name of each customer (from the Customer table) along with the number and name of the customer's book rep (from the Book Rep table). Both the Customer and Book Rep tables are required for this query. You need to **join** the tables to find records in the two tables that have identical values in matching fields (Figure 2–42). In this example, you need to find records in the Customer table and the Book Rep table that have the same value in the Book Rep Number fields.

BTW
Ad Hoc Relationships
When you join tables in a query, you are creating an ad hoc relationship, that is, a relationship between tables created for a specific purpose. In Chapter 3, you will create general-purpose relationships using the Relationships window.

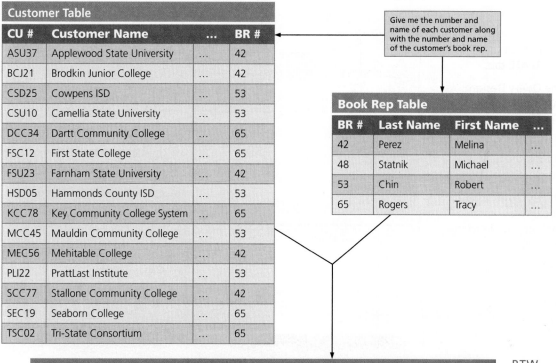

BTW
Join Line
If you do not get a join line automatically, there may be a problem with one of your table designs. Open each table in Design view and make sure that the data types are the same for the matching field in both tables and that one of the matching fields is the primary key in a table. Correct these errors and create the query again.

Give me the number and name of each customer along with the number and name of the customer's book rep.

Customer Table

CU #	Customer Name	...	BR #
ASU37	Applewood State University	...	42
BCJ21	Brodkin Junior College	...	42
CSD25	Cowpens ISD	...	53
CSU10	Camellia State University	...	53
DCC34	Dartt Community College	...	65
FSC12	First State College	...	65
FSU23	Farnham State University	...	42
HSD05	Hammonds County ISD	...	53
KCC78	Key Community College System	...	65
MCC45	Mauldin Community College	...	53
MEC56	Mehitable College	...	42
PLI22	PrattLast Institute	...	53
SCC77	Stallone Community College	...	42
SEC19	Seaborn College	...	65
TSC02	Tri-State Consortium	...	65

Book Rep Table

BR #	Last Name	First Name	...
42	Perez	Melina	...
48	Statnik	Michael	...
53	Chin	Robert	...
65	Rogers	Tracy	...

Customer Table

CU #	Customer Name	...	BR #	Last Name	First Name	...
ASU37	Applewood State University	...	42	Perez	Melina	...
BCJ21	Brodkin Junior College	...	42	Perez	Melina	...
CSD25	Cowpens ISD	...	53	Chin	Robert	...
CSU10	Camellia State University	...	53	Chin	Robert	...
DCC34	Dartt Community College	...	65	Rogers	Tracy	...
FSC12	First State College	...	65	Rogers	Tracy	...
FSU23	Farnham State University	...	42	Perez	Melina	...
HSD05	Hammonds County ISD	...	53	Chin	Robert	...
KCC78	Key Community College System	...	65	Rogers	Tracy	...
MCC45	Mauldin Community College	...	53	Chin	Robert	...
MEC56	Mehitable College	...	42	Perez	Melina	...
PLI22	PrattLast Institute	...	53	Chin	Robert	...
SCC77	Stallone Community College	...	42	Perez	Melina	...
SEC19	Seaborn College	...	65	Rogers	Tracy	...
TSC02	Tri-State Consortium	...	65	Rogers	Tracy	...

© 2014 Cengage Learning

Figure 2–42

To Join Tables

If you have determined that you need to join tables, you first will bring field lists for both tables to the upper pane of the Query window while working in Design view. Access will draw a line, called a **join line**, between matching fields in the two tables, indicating that the tables are related. You then can select fields from either table. Access joins the tables automatically.

The first step is to create a new query and add the Book Rep table to the query. Then, add the Customer table to the query. A join line should appear, connecting the Book Rep Number fields in the two field lists. **Why might the join line not appear?** *If the names of the matching fields differ from one table to the other, Access will not insert the line. You can insert it manually, however, by tapping or clicking one of the two matching fields and dragging the pointer to the other matching field.*

The following steps create a query to display information from both the Customer table and the Book Rep table.

1

- Tap or click CREATE on the ribbon to display the CREATE tab.

- Tap or click the Query Design button (CREATE tab | Queries group) to create a new query.

- If necessary, tap or click the Book Rep table (Show Table dialog box) to select the table.

- Tap or click the Add button (Show Table dialog box) to add a field list for the Book Rep Table to the query (Figure 2–43).

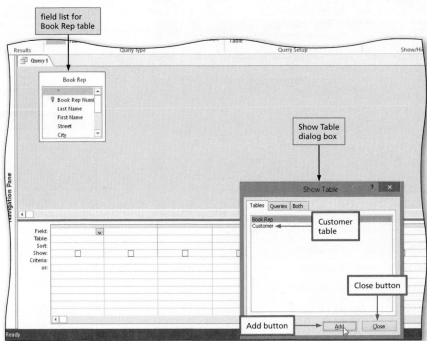

Figure 2–43

2

- Tap or click the Customer table (Show Table dialog box).

- Tap or click the Add button (Show Table dialog box) to add a field list for the Customer table.

- Close the Show Table dialog box by tapping or clicking the Close button.

- Expand the size of the two field lists so all the fields in the Book Rep and Customer tables appear (Figure 2–44).

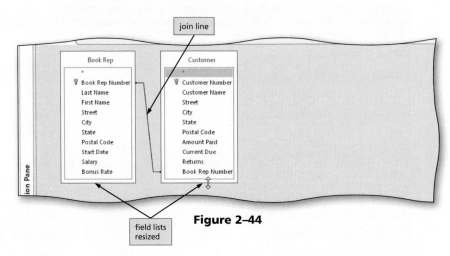

Figure 2–44

Q&A I did not get a join line. What should I do?

Ensure that the names of the matching fields are the same, the data types are the same, and the matching field is the primary key in one of the two tables. If all of these factors are true and you still do not have a join line, you can produce one by pointing to a matching field and dragging to the other matching field.

3

- In the design grid, include the Book Rep Number, Last Name, and First Name fields from the Book Rep Table as well as the Customer Number and Customer Name fields from the Customer table.

- Select Ascending as the sort order for both the Book Rep Number field and the Customer Number field (Figure 2–45).

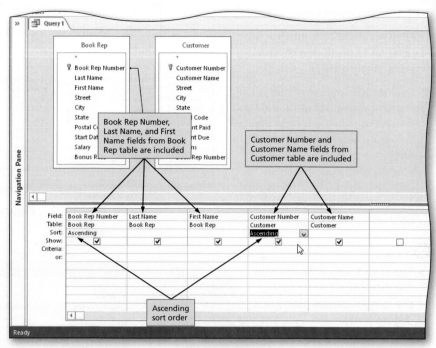

Figure 2–45

4

- Run the query (Figure 2–46).

5

- Tap or click the Save button on the Quick Access Toolbar to display the Save As dialog box.

- Type `Rep-Customer Query` as the query name.

6

- Tap or click the OK button (Save As dialog box) to save the query.

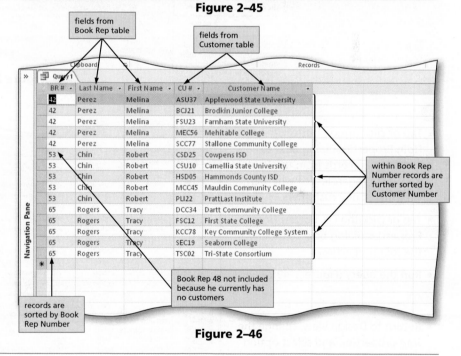

Figure 2–46

To Change Join Properties

1 CREATE QUERIES | 2 USE CRITERIA | 3 SORT DATA | 4 JOIN TABLES | 5 EXPORT RESULTS
6 PERFORM CALCULATIONS | 7 CREATE CROSSTAB | 8 CUSTOMIZE NAVIGATION PANE

Normally, records that do not match do not appear in the results of a join query. For example, the book rep named Michael Statnik does not appear in the results. ***Why?*** *He currently does not have any customers.* To cause such a record to be displayed, you need to change the **join properties**, which are the properties that indicate which records appear in a join. The following steps change the join properties of the Rep-Customer Query so that Bavant can include all book reps in the results, rather than only those reps who have already been assigned customers.

1

- Return to Design view.

- Press and hold or right-click the join line to produce a shortcut menu (Figure 2–47).

Q&A
I do not see Join Properties on my shortcut menu. What should I do?
If Join Properties does not appear on your shortcut menu, you did not point to the appropriate portion of the join line. You will need to point to the correct (middle) portion and press and hold or right-click again.

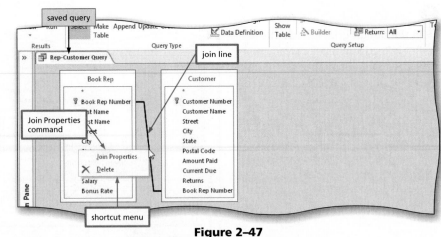

Figure 2–47

2

- Tap or click Join Properties on the shortcut menu to display the Join Properties dialog box (Figure 2–48).

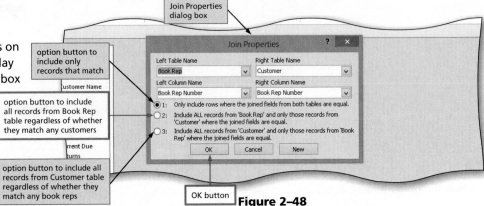

Figure 2–48

3

- Tap or click option button 2 (Join Properties dialog box) to include all records from the Book Rep Table regardless of whether they match any customers.

- Tap or click the OK button (Join Properties dialog box) to modify the join properties.

- Run the query (Figure 2–49).

Experiment

- Return to Design view, change the Join properties, and select option button 3. Run the query to see the effect of this option. When done, return to Design view, change the join properties, and once again select option button 2.

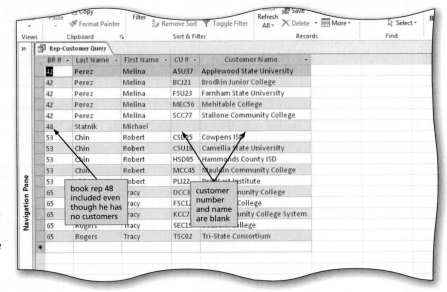

Figure 2–49

4

- Tap or click the Save button on the Quick Access Toolbar to save the changes to the query.

- Close the Rep-Customer Query.

Q&A
I see a dialog box that asks if I want to save the query. What should I do?
Tap or click the OK button to save the query.

To Create a Report from a Query

You can use queries in the creation of reports. The report in Figure 2–50 involves data from more than one table. *Why? The Last Name and First Name fields are in the Book Rep table. The Customer Number and Customer Name fields are in the Customer table. The Book Rep Number field is in both tables.* The easiest way to create such a report is to base it on a query that joins the two tables. The following steps use the Report Wizard and the Rep-Customer Query to create the report.

Rep-Customer Report

BR #	Last Name	First Name	CU #	Customer Name
42	Perez	Melina	ASU37	Applewood State University
42	Perez	Melina	BCJ21	Brodkin Junior College
42	Perez	Melina	FSU23	Farnham State University
42	Perez	Melina	MEC56	Mehitable College
42	Perez	Melina	SCC77	Stallone Community College
48	Statnik	Michael		
53	Chin	Robert	CSD25	Cowpens ISD
53	Chin	Robert	CSU10	Camellia State University
53	Chin	Robert	HSD05	Hammonds County ISD
53	Chin	Robert	MCC45	Mauldin Community College
53	Chin	Robert	PLI22	PrattLast Institute
65	Rogers	Tracy	DCC34	Dartt Community College
65	Rogers	Tracy	FSC12	First State College
65	Rogers	Tracy	KCC78	Key Community College System
65	Rogers	Tracy	SEC19	Seaborn College
65	Rogers	Tracy	TSC02	Tri-State Consortium

Figure 2–50

1

- Open the Navigation Pane, and then select the Rep-Customer Query in the Navigation Pane.

- Tap or click CREATE on the ribbon to display the CREATE tab.

- Tap or click the Report Wizard button (CREATE tab | Reports group) to display the Report Wizard dialog box (Figure 2–51).

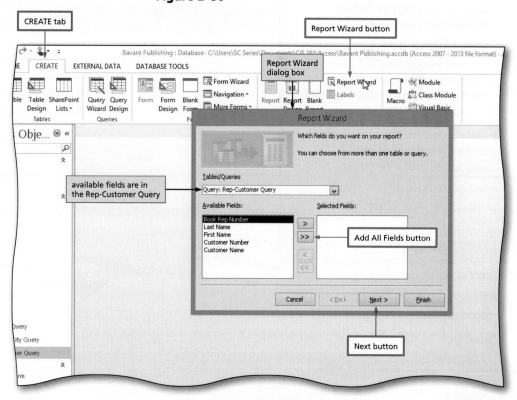

Figure 2–51

- Tap or click the Add All Fields button (Report Wizard dialog box) to add all the fields in the Rep-Customer Query.

- Tap or click the Next button to display the next Report Wizard screen (Figure 2–52).

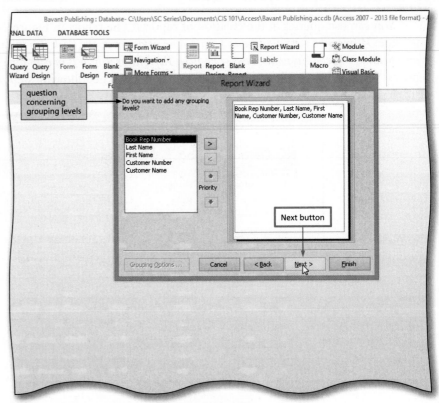

Figure 2–52

- Because you will not specify any grouping, tap or click the Next button in the Report Wizard dialog box to display the next Report Wizard screen.

- Because you already specified the sort order in the query, tap or click the Next button again to display the next Report Wizard screen.

- Make sure that Tabular is selected as the Layout and Portrait is selected as the Orientation.

- Tap or click the Next button to display the next Report Wizard screen.

- Erase the current title, and then type `Rep-Customer Report` as the new title.

- Tap or click the Finish button to produce the report (Figure 2–53).

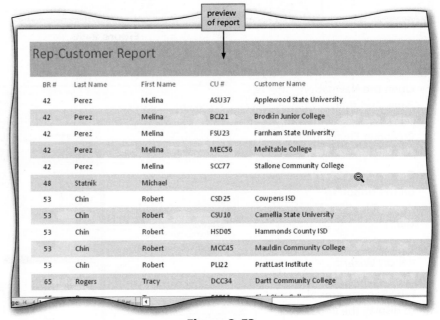

Figure 2–53

- Close the Rep-Customer Report.

To Print a Report

The following steps print a hard copy of the report.

1 With the Rep-Customer Report selected in the Navigation Pane, tap or click FILE on the ribbon to open the Backstage view.

2 Tap or click the Print tab in the Backstage view to display the Print gallery.

3 Tap or click the Quick Print button to print the report.

How would you approach the creation of a query that might involve multiple tables?

Examine the request to see if all the fields involved in the request are in one table. If the fields are in two (or more) tables, you need to join the tables.

If joining is required, identify the matching fields in the two tables that have identical values. Look for the same column name in the two tables or for column names that are similar.

Determine whether sorting is required. Queries that join tables often are used as the basis for a report. If this is the case, it may be necessary to sort the results. For example, the Rep-Customer Report is based on a query that joins the Book Rep and Customer tables. The query is sorted by book rep number and customer number.

Examine the request to see if there are any special restrictions. For example, the user only may want customers whose current due amount is $0.00.

Examine the request to see if you only want records from both tables that have identical values in matching fields. If you want to see records in one of the tables that do not have identical values, then you need to change the join properties.

Creating a Form for a Query

In the previous chapter, you created a form for the Customer table. You also can create a form for a query. Recall that a form in a database is a formatted document with fields that contain data. Forms allow you to view and maintain data.

To Create a Form for a Query

1 CREATE QUERIES | 2 USE CRITERIA | 3 SORT DATA | 4 JOIN TABLES | 5 EXPORT RESULTS
6 PERFORM CALCULATIONS | 7 CREATE CROSSTAB | 8 CUSTOMIZE NAVIGATION PANE

The following steps create a form, then save the form. *Why? The form will be available for future use in viewing the data in the query.*

1

- If necessary, select the Rep-Customer Query in the Navigation Pane.
- Tap or click CREATE on the ribbon to display the CREATE tab (Figure 2–54).

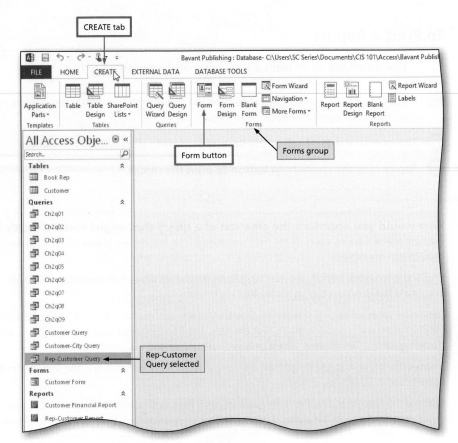

Figure 2–54

2

- Tap or click the Form button (CREATE tab | Forms group) to create a simple form (Figure 2–55).

Q&A
I see a field list also. What should I do?
Tap or click the Close button for the Field List.

3

- Tap or click the Save button on the Quick Access Toolbar to display the Save As dialog box.
- Type `Rep-Customer Form` as the form name.

4

- Tap or click the OK button to save the form.
- Tap or click the Close button for the form to close the form.

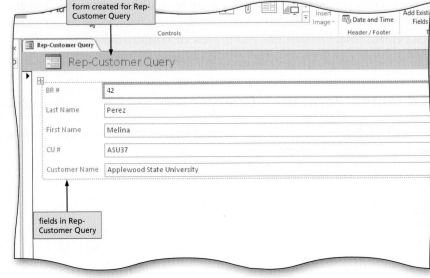

Figure 2–55

Using a Form

After you have saved a form, you can use it at any time by pressing and holding or right-clicking the form in the Navigation Pane and then tapping or clicking Open on the shortcut menu. If you plan to use the form to enter data, you must ensure you are viewing the form in Form view.

Exporting Data from Access to Other Applications

You can **export**, or copy, tables or queries from an Access database so that another application (for example, Excel or Word) can use the data. The application that will receive the data determines the export process to be used. You can export to text files in a variety of formats. For applications to which you cannot directly export data, you often can export an appropriately formatted text file that the other application can import. Figure 2–56 shows the workbook produced by exporting the Rep-Customer Query to Excel. The columns in the workbook have been resized to best fit the data.

BTW
**Distributing
a Document**
Instead of printing and distributing a hard copy of a document, you can distribute the document electronically. Options include sending the document via email; posting it on cloud storage (such as SkyDrive) and sharing the file with others; posting it on a social networking site, blog, or other website; and sharing a link associated with an online location of the document. You also can create and share a PDF or XPS image of the document, so that users can view the file in Acrobat Reader or XPS Viewer instead of in Access.

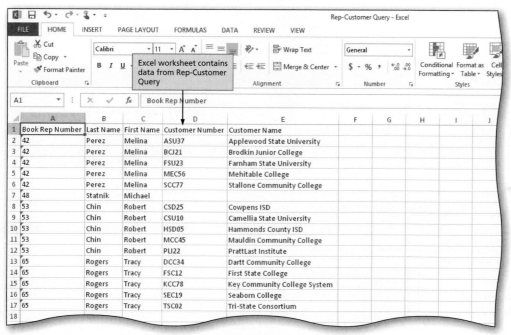

Figure 2–56

To Export Data to Excel

1 CREATE QUERIES | 2 USE CRITERIA | 3 SORT DATA | 4 JOIN TABLES | 5 EXPORT RESULTS
6 PERFORM CALCULATIONS | 7 CREATE CROSSTAB | 8 CUSTOMIZE NAVIGATION PANE

For Bavant Publishing to make the Rep-Customer Query available to Excel users, it needs to export the data. To export data to Excel, select the table or query to be exported and then tap or click the Excel button in the Export group on the EXTERNAL DATA tab. The steps on the next page export the Rep-Customer Query to Excel and save the export steps. ***Why save the export steps?*** *By saving the export steps, you could easily repeat the export process whenever you like without going through all the steps.* You would use the saved steps to export data in the future by tapping or clicking the Saved Exports button (EXTERNAL DATA tab | Export group) and then selecting the steps you saved.

1

- If necessary, tap or click the Rep-Customer Query in the Navigation Pane to select it.

- Tap or click EXTERNAL DATA on the ribbon to display the EXTERNAL DATA tab (Figure 2–57).

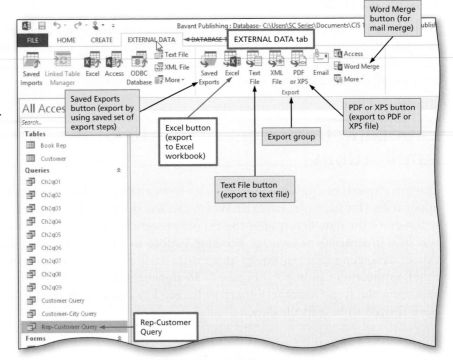

Figure 2–57

2

- Tap or click the Excel button (EXTERNAL DATA tab | Export group) to display the Export-Excel Spreadsheet dialog box.

- Tap or click the Browse button (Export-Excel Spreadsheet dialog box), and then navigate to the location where you wish to export the query (for example, the Access folder in the CIS 101 folder).

- Be sure the file name is Rep-Customer Query and then tap or click the Save button (File Save dialog box) to select the file name and location (Figure 2–58).

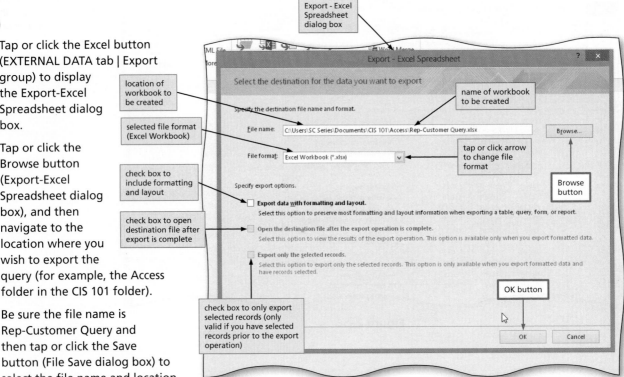

Figure 2–58

Q&A

Did I need to browse?
No. You could type the appropriate file location.

Could I change the name of the file?
You could change it. Simply replace the current file name with the one you want.

What if the file I want to export already exists?
Access will indicate that the file already exists and ask if you want to replace it. If you tap or click the Yes button, the file you export will replace the old file. If you tap or click the No button, you must either change the name of the export file or cancel the process.

3

- Tap or click the OK button (Export-Excel Spreadsheet dialog box) to export the data (Figure 2–59).

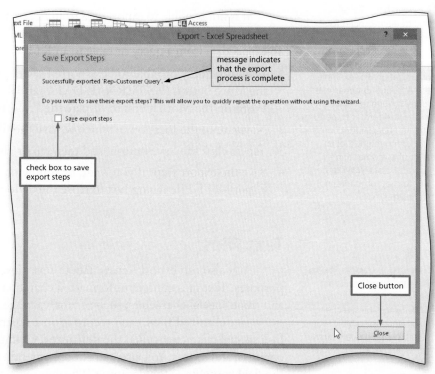

Figure 2–59

4

- Tap or click the 'Save export steps' check box (Export-Excel Spreadsheet dialog box) to display the Save Export Steps options.

- If necessary, type `Export-Rep-Customer Query` in the Save as text box.

- Type `Export the Rep-Customer Query without formatting` in the Description text box (Figure 2–60).

Q&A

How could I re-use the export steps?

You can use these steps to export data in the future by tapping or clicking the Saved Exports button (EXTERNAL DATA tab | Export group) and then selecting the steps you saved.

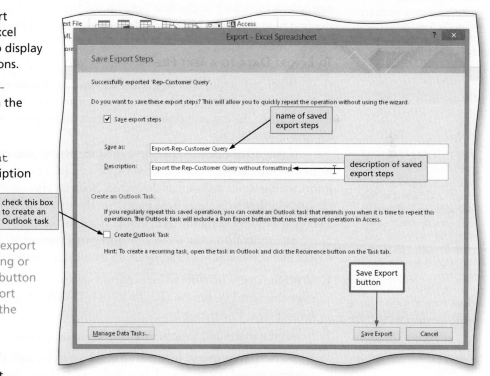

Figure 2–60

5

- Tap or click the Save Export button (Export-Excel Spreadsheet dialog box) to save the export steps.

Other Ways

1. Press and hold or right-click database object in Navigation Pane, tap or click Export

BTW
Exporting Data
You frequently need to export data so that it can be used in other applications and by other users in an organization. For example, the Accounting department might require financial data in an Excel format to perform certain financial functions. Marketing might require a list of customer names and addresses in Word or RTF format for marketing campaigns.

BTW
Saving Export Steps
Because query results are based on the data in the underlying tables, a change to an underlying table would result in a new query answer. For example, if the last name for book rep 42 changed from Perez to Smith, the change would be made in the Book Rep table. If you run the Rep-Customer Query again and export the query using the saved export steps, the Excel workbook would show the changed name.

BTW
Organizing Files and Folders
You should organize and store files in folders so that you easily can find the files later. For example, if you are taking an introductory computer class called CIS 101, a good practice would be to save all Access files in an Access folder in a CIS 101 folder. For a discussion of folders and detailed examples of creating folders, refer to the Office and Windows chapter at the beginning of this book.

TO EXPORT DATA TO WORD

It is not possible to export data from Access to the standard Word format. It is possible, however, to export the data as a rich text format (RTF) file, which Word can use. To export data from a query or table to an RTF file, you would use the following steps.

1. With the query or table to be exported selected in the Navigation Pane, tap or click the More button (EXTERNAL DATA tab | Export group) and then tap or click Word on the More menu to display the Export-RTF File dialog box.
2. Navigate to the location in which to save the file and assign a file name.
3. Tap or click the Save button, and then tap or click the OK button to export the data.
4. Save the export steps if you want, or simply tap or click the Close button in the Export-RTF File dialog box to close the dialog box without saving the export steps.

Text Files

You also can export Access data to text files, which can be used for a variety of purposes. Text files contain unformatted characters, including alphanumeric characters, and some special characters, such as tabs, carriage returns, and line feeds.

In **delimited files**, each record is on a separate line and the fields are separated by a special character, called the **delimiter**. Common delimiters are tabs, semicolons, commas, and spaces. You also can choose any other value that does not appear within the field contents as the delimiter. The comma-separated values (CSV) file often used in Excel is an example of a delimited file.

In **fixed-width files**, the width of any field is the same on every record. For example, if the width of the first field on the first record is 12 characters, the width of the first field on every other record also must be 12 characters.

TO EXPORT DATA TO A TEXT FILE

When exporting data to a text file, you can choose to export the data with formatting and layout. This option preserves much of the formatting and layout in tables, queries, forms, and reports. For forms and reports, this is the only option for exporting to a text file.

If you do not need to preserve the formatting, you can choose either delimited or fixed-width as the format for the exported file. The most common option, especially if formatting is not an issue, is delimited. You can choose the delimiter. You also can choose whether to include field names on the first row. In many cases, delimiting with a comma and including the field names is a good choice.

To export data from a table or query to a comma-delimited file in which the first row contains the column headings, you would use the following steps.

1. With the query or table to be exported selected in the Navigation Pane, tap or click the Text File button (EXTERNAL DATA tab | Export group) to display the Export-Text File dialog box.
2. Select the name and location for the file to be created.
3. If you need to preserve formatting and layout, be sure the 'Export data with formatting and layout' check box is checked. If you do not need to preserve formatting and layout, make sure the check box is not checked. Once you have made your selection, tap or click the OK button in the Export-Text File dialog box.
4. To create a delimited file, be sure the Delimited option button is selected in the Export Text Wizard dialog box. To create a fixed-width file, be sure the Fixed Width option button is selected. Once you have made your selection, tap or click the Next button.

5. a. If you are exporting to a delimited file, choose the delimiter that you want to separate your fields, such as a comma. Decide whether to include field names on the first row and, if so, tap or click the 'Include Field Names on First Row' check box. If you want to select a text qualifier, select it in the Text Qualifier list. When you have made your selections, tap or click the Next button.

   b. If you are exporting to a fixed-width file, review the position of the vertical lines that separate your fields. If any lines are not positioned correctly, follow the directions on the screen to reposition them. When you have finished, tap or click the Next button.

6. Tap or click the Finish button to export the data.

7. Save the export steps if you want, or simply tap or click the Close button in the Export-Text File dialog box to close the dialog box without saving the export steps.

BTW
Join Types
The type of join that finds records from both tables that have identical values in matching fields is called an inner join. An inner join is the default join in Access. Outer joins are used to show all the records in one table as well as the common records; that is, the records that share the same value in the join field. In a left outer join, all rows from the table on the left are included. In a right outer join, all rows from the table on the right are included.

Adding Criteria to a Join Query

Sometimes you will want to join tables, but you will not want to include all possible records. For example, you would like to create a report showing only those customers whose amount paid is greater than $20,000.00. In this case, you would relate the tables and include fields just as you did before. You also will include criteria. To include only those customers whose amount paid is more than $20,000.00, you will include >20000 as a criterion for the Amount Paid field.

To Restrict the Records in a Join

1 CREATE QUERIES | 2 USE CRITERIA | 3 SORT DATA | 4 JOIN TABLES | 5 EXPORT RESULTS
6 PERFORM CALCULATIONS | 7 CREATE CROSSTAB | 8 CUSTOMIZE NAVIGATION PANE

The following steps modify the Rep-Customer Query so that the results for Bavant Publishing include a criterion. **Why?** *Bavant wants to include only those customers whose amount paid is more than $20,000.00.*

- Open the Navigation Pane, if necessary, and then press and hold or right-click the Rep-Customer Query to produce a shortcut menu.

- Tap or click Design View on the shortcut menu to open the Rep-Customer Query in Design view.

- Close the Navigation Pane.

- Add the Amount Paid field to the query.

- Type >20000 as the criterion for the Amount Paid field (Figure 2–61).

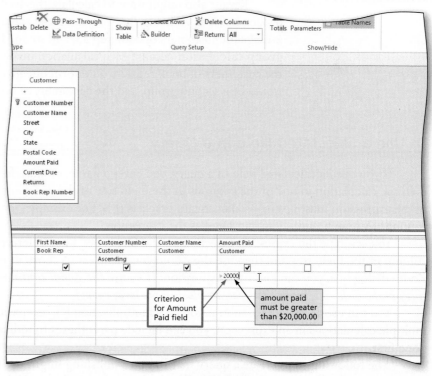

Figure 2–61

2

- Run the query (Figure 2–62).

3

- Close the query.

- When asked if you want to save your changes, tap or click the No button.

Q&A

What would happen if I saved the changes?
The next time you used this query, you would only see customers whose amount paid is more than $20,000.00.

BR #	Last Name	First Name	CU #	Customer Name	Amount Paid
42	Perez	Melina	ASU37	Applewood State University	$41,530.98
53	Chin	Robert	CSU10	Camellia State University	$63,246.88
65	Rogers	Tracy	DCC34	Dartt Community College	$21,345.50
65	Rogers	Tracy	FSC12	First State College	$34,557.25
65	Rogers	Tracy	KCC78	Key Community College System	$21,288.65
65	Rogers	Tracy	TSC02	Tri-State Consortium	$34,578.90

amount paid is greater than $20,000.00

Figure 2–62

BTW

Expression Builder
Access includes a tool to help you create complex expressions. If you click Build on the shortcut menu (see Figure 2–63), Access displays the Expression Builder dialog box, which includes an expression box, operator buttons, and expression elements. You can type parts of the expression directly and paste operator buttons and expression elements into the box. You also can use functions in expressions.

Calculations

If a special calculation is required for a query, you need to determine whether the calculation is **an individual record calculation** (for example, adding the values in two fields) or a **group calculation** (for example, finding the total of the values in a particular field on all the records).

Bavant Publishing might want to know the total amount (amount paid and current due) from each customer. This would seem to pose a problem because the Customer table does not include a field for total amount. You can calculate it, however, because the total amount is equal to the amount paid plus the current due. A field that can be computed from other fields is called a **calculated field** or a **computed field**. A calculated field is an individual record calculation because each calculation only involves fields in a single record.

Bavant also might want to calculate the average amount paid for the customers of each book rep. That is, they may want the average for customers of book rep 42, the average for customers of book rep 53, and so on. This type of calculation is called a **group calculation** because each calculation involves groups of records. In this example, the customers of book rep 42 would form one group, the customers of book rep 53 would be a second group, and the customers of book rep 65 would form a third group.

To Use a Calculated Field in a Query

1 CREATE QUERIES | 2 USE CRITERIA | 3 SORT DATA | 4 JOIN TABLES | 5 EXPORT RESULTS
6 PERFORM CALCULATIONS | 7 CREATE CROSSTAB | 8 CUSTOMIZE NAVIGATION PANE

If you need a calculated field in a query, you enter a name, or alias, for the calculated field, a colon, and then the calculation in one of the columns in the Field row of the design grid for the query. Any fields included in the expression must be enclosed in square brackets ([ ]). For example, for the total amount, you will type Total Amount:[Amount Paid]+[Current Due] as the expression.

You can type the expression directly into the Field row. The preferred method, however, is to select the column in the Field row and then use the Zoom command on its shortcut menu. When Access displays the Zoom dialog box, you can enter the expression. *Why use the Zoom command? You will not be able to see the entire entry in the Field row, because the space available is not large enough.*

You can use addition (+), subtraction (−), multiplication (*), or division (/) in calculations. If you have multiple calculations in an expression, you can include parentheses to indicate which calculations should be done first.

The following steps create a query that Bavant Publishing might use to obtain financial information on its customers, including the total amount (amount paid + current due), which is a calculated field.

①

- Create a query with a field list for the Customer table.

- Add the Customer Number, Customer Name, Amount Paid, and Current Due fields to the query.

- Press and hold or right-click the Field row in the first open column in the design grid to display a shortcut menu (Figure 2–63).

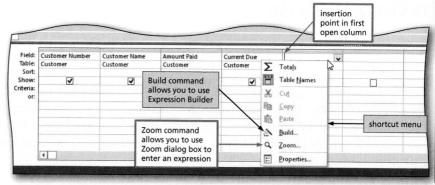

Figure 2–63

②

- Tap or click Zoom on the shortcut menu to display the Zoom dialog box.

- Type `Total Amount:[Amount Paid]+[Current Due]` in the Zoom dialog box (Figure 2–64).

Q&A Do I always need to put square brackets around field names?

If the field name does not contain spaces, square brackets are technically not required. It is a good practice, however, to get in the habit of using the brackets in field calculations.

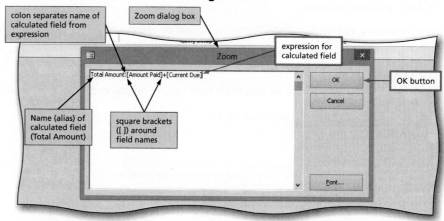

Figure 2–64

③

- Tap or click the OK button (Zoom dialog box) to enter the expression (Figure 2–65).

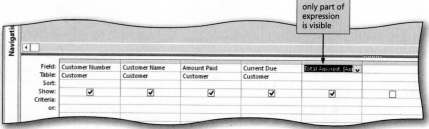

Figure 2–65

④

- Run the query (Figure 2–66).

Experiment

- Return to Design view and try other expressions. In at least one case, omit the Total Amount and the colon. In at least one case, intentionally misspell a field name. In each case, run the query to see the effect of your changes. When finished, reenter the original expression.

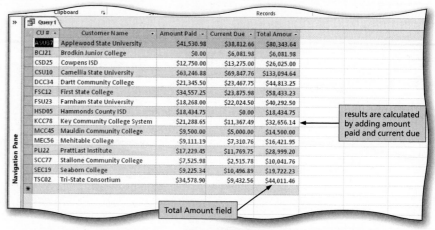

Figure 2–66

Other Ways

1. Press SHIFT+F2

To Change a Caption

In Chapter 1, you changed the caption for a field in a table. When you assigned a caption, Access displayed it in datasheets and forms. If you did not assign a caption, Access displayed the field name. You also can change a caption in a query. Access will display the caption you assign in the query results. When you omitted duplicates, you used the query property sheet. When you change a caption in a query, you use the property sheet for the field. In the property sheet, you can change other properties for the field, such as the format and number of decimal places. The following steps change the caption of the Amount Paid field to Paid and the caption of the Current Due field to Due. *Why? These changes give shorter, yet very readable, column headings for the fields.* The steps also save the query with a new name.

- Return to Design view.
- If necessary, tap or click DESIGN on the ribbon to display the QUERY TOOLS DESIGN tab.
- Tap or click the Amount Paid field in the design grid, and then tap or click the Property Sheet button (QUERY TOOLS DESIGN tab | Show/Hide group) to display the properties for the Amount Paid field.
- Tap or click the Caption box, and then type Paid as the caption (Figure 2–67).

◄ | My property sheet looks different. What should I do?
Q&A | Close the property sheet and repeat this step.

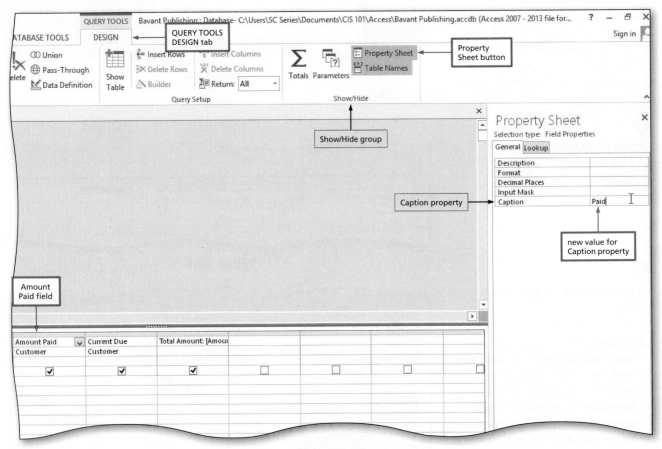

Figure 2–67

Close the property sheet by tapping or clicking the Property Sheet button a second time.

• Tap or click the Current Due field in the design grid, and then tap or click the Property Sheet button (QUERY TOOLS DESIGN tab | Show/Hide group).

• Tap or click the Caption box, and then type Due as the caption.

• Close the Property Sheet by tapping or clicking the Property Sheet button a second time.

• Run the query (Figure 2–68).

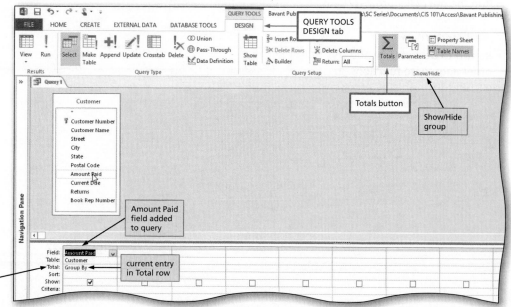

Figure 2–68

• Save the query as Ch2q10.

• Close the query.

Other Ways

1. Press and hold or right-click field in design grid, tap or click Properties on shortcut menu

To Calculate Statistics

1 CREATE QUERIES | 2 USE CRITERIA | 3 SORT DATA | 4 JOIN TABLES | 5 EXPORT RESULTS
6 PERFORM CALCULATIONS | 7 CREATE CROSSTAB | 8 CUSTOMIZE NAVIGATION PANE

For group calculations, Microsoft Access supports several built-in statistics: COUNT (count of the number of records), SUM (total), AVG (average), MAX (largest value), MIN (smallest value), STDEV (standard deviation), VAR (variance), FIRST (first value), and LAST (last value). These statistics are called aggregate functions. An **aggregate function** is a function that performs some mathematical function against a group of records. To use an aggregate function in a query, you include it in the Total row in the design grid. In order to do so, you must first include the Total row by tapping or clicking the Totals button on the DESIGN tab. *Why? The Total row usually does not appear in the grid.*

The following steps create a new query for the Customer table. The steps include the Total row in the design grid, and then calculate the average amount paid for all customers.

1

• Create a new query with a field list for the Customer table.

• Tap or click the Totals button (QUERY TOOLS DESIGN tab | Show/Hide group) to include the Total row in the design grid.

• Add the Amount Paid field to the query (Figure 2–69).

Figure 2–69

2

- Tap or click the Total row in the Amount Paid column to display the Total arrow.

- Tap or click the Total arrow to display the Total list (Figure 2–70).

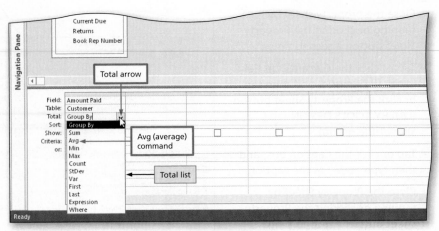

Figure 2–70

3

- Tap or click Avg to select the calculation that Access is to perform (Figure 2–71).

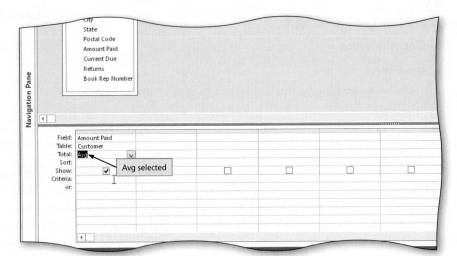

Figure 2–71

4

- Run the query (Figure 2–72).

🔍 **Experiment**

- Return to Design view and try other aggregate functions. In each case, run the query to see the effect of your selection. When finished, select Avg once again.

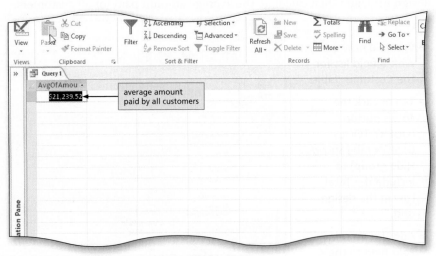

Figure 2–72

To Use Criteria in Calculating Statistics

Why? Sometimes calculating statistics for all the records in the table is appropriate. In other cases, however, you will need to calculate the statistics for only those records that satisfy certain criteria. To enter a criterion in a field, first you select Where as the entry in the Total row for the field, and then enter the criterion in the Criteria row. Access uses the word, Where, to indicate that you will enter a criterion. The following steps use this technique to calculate the average amount paid for customers of book rep 42. The steps also save the query with a new name.

- Return to Design view.
- Include the Book Rep Number field in the design grid.
- Tap or click the Total row in the Book Rep Number column.
- Tap or click the Total arrow in the Book Rep Number column to produce a Total list (Figure 2–73).

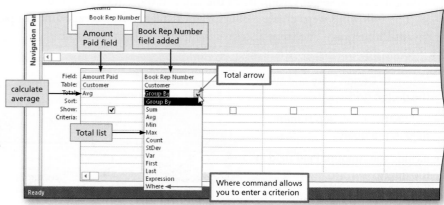

Figure 2–73

- Tap or click Where to be able to enter a criterion.
- Type 42 as the criterion for the Book Rep Number field (Figure 2–74).

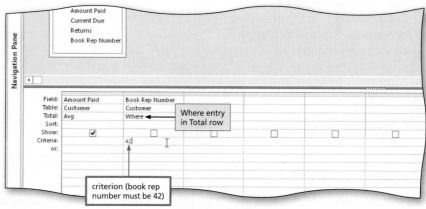

Figure 2–74

- Run the query (Figure 2–75).

- Save the query as Ch2q11.

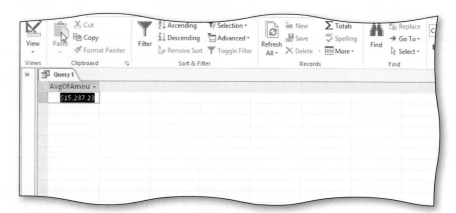

Figure 2–75

AC 118 **Access Chapter 2** Querying a Database

1 CREATE QUERIES | 2 USE CRITERIA | 3 SORT DATA | 4 JOIN TABLES | 5 EXPORT RESULTS
6 PERFORM CALCULATIONS | 7 CREATE CROSSTAB | 8 CUSTOMIZE NAVIGATION PANE

To Use Grouping

Why? *Statistics often are used in combination with grouping; that is, statistics are calculated for groups of records. For example, Bavant could calculate the average amount paid for the customers of each book rep, which would require the average for the customers of book rep 42, the average for customers of book rep 53, and so on.* **Grouping** means creating groups of records that share some common characteristic. In grouping by Book Rep Number, for example, the customers of book rep 42 would form one group, the customers of book rep 53 would form a second, and the customers of book rep 65 would form a third group. The calculations then are made for each group. To indicate grouping in Access, select Group By as the entry in the Total row for the field to be used for grouping.

The following steps create a query that calculates the average amount paid for customers of each book rep at Bavant Publishing. The steps also save the query with a new name.

1

- Return to Design view and clear the design grid.

- Include the Book Rep Number field in the query.

- Include the Amount Paid field in the query.

- Select Avg as the calculation in the Total row for the Amount Paid field (Figure 2–76).

Q&A Why was it not necessary to change the entry in the Total row for the Book Rep Number field?
Group By, which is the initial entry in the Total row when you add a field, is correct. Thus, you did not need to change the entry.

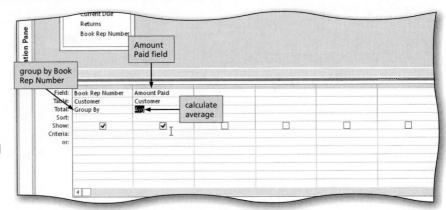

Figure 2–76

2

- Run the query (Figure 2–77).

3

- Save the query as Ch2q12.

- Close the query.

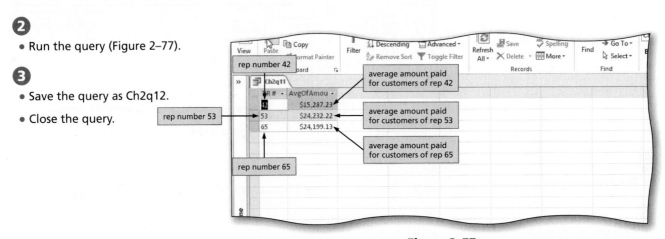

Figure 2–77

Crosstab Queries

A **crosstab query**, or simply, crosstab, calculates a statistic (for example, sum, average, or count) for data that is grouped by two different types of information. One of the types will appear down the side of the resulting datasheet, and the other will appear across the top. Crosstab queries are useful for summarizing data by category or group.

For example, if a query must summarize the sum of the returns grouped by both state and book rep number, you could have states as the row headings, that is, down the side. You could have book rep numbers as the column headings, that is, across the top. The entries within the datasheet represent the total of the returns. Figure 2–78 shows a crosstab in which the total of returns is grouped by both state and book rep number, with states down the left side and book rep numbers across the top. For example, the entry in the row labeled DE and in the column labeled 42 represents the total of the returns by all customers of book rep 42 who are located in Delaware.

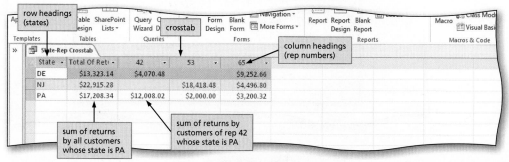

Figure 2–78

How do you know when to use a crosstab query?

If data is to be grouped by two different types of information, you can use a crosstab query. You will need to identify the two types of information. One of the types will form the row headings and the other will form the column headings in the query results.

To Create a Crosstab Query

1 CREATE QUERIES | 2 USE CRITERIA | 3 SORT DATA | 4 JOIN TABLES | 5 EXPORT RESULTS

6 PERFORM CALCULATIONS | **7 CREATE CROSSTAB** | 8 CUSTOMIZE NAVIGATION PANE

The following steps use the Crosstab Query Wizard to create a crosstab query. *Why? Bavant Publishing wants to group data on returns by two types of information: state and book rep.*

- Tap or click CREATE on the ribbon to display the CREATE tab.

- Tap or click the Query Wizard button (CREATE tab | Queries group) to display the New Query dialog box (Figure 2–79).

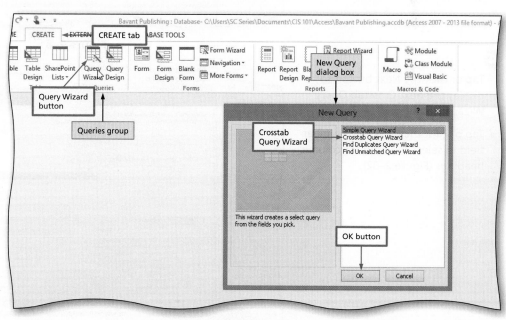

Figure 2–79

2

- Tap or click Crosstab Query Wizard (New Query dialog box).
- Tap or click the OK button to display the Crosstab Query Wizard dialog box (Figure 2–80).

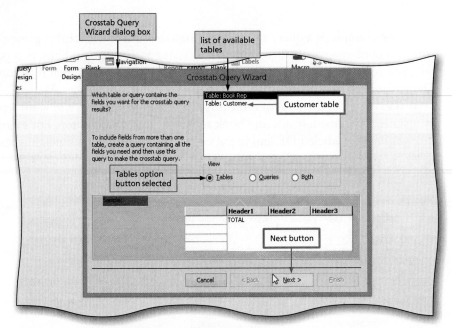

Figure 2–80

3

- With the Tables option button selected, tap or click Table: Customer to select the Customer table, and then tap or click the Next button to display the next Crosstab Query Wizard screen.
- Tap or click the State field, and then tap or click the Add Field button to select the State field for row headings (Figure 2–81).

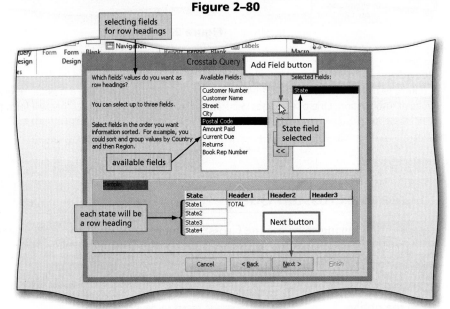

Figure 2–81

4

- Tap or click the Next button to display the next Crosstab Query Wizard screen.
- Tap or click the Book Rep Number field to select the field for column headings (Figure 2–82).

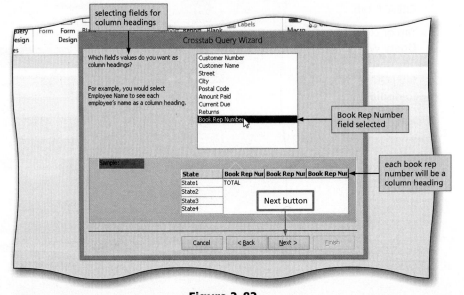

Figure 2–82

5

- Tap or click the Next button to display the next Crosstab Query Wizard screen.
- Tap or click the Returns field to select the field for calculations.

Experiment

- Tap or click other fields. For each field, examine the list of calculations that are available. When finished, tap or click the Returns field again.
- Tap or click Sum to select the calculation to be performed (Figure 2–83).

Q&A My list of functions is different. What did I do wrong?

Either you clicked the wrong field, or the Returns field has the wrong data type. For example, if you mistakenly assigned it the Short Text data type, you would not see Sum in the list of available calculations.

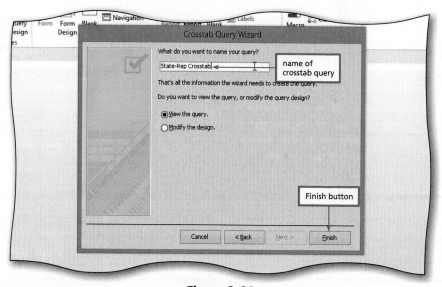

Figure 2–83

6

- Tap or click the Next button to display the next Crosstab Query Wizard screen.
- Erase the text in the name text box and type State-Rep Crosstab as the name of the query (Figure 2–84).

7

- If requested to do so by your instructor, name the crosstab query as FirstName LastName Crosstab where FirstName and LastName are your first and last names.
- Tap or click the Finish button to produce the crosstab shown in Figure 2–78 on page AC 119.
- Close the query.

Figure 2–84

Customizing the Navigation Pane

Currently, the entries in the Navigation Pane are organized by object type. That is, all the tables are together, all the queries are together, and so on. You might want to change the way the information is organized. For example, you might want to have the Navigation Pane organized by table, with all the queries, forms, and reports associated with a particular table appearing after the name of the table. You also can use the Search bar to restrict the objects that appear to only those that have a certain collection of characters in their name. For example, if you entered the letters, Cu, only those objects containing Cu somewhere within the name will be included.

BTW

Access Help

At any time while using Access, you can find answers to questions and display information about various topics through Access Help. Used properly, this form of assistance can increase your productivity and reduce your frustrations by minimizing the time you spend learning how to use Access. For instruction about Access Help and exercises that will help you gain confidence in using it, read the Office and Windows chapter at the beginning of this book.

To Customize the Navigation Pane

The following steps change the organization of the Navigation Pane. They also use the Search bar to restrict the objects that appear. *Why? Using the Search bar, you can reduce the number of objects that appear in the Navigation Pane and just show the ones in which you are interested.*

- If necessary, tap or click the 'Shutter Bar Open/Close Button' to open the Navigation Pane.

- Tap or click the Navigation Pane arrow to produce the Navigation Pane menu (Figure 2–85).

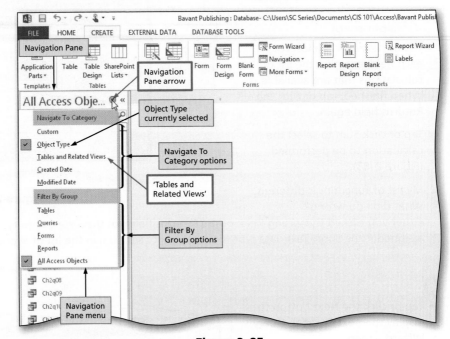

Figure 2–85

- Tap or click 'Tables and Related Views' to organize the Navigation Pane by table rather than by the type of object (Figure 2–86).

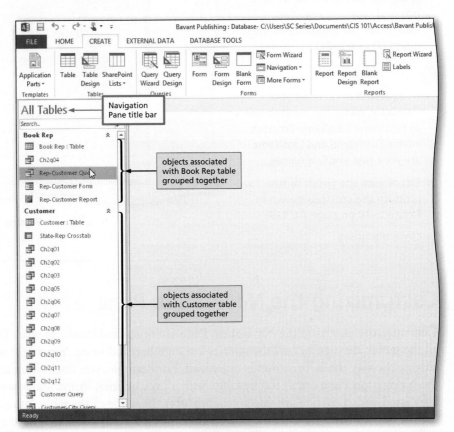

Figure 2–86

- Tap or click the Navigation Pane arrow to produce the Navigation Pane menu.

- Tap or click Object Type to once again organize the Navigation Pane by object type.

Experiment

- Select different Navigate To Category options to see the effect of the option. With each option you select, select different Filter By Group options to see the effect of the filtering. When you have finished experimenting, select the 'Object Type Navigate To Category' option and the 'All Access Objects Filter By Group' option.

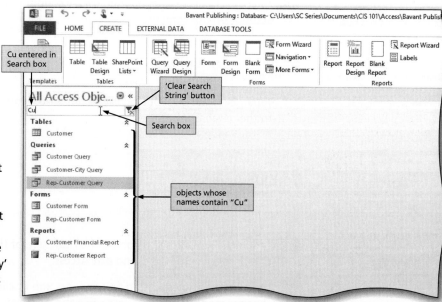

Figure 2–87

- If the Search bar does not appear, press and hold or right-click the Navigation Pane and tap or click Search Bar on the shortcut menu.

- Tap or click in the Search box to produce an insertion point.

- Type Cu as the search string to restrict the objects displayed to only those containing the desired string (Figure 2–87).

5

- Tap or click the 'Clear Search String' button to remove the search string and redisplay all objects.

Q&A Did I have to tap or click the button to redisplay all objects? Could I simply have erased the current string to achieve the same result?
You did not have to tap or click the button. You could have used the DELETE or BACKSPACE keys to erase the current search string.

To Sign Out of a Microsoft Account

If you are signed in to a Microsoft account and are using a public computer or otherwise wish to sign out of your Microsoft account, you should sign out of the account from the Account gallery in the Backstage view before exiting Access. Signing out of the account is the safest way to make sure that nobody else can access SkyDrive files or settings stored in your Microsoft account. The following steps sign out of a Microsoft account from Access. For a detailed example of the procedure summarized below, refer to the Office and Windows chapter at the beginning of this book.

1 If you wish to sign out of your Microsoft account, tap or click FILE on the ribbon to open the Backstage view and then tap or click the Account tab to display the Account gallery.

2 Tap or click the Sign out link, which displays the Remove Account dialog box. If a Can't remove Windows accounts dialog box appears instead of the Remove Account dialog box, click the OK button and skip the remaining steps.

Q&A Why does a Can't remove Windows accounts dialog box appear?
If you signed in to Windows using your Microsoft account, then you also must sign out from Windows, rather than signing out from within Access. When you are finished using Windows, be sure to sign out at that time.

BTW
Certification
The Microsoft Office Specialist (MOS) program provides an opportunity for you to obtain a valuable industry credential — proof that you have the Access 2013 skills required by employers. For more information, visit the Certification resource on the Student Companion Site located on www.cengagebrain.com. For detailed instructions about accessing available resources, visit www.cengage.com/ct/studentdownload or contact your instructor for information about accessing the required files.

BTW
Quick Reference
For a table that lists how to complete the tasks covered in this book using touch gestures, the mouse, ribbon, shortcut menu, and keyboard, see the Quick Reference Summary at the back of this book, or visit the Quick Reference resource on the Student Companion Site located on www.cengagebrain.com. For detailed instructions about accessing available resources, visit www.cengage.com/ct/studentdownload or contact your instructor for information about accessing the required files.

3 Tap or click the Yes button (Remove Account dialog box) to sign out of your Microsoft account on this computer.

Q&A Should I sign out of Windows after signing out of my Microsoft account?
When you are finished using the computer, you should sign out of your account for maximum security.

4 Tap or click the Back button in the upper-left corner of the Backstage view to return to the database.

To Exit Access

The following steps exit Access.

1 Tap or click the Close button on the right side of the title bar to close the open database, if there is one, and exit Access.

2 If a Microsoft Access dialog box appears, tap or click the Save button to save any changes made to the database since the last save.

Chapter Summary

In this chapter you have learned to create queries, enter fields, enter criteria, use text and numeric data in queries, use wildcards, use compound criteria, create parameter queries, sort data in queries, join tables in queries, perform calculations in queries, and create crosstab queries. You also learned to create a report and a form that used a query, to export a query, and to customize the Navigation Pane. The items listed below include all the new Access skills you have learned in this chapter, with tasks grouped by activity.

Calculations in Queries
Use a Calculated Field in a Query (AC 112)
Calculate Statistics (AC 115)
Use Criteria in Calculating Statistics (AC 117)
Use Grouping (AC 118)

Crosstab Query
Create a Crosstab Query (AC 119)

Criteria in Queries
Use Text Data in a Criterion (AC 81)
Use a Wildcard (AC 83)
Use Criteria for a Field Not Included in the Results (AC 85)
Use a Number in a Criterion (AC 89)
Use a Comparison Operator in a Criterion (AC 90)
Use a Compound Criterion Involving AND (AC 91)
Use a Compound Criterion Involving OR (AC 92)

Design Grid
Clear the Design Grid (AC 93)

Export Data
Export Data to Excel (AC 107)
Export Data to Word (AC 110)
Export Data to a Text File (AC 110)

Form Creation
Create a Form for a Query (AC 105)

Join Queries
Join Tables (AC 100)
Change Join Properties (AC 101)
Restrict the Records in a Join (AC 111)

Navigation Pane
Customize the Navigation Pane (AC 122)

Parameter Query
Create and View a Parameter Query (AC 87)
Use a Parameter Query (AC 88)

Query Creation
Create a Query in Design View (AC 78)
Add Fields to the Design Grid (AC 79)
Change a Caption (AC 114)

Report Creation
Create a Report from a Query (AC 103)

Sort in Queries
Sort Data in a Query (AC 94)
Omit Duplicates (AC 94)
Sort on Multiple Keys (AC 96)
Create a Top-Values Query (AC 98)

What decisions will you need to make when creating queries?

Use these guidelines as you complete the assignments in this chapter and create your own queries outside of this class.

1. Identify the fields by examining the question or request to determine which fields from the tables in the database are involved.

2. Identify restrictions or the conditions that records must satisfy to be included in the results.

3. Determine whether special order is required.

    a) Determine the sort key(s).

    b) If using two sort keys, determine the major and minor key.

    c) Determine sort order. If there are no words to imply a particular order, you would typically use Ascending.

    d) Determine restrictions, such as excluding duplicates.

4. Determine whether more than one table is required.

    a) Determine which tables to include.

    b) Determine the matching fields.

    c) Determine whether sorting is required.

    d) Determine restrictions.

    e) Determine join properties.

5. Determine whether calculations are required.

    a) For individual record calculations, determine the calculation and a name for the calculated field.

    b) For group calculations, determine the calculation as well as the field to be used for grouping.

6. If data is to be summarized and the data is to be grouped by two different types of information, create a crosstab query.

How should you submit solutions to questions in the assignments identified with a ✳ symbol?

Every assignment in this book contains one or more questions identified with a ✳ symbol. These questions require you to think beyond the assigned database. Present your solutions to the questions in the format required by your instructor. Possible formats may include one or more of these options: write the answer; create a document that contains the answer; present your answer to the class; discuss your answer in a group; record the answer as audio or video using a webcam, smartphone, or portable media player; or post answers on a blog, wiki, or website.

Apply Your Knowledge

Reinforce the skills and apply the concepts you learned in this chapter.

Using Wildcards in a Query, Creating a Parameter Query, Joining Tables, and Creating a Report

Instructions: Start Access. Open the Apply Cosmetics Naturally database that you modified in Apply Your Knowledge in Chapter 1 on page AC 65. (If you did not complete the exercise, see your instructor for a copy of the modified database.)

Perform the following tasks:

1. Create a query for the Customer table and add the Customer Number, Customer Name, Amount Paid, and Balance fields to the design grid. Add a criterion to find all customers whose names start with the letter C. Run the query and then save it as Apply 2 Step 1 Query.

2. Create a query for the Customer table and add the Customer Number, Customer Name, Amount Paid, and Sales Rep Number fields to the design grid. Sort the records in descending order by Amount Paid. Add a criterion for the Sales Rep Number field that allows the user to enter a different sales rep each time the query is run. Run the query and enter 41 as the sales rep number to test the query. Save the query as Apply 2 Step 2 Query.

Continued >

Apply Your Knowledge *continued*

3. Create a query that joins the Sales Rep and Customer tables. Add the Sales Rep Number, Last Name, and First Name fields from the Sales Rep table and the Customer Number and Customer Name fields from the Customer table to the design grid. Sort the records in ascending order by Customer Number within Sales Rep Number. All sales reps should appear in the result, even if they currently have no customers. Run the query and save it as Rep-Customer Query.

4. Create the report shown in Figure 2–88. The report uses the Rep-Customer Query.

Rep-Customer Report

SR #	Last Name	First Name	CU #	Customer Name
34	Johnson	Bobbi	AS24	Ashley's Salon
34	Johnson	Bobbi	DB14	Della's Beauty Place
34	Johnson	Bobbi	EY07	Environmentally Yours
34	Johnson	Bobbi	NC25	Nancy's Place
34	Johnson	Bobbi	TT21	Tan and Tone
39	Gutaz	Nicholas	BL15	Blondie's on Main
39	Gutaz	Nicholas	CY12	Curlin Yoga Studio
39	Gutaz	Nicholas	JN34	Just Natural
39	Gutaz	Nicholas	LB20	Le Beauty
39	Gutaz	Nicholas	UR23	U R Beautiful
41	Orlon	Jake	BA35	Beauty for All
41	Orlon	Jake	CL09	Casual Looks
41	Orlon	Jake	FN19	Fitness Counts
41	Orlon	Jake	RD03	Rose's Day Spa
41	Orlon	Jake	TW56	The Workout Place
55	Sinson	Terry		

Figure 2–88

5. If requested to do so by your instructor, rename the Rep-Customer Report in the Navigation Pane as LastName-Customer Report where LastName is your last name.

6. Submit the revised database in the format specified by your instructor.

7. ✸ What criteria would you enter in the Customer Name field if you wanted to find all customers who had the word Beauty somewhere in their name?

Extend Your Knowledge

Extend the skills you learned in this chapter and experiment with new skills. You may need to use Help to complete the assignment.

Creating Crosstab Queries Using Criteria, and Exporting a Query

Note: To complete this assignment, you will be required to use the Data Files for Students. Visit www.cengage.com/ct/studentdownload for detailed instructions or contact your instructor for information about accessing the required files.

Instructions: Start Access. Open the Extend Janitorial Services database. Janitorial Services is a small business that provides janitorial services to commercial businesses. The owner has created an Access database in which to store information about the customers she serves and the cleaning staff she employs. You will create the crosstab query shown in Figure 2–89. You also will query the database using specified criteria, and export a query.

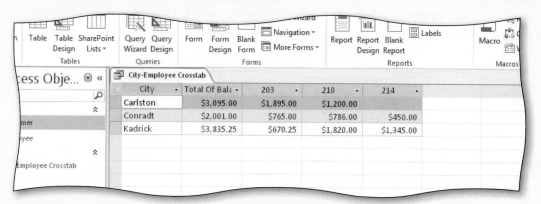

Figure 2–89

Perform the following tasks:

1. Create the crosstab query shown in Figure 2–89. The crosstab groups the total of customers' balance by city and employee number.

2. Create a query to find all customers who are not located in Kadrick. Include the Customer Number, Customer Name, and Balance fields in the query results. Save the query as Extend 2 Step 2 Query.

3. Create a query to find all employees whose first name is either Timmy or Tammy. Include the Employee Number, First Name, and Last Name in the query results. Save the query as Extend 2 Step 3 Query.

4. Create a query to find all customers where the employee number is either 210 or 214 and the balance is greater than $1,000.00. Include the Customer Number, Customer Name, Balance, and Employee Number fields in the design grid. Use the IN operator in your query design. Save the query as Extend 2 Step 4 Query.

5. Export the City-Employee Crosstab as a Word file with the name City-Employee Crosstab.rtf and save the export steps.

6. Open the Customer table and change the balance for customer AT23 to $755.

7. If requested to do so by your instructor, change the customer name of customer AT23 from Atlas Repair to Last Name Repair where Last Name is your last name.

8. Use the saved export steps to export the City-Employee Crosstab again. When asked if you want to replace the existing file, click Yes.

9. Submit the revised database and the exported RTF file in the format specified by your instructor.

10. ✳ How would you create the query in Step 4 without using the IN operator?

Analyze, Correct, Improve

Analyze a database, correct all errors, and improve the design.

Correcting Errors in the Table Structure

Note: To complete this assignment, you will be required to use the Data Files for Students. Visit www.cengage.com/ct/studentdownload for detailed instructions or contact your instructor for information about accessing the required files.

Instructions: Analyze Fitness is a database maintained by the Sports Science department at your university. Graduate students work with local residents as personal trainers to earn the necessary hours required for certification. The department chair has asked you to correct and improve two of the queries she created. Start Access and open the Analyze Fitness database from the Data Files for Students.

1. Correct The query shown in Figure 2–90 returns 0 results, and the department chair knows that is not correct. She wants to find all customers who live on Levick. Open the query in Design view, correct the errors, and save as Corrected Criteria Query.

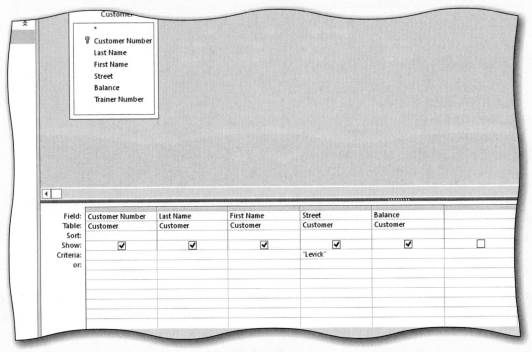

Figure 2–90

2. Improve The department chair also created the query shown in Figure 2–91. The query is sorted correctly, but she wanted Trainer Number to appear as the last field in the query result. She also would like to change the caption for the Balance field to Due. Improve the query to display the results in the desired order. Save the query as Improved Sort Query. Submit the revised database in the format specified by your instructor.

3. ✳ Why does the query shown in Figure 2–90 return 0 results?

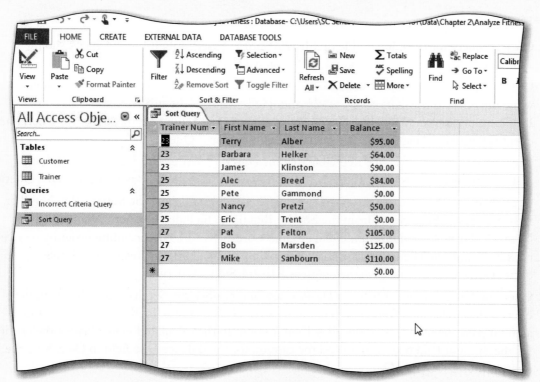

Figure 2–91

In the Labs

Design, create, modify, and/or use a database following the guidelines, concepts, and skills presented in this chapter. Labs are listed in order of increasing difficulty. Labs 1 and 2, which increase in difficulty, require you to create solutions based on what you learned in the chapter; Lab 3 requires you to create a solution, which uses cloud and web technologies, by learning and investigating on your own from general guidance.

Lab 1: Querying the Dartt Offsite Services Database

Problem: The management of Dartt Offsite Services has determined a number of questions it wants the database management system to answer. You must obtain the answers to these questions.

Note: Use the database modified in Lab 1 of Chapter 1 on page AC 68 for this assignment, or see your instructor for information on accessing the required files.

Instructions: Perform the following tasks:

1. Start Access. Open the Lab 1 Dartt Offsite Services database and create a new query for the Client table. Add the Client Number, Client Name, Amount Paid, Balance Due, and Service Rep Number fields to the design grid, and restrict the query results to only those clients where the service rep number is 37. Save the query as Lab 2-1 Step 1 Query.

2. Create a query for the Client table that includes the Client Number, Client Name, and Balance Due fields for all clients located in North Carolina (NC) with a balance due less than $1,000.00. Save the query as Lab 2-1 Step 2 Query.

3. Create a query for the Client table that includes the Client Number, Client Name, Street, City, and State field for all clients whose names begin with Ba. Save the query as Lab 2-1 Step 3 Query.

Continued >

In the Labs *continued*

4. Create a query for the Client table that lists all cities in ascending order. Each city should appear only once. Save the query as Lab 2-1 Step 4 Query.

5. Create a query for the Client table that allows the user to type the name of the desired city when the query is run. The query results should display the Client Number, Client Name, Balance Due, and Amount Paid fields. Test the query by searching for those records where the client is located in Austin. Save the query as Lab 2-1 Step 5 Query.

6. Create a query for the Service Rep table that includes the First Name, Last Name, and Start Date for all service reps who started after May 1, 2013. Save the query as Lab 2-1 Step 6 Query.

7. Create a query that joins the Service Rep and Client tables. Include the Service Rep Number, Last Name, and First Name from the Service Rep table. Include the Client Number, Client Name, and Amount Paid from the Client table. Sort the records in ascending order by service rep's last name and client name. All service reps should appear in the result even if they currently have no clients. Save the query as Lab 2-1 Step 7 Query.

8. Open the Lab 2-1 Step 7 Query in Design view and remove the Service Rep table from the query. Add the Balance Due field to the design grid. Calculate the total of the balance and amount paid amounts. Assign the alias Total Amount to the calculated field. Change the caption for the Amount Paid field to Paid and the caption for the Balance Due field to Owe. Save the query as Lab 2-1 Step 8 Query.

9. Create a query for the Client table to display the total amount paid amount for service rep 24. Save the query as Lab 2-1 Step 9 Query.

10. Create a query for the Client table to display the average balance amount for each service rep. Save the query as Lab 2-1 Step 10 Query.

11. Create the crosstab query shown in Figure 2–92. The crosstab groups the average of clients' amount paid amounts by state and service rep number. Save the crosstab as State-Service Rep Crosstab.

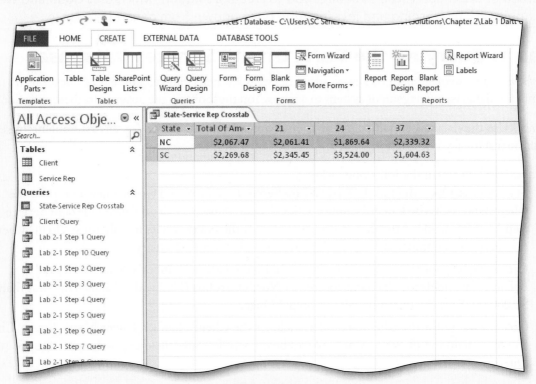

Figure 2–92

12. If requested to do so by your instructor, open the Lab 2-1 Step 1 query and change the caption for the Service Rep Number field to your last name.

13. Submit the revised database in the format specified by your instructor.

14. ✸ How would you modify the query in Step 7 to include only service reps that currently have clients?

Lab 2: Querying the Tennis Logos Database

Problem: The manager of Tennis Logos has determined a number of questions he wants the database management system to answer. You must obtain answers to these questions.

Note: Use the database created in Lab 2 of Chapter 1 on page AC 69 for this assignment or see your instructor for information on accessing the required files.

Instructions: Perform the following tasks:

1. Start Access. Open the Lab 2 Tennis Logos database and create a query for the Item table that includes all fields and all records in the Item table. Name the query Lab 2-2 Step 1 Query.

2. Create a query for the Item table that includes the Item Number, Description, Wholesale Price, and Supplier Code fields for all records where the supplier code is SD. Save the query as Lab 2-2 Step 2 Query.

3. Create a query for the Item table that includes the Item Number and Description fields for all items where the description starts with C. Save the query as Lab 2-2 Step 3 Query.

4. Create a query for the Item table that includes the Item Number and Description for all items with a Base Cost greater than $10.00. Save the query as Lab 2-2 Step 4 Query.

5. Create a query for the Item table that includes the Item Number, Description, and Wholesale Price fields for all items with a Wholesale Price between $1.00 and $4.00. Save the query as Lab 2-2 Step 5 Query.

6. Create a query for the Item table that includes the Item Number, Description, On Hand, and Wholesale Price fields for all items where the number on hand is less than 100 and the wholesale price is less than $3.00. Save the query as Lab 2-2 Step 6 Query.

7. Create a query for the Item table that includes the Item Number, Description, Wholesale Price, and Supplier Code for all items that have a Wholesale Price greater than $10.00 or a Supplier Code of LM. Save the query as Lab 2-2 Step 7 Query.

8. Create a query that joins the Supplier and the Item tables. Include the Supplier Code and Supplier Name from the Supplier table and the Item Number, Description, Wholesale Price, and Base Cost fields from the Item table. Sort the query in ascending order by Supplier Code and Description. Save the query as Supplier-Item Query.

9. Create a form for the Supplier-Item Query. Save the form as Supplier-Item Form.

10. If requested to do so by your instructor, rename the form in the Navigation Pane as LastName-Item Form where LastName is your last name.

11. Create the report shown in Figure 2–93. The report uses the Supplier-Item Query but does not use all the fields in the query.

12. Create a query for the Item table that includes the Item Number, Description, Base Cost, and Wholesale Price. Calculate the difference between Base Cost and Wholesale Price (Base Cost – Wholesale Price). Assign the alias Cost Difference to the calculated field. Save the query as Lab 2-2 Step 12 Query.

Continued >

In the Labs continued

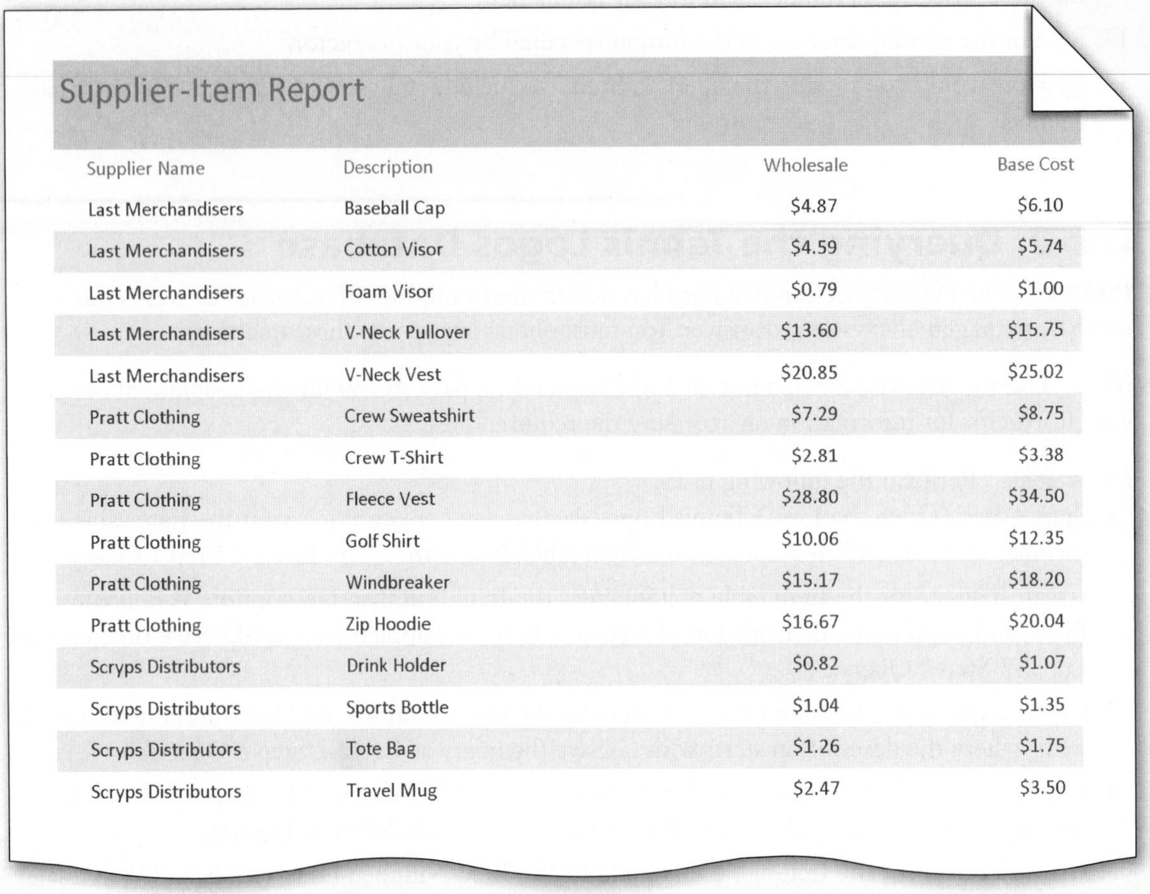

Supplier-Item Report

Supplier Name	Description	Wholesale	Base Cost
Last Merchandisers	Baseball Cap	$4.87	$6.10
Last Merchandisers	Cotton Visor	$4.59	$5.74
Last Merchandisers	Foam Visor	$0.79	$1.00
Last Merchandisers	V-Neck Pullover	$13.60	$15.75
Last Merchandisers	V-Neck Vest	$20.85	$25.02
Pratt Clothing	Crew Sweatshirt	$7.29	$8.75
Pratt Clothing	Crew T-Shirt	$2.81	$3.38
Pratt Clothing	Fleece Vest	$28.80	$34.50
Pratt Clothing	Golf Shirt	$10.06	$12.35
Pratt Clothing	Windbreaker	$15.17	$18.20
Pratt Clothing	Zip Hoodie	$16.67	$20.04
Scryps Distributors	Drink Holder	$0.82	$1.07
Scryps Distributors	Sports Bottle	$1.04	$1.35
Scryps Distributors	Tote Bag	$1.26	$1.75
Scryps Distributors	Travel Mug	$2.47	$3.50

Figure 2–93

13. Create a query for the Item table that displays the average Wholesale Price and the average Base Cost of all items. Save the query as Lab 2-2 Step 13 Query.

14. Submit the revised database in the format specified by your instructor.

15. ✹ There are two ways to create the query in step 1. What are they? Which one did you use?

Lab 3: Expand Your World: Cloud and Web Technologies
Creating Queries, Customizing the Navigation Pane, and Using the Excel Web App

Problem: Shopper is a small business that does personal shopping for clients. You will create two queries for the owner, customize the Navigation Pane, export a query in CSV format, open the exported file, and then modify the file using the Excel Web app.

Note: To complete this assignment, you will be required to use the Data Files for Students. Visit www.cengage.com/ct/studentdownload for detailed instructions or contact your instructor for information about accessing the required files.

Instructions: Perform the following tasks:
  1. Open the Lab 3 Shopper database. Create and save a query that joins the Shopper and Client tables. Include the Last Name and First Name from the Shopper table and the Client Number, Last Name, First Name, and Balance fields from the Client table. Sort the query by shopper Last Name and Client Number.

2. Create and save a query for the Client table. The query result should display the Last Name, First Name, Amount Paid, Balance, and Shopper Number in that order. Sort the query by Last Name within Shopper Number.

3. Change the organization of the Navigation Pane so that all objects associated with the Client table are grouped together and all objects associated with the Shopper table are grouped together.

4. Export the query you created in Step 2 above as a CSV file. Do not save the export steps.

5. Upload the CSV file to your SkyDrive and open the file in the Excel Web app.

6. Delete the Shopper Number column and resize the remaining columns.

7. If requested to do so by your instructor, change the last name and first name of the first client to your last name and first name.

8. Save and close the Excel workbook.

9. Submit the revised database and Excel workbook in the format specified by your instructor.

10. ✸ Study the query result from Step 2 above. What do you notice about the first name and last name field headings? Why do they appear as they do?

✸ Consider This: Your Turn

Apply your creative thinking and problem solving skills to design and implement a solution.

1: Querying the Craft Database

Personal/Academic

Instructions: Open the Craft database you created in Chapter 1 on page AC 73. If you did not create this database, contact your instructor for information about accessing the required files.

Part 1: Use the concepts and techniques presented in this chapter to create queries for the following. Save each query.

a. Find the item number and description of all items that contain the word, Rack.

b. Find the item number and description of all items made by students with a student code of 3962 or 7568.

c. Find the item number, description, and price of all items that have a price between $20.00 and $40.00.

d. Find the total price (price * on hand) of each item available for sale. Show the item number, description, price, on hand, and total price in the result. Change the caption for the On Hand field to Quantity.

e. Find the seller of each item. Show the student's last name and first name as well as the item number, description, price, and on hand. Sort the results by description within student last name.

f. Create a form based on the query you created in Step e.

g. Determine the average price of items grouped by student code.

h. Determine the two most expensive items for sale. Show the description and price.

Submit your assignment in the format specified by your instructor.

Part 2: ✸ You made several decisions while creating the queries in this assignment, including the query in Step b. What was the rationale behind your decisions? There are two ways to create the query in Step b. What are they? Which one did you use?

Continued >

Consider This: Your Turn *continued*

2: Querying the Mums Landscaping Database
Professional

Instructions: Open the Mums Landscaping database you created in Chapter 1 on page AC 73. If you did not create this database, contact your instructor for information about accessing the required files.

Part 1: Use the concepts and techniques presented in this chapter to create queries for the following. Save each query.

   a. Find all supervisors who started prior to January 1, 2013. Show the supervisor's first name, last name, and hourly rate.
   b. Find the customer name and address of all customers located on Cantor.
   c. Find the customer number, customer name, amount paid, and balance for all customers whose amount paid is $0.00 or whose balance is $0.00.
   d. Create a parameter query for the Customer table that will allow the user to enter a different postal code each time the query is run. The user should see all fields in the query result.
   e. Create a crosstab query that groups the total of customer's balance amounts by postal code and supervisor number.
   f. Find the supervisor for each customer. List the supervisor number, last name, first name, customer number, customer name, and balance. Sort the results by customer number within supervisor number.
   g. Open the query you created in Step f above and restrict retrieval to only those customers whose balance is greater than $500.00.
   h. Estimate the weekly pay for each supervisor by multiplying the hourly rate by 40. Show the supervisor's first name, last name, hourly rate, and weekly pay.

Submit your assignment in the format specified by your instructor.

Part 2: ✳ You made several decisions while creating the queries in this assignment, including the calculation in Step h above. What was the rationale behind your decisions, and how could you modify the query in Step h if the Supervisor table included a field called Hours Worked in which the actual hours worked was stored?

3: Creating Queries to Analyze Data
Research and Collaboration

Part 1: Examine a website that contains weather data, such as weather.com or Bing weather, and, as a team, select 30 cities of interest in your state or province. Create a database that contains one table and has the following fields: City, State or Province, High Temp, Low Temp, and Conditions. Use standard weather terms for the Conditions field, such as rainy, snowy, cloudy, clear, and so on. Create queries that do the following:

   a. Display the five cities with the highest high temperature.
   b. Display the five cities with the lowest low temperature.
   c. Display the average high and low temperatures for all cities.
   d. Display the average high and low temperatures for all cities where the conditions were clear.
   e. Calculate the difference between the high and low temperatures for each city.
   f. Display the high and low temperatures for each city in both Fahrenheit and Celsius.

Submit your assignment in the format specified by your instructor.

Part 2: ✹ You made several decisions while creating the queries in this assignment, including the grouping in Steps c and d and the calculations in Steps e and f. What was the rationale behind your decisions? How would you modify the query in Step d above to show the average high and low temperatures in cities grouped by Condition?

Learn Online

Reinforce what you learned in this chapter with games, exercises, training, and many other online activities and resources.

Student Companion Site   Reinforcement activities and resources are available at no additional cost on www.cengagebrain.com. Visit www.cengage.com/ct/studentdownload for detailed instructions about accessing the resources available at the Student Companion Site.

SAM   Put your skills into practice with SAM! If you have a SAM account, go to www.cengage.com/sam2013 to access SAM assignments for this chapter.

3 | Maintaining a Database

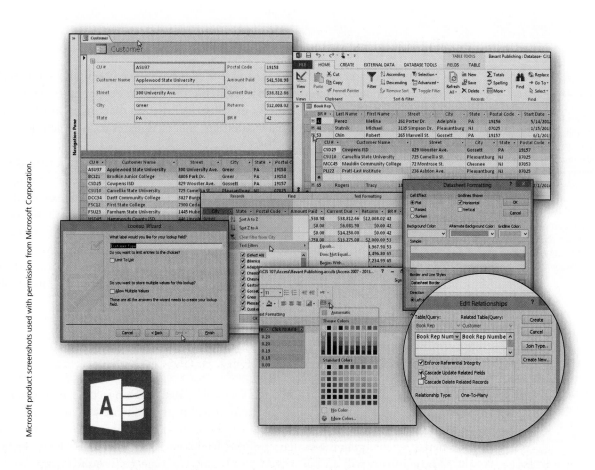

Objectives

You will have mastered the material in this chapter when you can:

- Add, change, and delete records
- Search for records
- Filter records
- Update a table design
- Use action queries to update records
- Use delete queries to delete records
- Specify validation rules, default values, and formats

- Create and use single-valued lookup fields
- Create and use multivalued lookup fields
- Add new fields to an existing report
- Format a datasheet
- Specify referential integrity
- Use a subdatasheet
- Sort records

3 | Maintaining a Database

Introduction

Once you have created a database and loaded it with data, you must maintain it. **Maintaining the database** means modifying the data to keep it up to date by adding new records, changing the data for existing records, and deleting records. Updating can include mass updates or mass deletions, that is, updates to, or deletions of, many records at the same time.

Maintenance of a database also can involve the need to **restructure the database** periodically, that is, to change the database structure. Restructuring can include adding new fields to a table, changing the characteristics of existing fields, and removing existing fields. Restructuring also includes the creation of validation rules and referential integrity. Validation rules ensure the validity of the data in the database, whereas referential integrity ensures the validity of the relationships. Maintaining a database also can include filtering records, a process that ensures that only the records that satisfy some criterion appear when viewing and updating the data in a table. Changing the appearance of a datasheet is a maintenance activity.

Project — Maintaining a Database

Bavant Publishing faces the task of keeping its database up to date. As the company takes on new customers and book reps, it will need to add new records, make changes to existing records, and delete records. Bavant believes that it can serve its customers better by changing the structure of the database to categorize the customers by type. The company will do this by adding a Customer Type field to the Customer table. Book reps believe they can maintain better customer relationships if the database includes the list of resources that are of interest to each customer. The company will do so by adding a Resources Needed field to the Customer table. Because customers may need more than one resource, this field will be a multivalued field, which is a field that can store multiple values or entries. Along with these changes, Bavant staff wants to change the appearance of a datasheet when displaying data.

Bavant would like the ability to make mass updates, that is, to update or delete many records in a single operation. It wants rules that make sure users can enter only valid, or appropriate, data into the database. Bavant also wants to ensure that the database cannot contain the name of a customer who is not associated with a specific book rep.

Figure 3–1 summarizes some of the various types of activities involved in maintaining the Bavant Publishing database.

Figure 3–1

Roadmap

In this chapter, you will learn how to maintain a database by performing the tasks shown in Figure 3–1. The following roadmap identifies general activities you will perform as you progress through this chapter:

1. UPDATE RECORDS using a form.
2. FILTER RECORDS using various filtering options.
3. CHANGE the STRUCTURE of a table.
4. Make MASS CHANGES to a table.
5. Create VALIDATION RULES.
6. CHANGE the APPEARANCE of a datasheet.
7. Specify REFERENTIAL INTEGRITY.
8. ORDER RECORDS in a datasheet.

At the beginning of step instructions throughout the chapter, you will see an abbreviated form of this roadmap. The abbreviated roadmap uses colors to indicate chapter progress: gray means the chapter is beyond that activity; blue means the task being shown is covered in that activity, and black means that activity is yet to be covered. For example, the following abbreviated roadmap indicates the chapter would be showing a task in the 3 CHANGE STRUCTURE activity.

1 UPDATE RECORDS | 2 FILTER RECORDS | 3 CHANGE STRUCTURE | 4 MASS CHANGES | 5 VALIDATION RULES

6 CHANGE APPEARANCE | 7 REFERENTIAL INTEGRITY | 8 ORDER RECORDS

Use the abbreviated roadmap as a progress guide while you read or step through the instructions in this chapter.

For an introduction to Windows and instruction about how to perform basic Windows tasks, read the Office and Windows chapter at the beginning of this book, where you can learn how to resize windows, change screen resolution, create folders, move and rename files, use Windows Help, and much more.

For an introduction to Office and instruction about how to perform basic tasks in Office apps, read the Office and Windows chapter at the beginning of this book, where you can learn how to run an application, use the ribbon, save a file, open a file, exit an application, use Help, and much more.

To Run Access

If you are using a computer to step through the project in this chapter and you want your screens to match the figures in this book, you should change your screen's resolution to 1366 × 768. For information about how to change a computer's resolution, refer to the Office and Windows chapter at the beginning of this book.

The following steps, which assume Windows 8 is running, use the Start screen or the search box to run Access based on a typical installation. You may need to ask your instructor how to run Access on your computer. For a detailed example of the procedure summarized below, refer to the Office and Windows chapter.

1 Scroll the Start screen for an Access 2013 tile. If your Start screen contains an Access 2013 tile, tap or click it to run Access and then proceed to Step 5; if the Start screen does not contain the Access 2013 tile, proceed to the next step to search for the Access app.

2 Swipe in from the right edge of the screen or point to the upper-right corner of the screen to display the Charms bar, and then tap or click the Search charm on the Charms bar to display the Search menu.

3 Type **Access** as the search text in the Search text box and watch the search results appear in the Apps list.

4 Tap or click Access 2013 in the search results to run Access.

5 If the Access window is not maximized, tap or click the Maximize button on its title bar to maximize the window.

To Open a Database from Access

The following steps open the Bavant Publishing database from the location you specified when you first created it (for example, the Access folder in the CIS 101 folder). For a detailed example of the procedure summarized below, refer to the Office and Windows chapter at the beginning of this book.

One of the few differences between Windows 7 and Windows 8 occurs in the steps to run Access. If you are using Windows 7, click the Start button, type **Access** in the 'Search programs and files' box, click Access 2013, and then, if necessary, maximize the Access window. For detailed steps to run Access in Windows 7, refer to the Office and Windows chapter at the beginning of this book. For a summary of the steps, refer to the Quick Reference located at the back of this book.

1 Tap or click FILE on the ribbon to open the Backstage view, if necessary.

2 If the database you want to open is displayed in the Recent list, tap or click the file name to open the database and display the opened database in the Access window; then skip to Step 7. If the database you want to open is not displayed in the Recent list or if the Recent list does not appear, tap or click 'Open Other Files' to display the Open Gallery.

3 If the database you want to open is displayed in the Recent list in the Open gallery, tap or click the file name to open the database and display the opened database in the Access window; then skip to Step 7.

4 Tap or click Computer, SkyDrive, or another location in the left pane and then navigate to the location of the database to be opened (for example, the Access folder in the CIS 101 folder).

5 Tap or click Bavant Publishing to select the database to be opened.

6 Tap or click the Open button (Open dialog box) to open the selected file and display the opened database in the Access window.

7 If a SECURITY WARNING appears, tap or click the Enable Content button.

Updating Records

Keeping the data in a database up to date requires updating records in three ways: adding new records, changing the data in existing records, and deleting existing records. In Chapter 1, you added records to a database using Datasheet view; that is, as you added records, the records appeared on the screen in a datasheet. The data looked like a table. When you need to add additional records, you can use the same techniques.

In Chapter 1, you used a simple form to view records. You also can use a **split form**, a form that allows you to simultaneously view both simple form and datasheet views of the data. You can use either portion of a split form to add or update records. To add new records, change existing records, or delete records, you use the same techniques you used in Datasheet view.

BTW
The Ribbon and Screen Resolution
Access may change how the groups and buttons within the groups appear on the ribbon, depending on the computer's screen resolution. Thus, your ribbon may look different from the ones in this book if you are using a screen resolution other than 1366 × 768.

To Create a Split Form

1 UPDATE RECORDS | 2 FILTER RECORDS | 3 CHANGE STRUCTURE | 4 MASS CHANGES | 5 VALIDATION RULES
6 CHANGE APPEARANCE | 7 REFERENTIAL INTEGRITY | 8 ORDER RECORDS

The following steps create a split form. *Why? With a split form, you have the advantage of seeing a single record in a form, while simultaneously viewing several records in a datasheet.*

- Open the Navigation Pane if it is currently closed.
- If necessary, tap or click the Customer table in the Navigation Pane to select it.
- Tap or click CREATE on the ribbon to display the CREATE tab.
- Tap or click the More Forms button (CREATE tab | Forms group) to display the More Forms menu (Figure 3–2).

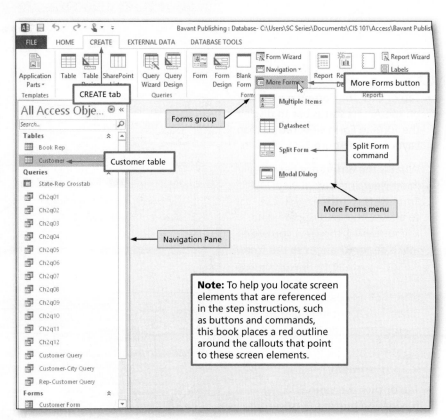

Figure 3–2

2

- Tap or click Split Form to create a split form based on the Customer table.

- Close the Navigation Pane (Figure 3–3).

Q&A Is the form automatically saved?
No. You will take specific actions later to save the form.

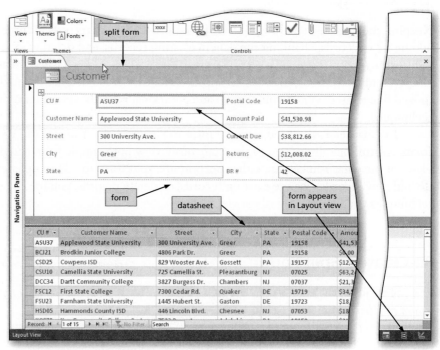

Figure 3–3

3

- Tap or click the Form View button on the Access status bar to display the form in Form view rather than Layout view (Figure 3–4).

Q&A What is the difference between Form view and Layout view?
Form view is the view you use to view, enter, and update data. Layout view is the view you use to make design changes to the form. It shows you the form with data in it so you can immediately see the effects of any design changes you make, but is not intended to be used to enter and update data.

 **Experiment**

- Tap or click the various Navigation buttons (First record, Next record, Previous record, Last record, and, 'New (blank) record') to see each button's effect. Tap or click the Current Record box, change the record number, and press the ENTER key to see how to move to a specific record.

Figure 3–4

4

- Tap or click the Save button on the Quick Access Toolbar to display the Save As dialog box.

- Type **Customer Split Form** as the form name (Figure 3–5).

5

- Tap or click the OK button (Save As dialog box) to save the form.

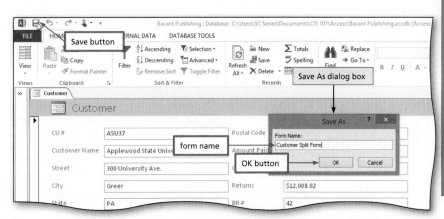

Figure 3–5

Other Ways

1. Press and hold or right-click tab for form, tap or click Form View on shortcut menu

---

To Use a Form to Add Records

1 UPDATE RECORDS | 2 FILTER RECORDS | 3 CHANGE STRUCTURE | 4 MASS CHANGES | 5 VALIDATION RULES
6 CHANGE APPEARANCE | 7 REFERENTIAL INTEGRITY | 8 ORDER RECORDS

Once a form or split form is open in Form view, you can add records using the same techniques you used to add records in Datasheet view. In a split form, the changes you make on the form are automatically made on the datasheet. You do not need to take any special action. The following steps use the split form that you just created to add records. **Why?** *With a split form, as you add a record, you can immediately see the effect of the addition on the datasheet.*

1

- Tap or click the 'New (blank) record' button on the Navigation bar to enter a new record, and then type the data for the new record, as shown in Figure 3–6. Press the TAB key after typing the data in each field, except after typing the data for the final field (Book Rep Number).

2

- Press the TAB key to complete the entry of the record.

- Close the form.

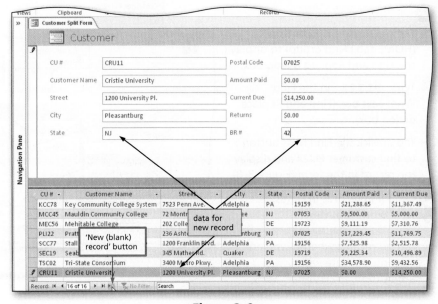

Figure 3–6

Other Ways

1. Tap or click New button (HOME tab | Records group) 2. Press CTRL+PLUS SIGN (+)

To Search for a Record

1 UPDATE RECORDS | 2 FILTER RECORDS | 3 CHANGE STRUCTURE | 4 MASS CHANGES | 5 VALIDATION RULES
6 CHANGE APPEARANCE | 7 REFERENTIAL INTEGRITY | 8 ORDER RECORDS

In the database environment, **searching** means looking for records that satisfy some criteria. Looking for the customer whose number is PLI22 is an example of searching. The queries in Chapter 2 also were examples of searching. Access had to locate those records that satisfied the criteria.

You can perform a search in Form view or Datasheet view without creating a query. The following steps search for the customer whose number is PLI22. *Why? You want to locate the record quickly so you can update this customer's record.*

- Open the Navigation Pane.

- Scroll down in the Navigation Pane, if necessary, so that Customer Split Form appears on your screen, press and hold or right-click Customer Split Form to display a shortcut menu, and then tap or click Open on the shortcut menu to open the form in Form view.

Q&A Which command on the shortcut menu gives me Form view? I see both Layout View and Design View, but no option for Form View.
The Open command opens the form in Form view.

- Close the Navigation Pane (Figure 3–7).

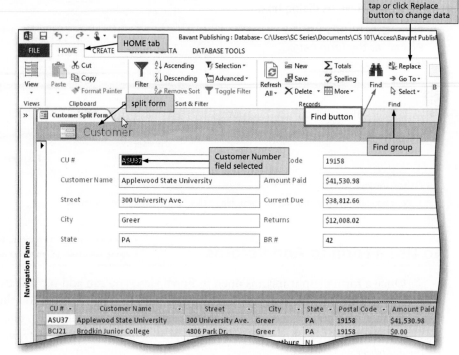

Figure 3–7

- Tap or click the Find button (HOME tab | Find group) to display the Find and Replace dialog box.

- Type **PLI22** in the Find What text box (Find and Replace dialog box).

- Tap or click the Find Next button to find customer PLI22 and display the record in the form (Figure 3–8).

Q&A Can I find records in Datasheet view or in Form view?
Yes. You use the same process to find records whether you are viewing the data with a split form, in Datasheet view, or in Form view.

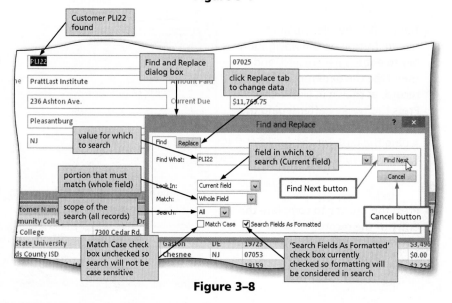

Figure 3–8

- Tap or click the Cancel button (Find and Replace dialog box) to remove the dialog box from the screen.

Q&A Why does the button in the dialog box read, Find Next, rather than simply Find?
In some cases, after locating a record that satisfies a criterion, you might need to find the next record that satisfies the same criterion. For example, if you just found the first customer whose book rep number is 42, you then may want to find the second such customer, then the third, and so on. To do so, tap or click the Find Next button. You will not need to retype the value each time.

Other Ways

1. Press CTRL+F

CONSIDER THIS

Can you replace one value with another using the Find and Replace dialog box?
Yes. Either tap or click the Replace button (HOME tab | Find group) or tap or click the Replace tab in the Find and Replace dialog box. You then can enter both the value to find and the new value.

To Update the Contents of a Record

1 UPDATE RECORDS | 2 FILTER RECORDS | 3 CHANGE STRUCTURE | 4 MASS CHANGES | 5 VALIDATION RULES
6 CHANGE APPEARANCE | 7 REFERENTIAL INTEGRITY | 8 ORDER RECORDS

The following step uses Form view to change the name of customer PLI22 from PrattLast Institute to Pratt-Last Institute. *Why? Bavant determined that this customer's name was missing the hyphen.* After locating the record to be changed, select the field to be changed by clicking the field. You also can press the TAB key repeatedly until the desired field is selected. Then make the appropriate changes. (Clicking the field automatically produces an insertion point. If you use the TAB key, you will need to press F2 to produce an insertion point.)

- Tap or click in the Customer Name field in the form for customer PLI22 immediately to the left of the L in the word, PrattLast.

- Type a hyphen (-) before Last.

- Press the TAB key to complete the change and move to the next field (Figure 3–9).

Q&A
Could I have changed the contents of the field in the datasheet portion of the split form?
Yes. You will first need to ensure the record to be changed appears in the datasheet. You then can change the value just as in the form.

Do I need to save my change?
No. Once you move to another record or close this form, the change to the name will become permanent.

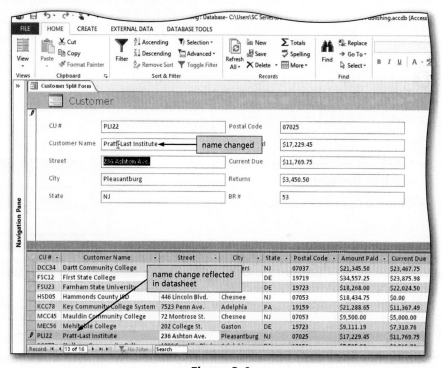

Figure 3–9

To Delete a Record

1 UPDATE RECORDS | 2 FILTER RECORDS | 3 CHANGE STRUCTURE | 4 MASS CHANGES | 5 VALIDATION RULES
6 CHANGE APPEARANCE | 7 REFERENTIAL INTEGRITY | 8 ORDER RECORDS

When records no longer are needed, you should delete the records (remove them) from the table. The steps on the next page delete customer HSD05. *Why? Customer HSD05 no longer is served by Bavant Publishing and its final payment has been received, so the record can be deleted.*

1

- With the Customer Split Form open, tap or click the record selector in the datasheet for customer HSD05 to select the record (Figure 3–10).

Q&A

That technique works in the datasheet portion. How do I select the record in the form portion?

With the desired record appearing in the form, tap or click the record selector (the triangle in front of the record) to select the entire record.

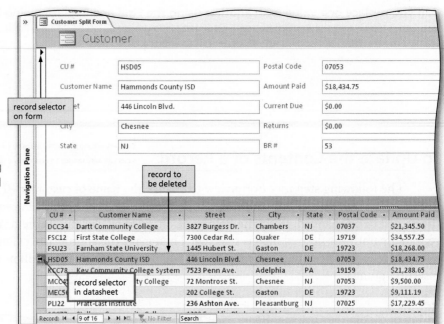

Figure 3–10

2

- Press the DELETE key to delete the record (Figure 3–11).

3

- Tap or click the Yes button to complete the deletion.

- Close the Customer Split Form.

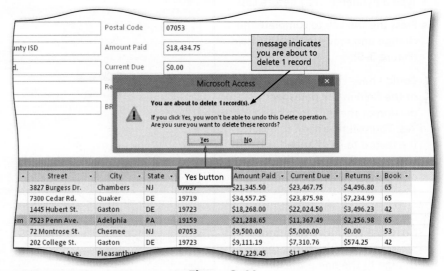

Figure 3–11

Other Ways

1. Tap or click Delete arrow (HOME tab | Records group), tap or click Delete Record on Delete menu

Filtering Records

You can use the Find button in either Datasheet view or Form view to locate a record quickly that satisfies some criterion (for example, the customer number is PLI22). All records appear, however, not just the record or records that satisfy the criterion. To have only the record or records that satisfy the criterion appear, use a **filter**. Four types of filters are available: Filter By Selection, Common Filters, Filter By Form, and Advanced Filter/Sort. You can use a filter in either Datasheet view or Form view.

To Use Filter By Selection

1 UPDATE RECORDS | 2 FILTER RECORDS | 3 CHANGE STRUCTURE | 4 MASS CHANGES | 5 VALIDATION RULES
6 CHANGE APPEARANCE | 7 REFERENTIAL INTEGRITY | 8 ORDER RECORDS

To use Filter By Selection, you give Access an example of the data you want by selecting the data within the table. You then choose the option you want on the Selection menu. The following steps use Filter By Selection in Datasheet view to display only the records for customers in Greer. **Why?** *Filter by Selection is appropriate for displaying these records and is the simplest type of filter.*

1

- Open the Navigation Pane.

- Open the Customer table, and close the Navigation Pane.

- Tap or click the City field on the first record to specify Greer as the city (Figure 3–12).

Q&A Could I have selected the City field on another record where the city is also Greer to select the same city? Yes. It does not matter which record you select as long as the city is Greer.

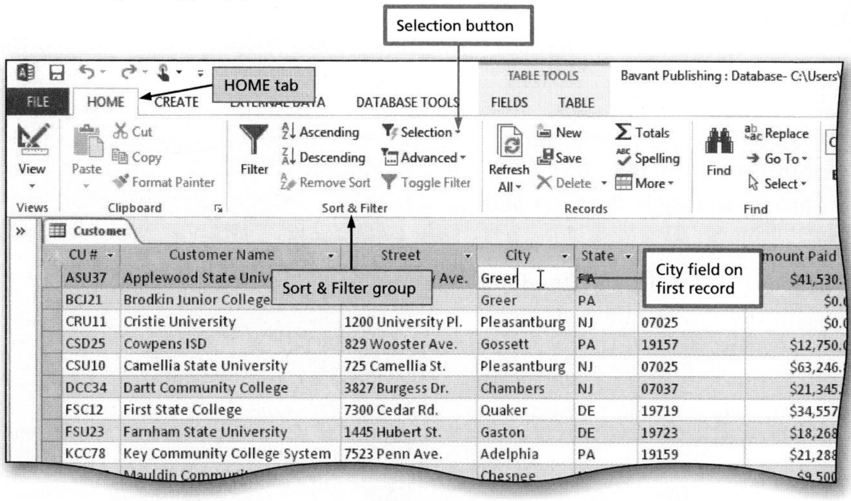

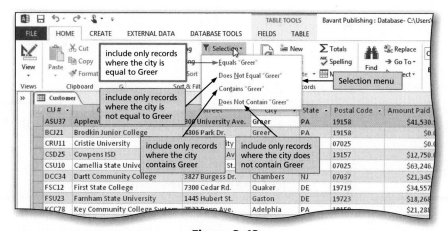

Figure 3–12

2

- Tap or click the Selection button (HOME tab | Sort & Filter group) to display the Selection menu (Figure 3–13).

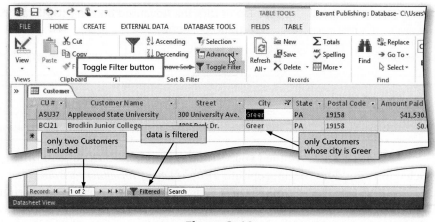

Figure 3–13

3

- Tap or click Equals "Greer" to select only those customers whose city is Greer (Figure 3–14).

Q&A Can I also filter in Form view? Yes. Filtering works the same whether you are viewing the data with a split form, in Datasheet view, or in Form view.

Figure 3–14

To Toggle a Filter

The Toggle Filter button toggles between filtered and unfiltered displays of the records in the table. That is, if only filtered records currently appear, clicking the Toggle Filter button will redisplay all records. If all records are currently displayed and there is a filter that is in effect, clicking the Toggle Filter button will display only the filtered records. If no filter is active, the Toggle Filter button will be dimmed, so clicking it would have no effect.

The following step toggles the filter. *Why? Bavant wants to once again view all the records.*

1

- Tap or click the Toggle Filter button (HOME tab | Sort & Filter group) to toggle the filter and redisplay all records (Figure 3–15).

Q&A Does that action clear the filter? No. The filter is still in place. If you tap or click the Toggle Filter button a second time, you will again see only the filtered records.

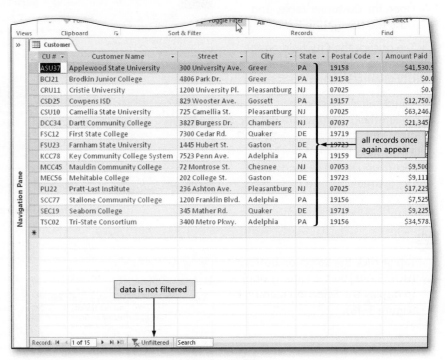

Figure 3–15

To Clear a Filter

Once you have finished using a filter, you can clear the filter. After doing so, you no longer will be able to use the filter by clicking the Toggle Filter button. The following steps clear the filter.

1 Tap or click the Advanced button (HOME tab | Sort & Filter group) to display the Advanced menu.

2 Tap or click 'Clear All Filters' on the Advanced menu.

To Use a Common Filter

If you have determined you want to include those customers whose city begins with G, Filter By Selection would not be appropriate. *Why? None of the options within Filter by Selection would support this type of criterion.* You can filter individual fields by clicking the arrow to the right of the field name and using one of the **common filters** that are available for the field. You can modify a common filter by customizing it for the specific field. The following steps customize a common filter to include only those customers whose city begins with G.

1

- Tap or click the City arrow to display the common filter menu.

- Point to the Text Filters command to display the custom text filters (Figure 3–16).

Q&A I selected the City field and then clicked the Filter button on the HOME tab | Sort & Filter group. My screen looks the same. Is this right?
Yes. That is another way to display the common filter menu.

If I wanted certain cities included, could I use the check boxes?
Yes. Be sure the cities you want are the only ones checked.

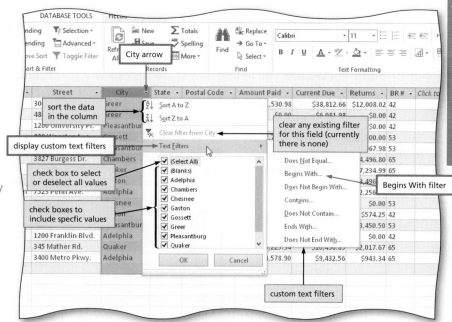

Figure 3–16

2

- Tap or click Begins With to display the Custom Filter dialog box.

- Type G as the 'City begins with' value (Figure 3–17).

🔍 **Experiment**

- Try other options in the common filter menu to see their effects. When done, once again select those customers whose city begins with G.

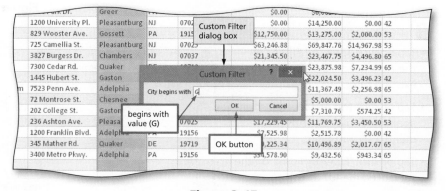

Figure 3–17

3

- Tap or click the OK button to filter the records (Figure 3–18).

Q&A Can I use the same technique in Form view?
In Form view, you would need to tap or click the field and then tap or click the Filter button to display the Common Filter menu. The rest of the process would be the same.

4

- Tap or click the Toggle Filter button (HOME tab | Sort & Filter group) to toggle the filter and redisplay all records.

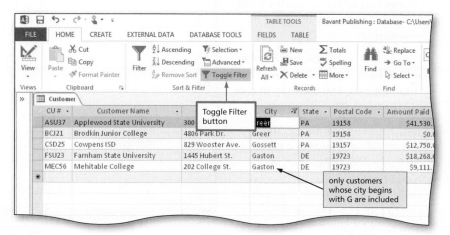

Figure 3–18

Other Ways

1. Press and hold or right-click field, tap or click Text Filters on shortcut menu

To Use Filter By Form

Filter By Selection and the common filters method you just used are quick and easy ways to filter by the value in a single field. For filters that involve multiple fields, however, these methods are not appropriate, so you would use Filter By Form. *Why? Filter By Form allows you to filter based on multiple fields and criteria.* For example, Filter By Form would allow you to find only those customers whose returns are $0.00 and whose book rep number is 42. The following steps use Filter By Form to restrict the records that appear.

1
- Tap or click the Advanced button (HOME tab | Sort & Filter group) to display the Advanced menu (Figure 3–19).

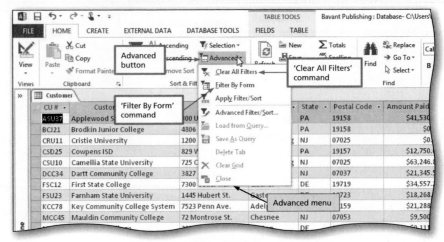

Figure 3–19

2
- Tap or click 'Clear All Filters' on the Advanced menu to clear the existing filter.
- Tap or click the Advanced button again to display the Advanced menu a second time.
- Tap or click 'Filter By Form' on the Advanced menu.
- Tap or click the blank row in the Returns field, tap or click the arrow that appears, and then tap or click 0 to specify the value in the Returns field.
- Tap or click the Book Rep Number (BR #) field, tap or click the arrow that appears, and then tap or click 42 (Figure 3–20).

Q&A
Is there any difference in the process if I am viewing a table in Form view rather than in Datasheet view?
In Form view, you will make your entries in a form rather than a datasheet. Otherwise, the process is the same.

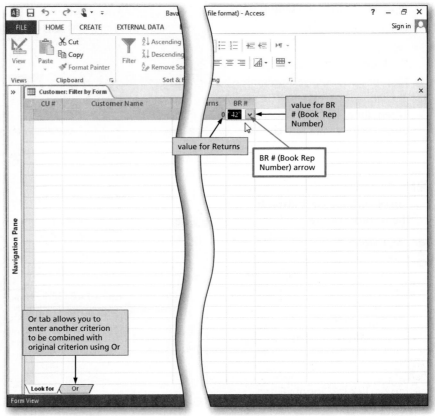

Figure 3–20

3

- Tap or click the Toggle Filter button (HOME tab | Sort & Filter group) to apply the filter (Figure 3–21).

🔍 **Experiment**

- Select 'Filter by Form' again and enter different criteria. In each case, toggle the filter to see the effect of your selection. When done, once again select those customers whose returns are 0 and whose book rep number is 42.

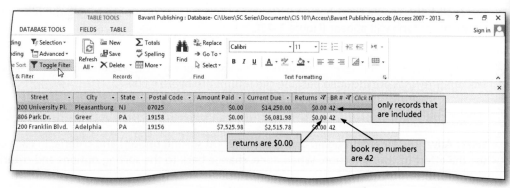

Figure 3–21

Other Ways

1. Tap or click the Advanced button (HOME tab | Sort & Filter group), tap or click Apply Filter/Sort on Advanced menu

---

To Use Advanced Filter/Sort

1 UPDATE RECORDS | 2 FILTER RECORDS | 3 CHANGE STRUCTURE | 4 MASS CHANGES | 5 VALIDATION RULES
6 CHANGE APPEARANCE | 7 REFERENTIAL INTEGRITY | 8 ORDER RECORDS

In some cases, your criteria will be too complex even for Filter By Form. You might decide you want to include any customer whose returns are 0 and whose book rep number is 42. Additionally, you might want to include any customer whose returns are greater than $4,000, no matter who the customer's book rep is. Further, you might want to have the results sorted by name. The following steps use Advanced Filter/Sort to accomplish this task. **Why?** *Advanced Filter/Sort supports complex criteria as well as the ability to sort the results.*

1

- Tap or click the Advanced button (HOME tab | Sort & Filter group) to display the Advanced menu, and then tap or click 'Clear All Filters' on the Advanced menu to clear the existing filter.

- Tap or click the Advanced button to display the Advanced menu a second time.

- Tap or click 'Advanced Filter/Sort' on the Advanced menu.

- Expand the size of the field list so all the fields in the Customer table appear.

- Include the Customer Name field and select Ascending as the sort order to specify the order in which the filtered records will appear.

- Include the Book Rep Number field and enter 42 as the criterion.

- Include the Returns field and enter 0 as the criterion in the Criteria row and >4000 as the criterion in the or row (Figure 3–22).

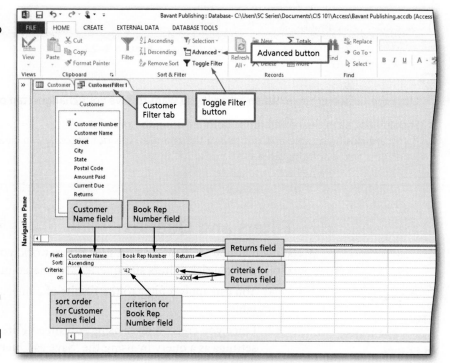

Figure 3–22

- Tap or click the Toggle Filter button (HOME tab | Sort & Filter group) to toggle the filter so that only records that satisfy the criteria will appear (Figure 3–23).

Q&A Why are those particular records included?
The second, fourth, and seventh records are included because the book rep number is 42 and the returns are $0.00. The other records are included because the returns are over $4,000.

Experiment

- Select Advanced Filter/Sort again and enter different sorting options and criteria. In each case, toggle the filter to see the effect of your selection. When done, change back to the sorting options and criteria you entered in Step 1.

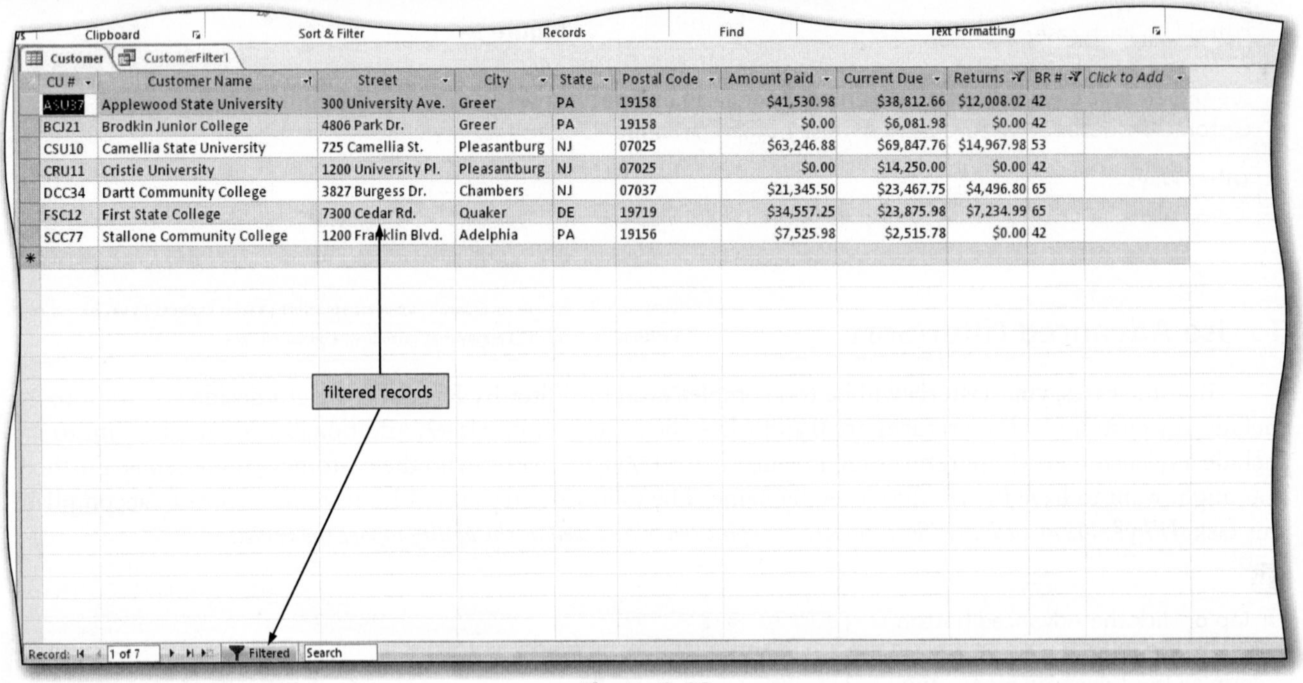
Clipboard
Sort & Filter
Records
Find
Text Formatting
Customer
CustomerFilter1
CU # | Customer Name | Street | City | State | Postal Code | Amount Paid | Current Due | Returns | BR # | Click to Add
ASU37 | Applewood State University | 300 University Ave. | Greer | PA | 19158 | $41,530.98 | $38,812.66 | $12,008.02 | 42
BCJ21 | Brodkin Junior College | 4806 Park Dr. | Greer | PA | 19158 | $0.00 | $6,081.98 | $0.00 | 42
CSU10 | Camellia State University | 725 Camellia St. | Pleasantburg | NJ | 07025 | $63,246.88 | $69,847.76 | $14,967.98 | 53
CRU11 | Cristie University | 1200 University Pl. | Pleasantburg | NJ | 07025 | $0.00 | $14,250.00 | $0.00 | 42
DCC34 | Dartt Community College | 3827 Burgess Dr. | Chambers | NJ | 07037 | $21,345.50 | $23,467.75 | $4,496.80 | 65
FSC12 | First State College | 7300 Cedar Rd. | Quaker | DE | 19719 | $34,557.25 | $23,875.98 | $7,234.99 | 65
SCC77 | Stallone Community College | 1200 Franklin Blvd. | Adelphia | PA | 19156 | $7,525.98 | $2,515.78 | $0.00 | 42
filtered records
Record: 1 of 7
Filtered
Search

Figure 3–23

3

- Close the Customer table. When asked if you want to save your changes, tap or click the No button.

Q&A Should I not have cleared all filters before closing the table?
If you are closing a table and not saving the changes, it is not necessary to clear the filter. No filter will be active when you next open the table.

Filters and Queries

Now that you are familiar with how filters work, you might notice similarities between filters and queries. Filters and queries are related in three ways.

1. You can apply a filter to the results of a query just as you can apply a filter to a table.
2. Once you create a filter using Advanced Filter/Sort, you can save the filter settings as a query by using the 'Save as Query' command on the Advanced menu.
3. You can restore filter settings that you previously saved in a query by using the 'Load from Query' command on the Advanced menu.

BTW
Using Wildcards in Filters
Both the question mark(?) and the asterisk (*) wildcards can be used in filters created using Advanced Filter/Sort.

How do you determine whether to use a query or a filter?
The following guidelines apply to this decision.

If you think that you will frequently want to display records that satisfy this exact criterion, you should consider creating a query whose results only contain the records that satisfy the criterion. To display those records in the future, simply open the query.

If you are viewing data in a datasheet or form and decide you want to restrict the records to be included, it is easier to create a filter than a query. You can create and use the filter while you are viewing the data.

If you have created a filter that you would like to be able to use again, you can save the filter as a query.

Once you have decided to use a filter, how do you determine which type of filter to use?
If your criterion for filtering is that the value in a particular field matches or does not match a certain specific value, you can use Filter By Selection.

If your criterion only involves a single field but is more complex (for example, the criterion specifies that the value in the field begins with a certain collection of letters) you can use a common filter.

If your criterion involves more than one field, use Filter By Form.

If your criterion involves more than a single And or Or, or if it involves sorting, you will probably find it simpler to use Advanced Filter/Sort.

Break Point: If you wish to take a break, this is a good place to do so. You can quit Access now. To resume at a later time, start Access, open the database called Bavant Publishing, and continue following the steps from this location forward.

Changing the Database Structure

When you initially create a database, you define its **structure**; that is, you assign names and types to all the fields. In many cases, the structure you first define will not continue to be appropriate as you use the database.

Perhaps a field currently in the table no longer is necessary. If no one ever uses a particular field, it is not needed in the table. Because it is occupying space and serving no useful purpose, you should remove it from the table. You also would need to delete the field from any forms, reports, or queries that include it.

More commonly, an organization will find that it needs to maintain additional information that was not anticipated at the time the database was first designed. The organization's own requirements may have changed. In addition, outside regulations that the organization must satisfy may change as well. Either case requires the addition of fields to an existing table.

Although you can make some changes to the database structure in Datasheet view, it is usually easier and better to make these changes in Design view.

TO DELETE A FIELD

If a field in one of your tables no longer is needed, you should delete the field; for example, it may serve no useful purpose, or it may have been included by mistake. To delete a field, you would use the following steps.

1. Open the table in Design view.
2. Tap or click the row selector for the field to be deleted.
3. Press the DELETE key.
4. When Access displays the dialog box requesting confirmation that you want to delete the field, tap or click the Yes button.

BTW
Changing Data Types
It is possible to change the data type for a field that already contains data. Before doing so, you should consider the effect on other database objects, such as forms, queries, and reports. For example, you could convert a Short Text field to a Long Text field if you find that you do not have enough space to store the data that you need. You also could convert a Number field to a Currency field or vice versa.

BTW
Organizing Files and Folders
You should organize and store files in folders so that you easily can find the files later. For example, if you are taking an introductory computer class called CIS 101, a good practice would be to save all Access files in an Access folder in a CIS 101 folder. For a discussion of folders and detailed examples of creating folders, refer to the Office and Windows chapter at the beginning of this book.

BTW
Database Backup
If you are doing mass
changes to a database, be
sure to back up the database
prior to doing the updates.

TO MOVE A FIELD

If you decide you would rather have a field in one of your tables in a different position, you can move it. To move a field, you would use the following steps.

1. Open the table in Design view.
2. Tap or click the row selector for the field to be deleted.
3. Drag the field to the desired position.
4. Release the mouse button or lift your finger to place the field in the new position.

To Add a New Field

1 UPDATE RECORDS | 2 FILTER RECORDS | 3 CHANGE STRUCTURE | 4 MASS CHANGES | 5 VALIDATION RULES
6 CHANGE APPEARANCE | 7 REFERENTIAL INTEGRITY | 8 ORDER RECORDS

You can add fields to a table in a database. The following steps add the Customer Type field to the Customer table immediately after the Postal Code field. *Why? Bavant Publishing has decided that it needs to categorize its customers by adding an additional field, Customer Type. The possible values for Customer Type are HS (which indicates the customer is a high school or an intermediate school district), COM (which indicates the customer is a community college), or UNI (which indicates the customer is a university or four-year college).*

● If necessary, open the Navigation Pane, open the Customer table in Design view, and then close the Navigation Pane.

● Tap or click the row selector for the Amount Paid field, and then press the INSERT key to insert a blank row above the selected field (Figure 3–24).

● Tap or click the Field Name column for the new field to produce an insertion point.

● Type **Customer Type** as the field name and then press the TAB key.

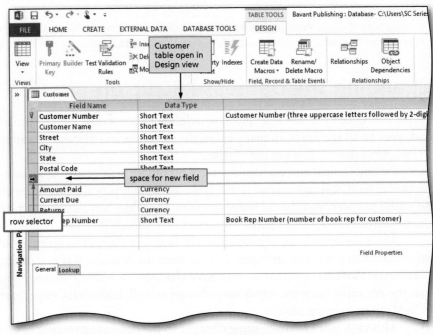

Figure 3–24

Other Ways

1. Tap or click Insert Rows button (TABLE TOOLS Design tab | Tools group)

To Create a Lookup Field

1 UPDATE RECORDS | 2 FILTER RECORDS | 3 CHANGE STRUCTURE | 4 MASS CHANGES | 5 VALIDATION RULES
6 CHANGE APPEARANCE | 7 REFERENTIAL INTEGRITY | 8 ORDER RECORDS

A **lookup field** allows the user to select from a list of values when updating the contents of the field. The following steps make the Customer Type field a lookup field. *Why? The Customer Type field has only three possible values, making it an appropriate lookup field.*

1

- If necessary, tap or click the Data Type column for the Customer Type field, and then tap or click the Data Type arrow to display the menu of available data types (Figure 3–25).

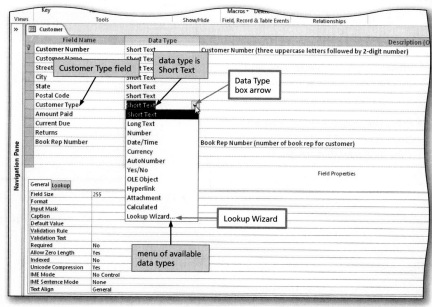

Figure 3–25

2

- Tap or click Lookup Wizard, and then tap or click the 'I will type in the values that I want.' option button (Lookup Wizard dialog box) to indicate that you will type in the values (Figure 3–26).

Q&A When would I use the other option button?

You would use the other option button if the data to be entered in this field were found in another table or query.

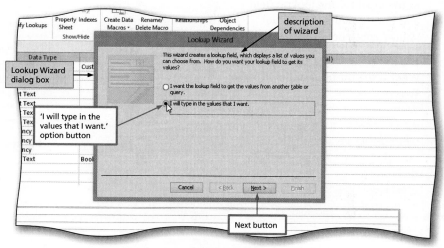

Figure 3–26

3

- Tap or click the Next button to display the next Lookup Wizard screen (Figure 3–27).

Q&A Why did I not change the field size for the Customer Type field?

You could have changed the field size to 3, but it is not necessary. When you create a lookup field and indicate specific values for the field, you automatically restrict the field size.

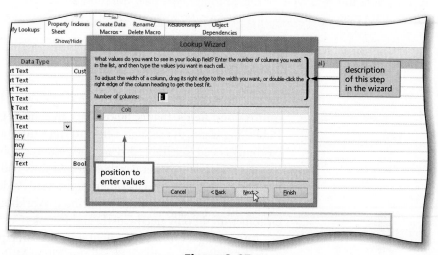

Figure 3–27

● Tap or click the first row of the table (below Col1), and then type **HS** as the value in the first row.

● Press the DOWN ARROW key, and then type **COM** as the value in the second row.

● Press the DOWN ARROW key, and then type **UNI** as the value in the third row (Figure 3–28).

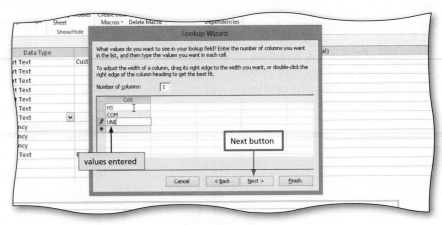

Figure 3–28

● Tap or click the Next button to display the next Lookup Wizard screen.

● Ensure Customer Type is entered as the label for the lookup field and that the 'Allow Multiple Values' check box is NOT checked (Figure 3–29).

Q&A

What is the purpose of the 'Limit To List' check box?

With a lookup field, users can select from the list of values, in which case they can only select items in the list. They can also type their entry, in which case they are not necessarily limited to items in the list. If you check the 'Limit To List' check box, users would be limited to items in the list, even if they type their entry. You will accomplish this same restriction later in this chapter with a validation rule, so you do not need to check this box.

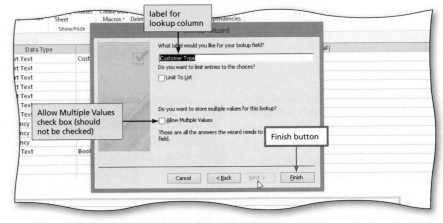

Figure 3–29

● Tap or click the Finish button to complete the definition of the lookup field.

Q&A

Why does the data type for the Customer Type field still show Short Text?

The data type is still Short Text because the values entered in the wizard were entered as text.

To Add a Multivalued Field

Normally, fields contain only a single value. In Access, it is possible to have **multivalued fields**, that is, fields that can contain more than one value. Bavant Publishing wants to use such a field to store the abbreviations of the various resources its customers need (see Table 3–1 for the resource abbreviations and descriptions). Unlike the Customer Type, where each customer only had one type, customers can require multiple resources. One customer might need Audio, PrMan, PrWrk, and Txt (Audio CD, Printed Laboratory Manual, Printed Workbook, and Printed Textbook). Another customer might only need CustD and Ebook (Custom Digital and Electronic Textbook).

Creating a multivalued field uses the same process as creating a lookup field, with the exception that you check the 'Allow Multiple Values' check box. The following steps create a multivalued field.

Table 3–1 Resource Abbreviations and Descriptions	
Resource Abbreviation	**Description**
Audio	Audio CD
CDVD	Culture DVD
CustD	Custom Digital
CustP	Custom Print
Ebook	Electronic Textbook
OlMan	Online Laboratory Manual
OlWrk	Online Workbook
PrMan	Printed Laboratory Manual
PrWrk	Printed Workbook
SDVD	Sitcom DVD
Txt	Printed Textbook

© 2014 Cengage Learning

1 Tap or click the row selector for the Amount Paid field, and then press the INSERT key to insert a blank row.

2 Tap or click the Field Name column for the new field, type **Resources Needed** as the field name, and then press the TAB key.

3 Tap or click the Data Type arrow to display the menu of available data types for the Resources Needed field, and then tap or click Lookup Wizard in the menu of available data types to start the Lookup Wizard.

4 Tap or click the 'I will type in the values that I want.' option button to indicate that you will type in the values.

5 Tap or click the Next button to display the next Lookup Wizard screen.

6 Tap or click the first row of the table (below Col1), and then type **Audio** as the value in the first row.

7 Enter the remaining values from the first column in Table 3–1. Before typing each value, press the DOWN ARROW key to move to a new row.

8 Tap or click the Next button to display the next Lookup Wizard screen.

9 Ensure that Resources Needed is entered as the label for the lookup field.

10 Tap or click the 'Allow Multiple Values' check box to allow the user to enter multiple values.

11 Tap or click the Finish button to complete the definition of the Lookup Wizard field.

BTW

Modifying Table Properties
You can change the properties of a table by opening the table in Design view and then clicking the Property Sheet button. To display the records in a table in an order other than primary key (the default sort order), use the Order By property. For example, to display the Customer table automatically in Customer Name order, change the Order By property setting to Customer. Customer Name in the property box, close the property sheet, and save the change to the table design. When you open the Customer table in Datasheet view, the records will be sorted in Customer Name order.

BTW

Multivalued Fields
Do not use multivalued fields if you plan to move your data to another relational database management system, such as SQL Server at a later date. SQL Server and other relational DMBSs do not support multivalued fields.

TO MODIFY SINGLE OR MULTIVALUED LOOKUP FIELDS

At some point you might want to change the list of choices in a lookup field. If you need to modify a single or multivalued lookup field, you would use the following steps.

1. Open the table in Design view and select the field to be modified.

2. Tap or click the Lookup tab in the Field Properties pane.

3. Change the list in the Row Source property to the desired list of values.

To Add a Calculated Field

A field that can be computed from other fields is called a **calculated field** or a **computed field**. In Chapter 2, you created a calculated field in a query that provided total amount data. In Access 2013, it is also possible to include a calculated field in a table. Users will not be able to update this field. *Why? Access will automatically perform the necessary calculation and display the appropriate value whenever you display or use this field in any way.* The following steps add to the Customer table a field that calculates the sum of the Amount Paid and Current Due fields.

- Tap or click the row selector for the Returns field, and then press the INSERT key to insert a blank row above the selected field.

- Tap or click the Field Name column for the new field.

- Type **Total Amount** as the field name, and then press the TAB key.

- Tap or click the Data Type arrow to display the menu of available data types (Figure 3–30).

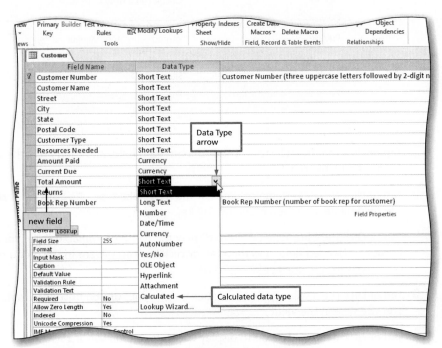

Figure 3–30

- Tap or click Calculated to select the Calculated data type and display the Expression Builder dialog box (Figure 3–31).

Q&A
I do not have the list of fields in the Expression Categories area. What should I do?
Tap or click Customer in the Expression Elements area.

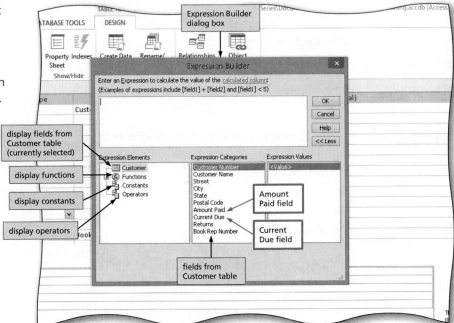

Figure 3–31

- Double-tap or double-click the Amount Paid field in the Expression Categories area (Expression Builder dialog box) to add the field to the expression.

- Type a plus sign (+).

Q&A Could I select the plus sign from a list rather than typing it?
Yes. Tap or click Operators in the Expression Elements area to display available operators, and then double-tap or double-click the plus sign.

- Double-tap or double-click the Current Due field in the Expression Categories area (Expression Builder dialog box) to add the field to the expression (Figure 3–32).

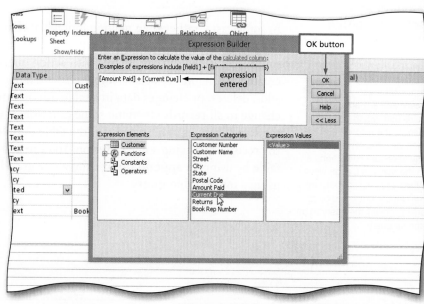

Figure 3–32

- Tap or click the OK button (Expression Builder dialog box) to enter the expression in the Expression property of the Total Amount (Figure 3–33).

Q&A Could I have typed the expression in the Expression Builder dialog box rather than selecting the fields from a list?
Yes. You can use whichever technique you find more convenient.

When I entered a calculated field in a query, I typed the expression in the Zoom dialog box. Could I have used the Expression Builder instead?
Yes. To do so, you would tap or click Build rather than Zoom on the shortcut menu.

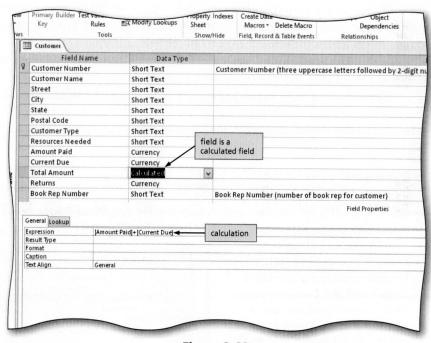

Figure 3–33

To Save the Changes and Close the Table

The following steps save the changes; that is, they save the addition of the new fields and close the table.

1 Tap or click the Save button on the Quick Access Toolbar to save the changes.

2 Close the Customer table.

BTW
Calculated Fields
You can use the the Result Type field property to format the calculated field values.

BTW
Viewing Records
Before Updating
You can view records affected
by an update query before
running the query. To do
so, use the Select button to
convert the query to a select
query, add any additional
fields that would help you
identify the records, and
then view the results. Make
any necessary corrections
to the query in Design view.
When you are satisfied, use
the Update button to once
again convert the query to an
update query.

Mass Changes

In some cases, rather than making individual changes to records, you will want to make mass changes. That is, you will want to add, change, or delete many records in a single operation. You can do this with action queries. Unlike the select queries that you created in Chapter 2, which simply presented data in specific ways, an **action query** adds, deletes, or changes data in a table. An **update query** allows you to make the same change to all records satisfying some criterion. If you omit the criterion, you will make the same changes to all records in the table. A **delete query** allows you to delete all the records satisfying some criterion. You can add the results of a query to an existing table by using an **append query**. You also can add the query results to a new table by using a **make-table query**.

To Use an Update Query

1 UPDATE RECORDS | 2 FILTER RECORDS | 3 CHANGE STRUCTURE | 4 MASS CHANGES | **5 VALIDATION RULES**
6 CHANGE APPEARANCE | 7 REFERENTIAL INTEGRITY | 8 ORDER RECORDS

The new Customer Type field is blank on every record in the Customer table. One approach to entering the information for the field would be to step through the entire table, assigning each record its appropriate value. If most of the customers have the same type, it would be more convenient to use an update query to assign a single value to all customers and then update the Customer Type for those customers whose type differs. An update query makes the same change to all records satisfying a criterion.

In the Bavant Publishing database, for example, most customers are type UNI. Initially, you can set all the values to UNI. Later, you can change the type for community colleges and high schools.

The following steps use an update query to change the value in the Customer Type field to UNI for all the records. Because all records are to be updated, criteria are not required. *Why? If there is a criterion, the update only takes place on those records that satisfy the criterion. Without a criterion, the update applies to all records.*

1

- Create a new query for the Customer table, and ensure the Navigation Pane is closed.

- Tap or click the Update button (QUERY TOOLS DESIGN tab | Query Type group) to specify an update query, double-tap or double-click the Customer Type field to select the field, tap or click the Update To row in the first column of the design grid, and then type UNI as the new value (Figure 3–34).

Q&A
If I change my mind and do not want an update query, how can I change the query back to a select query?
Tap or click the Select button (QUERY TOOLS DESIGN tab | Query Type group).

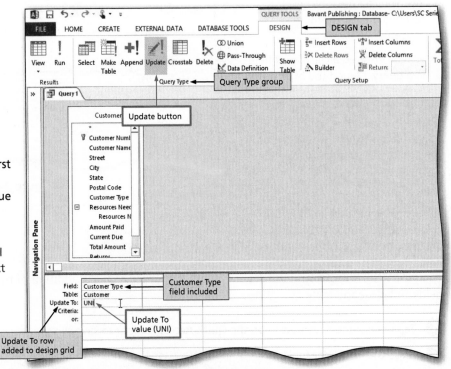

Figure 3–34

2

- Tap or click the Run button (QUERY TOOLS DESIGN tab | Results group) to run the query and update the records (Figure 3–35).

Q&A The dialog box did not appear on my screen when I ran the query. What happened?
If the dialog box did not appear, it means that you did not tap or click the Enable Content button when you first opened the database. Close the database, open it again, and enable the content. Then, create and run the query again.

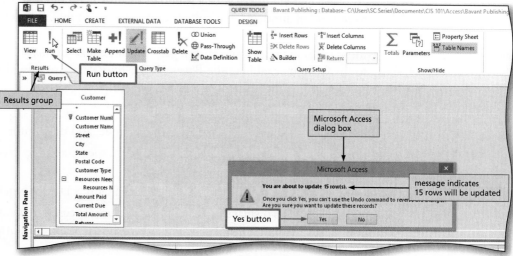

Figure 3–35

3

- Tap or click the Yes button to make the changes.

Experiment

- Create an update query to change the customer type to COM. Enter a criterion to restrict the records to be updated, and then run the query. Open the table to view your changes. When finished, create and run an update query to change the customer type to UNI on all records.

- Close the query. Because you do not need to use this update query again, do not save the query.

Other Ways

1. Press and hold or right-click any open area in upper pane, point to Query Type on shortcut menu, tap or click Update Query on Query Type submenu

TO USE A DELETE QUERY

In some cases, you might need to delete several records at a time. If, for example, all high school customers are to be serviced by another publisher, the customers with this customer type can be deleted from the Bavant Publishing database. Instead of deleting these customers individually, which could be very time-consuming in a large database, you can delete them in one operation by using a delete query, which is a query that deletes all the records satisfying the criteria entered in the query. To create a delete query, you would use the following steps.

1. Create a query for the table containing the records to be deleted.
2. In Design view, indicate the fields and criteria that will specify the records to delete.
3. Tap or click the Delete button (QUERY TOOLS DESIGN tab | Query Type group).
4. Run the query by clicking the Run button (QUERY TOOLS DESIGN tab | Results group).
5. When Access indicates the number of records to be deleted, tap or click the Yes button.

BTW
Delete Queries
If you do not specify any criteria in a delete query, Access will delete all the records in the table.

TO USE AN APPEND QUERY

An append query adds a group of records from one table, called the Source table, to the end of another table, called the Destination table. For example, suppose that Bavant Publishing acquires some new customers and a database containing a table with those customers. To avoid entering all this information manually, you can append it to the Customer table in the Bavant Publishing database using the append query. To create an append query, you would use the following steps.

1. Create a query for the Source table.
2. In Design view, indicate the fields to include, and then enter any necessary criteria.
3. View the query results to be sure you have specified the correct data, and then return to Design view.
4. Tap or click the Append button (QUERY TOOLS DESIGN tab | Query Type group).
5. When Access displays the Append dialog box, specify the name of the Destination table and its location. Run the query by clicking the Run button (QUERY TOOLS DESIGN tab | Results group).
6. When Access indicates the number of records to be appended, tap or click the OK button.

TO USE A MAKE-TABLE QUERY

In some cases, you might want to create a new table that contains only records copied from an existing table. If so, use a make-table query to add the records to a new table. To create a make-table query, you would use the following steps.

1. Create a query for the Source table.
2. In Design view, indicate the fields to include, and then enter any necessary criteria.
3. View the query results to be sure you have specified the correct data, and then return to Design view.
4. Tap or click the Make Table button (QUERY TOOLS DESIGN tab | Query Type group).
5. When Access displays the Make Table dialog box, specify the name of the Destination table and its location. Run the query by clicking the Run button (QUERY TOOLS DESIGN tab | Results group).
6. When Access indicates the number of records to be inserted, tap or click the OK button.

BTW
Archive Tables
You can use a make table query to create an archive table. An archive table is a table that contains data that is no longer used in operations but that might still be needed by the organization.

Break Point: If you wish to take a break, this is a good place to do so. You can quit Access now. To resume at a later time, start Access, open the database called Bavant Publishing, and continue following the steps from this location forward.

Validation Rules

You now have created, loaded, queried, and updated a database. Nothing you have done so far, however, restricts users to entering only valid data, that is, data that follows the rules established for data in the database. An example of such a rule would be that customer types can only be HS, COM, or UNI. To ensure the entry of valid data, you create **validation rules**, that is, rules that a user must follow when entering the data. As you will see, Access will prevent users from entering data that does not follow the rules. The steps also specify **validation text**, which is the message that will appear if a user attempts to violate the validation rule.

Validation rules can indicate a **required field**, a field in which the user *must* enter data; failing to enter data into a required field generates an error. Validation rules can restrict a user's entry to a certain **range of values**; for example, the values in the Returns field must be between $0 and $30,000. They can specify a **default value**, that

BTW
Database Design:
Validation
In most organizations, decisions about what is valid and what is invalid data are made during the requirements gathering process and the database design process.

is, a value that Access will display on the screen in a particular field before the user begins adding a record. To make data entry of customer numbers more convenient, you also can have lowercase letters appear automatically as uppercase letters. Finally, validation rules can specify a collection of acceptable values.

To Change a Field Size

The Field Size property for text fields represents the maximum number of characters a user can enter in the field. Because the field size for the Customer Number field is five, for example, a user would not be able to enter a sixth character in the field. Occasionally, you will find that the field size that seemed appropriate when you first created a table is no longer appropriate. In the Customer table, there is a street name that needs to be longer than 20 characters. To allow this name in the table, you need to change the field size for the Street field to a number that is large enough to accommodate the new name. The following step changes the field size for the Street field from 20 to 25.

BTW

Using Wildcards in Validation Rules
You can include wildcards in validation rules. For example, if you enter the expression, like T?, in the Validation Rule for the State field, the only valid entries for the field will be TN or TX.

1 Open the Customer table in Design view and close the Navigation Pane.

2 Select the Street field by clicking its row selector.

3 Tap or click the Field Size property to select it, delete the current entry (20), and then type **25** as the new field size.

To Specify a Required Field

1 UPDATE RECORDS | 2 FILTER RECORDS | 3 CHANGE STRUCTURE | 4 MASS CHANGES | 5 VALIDATION RULES
6 CHANGE APPEARANCE | 7 REFERENTIAL INTEGRITY | 8 ORDER RECORDS

To specify that a field is to be required, change the value for the Required property from No to Yes. The following step specifies that the Customer Name field is to be a required field. *Why? Users will not be able to leave the Customer Name field blank when entering or editing records.*

1

- Select the Customer Name field by clicking its row selector.

- Tap or click the Required property box in the Field Properties pane, and then tap or click the down arrow that appears.

- Tap or click Yes in the list to make Customer Name a required field (Figure 3–36).

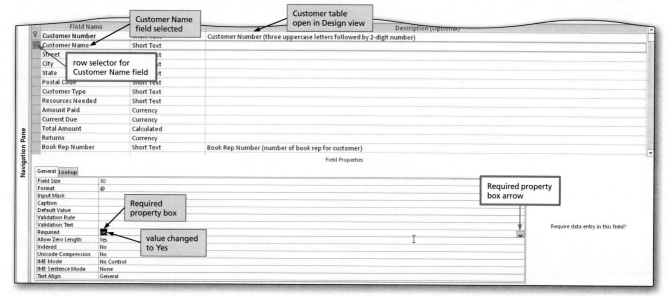

Figure 3–36

To Specify a Range

The following step specifies that entries in the Returns field must be between $0 and $30,000. To indicate this range, the criterion specifies that the returns amount must be both >= 0 (greater than or equal to 0) and <= 30000 (less than or equal to 30,000). ***Why?*** *Combining these two criteria with the word, and, is logically equivalent to being between $0.00 and $30,000.00.*

- Select the Returns field by clicking its row selector, tap or click the Validation Rule property box to produce an insertion point, and then type `>=0 and <=30000` as the rule.

- Tap or click the Validation Text property box to produce an insertion point, and then type **Must be at least $0.00 and at most $30,000.00** as the text (Figure 3–37).

Q&A What is the effect of this change?
Users now will be prohibited from entering a returns amount that is either less than $0.00 or greater than $30,000.00 when they add records or change the value in the Returns field.

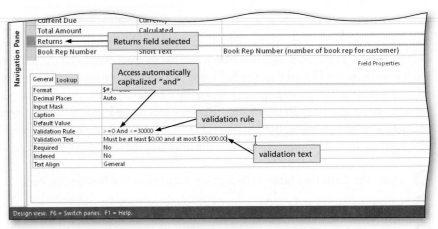

Figure 3–37

To Specify a Default Value

To specify a default value, enter the value in the Default Value property box. The following step specifies UNI as the default value for the Customer Type field. ***Why?*** *More customers at Bavant have type UNI than either of the other types. By making it the default value, if users do not enter a customer type, the type will be UNI.*

- Select the Customer Type field, tap or click the Default Value property box to produce an insertion point, and then type `=UNI` as the value (Figure 3–38).

Q&A Do I need to type the equal (=) sign?
No. You could enter UNI as the default value.

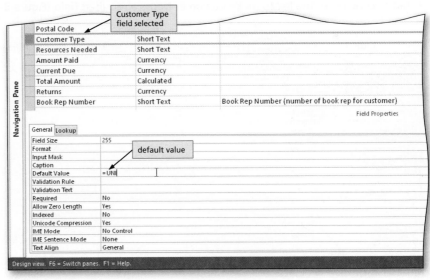

Figure 3–38

To Specify a Collection of Legal Values

1 UPDATE RECORDS | 2 FILTER RECORDS | 3 CHANGE STRUCTURE | 4 MASS CHANGES | 5 VALIDATION RULES
6 CHANGE APPEARANCE | 7 REFERENTIAL INTEGRITY | 8 ORDER RECORDS

The only **legal values**, or **allowable values**, for the Customer Type field are HS, COM, and UNI. The following step creates a validation rule to specify these as the only legal values for the Customer Type field. ***Why?*** *The validation rule prohibits users from entering any other value in the Customer Type field.*

1

- With the Customer Type field selected, tap or click the Validation Rule property box to produce an insertion point and then type `=HS or =COM or =UNI` as the validation rule.

- Tap or click the Validation Text property box, and then type `Must be HS, COM, or UNI` as the validation text (Figure 3–39).

Q&A
What is the effect of this change?
Users now will be allowed to enter only HS, COM, or UNI in the Customer Type field when they add records or make changes to this field.

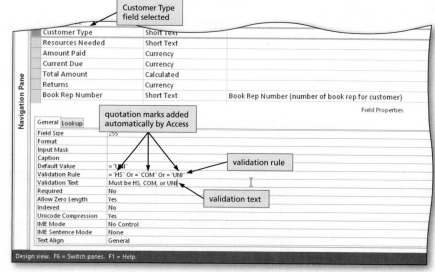

Figure 3–39

To Specify a Format

1 UPDATE RECORDS | 2 FILTER RECORDS | 3 CHANGE STRUCTURE | 4 MASS CHANGES | 5 VALIDATION RULES
6 CHANGE APPEARANCE | 7 REFERENTIAL INTEGRITY | 8 ORDER RECORDS

To affect the way data appears in a field, you can use a **format**. To use a format with a Short Text field, you enter a special symbol, called a **format symbol**, in the field's Format property box. The Format property uses different settings for different data types. The following step specifies a format for the Customer Number field using the > symbol. ***Why?*** *The > format symbol causes Access to display lowercase letters automatically as uppercase letters, which is appropriate for the Customer Number field.* There is another symbol, the < symbol, which causes Access to display uppercase letters automatically as lowercase letters.

1

- Select the Customer Number field.

- Tap or click the Format property box, erase the current format (@), if it appears on your screen, and then type `>` (Figure 3–40).

Q&A
Where did the current format (@) come from and what does it mean?
Access added this format when you created the table by importing data from an Excel workbook. It simply means any character or a space. It is not needed here.

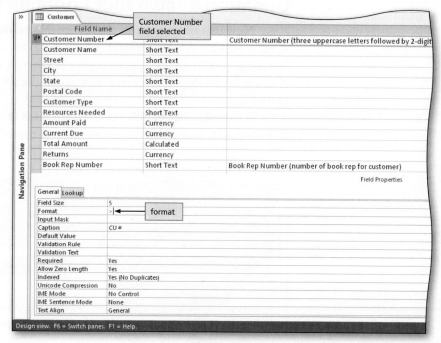

Figure 3–40

To Save the Validation Rules, Default Values, and Formats

BTW
Using the BETWEEN Operator in Validation Rules
You can use the BETWEEN operator to specify a range of values. For example, to specify that entries in the Returns field must be between \$0 and \$30,000, type BETWEEN 0 and 30000 as the rule.

The following steps save the validation rules, default values, and formats.

1 Tap or click the Save button on the Quick Access Toolbar to save the changes (Figure 3–41).

2 If a Microsoft Access dialog box appears, tap or click the No button to save the changes without testing current data.

Q&A When would you want to test current data?
If you have any doubts about the validity of the current data, you should be sure to test the current data.

3 Close the Customer table.

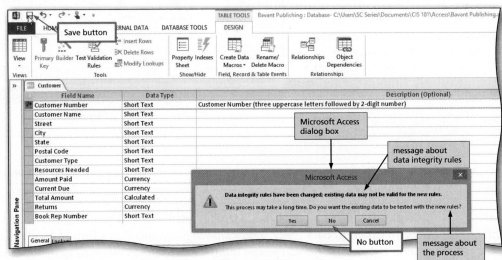

Figure 3–41

Updating a Table that Contains Validation Rules

Now that the Bavant database contains validation rules, Access restricts the user to entering data that is valid and is formatted correctly. If a user enters a number that is out of the required range, for example, or enters a value that is not one of the possible choices, Access displays an error message in the form of a dialog box. The user cannot update the database until the error is corrected.

If the customer number entered contains lowercase letters, such as wip22 (Figure 3–42), Access will display the data automatically as WIP22 (Figure 3–43).

Figure 3–42

Figure 3–43

If the customer type is not valid, such as xxx, Access will display the text message you specified (Figure 3–44) and prevent the data from entering the database.

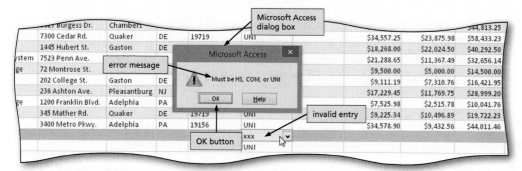

Figure 3–44

If the returns amount is not valid, such as 40000, which is too large, Access also displays the appropriate message (Figure 3–45) and refuses to accept the data.

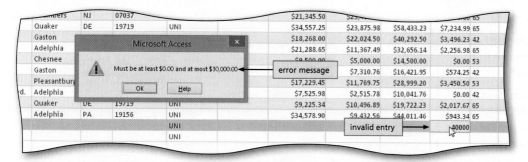

Figure 3–45

If a required field contains no data, Access indicates this by displaying an error message as soon as you attempt to leave the record (Figure 3–46). The field must contain a valid entry before Access will move to a different record.

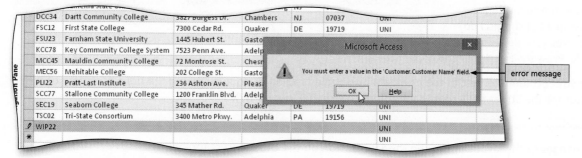

Figure 3–46

CONSIDER THIS

When entering invalid data into a field with a validation rule, is it possible that you could not enter the data correctly? What would cause this? If it happens, what should you do?

If you cannot remember the validation rule you created or if you created the rule incorrectly, you might not be able to enter the data. In such a case, you will be unable to leave the field or close the table because you have entered data into a field that violates the validation rule.

If this happens, first try again to type an acceptable entry. If this does not work, repeatedly press the BACKSPACE key to erase the contents of the field and then try to leave the field. If you are unsuccessful using this procedure, press the ESC key until the record is removed from the screen. The record will not be added to the database.

Should the need arise to take this drastic action, you probably have a faulty validation rule. Use the techniques of the previous sections to correct the existing validation rules for the field.

Making Additional Changes to the Database

Now that you have changed the structure and created validation rules, there are additional changes to be made to the database. You will use both the lookup and multivalued lookup fields to change the contents of the fields. You also will update both the form and the report to reflect the changes in the table.

To Change the Contents of a Field

1 UPDATE RECORDS | 2 FILTER RECORDS | 3 CHANGE STRUCTURE | 4 MASS CHANGES | 5 VALIDATION RULES
6 CHANGE APPEARANCE | 7 REFERENTIAL INTEGRITY | 8 ORDER RECORDS

Now that the size for the Street field has been increased, you can change the name for customer TSC02 from 3400 Metro Pkwy. to 3400 Metropolitan Pkwy. and then resize the column, just as you resized columns in Chapter 1 on page AC 28. *Why? Changing the field size for the field does not automatically increase the width of the corresponding column in the datasheet.* The following steps change the Street name and resize the column in the datasheet to accommodate the new name.

1

- Open the Customer table in Datasheet view and ensure the Navigation Pane is closed.

- Tap or click in the Street field for customer TSC02 immediately to the right of the letter, o, of Metro to produce an insertion point.

- Change the street from 3400 Metro Pkwy. to 3400 Metropolitan Pkwy. by typing **politan** and pressing the TAB key.

 I cannot add the extra characters. Whatever I type replaces what is currently in the cell. What happened and what should I do? You are in Overtype mode, not Insert mode. Press the INSERT key and correct the entry.

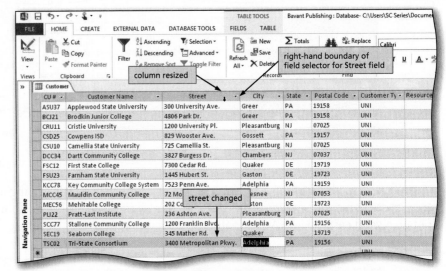

Figure 3–47

- Resize the Street column to best fit the new data by double-tapping or double-clicking the right boundary of the field selector for the Street field, that is, the column heading (Figure 3–47).

2

- Save the changes to the layout by clicking the Save button on the Quick Access Toolbar.

- Close the Customer table.

To Use a Lookup Field

Earlier, you changed all the entries in the Customer Type field to UNI. You have created a rule that will ensure that only legitimate values (HS, COM, or UNI) can be entered in the field. You also made Customer Type a lookup field. *Why? You can make changes to a lookup field for individual records by simply clicking the field to be changed, clicking the arrow that appears in the field, and then selecting the desired value from the list.* The following steps change the incorrect Customer Type values to the correct values.

- Open the Customer table in Datasheet view and ensure the Navigation Pane is closed.

- Tap or click in the Customer Type field on the second record to display an arrow.

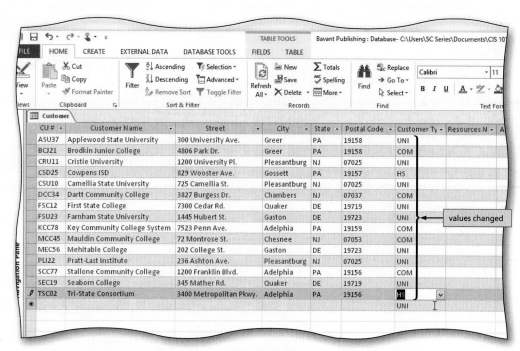

Figure 3–48

- Tap or click the
arrow to display the drop-down list of available choices for the Customer Type field (Figure 3–48).

Q&A I got the drop-down list as soon as I clicked. I did not need to tap or click the arrow. What happened?
If you tap or click in the position where the arrow would appear, you will get the drop-down list. If you tap or click anywhere else, you would need to tap or click the arrow.

Could I type the value instead of selecting it from the list?
Yes. Once you have either deleted the previous value or selected the entire previous value, you can begin typing. You do not have to type the full entry. When you begin with the letter, C, for example, Access will automatically add the OM.

- Tap or click COM to change the value.

- In a similar fashion, change the values on the other records to match those shown in Figure 3–49.

Figure 3–49

To Use a Multivalued Lookup Field

Using a multivalued lookup field is similar to using a regular lookup field. The difference is that when you drop down the list, the entries all will be preceded by check boxes. *Why? Having the check boxes allows you to make multiple selections. You check all the entries that you want.* The appropriate entries are shown in Figure 3–50. As indicated in the figure, the resources needed for customer ASU37 are CDVD, Ebook, OlMan, OlWrk, SDVD, and Txt.

Customer Number	Customer Name	Resources Needed
ASU37	Applewood State University	CDVD, Ebook, OlMan, OlWrk, SDVD, Txt
BCJ21	Brodkin Junior College	Audio, PrMan, PrWrk, Txt
CRU11	Cristie University	CustD, Ebook
CSD25	Cowpens ISD	CDVD, PrWrk, SDVD, Txt
CSU10	Camellia State University	Audio, CDVD, Ebook, OlMan, OlWrk, PrMan, PrWrk, SDVD, Txt
DCC34	Dartt Community College	CDVD, Ebook, OlMan, OlWrk, SDVD
FSC12	First State College	Audio, CDVD, PrMan, PrWrk, SDVD, Txt
FSU23	Farnham State University	CDVD, CustD, CustP, Ebook, OlMan, OlWrk, SDVD
KCC78	Key Community College System	Audio, CDVD, Ebook, OlMan, OlWrk, PrMan, PrWrk, SDVD, Txt
MCC45	Mauldin Community College	Audio, PrMan, PrWrk, Txt
MEC56	Mehitable College	Audio, CDVD, PrMan, PrWrk, SDVD, Txt
PLI22	Pratt-Last Institute	CDVD, CustD, CustP, Ebook, OlMan, OlWrk, SDVD
SCC77	Stallone Community College	Audio, PrMan, PrWrk, Txt
SEC19	Seaborn College	CDVD, CustD, CustP, SDVD
TSC02	Tri-State Consortium	Audio, CDVD, Ebook, OlMan, OlWrk, PrMan, PrWrk, SDVD, Txt

Figure 3–50

The following steps make the appropriate entries for the Resources Needed field.

1

- Tap or click the Resources Needed field on the first record to display the arrow.
- Tap or click the arrow to display the list of available resources (Figure 3–51).

Q&A

All the resources currently appear in the box. What if there were too many resources to fit?

Access would automatically include a scroll bar that you could use to scroll through all the choices.

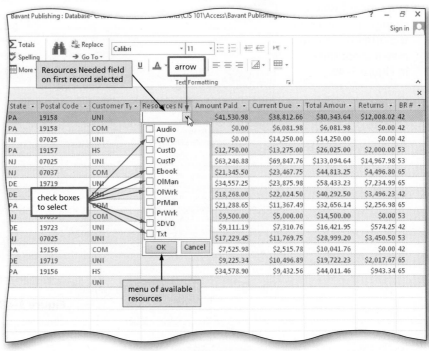

Figure 3–51

- Tap or click the CDVD, Ebook, OlMan, OlWrk, SDVD, and Txt check boxes to select the resources for the first customer (Figure 3–52).

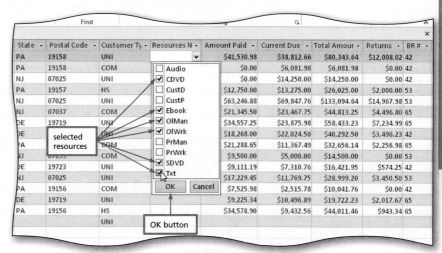

Figure 3–52

- Tap or click the OK button to complete the selection.
- Using the same technique, enter the resources given in Figure 3–50 for the remaining customers.
- Double-tap or double-click the right boundary of the field selector for the Resources Needed field to resize the field so that it best fits the data (Figure 3–53).

4

- Save the changes to the layout by clicking the Save button on the Quick Access Toolbar.
- Close the Customer table.

Q&A What if I closed the table without saving the layout changes?
You would be asked if you want to save the changes.

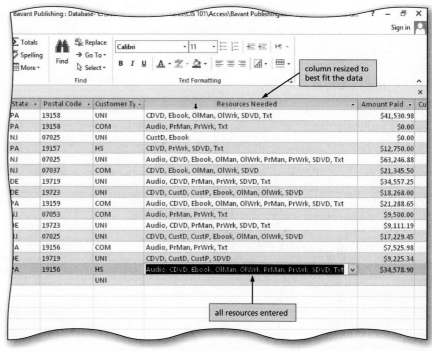

Figure 3–53

To Update a Form to Reflect the Changes in the Table

In the first chapter, on page AC 46, you clicked the Form button (CREATE tab | Forms group) to create a simple form that contained all the fields in the Customer table. Now that you have added fields, the form you created, Customer Form, no longer contains all the fields in the table. The steps on the next page delete the Customer Form and then create it a second time.

① Open the Navigation Pane, and then press and hold or right-click the Customer Form in the Navigation Pane to display a shortcut menu.

② Tap or click Delete on the shortcut menu to delete the selected form, and then tap or click the Yes button in the Microsoft Access dialog box to confirm the deletion.

③ Tap or click the Customer table in the Navigation Pane to select the table.

④ If necessary, tap or click CREATE on the ribbon to display the CREATE tab.

⑤ Tap or click the Form button (CREATE tab | Forms group) to create a simple form (Figure 3–54).

⑥ Tap or click the Save button on the Quick Access Toolbar to save the form.

⑦ Type **Customer Form** as the form name, and then tap or click the OK button to save the form.

⑧ Close the form.

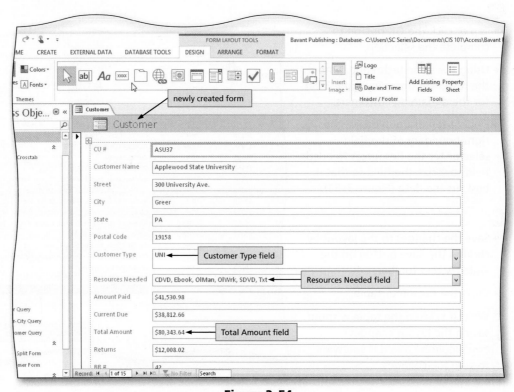

Figure 3–54

To Update a Report to Reflect the Changes in the Table

1 UPDATE RECORDS | 2 FILTER RECORDS | 3 CHANGE STRUCTURE | 4 MASS CHANGES | 5 VALIDATION RULES
6 CHANGE APPEARANCE | 7 REFERENTIAL INTEGRITY | 8 ORDER RECORDS

You also may want to include the new fields in the Customer Financial Report you created earlier. Just as you did with the form, you could delete the current version of the report and then create it all over again. It would be better, however, to modify the report in Layout view. *Why? There are several steps involved in creating the Customer Financial report, so it is more complicated than the process of re-creating the form.* In Layout view, you easily can add new fields. The following steps modify the Customer Financial Report by adding the Customer Type and Total Amount fields. To accommodate the extra fields, the steps also change the orientation of the report from Portrait to Landscape.

1

- Open the Navigation Pane, if necessary, and then press and hold or right-click the Customer Financial Report in the Navigation Pane to display a shortcut menu.

- Tap or click Layout View on the shortcut menu to open the report in Layout view.

- Close the Navigation Pane.

- Tap or click the 'Add Existing Fields' button (REPORT LAYOUT TOOLS DESIGN tab | Tools group) to display a field list (Figure 3–55).

Q&A

Why are there two Resources Needed fields in the list?

They serve different purposes. If you were to select Resources Needed, you would get all the resources for a given customer on one line. If you were to select Resources Needed.Value, each resource would be on a separate line. You are not selecting either one for this report.

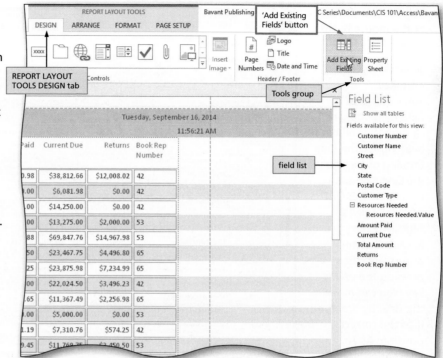

Figure 3–55

2

- Drag the Customer Type field in the field list until the line to the left of the pointer is between the Customer Name and Amount Paid fields (Figure 3–56).

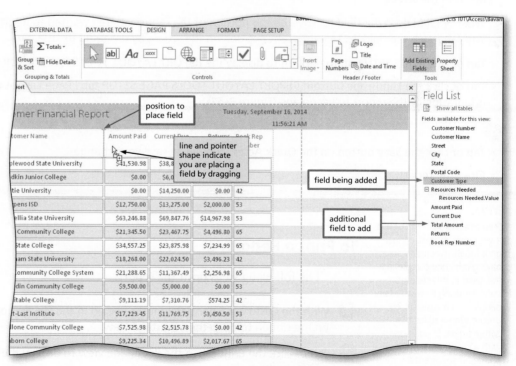

Figure 3–56

③

- Release your finger or the mouse button to place the field.

Q&A What if I make a mistake?

You can delete the field by tapping or clicking the column heading for the field, tapping or clicking the Select Column command (REPORT LAYOUT TOOLS ARRANGE tab | Rows & Columns group) and then pressing the DELETE key. You can move the field by dragging it to the correct position. As an alternative, you can close the report without saving it and then open it again in Layout view.

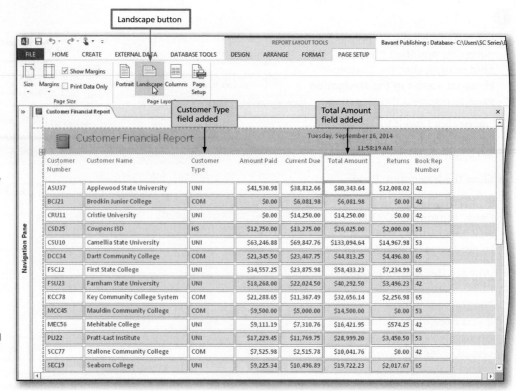

Figure 3–57

- Using the same technique, add the Total Amount field between the Current Due and Returns fields.

- Tap or click the 'Add Existing Fields' button (REPORT LAYOUT TOOLS DESIGN tab | Tools group) to remove the field list from the screen.

Q&A What would I do if the field list covered the portion of the report where I wanted to insert a new field?

You can move the field list to a different position on the screen by dragging its title bar.

- Tap or click PAGE SETUP on the ribbon to display the REPORT LAYOUT TOOLS PAGE SETUP tab.

- Tap or click the Landscape button (REPORT LAYOUT TOOLS PAGE SETUP tab | Page Layout group) to change the orientation of the report to Landscape (Figure 3–57).

④

- Tap or click the Save button on the Quick Access Toolbar to save your changes.

- Close the report.

BTW

Problems with Touch

If you are using your finger on a touch screen and are having difficulty completing the steps in this chapter, consider using a stylus. Many people find it easier to be precise with a stylus than with a finger. In addition, with a stylus you see the pointer. If you are still having trouble completing the steps with a stylus, try using a mouse.

To Print a Report

The following steps print the report.

① With the Customer Financial Report selected in the Navigation Pane, tap or click FILE on the ribbon to open the Backstage view.

② Tap or click the Print tab in the Backstage view to display the Print gallery.

③ Tap or click the Quick Print button to print the report.

Changing the Appearance of a Datasheet

You can change the appearance of a datasheet in a variety of ways. You can include totals in the datasheet. You can also change the appearance of gridlines. You can change the text colors and font.

To Include Totals in a Datasheet

1 UPDATE RECORDS | 2 FILTER RECORDS | 3 CHANGE STRUCTURE | 4 MASS CHANGES | 5 VALIDATION RULES
6 CHANGE APPEARANCE | 7 REFERENTIAL INTEGRITY | 8 ORDER RECORDS

The following steps first include an extra row, called the Total row, in the datasheet for the Book Rep table. *Why? It is possible to include totals and other statistics at the bottom of a datasheet in the Total row.* The steps then display the total of the salary for all the book reps.

- Open the Book Rep table in Datasheet view and close the Navigation Pane.
- Tap or click the Totals button (HOME tab | Records group) to include the Total row in the datasheet.
- Tap or click the Total row in the Salary column to display an arrow.
- Tap or click the arrow to display a menu of available calculations (Figure 3–58).

Q&A
Will I always get the same list? No. You will only get the items that are applicable to the type of data in the column. You cannot calculate the sum of text data, for example.

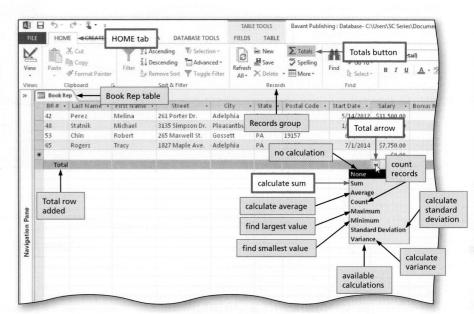

Figure 3–58

- Tap or click Sum to calculate the total of the salary amounts (Figure 3–59).

Experiment

- Experiment with other statistics. When finished, once again select the sum.

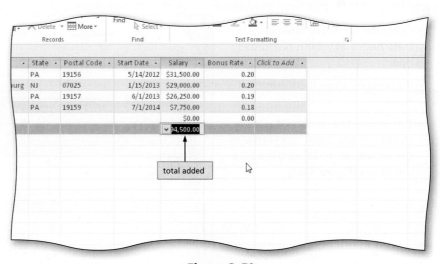

Figure 3–59

BTW
**Distributing a
Document**
Instead of printing and
distributing a hard copy of a
document, you can distribute
the document electronically.
Options include sending the
document via email; posting
it on cloud storage (such as
SkyDrive) and sharing the
file with others; posting it
on a social networking site,
blog, or other website; and
sharing a link associated
with an online location of
the document. You also can
create and share a PDF or
XPS image of the document,
so that users can view the
file in Acrobat Reader or XPS
Viewer instead of in Access.

To Remove Totals from a Datasheet

If you no longer want the totals to appear as part of the datasheet, you can remove the Total row. The following step removes the Total row.

 Tap or click the Totals button (HOME tab | Records group), which is shown in Figure 3–58 on the previous page, to remove the Total row from the datasheet.

Figure 3–60 shows the various buttons, found in the Text Formatting group on the HOME tab, that are available to change the datasheet appearance. The changes to the datasheet will be reflected not only on the screen, but also when you print or preview the datasheet.

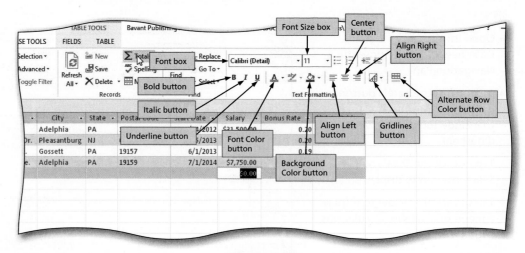

Figure 3–60

To Change Gridlines in a Datasheet

1 UPDATE RECORDS | 2 FILTER RECORDS | 3 CHANGE STRUCTURE | 4 MASS CHANGES | 5 VALIDATION RULES
6 CHANGE APPEARANCE | 7 REFERENTIAL INTEGRITY | 8 ORDER RECORDS

The following steps change the datasheet so that only horizontal gridlines are included. *Why? You might prefer the appearance of the datasheet with only horizontal gridlines.*

- Open the Book Rep table in Datasheet view, if it is not already open.

- If necessary, close the Navigation Pane.

- Tap or click the datasheet selector, the box in the upper-left corner of the datasheet, to select the entire datasheet (Figure 3–61).

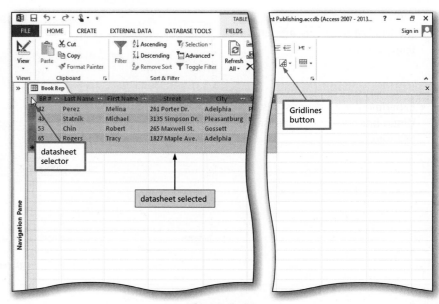

Figure 3–61

2

- Tap or click the Gridlines button (HOME tab | Text Formatting group) to display the Gridlines gallery (Figure 3–62).

Q&A Does it matter whether I tap or click the button or the arrow? In this case, it does not matter. Either action will display the gallery.

3

- Tap or click Gridlines: Horizontal in the Gridlines gallery to include only horizontal gridlines.

Experiment

- Experiment with other gridline options. When finished, once again select horizontal gridlines.

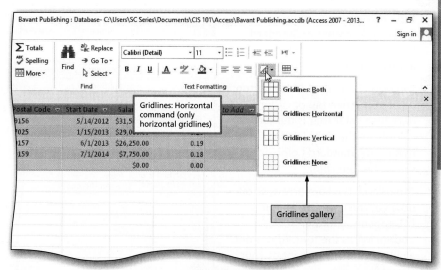

Figure 3–62

To Change the Colors and Font in a Datasheet

1 UPDATE RECORDS | 2 FILTER RECORDS | 3 CHANGE STRUCTURE | 4 MASS CHANGES | 5 VALIDATION RULES
6 CHANGE APPEARANCE | 7 REFERENTIAL INTEGRITY | 8 ORDER RECORDS

You also can modify the appearance of the datasheet by changing the colors and the font. The following steps change the Alternate Fill color, a color that appears on every other row in the datasheet. *Why? Having rows appear in alternate colors is an attractive way to visually separate the rows.* The steps also change the font color, the font, and the font size.

1

- With the datasheet for the Book Rep table selected, tap or click the Alternate Row Color button arrow (HOME tab | Text Formatting group) to display the color palette (Figure 3–63).

Q&A Does it matter whether I tap or click the button or the arrow? Yes. Clicking the arrow produces a color palette. Clicking the button applies the currently selected color. When in doubt, you should tap or click the arrow.

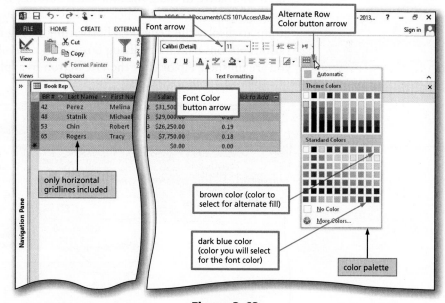

Figure 3–63

2

- Tap or click Brown in the upper-right corner of Standard Colors to select brown as the alternate color.

- Tap or click the Font Color button arrow, and then tap or click the dark blue color that is the second color from the right in the bottom row in the Standard Colors to select the font color.

- Tap or click the Font arrow, scroll down in the list until Bodoni MT appears, and then select Bodoni MT as the font. (If it is not available, select any font of your choice.)

- Tap or click the Font Size arrow and select 10 as the font size (Figure 3–64).

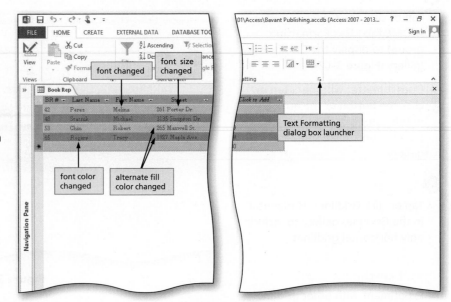

Figure 3–64

Q&A
Does the order in which I make these selections make a difference?
No. You could have made these selections in any order.

Experiment

- Experiment with other colors, fonts, and font sizes. When finished, return to the options selected in this step.

Using the Datasheet Formatting Dialog Box

As an alternative to using the individual buttons, you can tap or click the Datasheet Formatting dialog box launcher, which is the arrow at the right of the Text Formatting group, to display the Datasheet Formatting dialog box (Figure 3–65). You can use the various options within the dialog box to make changes to the datasheet format. Once you are finished, tap or click the OK button to apply your changes.

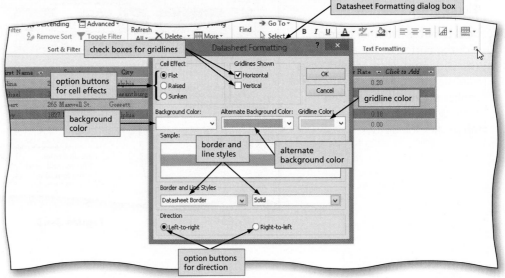

Figure 3–65

To Close the Datasheet without Saving the Format Changes

The following steps close the datasheet without saving the changes to the format. Because the changes are not saved, the next time you open the Book Rep table in Datasheet view, it will appear in the original format. If you had saved the changes, the changes would be reflected in its appearance.

1 Close the Book Rep table.

2 Tap or click the No button in the Microsoft Access dialog box when asked if you want to save your changes.

CONSIDER THIS

What kind of decisions should I make in determining whether to change the format of a datasheet?

• Would totals or other calculations be useful in the datasheet? If so, include the Total row and select the appropriate computations.

• Would another gridline style make the datasheet more useful? If so, change to the desired gridlines.

• Would alternating colors in the rows make them easier to read? If so, change the alternate fill color.

• Would a different font and/or font color make the text stand out better? If so, change the font color and/or the font.

• Is the font size appropriate? Can you see enough data at one time on the screen and yet have the data be readable? If not, change the font size to an appropriate value.

• Is the column spacing appropriate? Are some columns wider than they need to be? Do some columns not display all the data? Change the column sizes as necessary.

As a general guideline, once you have decided on a particular look for a datasheet, all datasheets in the database should have the same look, unless there is a compelling reason for a datasheet to differ.

Multivalued Fields in Queries

You can use multivalued fields in queries in the same way you use other fields in queries. You can choose to display the multiple values either on a single row or on multiple rows in the query results.

BTW

Using Criteria with Multivalued Fields
To enter criteria in a multivalued field, simply enter the criteria in the Criteria row. For example, to find all customers who need audio, enter Audio in the Criteria row.

To Include Multiple Values on One Row of a Query

1 UPDATE RECORDS | 2 FILTER RECORDS | 3 CHANGE STRUCTURE | 4 MASS CHANGES | 5 VALIDATION RULES
6 CHANGE APPEARANCE | 7 REFERENTIAL INTEGRITY | 8 ORDER RECORDS

To include a multivalued field in the results of a query, place the field in the query design grid just like any other field. *Why? When you treat the multivalued field like any other field, the results will list all of the values for the multivalued field on a single row.* The following steps create a query to display the customer number, customer name, customer type, and resources needed for all customers.

1

• Create a query for the Customer table and close the Navigation Pane.

• Include the Customer Number, Customer Name, Customer Type, and Resources Needed fields (Figure 3–66).

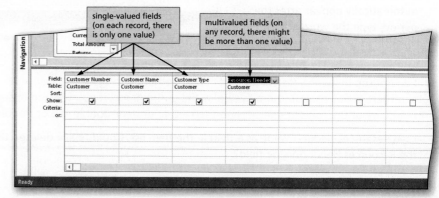

Figure 3–66

2

- Run the query and view the results (Figure 3–67).

Q&A

Can I include criteria for the multivalued field?

Yes. You can include criteria for the multivalued field.

3

- Save the query as Ch3q01.

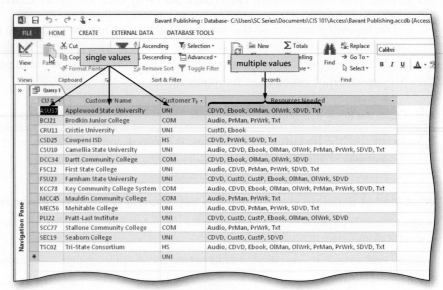

Figure 3–67

To Include Multiple Values on Multiple Rows of a Query

1 UPDATE RECORDS | 2 FILTER RECORDS | 3 CHANGE STRUCTURE | 4 MASS CHANGES | 5 VALIDATION RULES
6 CHANGE APPEARANCE | 7 REFERENTIAL INTEGRITY | 8 ORDER RECORDS

You may want to see the multiple resources needed for a customer on separate rows rather than a single row. *Why? Each row in the results will focus on one specific resource that is needed.* To do so, you need to use the Value property of the Resources Needed field, by following the name of the field with a period and then the word, Value. The following steps use the Value property to display each resource on a separate row.

1

- Return to Design view and ensure that the Customer Number, Customer Name, Customer Type, and Resources Needed fields are included in the design grid.

- Tap or click the Resources Needed field to produce an insertion point, press the RIGHT ARROW key as necessary to move the insertion point to the end of the field name, and then type a period.

- If the word, Value, did not automatically appear after the period, type the word `value` after the period following the word, Needed, to use the Value property (Figure 3–68).

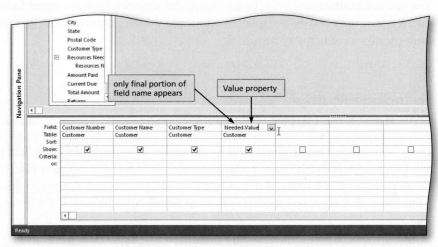

Figure 3–68

Q&A

I do not see the word, Resources. Did I do something wrong?

No. There is not enough room to display the entire name. If you wanted to see it, you could point to the right boundary of the column selector and then either drag or double-tap or double-click.

I see Resources Needed.Value as a field in the field list. Could I have deleted the Resources Needed field and added the Resources Needed.Value field?

Yes. Either approach is fine.

2

- Run the query and view the results (Figure 3–69).

Q&A Can I now include criteria for the multivalued field?
Yes. You could enter a criterion just like in any other query.

3

- Save the query as a new object in the database named Ch3q02.

- Close the query.

each row contains only one resource

the six resources needed by Customer ASU37 now appear on six rows

CU #	Customer Name	Customer Ty	
CRU11	Cristie University	UNI	CustD
CRU11	Cristie University	UNI	Ebook
ASU37	Applewood State University	UNI	CDVD
ASU37	Applewood State University	UNI	Ebook
ASU37	Applewood State University	UNI	OlMan
ASU37	Applewood State University	UNI	OlWrk
ASU37	Applewood State University	UNI	SDVD
ASU37	Applewood State University	UNI	Txt
BCJ21	Brodkin Junior College	COM	Audio
BCJ21	Brodkin Junior College	COM	PrMan
BCJ21	Brodkin Junior College	COM	PrWrk
BCJ21	Brodkin Junior College	COM	Txt
CSD25	Cowpens ISD	HS	CDVD
CSD25	Cowpens ISD	HS	PrWrk
CSD25	Cowpens ISD	HS	SDVD
CSD25	Cowpens ISD	HS	Txt
CSU10	Camellia State University	UNI	Audio
CSU10	Camellia State University	UNI	CDVD
CSU10	Camellia State University	UNI	Ebook
CSU10	Camellia State University	UNI	OlMan
CSU10	Camellia State University	UNI	OlWrk
CSU10	Camellia State University	UNI	PrMan
CSU10	Camellia State University	UNI	PrWrk
CSU10	Camellia State University	UNI	SDVD
CSU10	Camellia State University	UNI	Txt

Figure 3–69

Break Point: If you wish to take a break, this is a good place to do so. You can quit Access now. To resume at a later time, start Access, open the database called Bavant Publishing, and continue following the steps from this location forward.

Referential Integrity

When you have two related tables in a database, it is essential that the data in the common fields match. There should not be a customer in the Customer table whose book rep number is 42, for example, unless there is a record in the Book Rep table whose number is 42. This restriction is enforced through **referential integrity**, which is the property that ensures that the value in a foreign key must match that of another table's primary key.

A **foreign key** is a field in one table whose values are required to match the *primary key* of another table. In the Customer table, the Book Rep Number field is a foreign key that must match the primary key of the Book Rep table; that is, the book rep number for any customer must be a book rep currently in the Book Rep table. A customer whose book rep number is 92, for example, should not be stored because no such book rep exists.

In Access, to specify referential integrity, you must explicitly define a relationship between the tables by using the Relationships button. As part of the process of defining a relationship, you indicate that Access is to enforce referential integrity. Access then prohibits any updates to the database that would violate the referential integrity.

The type of relationship between two tables specified by the Relationships command is referred to as a **one-to-many relationship**. This means that *one* record in the first table is related to, or matches, *many* records in the second table, but each record in the second table is related to only *one* record in the first. In the Bavant Publishing database, for example, a one-to-many relationship exists between the Book Rep table and the Customer table. *One* book rep is associated with *many* customers, but each customer is associated with only a single book rep. In general, the table containing the foreign key will be the *many* part of the relationship.

BTW
Relationships
You also can use the Relationships window to specify a one-to-one relationship. In a one-to-one relationship, the matching fields are both primary keys. If Bavant Publishing maintained a company car for each book rep, the data concerning the cars might be kept in a Car table, in which the primary key is Book Rep Number — the same primary key as the Book Rep table. Thus, there would be a one-to-one relationship between book reps and cars.

CONSIDER THIS

When specifying referential integrity, what special issues do you need to address?

You need to decide how to handle deletions. In the relationship between customers and book reps, for example, deletion of a book rep for whom customers exist, such as book rep number 42, would violate referential integrity. Customers for book rep 42 no longer would relate to any book rep in the database. You can handle this in two ways. For each relationship, you need to decide which of the approaches is appropriate.

- The normal way to avoid this problem is to prohibit such a deletion.

- The other option is to **cascade the delete.** This means that Access would allow the deletion but then delete all related records. For example, it would allow the deletion of the book rep from the Book Rep table but then automatically delete any customers related to the deleted book rep. In this example, cascading the delete would obviously not be appropriate.

You also need to decide how to handle the update of the primary key. In the relationship between book reps and customers, for example, changing the book rep number for book rep 42 to 43 in the Book Rep table would cause a problem because some customers in the Customer table have book rep number 42. These customers no longer would relate to any book rep. You can handle this in two ways. For each relationship, you need to decide which of the approaches is appropriate.

- The normal way to avoid this problem is to prohibit this type of update.

- The other option is to **cascade the update.** This means to allow the change, but make the corresponding change in the foreign key on all related records. In the relationship between customers and book reps, for example, Access would allow the update but then automatically make the corresponding change for any customer whose book rep number was 42. It now will be 43.

To Specify Referential Integrity

1 UPDATE RECORDS | 2 FILTER RECORDS | 3 CHANGE STRUCTURE | 4 MASS CHANGES | 5 VALIDATION RULES
6 CHANGE APPEARANCE | 7 REFERENTIAL INTEGRITY | 8 ORDER RECORDS

The following steps use the Relationships button on the DATABASE TOOLS tab to specify referential integrity by explicitly indicating a relationship between the Book Rep and Customer tables. The steps also ensure that updates will cascade, but that deletes will not. *Why? By specifying that updates will cascade, it will be possible to change the Book Rep Number for a book rep, and the same change will automatically be made for all customers of that book rep. By not specifying that deletes will cascade, it will not be possible to delete a book rep who has related customers.*

1
- Tap or click DATABASE TOOLS on the ribbon to display the DATABASE TOOLS tab. (Figure 3–70).

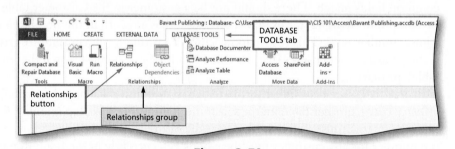

Figure 3–70

2
- Tap or click the Relationships button (DATABASE TOOLS tab | Relationships group) to open the Relationships window and display the Show Table dialog box (Figure 3–71).

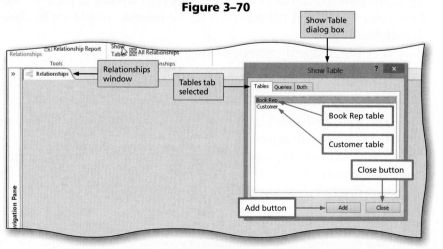

Figure 3–71

3

- If necessary, tap or click the Book Rep table (Show Table dialog box), and then tap or click the Add button to add a field list for the Book Rep table to the Relationships window.

- Tap or click the Customer table (Show Table dialog box), and then tap or click the Add button to add a field list for the Customer table to the Relationships window.

- Tap or click the Close button (Show Table dialog box) to close the dialog box.

- Resize the field lists that appear so all fields are visible (Figure 3–72).

Q&A Do I need to resize the field lists?
No. You can use the scroll bars to view the fields. Before completing the next step, however, you would need to make sure the Book Rep Number fields in both tables appear on the screen.

4

- Drag the Book Rep Number field in the Book Rep table field list to the Book Rep Number field in the Customer table field list to display the Edit Relationships dialog box to create a relationship.

Q&A Do I actually move the field from the Book Rep table to the Customer table?
No. The pointer will change shape to indicate you are in the process of dragging, but the field does not move.

- Tap or click the 'Enforce Referential Integrity' check box (Edit Relationships dialog box).

- Tap or click the 'Cascade Update Related Fields' check box (Figure 3–73).

Q&A The Cascade check boxes were dim until I clicked the 'Enforce Referential Integrity' check box. Is that correct?
Yes. Until you have chosen to enforce referential integrity, the cascade options are not applicable.

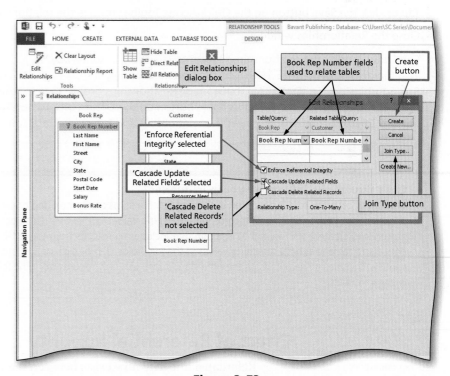

Figure 3–72

Figure 3–73

5

- Tap or click the Create button (Edit Relationships dialog box) to complete the creation of the relationship (Figure 3–74).

Q&A What is the symbol at the lower end of the join line?
It is the mathematical symbol for infinity. It is used here to denote the "many" end of the relationship.

Can I print a copy of the relationship?
Yes. Tap or click the Relationship Report button (RELATIONSHIP TOOLS DESIGN tab | Tools group) to produce a report of the relationship. You can print the report. You also can save it as a report in the database for future use. If you do not want to save it, close the report after you have printed it and do not save the changes.

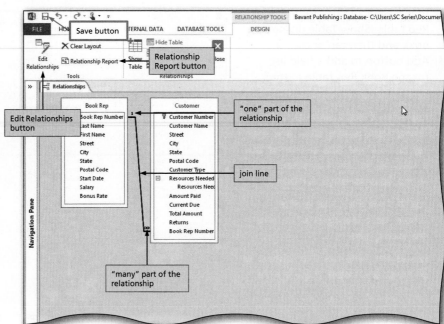

Figure 3–74

6

- Tap or click the Save button on the Quick Access Toolbar to save the relationship you created.

- Close the Relationships window.

Q&A Can I later modify the relationship if I want to change it in some way?
Yes. Tap or click DATABASE TOOLS on the ribbon to display the DATABASE TOOLS tab, and then tap or click the Relationships button (DATABASE TOOLS tab | Relationships group) to open the Relationships window. To add another table, tap or click the Show Table button on the Design tab. To remove a table, tap or click the Hide Table button. To edit a relationship, select the relationship and tap or click the Edit Relationships button.

CONSIDER THIS

Can I change the join type as I can in queries?
Yes. Tap or click the Join Type button in the Edit Relationships dialog box. Tap or click option button 1 to create an INNER join, that is, a join in which only records with matching values in the join fields appear in the result. Tap or click option button 2 to create a LEFT join, that is, a join that includes all records from the left-hand table, but only records from the right-hand table that have matching values in the join fields. Tap or click option button 3 to create a RIGHT join, that is, a join that includes all records from the right-hand table, but only records from the left-hand table that have matching values in the join fields.

BTW

Exporting a Relationship Report
You also can export a relationship report. To export a report as a PDF or XPS file, press and hold or right-click the report in the Navigation Pane, tap or click Export on the shortcut menu, and then tap or click PDF or XPS as the file type.

Effect of Referential Integrity

Referential integrity now exists between the Book Rep and Customer tables. Access now will reject any number in the Book Rep Number field in the Customer table that does not match a book rep number in the Book Rep table. Attempting to change the book rep number for a customer to one that does not match any book rep in the Book Rep table would result in the error message shown in Figure 3–75. Similarly, attempting to add a customer whose book rep number does not match would produce the same error message.

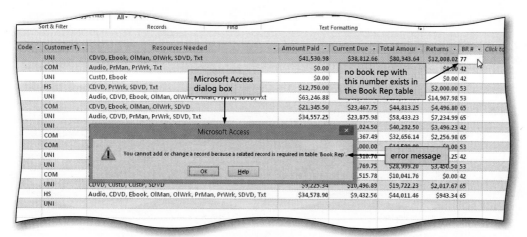

Figure 3–75

Access also will reject the deletion of a book rep for whom related customers exist. Attempting to delete book rep 42 from the Book Rep table, for example, would result in the message shown in Figure 3–76.

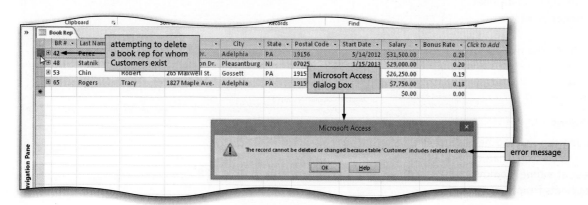

Figure 3–76

Access would, however, allow the change of a book rep number in the Book Rep table. Then it automatically makes the corresponding change to the book rep number for all the book rep's customers. For example, if you changed the book rep number of book rep 42 to 24, the same 24 would appear in the book rep number field for customers whose book rep number had been 42.

To Use a Subdatasheet

1 UPDATE RECORDS | 2 FILTER RECORDS | 3 CHANGE STRUCTURE | 4 MASS CHANGES | 5 VALIDATION RULES
6 CHANGE APPEARANCE | 7 REFERENTIAL INTEGRITY | 8 ORDER RECORDS

It is possible to view the customers of a given book rep when you are viewing the datasheet for the Book Rep table. **Why is data from one table visible when viewing the other table?** *The Book Rep table is now explicitly related to the Customer table.* One consequence of the tables being explicitly related is that the customers for a book rep can appear below the book rep in a **subdatasheet**. The availability of such a subdatasheet is indicated by a plus sign that appears in front of the rows in the Book Rep table. The steps on the next page display the subdatasheet for book rep 53.

1

- Open the Book Rep table in Datasheet view and close the Navigation Pane (Figure 3–77).

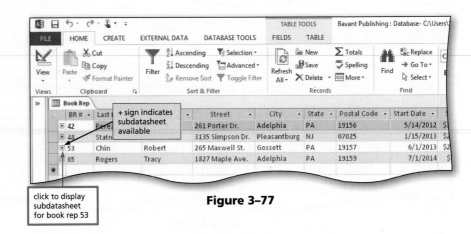

Figure 3–77

2

- Tap or click the plus sign in front of the row for book rep 53 to display the subdatasheet (Figure 3–78).

Q&A How do I hide the subdatasheet when I no longer want it to appear?

When you clicked the plus sign, it changed to a minus sign. Tap or click the minus sign.

 Experiment

- Display subdatasheets for other book reps. Display more than one subdatasheet at a time. Remove the subdatasheets from the screen.

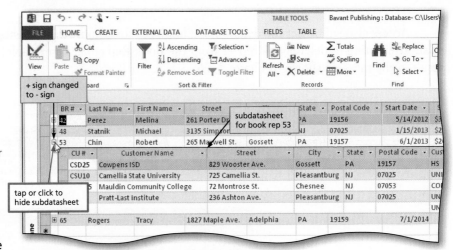

Figure 3–78

3

- If requested by your instructor, replace the city and state for book rep 53 with your city and state.
- Close the datasheet for the Book Rep table.

Handling Data Inconsistency

In many organizations, databases evolve and change over time. One department may create a database for its own internal use. Employees in another department may decide they need their own database containing much of the same information. For example, the Purchasing department of an organization may create a database of products that it buys and the Receiving department may create a database of products that it receives. Each department is keeping track of the same products. When the organization eventually merges the databases, they may find inconsistencies and duplication. The Find Duplicates Query Wizard and the Find Unmatched Query Wizard can assist in clearing the resulting database of duplication and errors.

TO FIND DUPLICATE RECORDS

One reason to include a primary key for a table is to eliminate duplicate records. A possibility still exists, however, that duplicate records can get into your database. You would use the following steps to find duplicate records using the Find Duplicates Query Wizard.

1. Tap or click CREATE on the ribbon, and then tap or click the Query Wizard button (CREATE tab | Queries group).
2. When Access displays the New Query dialog box, tap or click the Find Duplicates Query Wizard and then tap or click the OK button.
3. Identify the table and field or fields that might contain duplicate information.
4. Indicate any other fields you want displayed.
5. Finish the wizard to see any duplicate records.

TO FIND UNMATCHED RECORDS

Occasionally, you might need to find records in one table that have no matching records in another table. For example, you may want to determine which book reps currently have no customers. You would use the following steps to find unmatched records using the Find Unmatched Query Wizard.

1. Tap or click CREATE on the ribbon, and then tap or click the Query Wizard button (CREATE tab | Queries group).
2. When Access displays the New Query dialog box, tap or click the Find Unmatched Query Wizard and then tap or click the OK button.
3. Identify the table that might contain unmatched records, and then identify the related table.
4. Indicate the fields you want displayed.
5. Finish the wizard to see any unmatched records.

Ordering Records

Normally, Access sequences the records in the Customer table by customer number whenever listing them because the Customer Number field is the primary key. You can change this order, if desired.

To Use the Ascending Button to Order Records

1 UPDATE RECORDS | 2 FILTER RECORDS | 3 CHANGE STRUCTURE | 4 MASS CHANGES | 5 VALIDATION RULES
6 CHANGE APPEARANCE | 7 REFERENTIAL INTEGRITY | **8 ORDER RECORDS**

To change the order in which records appear, use the Ascending or Descending buttons. Either button reorders the records based on the field in which the insertion point is located.

The steps on the next page order the records by city using the Ascending button. *Why? Using the Ascending button is the quickest and easiest way to order records.*

1

- Open the Customer table in Datasheet view and close the Navigation Pane.

- Tap or click the City field on the first record to select the field (Figure 3–79).

Q&A Did I have to tap or click the field on the first record?

No. Any other record would have worked as well.

Figure 3–79

2

- Tap or click the Ascending button (HOME tab | Sort & Filter group) to sort the records by City (Figure 3–80).

3

- Close the Customer table.

- Tap or click the No button (Microsoft Access dialog box) when asked if you want to save your changes.

Q&A What if I saved the changes?

The next time you open the table the records will be sorted by city.

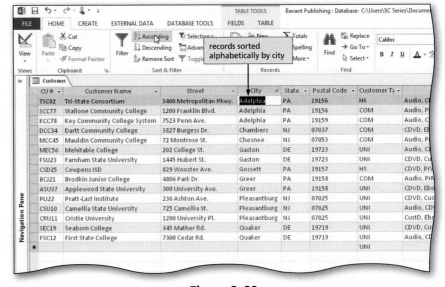

Figure 3–80

Other Ways

1. Press and hold or right-click field name, tap or click Sort A to Z (for ascending) or Sort Z to A (for descending)

TO USE THE ASCENDING BUTTON TO ORDER RECORDS ON MULTIPLE FIELDS

Just as you are able to sort the answer to a query on multiple fields, you also can sort the data that appears in a datasheet on multiple fields. To do so, the major and minor keys must be next to each other in the datasheet with the major key on the left. (If this is not the case, you can drag the columns into the correct position. Instead of dragging, however, usually it will be easier to use a query that has the data sorted in the desired order.)

To sort on a combination of fields where the major key is just to the left of the minor key, you would use the following steps.

1. Tap or click the field selector at the top of the major key column to select the entire column.
2. Hold down the SHIFT key and then tap or click the field selector for the minor key column to select both columns.
3. Tap or click the Ascending button to sort the records.

To Sign Out of a Microsoft Account

If you are signed in to a Microsoft account and are using a public computer or otherwise wish to sign out of your Microsoft account, you should sign out of the account from the Account gallery in the Backstage view before exiting Access. Signing out of the account is the safest way to make sure that nobody else can access SkyDrive files or settings stored in your Microsoft account. The following steps sign out of a Microsoft account from Access. For a detailed example of the procedure summarized below, refer to the Office and Windows chapter at the beginning of this book.

1 If you wish to sign out of your Microsoft account, tap or click FILE on the ribbon to open the Backstage view and then tap or click the Account tab to display the Account gallery.

2 Tap or click the Sign out link, which displays the Remove Account dialog box. If a Can't remove Windows accounts dialog box appears instead of the Remove Account dialog box, click the OK button and skip the remaining steps.

Q&A Why does a Can't remove Windows accounts dialog box appear?
If you signed in to Windows using your Microsoft account, then you also must sign out from Windows, rather than signing out from within Access. When you are finished using Windows, be sure to sign out at that time.

3 Tap or click the Yes button (Remove Account dialog box) to sign out of your Microsoft account on this computer.

Q&A Should I sign out of Windows after signing out of my Microsoft account?
When you are finished using the computer, you should sign out of your account for maximum security.

4 Tap or click the Back button in the upper-left corner of the Backstage view to return to the database.

To Exit Access

This project now is complete. The following steps exit Access.

1 Tap or click the Close button on the right side of the title bar to exit Access.

2 If a Microsoft Access dialog box appears, tap or click the Save button to save any changes made to the object since the last save.

BTW

Certification
The Microsoft Office Specialist (MOS) program provides an opportunity for you to obtain a valuable industry credential — proof that you have the Access 2013 skills required by employers. For more information, visit the Certification resource on the Student Companion Site located on www .cengagebrain.com. For detailed instructions about accessing available resources, visit www.cengage.com/ ct/studentdownload or contact your instructor for information about accessing the required files.

BTW

Quick Reference
For a table that lists how to complete the tasks covered in this book using touch gestures, the mouse, ribbon, shortcut menu, and keyboard, see the Quick Reference Summary at the back of this book, or visit the Quick Reference resource on the Student Companion Site located on www.cengagebrain.com. For detailed instructions about accessing available resources, visit www.cengage.com/ ct/studentdownload or contact your instructor for information about accessing the required files.

Chapter Summary

In this chapter you have learned how to use a form to add records to a table, search for records, delete records, filter records, create and use lookup fields, create calculated fields, create and use multivalued fields, make mass changes, create validation rules, change the appearance of a datasheet, specify referential integrity, and use subdatasheets. The items listed below include all the new Access skills you have learned in this chapter, with tasks grouped by activity.

Data Inconsistency
Find Duplicate Records (AC 187)
Find Unmatched Records (AC 187)

Datasheet Appearance
Include Totals in a Datasheet (AC 175)
Change Gridlines in a Datasheet (AC 176)
Change the Colors and Font in a Datasheet (AC 177)

Filter Records
Use Filter By Selection (AC 147)
Toggle a Filter (AC 148)
Use a Common Filter (AC 148)
Use Filter By Form (AC 150)
Use Advanced Filter/Sort (AC 151)

Form Creation and Use
Create a Split Form (AC 141)
Use a Form to Add Records (AC 143)

Lookup Field Use
Use a Lookup Field (AC 169)
Use a Multivalued Lookup Field (AC 170)

Mass Changes
Use an Update Query (AC 160)
Use a Delete Query (AC 161)
Use an Append Query (AC 162)
Use a Make-Table Query (AC 162)

Multivalued Fields
Include Multiple Values on One Row of a Query (AC 179)
Include Multiple Values on Multiple Rows of a Query (AC 180)

Referential Integrity
Specify Referential Integrity (AC 182)
Use a Subdatasheet (AC 185)

Sort Records
Use the Ascending Button to Order Records (AC 187)
Use the Ascending Button to Order Records on Multiple Fields (AC 188)

Structure Change
Delete a Field (AC 153)
Move a Field (AC 154)
Add a New Field (AC 154)
Create a Lookup Field (AC 154)
Modify Single or Multivalued Lookup Fields (AC 157)
Add a Calculated Field (AC 158)
Update a Report to Reflect the Changes in the Table (AC 172)

Table Update
Search for a Record (AC 143)
Update the Contents of a Record (AC 145)
Delete a Record (AC 145)
Change the Contents of a Field (AC 168)

Validation Rules
Specify a Required Field (AC 163)
Specify a Range (AC 164)
Specify a Default Value (AC 164)
Specify a Collection of Legal Values (AC 165)
Specify a Format (AC 165)

What decisions will you need to make when maintaining your own databases?

Use these guidelines as you complete the assignments in this chapter and maintain your own databases outside of this class.

1. Determine when it is necessary to add, change, or delete records in a database.

2. Determine whether you should filter records.

  a) If your criterion for filtering is that the value in a particular field matches or does not match a certain specific value, use Filter By Selection.

  b) If your criterion only involves a single field but is more complex, use a common filter.

  c) If your criterion involves more than one field, use Filter By Form.

  d) If your criterion involves more than a single And or Or, or if it involves sorting, use Advanced Filter/Sort.

3. Determine whether additional fields are necessary or whether existing fields should be deleted.

4. Determine whether validation rules, default values, and formats are necessary.

  a) Can you improve the accuracy of the data entry process by enforcing data validation?

  b) What values are allowed for a particular field?

  c) Are there some fields in which one particular value is used more than another?

  d) Are there some fields for which special formats would be appropriate?

5. Determine whether changes to the format of a datasheet are desirable.

  a) Would totals or other calculations be useful in the datasheet?

  b) Would different gridlines make the datasheet more useful?

  c) Would alternating colors in the rows make them easier to read?

  d) Would a different font and/or font color make the text stand out better?

  e) Is the font size appropriate?

  f) Is the column spacing appropriate?

6. Identify related tables in order to implement relationships between the tables.

  a) Is there a one-to-many relationship between the tables?

  b) If so, which table is the one table?

  c) Which table is the many table?

7. When specifying referential integrity, address deletion and update policies.

  a) Decide how to handle deletions. Should deletion be prohibited or should the delete cascade?

  b) Decide how to handle the update of the primary key. Should the update be prohibited or should the update cascade?

How should you submit solutions to questions in the assignments identified with a symbol?

Every assignment in this book contains one or more questions identified with a symbol. These questions require you to think beyond the assigned database. Present your solutions to the questions in the format required by your instructor. Possible formats may include one or more of these options: write the answer; create a document that contains the answer; present your answer to the class; discuss your answer in a group; record the answer as audio or video using a webcam, smartphone, or portable media player; or post answers on a blog, wiki, or website.

CONSIDER THIS

Apply Your Knowledge

Reinforce the skills and apply the concepts you learned in this chapter.

Adding Lookup Fields, Specifying Validation Rules, Updating Records, Updating Reports, and Creating Relationships

Instructions: Start Access. Open the Apply Cosmetics Naturally database that you modified in Apply Your Knowledge in Chapter 2 on page AC 125. (If you did not complete the exercise, see your instructor for a copy of the modified database.)

Continued >

Apply Your Knowledge *continued*

Perform the following tasks:

1. Open the Customer table in Design view.

2. Add a Lookup field called Customer Type to the Customer table. The field should appear after the Postal Code field. The field will contain data on the type of customer. The customer types are FIT (Fitness Centers, Exercise Studios), RET (retail stores), and SAL (salons, spas). Save the changes to the Customer table.

3. Create the following validation rules for the Customer table.

   a. Specify the legal values FIT, RET, and SAL for the Customer Type field. Enter `Must be FIT, RET, or SAL` as the validation text.

   b. Format the Customer Number field to ensure that any letters entered in the field appear as uppercase.

   c. Make the Customer Name field a required field.

4. Save the changes and close the table. You do not need to test the current data.

5. Create an update query for the Customer table. Change all the entries in the Customer Type field to SAL. Save the query as Customer Type Update Query.

6. Open the Customer table in Datasheet view, update the following records, and then close the table:

   a. Change the customer type for customers CY12, FN19, TT21, and TW56 to FIT.

   b. Change the customer type for customers BL15, EY07, and JN34 to RET.

7. Open the Customer Financial Report in Layout view and add the Customer Type field to the report as shown in Figure 3–81. Save the report.

Customer Financial Report				Tuesday, September 30, 2014 1:39:09 PM	
Customer Number	Customer Name	Customer Type	Amount Paid	Balance	Sales Rep Number
AS24	Ashley's Salon	SAL	$1,789.65	$236.99	34
BA35	Beauty for All	SAL	$0.00	$275.75	41
BL15	Blondie's on Main	RET	$1,350.00	$555.00	39
CL09	Casual Looks	SAL	$1,245.45	$297.95	41
CY12	Curlin Yoga Studio	FIT	$740.25	$175.86	39
DB14	Della's Beauty Place	SAL	$859.89	$341.78	34
EY07	Environmentally Yours	RET	$1,765.00	$0.00	34
FN19	Fitness Counts	FIT	$1,976.76	$349.95	41
JN34	Just Natural	RET	$810.78	$450.99	39
LB20	Le Beauty	SAL	$1,467.24	$215.99	39
NC25	Nancy's Place	SAL	$675.89	$345.89	34
RD03	Rose's Day Spa	SAL	$1,024.56	$0.00	41
TT21	Tan and Tone	FIT	$925.75	$265.85	34
TW56	The Workout Place	FIT	$154.95	$870.78	41
UR23	U R Beautiful	SAL	$0.00	$1,235.00	39
			$14,786.17	$5,617.78	

Figure 3–81

8. Establish referential integrity between the Sales Rep table (the one table) and the Customer table (the many table). Cascade the update but not the delete. Save the relationship.

9. Create a relationship report for the relationship, save the report, and close the report. (*Hint:* See the Q&A on page AC 184 for directions on creating a relationship report.)

10. If requested to do so by your instructor, rename the relationship report as Relationships for First Name Last Name where First Name Last Name is your name.

11. Submit the revised database in the format specified by your instructor.

12. ✳ The Customer Type field currently has three possible values. How would you add the value GRO to the Customer Type list?

Extend Your Knowledge

Extend the skills you learned in this chapter and experiment with new skills. You may need to use Help to complete the assignment.

Creating Action Queries and Adding Totals to a Datasheet

Note: To complete this assignment, you will be required to use the Data Files for Students. Visit www.cengage.com/ct/studentdownload for detailed instructions or contact your instructor for information about accessing the required files.

Instructions: Surplus is a small business that purchases merchandise closeouts and resells to the public. The owner has created an Access database in which to store information about the items he sells. He recently acquired some new inventory. The inventory is currently stored in the Additional Surplus database.

Perform the following tasks:

1. Start Access and open the Additional Surplus database from the Data Files for Students.

2. Create and run an append query to append the data in the Surplus table to the Item table in the Extend Surplus database. The result of the append query will be the Item table shown in Figure 3–82.

Item Code	Description	On Hand	Selling Price	Click to Add
3663	Air Deflector	8	$5.99	
3673	Energy Booklet	25	$2.99	
4553	Energy Saving Kit	7	$43.25	
4573	Faucet Aerator	20	$0.99	
4583	Fluorescent Light Bulb	18	$4.75	
5923	Low Flow Shower Head	11	$8.99	
6185	Luminescent Night Light	12	$4.50	
6234	Programmable Thermostat	3	$36.99	
6345	Rain Gauge	16	$3.15	
7123	Retractable Clothesline	10	$13.99	
7934	Shower Timer	15	$2.99	
8136	Smoke Detector	10	$6.50	
8344	Toilet Tank Water Saver	18	$3.50	
8590	Water Conservation Kit	8	$13.99	
9458	Windows Insulator Kit	10	$5.25	
BA35	Bat House	14	$30.99	
BL06	Bug Mister	9	$8.99	
GF12	Globe Feeder	12	$7.50	
LM05	Leaf Mister	5	$18.00	
SF03	Suet Feeder	8	$3.79	
WF10	Window Feeder	11	$8.49	

Figure 3–82

3. Open the Item table in the Extend Surplus database and sort the datasheet in ascending order by Description.

4. Add a totals row to the datasheet and display the sum of the items on hand and the average selling price. Save the changes to the table layout and close the table.

5. Create and run a make-table query for the Item table to create a new table, Discount Items, in the Extend Surplus database. Only items where the number on hand is fewer than 10 should be included in the Discount Items table.

6. If requested to do so by your instructor, change the description for BA35 in the Item table to First Name Last Name House where First Name and Last Name are your first and last names.

7. Submit the revised database in the format specified by your instructor.

8. ✳ If the additional surplus items were in an Excel workbook, how would you add them to the Item table?

Analyze, Correct, Improve

Analyze a database, correct all errors, and improve the design.

Correcting the Database Structure and Improving the Appearance of a Datasheet

Note: To complete this assignment, you will be required to use the Data Files for Students. Visit www.cengage.com/ct/studentdownload for detailed instructions or contact your instructor for information about accessing the required files.

Instructions: Analyze Travel is a database maintained by the International Studies department at your university. The department keeps a database of students interested in Study Abroad programs. The Student table shown in Figure 3–83 contains errors that must be corrected. Some improvements to the table's appearance would make it easier for student workers to use. Start Access and open the Analyze Travel database from the Data Files for Students.

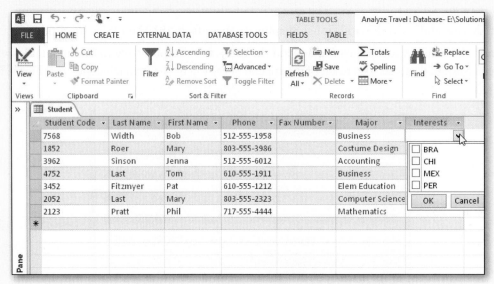

Figure 3–83

1. Correct Interests is a multi-valued field to indicate trips of interest. A trip to Belize (BEL) was omitted from the list and needs to be added. The Fax Number field was added by mistake and must be deleted.

2. Improve Different individuals update this database. Some have complained that the small font combined with the fluorescent lighting makes it difficult to view the table. Change the appearance of the table by changing the font to Arial, the font size to 12, and the alternate fill color to White, Background 1, Darker 15%. Bold the datasheet and sort the table by student last name and first name in ascending order. If instructed to do so by your instructor, change the first name and last name of student 3452 to your first and last name. Save the changes to the layout of the table.

3. ☀ What other reasons would a user have for changing the appearance of a datasheet?

In the Labs

Design, create, modify, and/or use a database following the guidelines, concepts, and skills presented in this chapter. Labs are listed in order of increasing difficulty. Labs 1 and 2, which increase in difficulty, require you to create solutions based on what you learned in the chapter; Lab 3 requires you to create a solution, which uses cloud and web technologies, by learning and investigating on your own from general guidance.

Lab 1: **Maintaining the Dartt Offsite Services Database**

Problem: Dartt Offsite Services is expanding rapidly and needs to make some database changes to handle the expansion. The company needs to know more about its customers, such as services needed. It also needs to add validation rules, and update records in the database.

Note: Use the database modified in Lab 1 of Chapter 2 for this assignment, or see your instructor for information on accessing the files required for this book.

Instructions: Perform the following tasks:

1. Open the Lab 1 Dartt Offsite Services database and open the Client table in Design view.

2. Add a multivalued lookup field, Services Needed, to the Client table. The field should appear after the Postal Code field. Table 3–2 lists the services abbreviations and descriptions that management would like in the multivalued field. Save the change to the table.

Table 3–2 Services Abbreviations and Descriptions

Services Abbreviation	Description
Arch	Archival Storage
Data	Data Backup
Drec	Disaster Recovery
Net	Network Backup
Shrd	Shred Documents
Web	Website Backup

© 2014 Cengage Learning

3. Add a calculated field named Total Amount (Amount Paid + Balance Due) to the Client table. The field should follow the Balance Due field. Save the change to the table.

4. Create the following rules for the Client table and save the changes:

   a. Ensure that any letters entered in the Client Number field appear as uppercase.

   b. Make Client Name a required field.

   c. Ensure that only the values SC and NC can be entered in the State field. Include validation text.

   d. Assign a default value of NC to the State field.

5. Use Filter By Form to find all records where the city is Kyle and the balance due is $0.00. Delete the record(s). Do not save the filter.

6. Open the Client table in Datasheet view and add the data shown in Figure 3–84 to the Services Needed field. Resize the field to best fit and save the changes to the layout of the table.

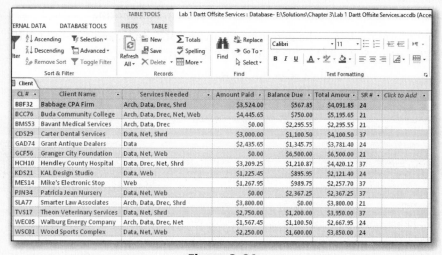

Figure 3–84

Continued >

In the Labs *continued*

7. Open the Service Rep table in Design view and change the field size for the Last Name field to 20. Save the changes and close the table.

8. Open the Service Rep table in Datasheet view, find the record for service rep 21, and change the last name to Kelly-Williamson. Resize the column to best fit.

9. If requested to do so by your instructor, change the last name for service rep 45 to your last name. If your last name is longer than 20 characters, simply enter as much as you can.

10. Save the changes to the layout of the table and close the Service Rep table.

11. Establish referential integrity between the Service Rep table (the one table) and the Client table (the many table). Cascade the update but not the delete.

12. Submit the revised database in the format specified by your instructor.

13. ✷ What would the validation rule be if the only allowable values in the State field were NC, SC, or TN?

Lab 2: **Maintaining the Tennis Logos Database**

Problem: The manager of Tennis Logos needs to change the database structure, add validation rules, and update records.

Note: Use the database modified in Lab 2 of Chapter 2 on page AC 131 for this assignment or see your instructor for information on accessing the files required for this book.

Instructions: Perform the following tasks:

1. Open the Tennis Logos database, and then open the Item table in Design view.

2. Add a lookup field, Item Type, to the Item table. The field should appear after the Description field. The field will contain data on the type of item for sale. The item types are CAP (caps, hats, visors), CLO (clothing), and NOV (novelties).

3. Add the following validation rules to the Item table and save the changes:
   a. Make Description a required field.
   b. Specify the legal values CAP, CLO, and NOV for the Item Type field. Include validation text.
   c. Assign CLO as the default value for the Item Type field.
   d. Specify that number on hand must be between 0 and 250. Include validation text.

4. Using a query, assign the value CLO to the Item Type field for all records. Save the query as Update Query.

5. Create a split form for the Item table and save it as Item Split Form.

6. Use the split form to change the item type for items 3363, 3673, and 6234 to CAP. Change the item type for items 5923, 7123, 7934, and 8136 to NOV.

7. Add the items shown in Table 3–3 to the Item table.

Table 3–3 Additional Records for Item table						
Item Number	**Description**	**Item Type**	**On Hand**	**Wholesale Price**	**Base Cost**	**Supplier Code**
6523	Mouse Pad	NOV	100	$1.29	$1.59	SD
6974	Pen	NOV	225	$0.49	$0.79	SD
8206	Turtleneck	CLO	55	$11.29	$11.59	PC

8. Create an advanced filter for the Item table. Filter the table to find all items with fewer than 75 items on hand. Sort the filter by Item Type and Description. Save the filter settings as a query and name the filter Reorder Filter.

9. Using a query, delete all records in the Item table where the description starts with the letter Z. Save the query as Delete Query.

10. If requested to do so by your instructor, right-click the Item table in the Navigation Pane, click Table Properties, and add a description for the Item table that includes your first and last name and the date you completed this assignment. Save the change to the table property.

11. Specify referential integrity between the Supplier table (the one table) and the Item table (the many table). Cascade the update but not the delete.

12. Add the Item Type field to the Inventory Status Report. It should follow the Description field.

13. Submit the revised database in the format specified by your instructor.

14. ✸ There are two ways to enter the validation rule in Step 3d. What are they? Which one did you use?

Lab 3: Expand Your World: Cloud and Web Technologies
Filtering Records, Editing Relationships, and Exporting Relationship Reports

Problem: As a way to earn money for college, you and a few friends have started a dog walking business. You use Access to manage your business and are still learning how to create and edit relationships. You want to be able to export a relationship report to share your knowledge with your friends.

Note: To complete this assignment, you will be required to use the Data Files for Students. Visit www.cengage.com/ct/studentdownload for detailed instructions or contact your instructor for information about accessing the required files.

Instructions: Perform the following tasks:
1. Open the Lab 3 Dog Walkers database from the Data Files for Students.

2. In the Relationships window, edit the relationship to cascade the update.

3. Create a relationship report for the relationship and save the report with the name Relationship Report for First Name Last Name where first and last name are your first and last name.

4. Change the Walker Number for Alice Kerdy to 101.

5. In the Walker table, move the First Name field so that it appears before the Last Name field.

6. Export the relationship report as a PDF file and upload to your SkyDrive.

7. Share the PDF file with your instructor.

8. Submit the revised database in the format specified by your instructor.

9. ✸ What happened in the Customer table when you changed the Walker Number to 101?

✸ Consider This: Your Turn

Apply your creative thinking and problem solving skills to design and implement a solution.

1: Maintaining the Craft Database

Personal/Academic

Instructions: Open the Craft database you used in Chapter 2 on page AC 133. If you did not create this database, contact your instructor for information about accessing the required files.

Part 1: Use the concepts and techniques presented in this chapter to modify the database as follows:

a. The minimum price of any item is $4.00.
b. The Description field should always contain data.
c. Ten oven pulls have been sold. Use an update query to change the on hand value from 25 to 15. Save the update query.
d. Tom Last (student code 4752) has created the items shown in Table 3–4. Use a split form to add these items to the Item table.

Table 3–4 Additional Records for Item table				
Item Number	**Description**	**Price**	**On Hand**	**Student Code**
W128	Child's Stool	$115.00	3	4752
W315	Harmony Stool	$81.00	4	4752
W551	Skittle Pins	$4.00	15	4752

© 2014 Cengage Learning

e. A Total Value (On Hand * Price) calculated field should be added to the Item table before the Student Code field. Set the Result Type to Currency and the Decimal Places to 2. (*Hint:* Result Type is a field property for calculated fields.)
f. Specify referential integrity. Cascade the delete but not the update.
g. Add the Total Value field to the Wood Crafts for Sale report created in Chapter 1.
h. All the magazine racks have been sold and Tom Last does not want to make any more. Use a delete query to remove the item. Save the delete query.

Submit your assignment in the format specified by your instructor.

Part 2: ✸ You made several decisions while completing this assignment, including specifying referential integrity. What was the rationale behind your decisions? What would happen if you deleted the record for Tom Last (student code 4752) from the Student table?

2: Maintaining the Mums Landscaping Database

Professional

Instructions: Open the Mums Landscaping database you used in Chapter 2 on page AC 134. If you did not create this database, contact your instructor for information about accessing the required files.

Part 1: Use the concepts and techniques presented in this chapter to modify the database according to the following requirements:

a. Mums could better serve its customers by adding a field that would list the type of services each customer needs. Table 3–5 lists the service abbreviations and descriptions that should appear in the field.

Table 3–5 Services Abbreviations and Descriptions	
Services Abbreviation	**Description**
IRR	Irrigation
LND	Landscaping
LWN	Lawn Care
PLT	Plant Maintenance
TRE	Tree Pruning

© 2014 Cengage Learning

b. A Total Amount field that summed the Amount Paid and Balance fields would be beneficial for the reports that Mums needs.

c. Hill Accessories is no longer a customer of Mums. Use Find or Filter By Selection to delete this record.

d. Add the data for the services needed multivalued field as shown in Figure 3–85.

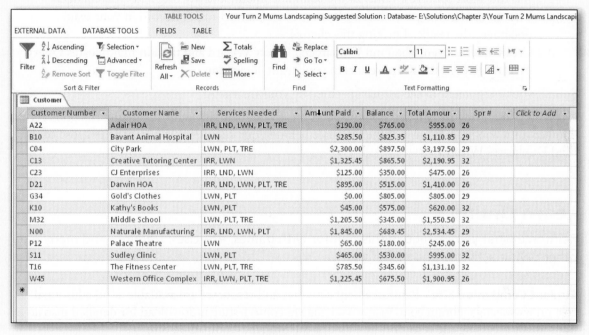

Customer Number	Customer Name	Services Needed	Amount Paid	Balance	Total Amount	Spr #	Click to Add
A22	Adair HOA	IRR, LND, LWN, PLT, TRE	$190.00	$765.00	$955.00	26	
B10	Bavant Animal Hospital	LWN	$285.50	$825.35	$1,110.85	29	
C04	City Park	LWN, PLT, TRE	$2,300.00	$897.50	$3,197.50	29	
C13	Creative Tutoring Center	IRR, LWN	$1,325.45	$865.50	$2,190.95	32	
C23	CJ Enterprises	IRR, LND, LWN	$125.00	$350.00	$475.00	26	
D21	Darwin HOA	IRR, LND, LWN, PLT, TRE	$895.00	$515.00	$1,410.00	26	
G34	Gold's Clothes	LWN, PLT	$0.00	$805.00	$805.00	29	
K10	Kathy's Books	LWN, PLT	$45.00	$575.00	$620.00	32	
M32	Middle School	LWN, PLT, TRE	$1,205.50	$345.00	$1,550.50	32	
N00	Naturale Manufacturing	IRR, LND, LWN, PLT	$1,845.00	$689.45	$2,534.45	29	
P12	Palace Theatre	LWN	$65.00	$180.00	$245.00	26	
S11	Sudley Clinic	LWN, PLT	$465.00	$530.00	$995.00	32	
T16	The Fitness Center	LWN, PLT, TRE	$785.50	$345.60	$1,131.10	32	
W45	Western Office Complex	IRR, LWN, PLT, TRE	$1,225.45	$675.50	$1,900.95	26	

Figure 3–85

e. Add the Total Amount field to the Customer Financial Report.

f. An entry should always appear in the Customer Name field. Any letters in the Customer Number field should appear in uppercase.

g. A customer's balance should never equal or exceed $1,000.00.

h. Specify referential integrity. Cascade the update but not the delete.

Submit your assignment in the format specified by your instructor.

Part 2: ✳ You made several decisions while including adding a calculated field, Total Amount, to the database. What was the rationale behind your decisions? Does the calculated field actually exist in the database? Are there any issues that you need to consider when you create a calculated field?

Continued >

Consider This: Your Turn *continued*

3: Understanding Database Maintenance
Research and Collaboration

Part 1:   Before you begin this assignment, you and your teammates need to decide on a team name. Once you have agreed on a name, save the Bavant Publishing database as Team Name Publishing where Team Name is the name of your team. Use this database for this assignment. As your group completes the assignment, complete the following tasks, keeping track of problems you encounter, the solutions you apply, and any other observations. Create a blog, a Google document, or a Word document on the SkyDrive on which to store the team's observations.

   a.   For every member in the team, add a record to the Book Rep table. Use your own names but fictitious data for the remaining fields. Record in the team document or blog what happened when you added the records. For example, was someone's name too long to fit within the allotted field size?

   b.   Based on the records currently in the Book Rep table, change the field size for any field that was too short to store a value. In the team document, identify the fields you changed.

   c.   Change the book rep number for Robert Chin from 53 to 56. Record in your team document the result of making this change.

   d.   Create queries using the Find Unmatched Query Wizard and the Find Duplicates Query Wizard. Record the query results in your team document.

Submit your assignment in the format specified by your instructor.

Part 2:   ✳ You made several decisions while in this assignment, including changing the book rep number for a book rep. What was the rationale behind your decisions? What is the purpose of the Find Duplicates Wizard?

Learn Online

Reinforce what you learned in this chapter with games, exercises, training, and many other online activities and resources.

Student Companion Site   Reinforcement activities and resources are available at no additional cost on www.cengagebrain.com. Visit www.cengage.com/ct/studentdownload for detailed instructions about accessing the resources available at the Student Companion Site.

SAM   Put your skills into practice with SAM! If you have a SAM account, go to www.cengage.com/sam2013 to access SAM assignments for this chapter.

Index

Note: Please note that boldfaced page numbers indicate key terms.

A

Access, **OFF 63**
See also databases
date format, AC 90
exiting, AC 24, AC 56, AC 189
exporting data to Excel, AC 107–109
exporting data to Word, AC 110
Help, AC 42, AC 121, AC 172
importing data from other applications into, AC 32–37
introduction to, OFF 63–64
opening databases from, AC 77, AC 140
running, AC 76–77, AC 140
running in Windows 7, Windows 8, AC 6
starting, OFF 63, AC 24–25
unique elements of, OFF 64
views, AC 49, AC 142, AC 144
Access window, AC 7–8
Access work area, **OFF 64, AC 8**
accounts
signing in to Microsoft, OFF 37–38
signing out of Microsoft, AC 55, AC 123–124
action query, **AC 160**
active cell, **OFF 59**, OFF 60
Active Directory Synchronization, **CLD 8**
ad hoc relationships, AC 99
adding
calculated field, AC 158–159
criteria to join queries, AC 111–112
fields to design grid, AC 79–80
multivalued fields, AC 156–157
new fields, AC 154
records to tables, AC 20–23
records to tables containing data, AC 26–27
records using form, AC 143
totals to reports, AC 53
address bar, folder windows, OFF 27
Adobe Reader, **AC 29**, AC 107
Advanced Filter/Sort, AC 151–152
aggregate function, **AC 115**
allowable values, **AC 165**
AND criterion, **AC 91**
AND operator, **AC 92**
app, **OFF 3**
App bar, **OFF 8**
append query, **AC 160**, AC 162
Apple iPads, iPhones, access to Office 365, CLD 8

apps

exiting Office, with one document open, OFF 42–43
importing data from other applications into Access, AC 32–37
Microsoft Office 2013, OFF 9
pinning, unpinning, OFF 8
running, OFF 63
running from File Explorer, OFF 57–59
running from Start screen, OFF 11–12
running using Search box, OFF 46–48
running using Start menu using Windows 7, OFF 12
switching between Start screen and, OFF 13
switching from one to another, OFF 30–31
archive tables, AC 162
ascending order of records, AC 187–189
ascending sort order, AC 94, AC 96
assignments, OFF 83
asterisk (*), **AC 83**
at sign (@), AC 165
AutoCorrect feature, AC 23
AutoIncrement fields, AC 9
automatically updated properties, **AC 54**
AutoNumber fields, AC 9
AVG function, AC 115, AC 116

B

backing up, **AC 56**
databases, AC 56–57, AC 154
with different name, AC 58
Backstage view, **OFF 31**
closing Office files using, OFF 53–54
creating new Office documents from, OFF 51–52
backup copy, **AC 56**
BETWEEN operator
described, **AC 92**
using in validation rules, AC 166
Blackberry phones, access to Office 365, CLD 8
brochures, creating, OFF 70
BTWs, OFF 4
business teams using Office 365 in, CLD 9
buttons, mouse, OFF 4

C

calculated field, **AC 112**, AC 112–113, **AC 158**, AC 159
calculating statistics, AC 115–117

calculations

with Access, AC 112
using calculated fields in queries, AC 112–113
calendars, Office 365, CLD 7, CLD 10
captions
changing field, AC 114–115
described, **AC 10**
cascading deletes, updates, AC 182
cell, **OFF 59**
cell reference, **OFF 59**
chapter roadmaps, OFF 2
charts, **OFF 55**
clearing
design grid, AC 93
filters, AC 148
click mouse operations, OFF 5
Click-to-Run, **CLD 6**
closing
database tables, AC 20, AC 24
databases without exiting Access, AC 57
Office files, OFF 66
Office files using Backstage view, OFF 53–54
tables, AC 159
cloud computing, **CLD 2**
Office 365. *See* Office 365
overview of, CLD 2–3
collaboration using SharePoint, CLD 10
collapsing
folders, OFF 30
ribbon, OFF 19
colors, changing in datasheets, AC 177–178
column heading, **OFF 59**
column headings, **AC 32**
columns (datasheet), resizing, AC 28, AC 39
columns (report), modifying headings, resizing, AC 50–53
commands
Access tabs, OFF 64
dimmed, OFF 61
Excel tabs, OFF 64
hiding from screen, OFF 20
on mini toolbar, OFF 17
on Quick Access Toolbar, OFF 17–18, OFF 22
on ribbon, ScreenTips, OFF 16
and shortcut menus, OFF 20–21
common filters, **AC 148–149**
compacting, repairing databases, AC 57
comparison operators, **AC 89**, AC 90
compound criterion, **AC 91**
using involving AND, AC 91
using involving OR, AC 92

Quick Reference Summary

Microsoft Office 2013 Access Introductory Quick Reference

Task	Page Number	Ribbon	Other On-Screen Areas	Shortcut Menu	Keyboard Shortcut
Advanced Filter/ Sort, Use	AC 151	Advanced button (HOME tab | Sort & Filter group), Advanced Filter/Sort			
Append Query, Use	AC 162	Append button (QUERY TOOLS DESIGN Tab | Query Type group)			
Ascending Button, Use to Order Records	AC 187	Select field, Ascending button (HOME tab | Sort & Filter group)	Sort A to Z (for ascending) or Sort Z to A (for descending)		
Back up Database	AC 56	FILE tab, Save As tab, 'Back Up Database', Save As button			
Calculated Field in Query, Use	AC 112			Press and hold or right-click field row, Zoom	
Calculated Field, Create	AC 158		In Design view, create new field, tap or click Data Type arrow, tap or click Calculated		
Caption, Change	AC 114	Property Sheet button (DESIGN tab | Show/Hide group), Caption box	Select field in design grid, tap or click Properties on shortcut menu	Press and hold or right-click field in design grid, tap or click Properties on shortcut menu	
Close Object	AC 20		Close button for object	Close	
Collection of Legal Values, Specify	AC 165		In Design view, enter values in Validation Rule property box in Field Properties pane		
Colors and Font, Change in Datasheet	AC 177	Font Color arrow (HOME tab | Text Formatting group)			
Column, Resize	AC 28		Double-click or double-tap right boundary of field selector in datasheet	Press and hold or right-click field name, Field Width	
Common Filter, Use	AC 148			Arrow for field, point to Text Filters	
Compact Database	AC 57	FILE tab, Info tab in Backstage view, 'Compact & Repair Database' button			

Task	Page Number	Ribbon	Other On-Screen Areas	Shortcut Menu	Keyboard Shortcut
Comparison Operator, Use	AC 90		Create query, enter comparison operator on Criteria row		
Compound Criterion Involving AND, Use	AC 91				Place criteria on same line
Compound Criterion Involving OR, USE	AC 92				Place criteria on separate lines
Criteria, Use in Calculating Statistics	AC 117	Totals button (QUERY TOOLS DESIGN tab | Show/Hide group), Total arrow, tap or click calculation			
Criterion, Use in a Query	AC 43		In Design View, tap or click Criteria row, enter criterion		
Crosstab Query, Create	AC 119	Query Wizard button (CREATE tab | Queries group), Crosstab Query Wizard			
Data, Export to Excel	AC 107	Excel button (EXTERNAL DATA tab | Export group)	Select object in Navigation Pane, tap or click Export		
Data, Import	AC 33	Button for imported data format (EXTERNAL DATA tab | Import & Link group)			
Data, Sort in Query	AC 94	Select field in design grid, tap or click Sort row, tap or click Sort arrow, select order			
Database Properties, Change	AC 55	View and edit database properties link (FILE tab | Info tab)			
Database, Create	AC 6	Blank desktop database thumbnail (FILE tab | New tab)			
Database, Create using Template	AC 7		FILE tab, New tab, select template		
Default Value, Specify	AC 164		In Design view, select field in upper pane, enter value in Default Value property box in Field Properties pane		
Delete Object	AC 58			Delete	
Delete Query, Use	AC 161		Create query, Delete button (QUERY TOOLS DESIGN tab | Results group)	Press and hold or right-click any open area in upper pane, point to Query Type, tap or click Delete Query	
Design Grid, Clear	AC 93		In Design view, select all columns, tap or click DELETE		
Duplicate Records, Find	AC 187	Query Wizard button (CREATE tab | Queries group), 'Find Duplicates Query Wizard'			
Duplicates, Omit	AC 94	In Design view, Property Sheet button (QUERY TOOLS DESIGN tab | Show/Hide group), tap or click Unique Values property, tap or click Yes			

Microsoft Office 2013 Access Introductory Quick Reference *(continued)*

Task	Page Number	Ribbon	Other On-Screen Areas	Shortcut Menu	Keyboard Shortcut
Exit Access	AC 24		Close button on right side of title bar		
Field Contents, Change	AC 168		In Datasheet view, tap or click in field, enter data		
Field in Query, Add to Design Grid	AC 79		Double-click or double-tap field in field list		
Field, Add New	AC 154	In Design view, Insert Rows button (TABLE TOOLS DESIGN tab | Tools group)			Design View, INSERT
Field, Delete	AC 158		In Design view, tap or click row selector for field, DELETE		
Field, Move	AC 154		In Design view, tap or click row selector for field to move, drag to new position		
Filter By Form, Use	AC 150	Advanced button (HOME tab | Sort & Filter group), 'Clear All Filters', Advanced button, 'Filter By Form'			
Filter By Selection, Use	AC 157	Selection button (HOME tab | Sort & Filter group) select criterion			
Filter, Clear	AC 148	Advanced button (HOME tab | Sort & Filter group), 'Clear All Filters'			
Filter, Toggle	AC 148	Toggle Filter button (HOME tab | Sort & Filter group)			
Form for Query, Create	AC 105	Select query, Form button (CREATE tab | Forms group)			
Form, Create	AC 45	Form button (CREATE tab | Forms group)			
Format, Specify	AC 165		In Design view, select field, tap or click Format property box in field grid, enter format		
Gridlines, Change in Datasheet	AC 176	Gridlines button (HOME tab | Text Formatting group)			
Grouping, Use	AC 118		Create query, select Group By in Total row, select field to group by		
Join Properties, Change	AC 101			In Design view, press and hold or right-click join line, click Join Properties	
Lookup Field, Create	AC 154		In Design view, select Data Type column for field, Data Type arrow, Lookup Wizard		
Make-Table Query, Use	AC 162	Create query, Make Table button (QUERY TOOLS DESIGN tab | Query Type group)			
Multiple Keys, Sort on	AC 96		Assign two sort keys in design grid		

Microsoft Office 2013 Access Introductory Quick Reference *(continued)*

Task	Page Number	Ribbon	Other On-Screen Areas	Shortcut Menu	Keyboard Shortcut
Multivalued Field, Query Showing Multiple Values on a Single Row	AC 179		Create query with specified fields		
Multivalued Lookup Field, Use	AC 170		In Datasheet view, tap or click field, tap or click check boxes, OK		
Navigation Pane, Customize	AC 122		Navigation Pane arrow		
Number Criterion, Use	AC 89		Create query, select table, enter number as criterion in field grid		
Open Database	AC 25	Open button (FILE tab)			
Open Table	AC 21		Double-click or double-tap table in Navigation Pane	Press and hold or right-click table in Navigation Pane, tap or click Open	
Parameter Query, Create	AC 87		In Design view, type parameter in square brackets in criterion row of field grid, Run button (QUERY TOOLS DESIGN tab | Results group)		
Parameter Query, Use	AC 87			Right-click or press and hold query in Navigation Pane, tap or click Open	
Preview or Print Object	AC 30	Print or Print Preview button (FILE tab | Print tab)			CTRL+P, ENTER
Primary Key, Modify	AC 11	Select field, Data Type arrow (TABLE TOOLS FIELDS tab | Formatting group), select data type			
Query, Create in Design View	AC 78	Query Design button (CREATE tab | Queries group)			
Query, Create using Simple Query Wizard	AC 40	Query Wizard button (CREATE tab | Queries group)			
Query, Export	AC 107		Select query in Navigation Pane, application button (EXTERNAL DATA tab | Export group)	Press and hold or right-click query in Navigation Pane, Export	
Range, Specify	AC 164		In Design view, select field, enter rule in Validation Rule property box in Field Properties pane		
Record, Add using a Form	AC 143	New button (HOME tab | Records Group)	'New (blank) record' button in Navigation buttons	Open, tap or click in field	CTRL+PLUS SIGN (+)

Microsoft Office 2013 Access Introductory Quick Reference *(continued)*

Task	Page Number	Ribbon	Other On-Screen Areas	Shortcut Menu	Keyboard Shortcut
Record, Delete	AC 145	Delete arrow (HOME tab | Records group), Delete Record	In Datasheet view, tap or click record selector, DELETE		DELETE
Record, Search for	AC 143	Find button (HOME tab | Find group)			CTRL+F
Record, Update	AC 143		In Form view, change desired data		In Datasheet, select field and edit
Records in a Join, Restrict	AC 111		In Design view, enter criterion for query		
Referential Integrity, Specify	AC 182	Relationships button (DATABASE TOOLS tab | Relationships group)			
Rename Object	AC 58			Press and hold or right-click object in Navigation Pane, Rename, enter new name, press ENTER	
Report Column Headings, Modify	AC 50			Press and hold or right-click field name, Rename Field	
Report, Create	AC 48	Report button (CREATE tab | Reports group)			
Required Field, Specify	AC 163		In Design view, select field, Required property box in Field Properties pane, down arrow, Yes		
Run Access	AC 5		Access 2013 tile on Windows Start screen or display Charms bar, tap or click Search charm, type Access, tap or click Access 2013		
Save Object	AC 16	FILE tab, Save	Save button on Quick Access Toolbar		CTRL+S
Save Object As	AC 45	FILE tab, Save As tab, 'Save Object As', Save As button			
Split Form, Create	AC 141	Select table in Navigation Pane, More Forms button (CREATE tab | Forms group), Split Form button			
Statistics, Calculate	AC 115	Create query, Totals button (QUERY TOOLS DESIGN tab | Show/Hide group), tap or click Total row, tap or click Total arrow, select calculation			
Subdatasheet, Use	AC 185		In Datasheet view, plus sign in front of row		
Table, Modify in Design View	AC 37	Table Design button (CREATE tab | Tables group)			
Table, View in Design View	AC 17	View arrow (TABLE TOOLS FIELDS tab | Views group), Design View	Design View button on status bar		

Microsoft Office 2013 Access Introductory Quick Reference *(continued)*

Task	Page Number	Ribbon	Other On-Screen Areas	Shortcut Menu	Keyboard Shortcut
Tables, Join	AC 100	Query Design button (CREATE tab | Queries group), add field lists for tables to join, add desired fields to design grid, run query			
Text Data Criterion, Use	AC 81		Create query, select table, enter text as criterion in field grid		
Top-Values Query, Create	AC 98	In Design view, Return arrow (QUERY TOOLS DESIGN tab | Query Setup group)			
Totals, Add to a Report	AC 53	Totals button (REPORT DESIGN TOOLS DESIGN tab | Grouping & Totals group)			
Totals, Include in a Datasheet	AC 175	In Datasheet view, Totals button (HOME tab | Records group), click Total row, click arrow			
Totals, Remove from a Datasheet	AC 176	Totals button (HOME tab | Records group)			
Unmatched Records, Find	AC 187	Query Wizard button (CREATE tab | Queries group), 'Find Unmatched Query Wizard'			
Update Query, Use	AC 160	Create query, Update button (QUERY TOOLS DESIGN tab | Query Type group), select field, click Update To row, enter new value, run query		Press and hold or right-click any open area in upper pane, point to Query Type, tap or click Update Query	
Wildcard, Use	AC 83		In Design view, tap or click Criteria row in design grid, type wildcard and text		

Important Notes for Windows 7 Users

The screen shots in this book show Microsoft Office 2013 running in Windows 8. If you are using Microsoft Windows 7, however, you still can use this book because Office 2013 runs virtually the same way on both platforms. You will encounter only minor differences if you are using Windows 7. Read this section to understand the differences.

Dialog Boxes

If you are a Windows 7 user, the dialog boxes shown in this book will look slightly different than what you see on your screen. Dialog boxes for Windows 8 have a title bar with a solid color, and the dialog box name is centered on the title bar. Beyond these superficial differences in appearance, however, the options in the dialog boxes across both platforms are the same. For instance, Figures 1 and 2 show the Font dialog box in Windows 7 and the Font dialog box in Windows 8.

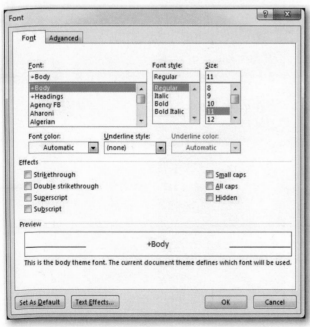

Figure 1 Font Dialog Box in Windows 7

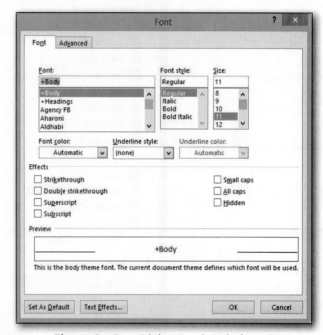

Figure 2 Font Dialog Box in Windows 8

Alternate Steps for Running an App in Windows 7

Nearly all of the steps in this book work exactly the same way for Windows 7 users; however, running an app (or program/application) requires different steps for Windows 7. The following steps show how to run an app in Windows 7.

Running an App (or Program/Application) Using Windows 7

1. Click the Start button on the taskbar to display the Start menu.
2. Click All Programs and then click the Microsoft Office 2013 folder (Figure 3).
3. If necessary, click the name of the folder containing the app you want to run.
4. Click the name of the app you want to run (such as Excel 2013).

Figure 3   Running an App Using the Windows 7 Start Menu